DATE DUE

			PRINTED IN U.S.A.

SOMETHING ABOUT THE AUTHOR

ISSN 0276-816X

something ABOUT THE AUTHOR

Facts and Pictures about Authors
and Illustrators of Books for Young People

EDITED BY
ANNE COMMIRE

VOLUME 44

GALE RESEARCH COMPANY
BOOK TOWER
DETROIT, MICHIGAN
48226

Editor: Anne Commire

Associate Editors: Agnes Garrett, Helga P. McCue

Assistant Editors: Dianne H. Anderson, Eunice L. Petrini, Linda Shedd

Sketchwriter: Rachel Koenig

Researchers: Kathleen Betsko, Catherine Ruello

Editorial Assistants: Lisa Bryon, Elisa Ann Ferraro

Permissions Assistant: Susan Pfanner

In cooperation with the Young People's Literature staff

Editor: Joyce Nakamura

Research Coordinator: Cynthia J. Walker

External Production Supervisor: Mary Beth Trimper

External Production Assistant: Michael B. Vargas

Internal Production Associate: Louise Gagné

Internal Senior Production Assistant: Sandy Rock

Layout Artist: Elizabeth Lewis Patryjak

Art Director: Arthur Chartow

Special acknowledgment is due to the members of the *Contemporary Authors* staff
who assisted in the preparation of this volume.

Publisher: Frederick G. Ruffner

Executive Vice-President/Editorial Director: Dedria Bryfonski

Director, Literature Division: Christine Nasso

Senior Editor, Something about the Author: Adele Sarkissian

Library of Congress Catalog Card Number 72-27107

ISBN 0-8103-2254-4

ISSN 0276-816X

Computerized photocomposition by
Typographics, Incorporated
Kansas City, Missouri

Printed in the United States

Contents

Introduction

As the only ongoing reference series that deals with the lives and works of authors and illustrators of children's books, *Something about the Author (SATA)* is a unique source of information. The *SATA* series includes not only well-known authors and illustrators whose books are most widely read, but also those less prominent people whose works are just coming to be recognized. *SATA* is often the only readily available information source for less well-known writers or artists. You'll find *SATA* informative and entertaining whether you are:

— a student in junior high school (or perhaps one to two grades higher or lower) who needs information for a book report or some other assignment for an English class;

— a children's librarian who is searching for the answer to yet another question from a young reader or collecting background material to use for a story hour;

— an English teacher who is drawing up an assignment for your students or gathering information for a book talk;

— a student in a college of education or library science who is studying children's literature and reference sources in the field;

— a parent who is looking for a new way to interest your child in reading something more than the school curriculum prescribes;

— an adult who enjoys children's literature for its own sake, knowing that a good children's book has no age limits.

Scope

In *SATA* you will find detailed information about authors and illustrators who span the full time range of children's literature, from early figures like John Newbery and L. Frank Baum to contemporary figures like Judy Blume and Richard Peck. Authors in the series represent primarily English-speaking countries, particularly the United States, Canada, and the United Kingdom. Also included, however, are authors from around the world whose works are available in English translation, for example: from France, Jean and Laurent De Brunhoff; from Italy, Emanuele Luzzati; from the Netherlands, Jaap ter Haar; from Germany, James Krüss; from Norway, Babbis Friis-Baastad; from Japan, Toshiko Kanzawa; from the Soviet Union, Kornei Chukovsky; from Switzerland, Alois Carigiet, to name only a few. Also appearing in *SATA* are Newbery medalists from Hendrik Van Loon (1922) to Patricia MacLachlan (1986). The writings represented in *SATA* include those created intentionally for children and young adults as well as those written for a general audience and known to interest younger readers. These writings cover the spectrum from picture books, humor, folk and fairy tales, animal stories, mystery and adventure, science fiction and fantasy, historical fiction, poetry and nonsense verse, to drama, biography, and nonfiction.

Information Features

In *SATA* you will find full-length entries that are being presented in the series for the first time. This volume, for example, marks the first full-length appearance of Arlene Alda, H. M. Hoover, Ethel Kessler, Doris Lee, Sonia O. Lisker, Malvina Reynolds, Ann Schlee, Craig Kee Strete, and Kit Williams, among others. Since Volume 25, each *SATA* volume also includes newly revised and updated biographies for a selection of early *SATA* listees who remain of interest to today's readers and who have been active enough to require extensive revision of their earlier entries. The entry for a given biographee may be revised as often as there is substantial new information to provide. In Volume 44 you'll find revised entries for Arna Bontemps, Phyllis McGinley, Jean Lowery Nixon, and Rosemary Sutcliff.

Brief Entries, first introduced in Volume 27, are another regular feature of *SATA*. Brief Entries present essentially the same types of information found in a full entry but do so in a capsule form and without illustration. These entries are intended to give you useful and timely information while the more time-consuming process of compiling a full-length biography is in progress. In this volume you'll find Brief Entries for Anthony Browne, W. J. Corbett, Chris L. Demarest, Lyn Littlefield Hoopes, Jason Lauré, Jan Ormerod, Cynthia Rylant, James Skofield, and James Alfred Wight, among others.

Obituaries have been included in *SATA* since Volume 20. An Obituary is intended not only as a death notice but also as a concise view of a person's life and work. Obituaries may appear for persons who have entries in earlier *SATA* volumes, as well as for people who have not yet appeared in the series. In this volume Obituaries mark the recent deaths of Jane E. Bayer, Rebecca Caudill, Helen MacInnes, and E. B. White.

Each *SATA* volume provides a cumulative index in two parts: first, the Illustrations Index, arranged by the name of the illustrator, gives the number of the volume and page where the illustrator's work appears in the current volume as well as all preceding volumes in the series; second, the Author Index gives the number of the volume in which a person's biographical sketch, Brief Entry, or Obituary appears in the current volume as well as all preceding volumes in the series. These indexes also include references to authors and illustrators who appear in *Yesterday's Authors of Books for Children.* Beginning with Volume 36, the *SATA* Author Index provides cross-references to authors who are included in *Children's Literature Review.*

You will also find cross-references to authors who are included in the *Something about the Author Autobiography Series,* starting with Volume 42. This companion series to *SATA* is described in detail below.

Illustrations

While the textual information in *SATA* is its primary reason for existing, photographs and illustrations not only enliven the text but are an integral part of the information that *SATA* provides. Illustrations and text are wedded in such a special way in children's literature that artists and their works naturally occupy a prominent place among *SATA*'s listees. The illustrators that you'll find in the series include such past masters of children's book illustration as Randolph Caldecott, Kate Greenaway, Walter Crane, Arthur Rackham, and Ernest L. Shepard, as well as such noted contemporary artists as Maurice Sendak, Edward Gorey, Tomie de Paola, and Margot Zemach. There are Caldecott medalists from Dorothy Lathrop (the first recipient in 1938) to Chris Van Allsburg (the latest winner in 1986); cartoonists like Charles Schulz, ("Peanuts"), Walt Kelly ("Pogo"), Hank Ketcham ("Dennis the Menace"), and Georges Rémi ("Tintin"); photographers like Jill Krementz, Tana Hoban, Bruce McMillan, and Bruce Curtis; and filmmakers like Walt Disney, Alfred Hitchcock, and Steven Spielberg.

In more than a dozen years of recording the metamorphosis of children's literature from the printed page to other media, *SATA* has become something of a repository of photographs that are unique in themselves and exist nowhere else as a group, particularly many of the classics of motion picture and stage history and photographs that have been specially loaned to us from private collections.

What a *SATA* Entry Provides

Whether you're already familiar with the *SATA* series or just getting acquainted, you will want to be aware of the kind of information that an entry provides. In every *SATA* entry the editors attempt to give as complete a picture of the person's life and work as possible. In some cases that full range of information may simply be unavailable, or a biographee may choose not to reveal complete personal details. The information that the editors attempt to provide in every entry is arranged in the following categories:

1. The "head" of the entry gives

        —the most complete form of the name,
        —any part of the name not commonly used, included in parentheses,
        —birth and death dates, if known; a (?) indicates a discrepancy in published sources,

—pseudonyms or name variants under which the person has had books published or is publicly known, in parentheses in the second line.

2. "Personal" section gives

   —date and place of birth and death,
   —parents' names and occupations,
   —name of spouse, date of marriage, and names of children,
   —educational institutions attended, degrees received, and dates,
   —religious and political affiliations,
   —agent's name and address,
   —home and/or office address.

3. "Career" section gives

   —name of employer, position, and dates for each career post,
   —military service,
   —memberships,
   —awards and honors.

4. "Writings" section gives

   —title, first publisher and date of publication, and illustration information for each book written; revised editions and other significant editions for books with particularly long publishing histories; genre, when known.

5. "Adaptations" section gives

   —title, major performers, producer, and date of all known reworkings of an author's material in another medium, like movies, filmstrips, television, recordings, plays, etc.

6. "Sidelights" section gives

   —commentary on the life or work of the biographee either directly from the person (and often written specifically for the *SATA* entry), or gathered from biographies, diaries, letters, interviews, or other published sources.

7. "For More Information See" section gives

   —books, feature articles, films, plays, and reviews in which the biographee's life or work has been treated.

How a *SATA* Entry Is Compiled

A *SATA* entry progresses through a series of steps. If the biographee is living, the *SATA* editors try to secure information directly from him or her through a questionnaire. From the information that the biographee supplies, the editors prepare an entry, filling in any essential missing details with research. The author or illustrator is then sent a copy of the entry to check for accuracy and completeness.

If the biographee is deceased or cannot be reached by questionnaire, the *SATA* editors examine a wide variety of published sources to gather information for an entry. Biographical sources are searched with the aid of Gale's *Biography and Genealogy Master Index*. Bibliographic sources like the *National Union Catalog*, the *Cumulative Book Index*, *American Book Publishing Record*, and the *British Museum Catalogue* are consulted, as are book reviews, feature articles, published interviews, and material sometimes obtained from the biographee's family, publishers, agent, or other associates.

For each entry presented in *SATA*, the editors also attempt to locate a photograph of the biographee as well as representative illustrations from his or her books. After surveying the available books which the biographee has written and/or illustrated, and then making a selection of appropriate photographs and illustrations, the editors request permission of the current copyright holders to reprint the material. In the case of older books for which the copyright may have passed through several hands, even locating the current copyright holder is often a long and involved process.

We invite you to examine the entire *SATA* series, starting with this volume. Described below are some of the people in Volume 44 that you may find particularly interesting.

Highlights of This Volume

KAREN BLIXEN......Danish writer who was equally well known under her pseudonym, Isak Dinesen. Blixen grew up during the late 1800s at her family's historic inn, Rungstedlund, which was located on the sea near Copenhagen. She later traveled to British East Africa where she and her husband were managers of a coffee farm. Blixen spent nearly twenty years in Africa, and it was the memorable events of those years that she chronicled in her best-known book, *Out of Africa.* When Blixen finally left Africa in 1931, she took with her an eternal love for the land where she had been "strengthened by the air of the high mountain region, tanned by its sun, filled with its wild, free, magnificent beauty. . . ." Often described by critics as a "courageous" writer, Blixen dealt with themes of aristocratic pride and acceptance of fate in all her works, including *Seven Gothic Tales* and *Winter's Tales.*

ARNA BONTEMPS......a librarian and educator who was among the first black writers to realistically portray black life in America. Growing up in Louisiana and California, Bontemps found he had one of two choices—either to reject his ethnic background or embrace it. Deciding that "the shedding of his Negro-ness" was "not only impossible but unthinkable," Bontemps traveled to New York City where, along with contemporaries like Langston Hughes and Jean Toomer, he became part of the Harlem Renaissance movement that flourished during the 1920s. In subsequent years, Bontemps produced novels, poems, biographies, and plays, as well as children's books like *Sad-Faced Boy, The Fast Sooner Hound,* and the Newbery Award Honor Book, *Story of the Negro.*

BOB CLAMPETT......creator of "Beany and Cecil." This Emmy Award-winning animator was part of the Warner Brothers team that produced such memorable cartoon characters as Daffy Duck, Tweety and Sylvester, Porky Pig, and, of course, Bugs Bunny. After years of drawing "Loony Tunes" and "Merrie Melodies" short subjects, Clampett decided to try his hand at creating his own characters. Thus was born Cecil the Seasick Serpent, Beany, and the villainous Dishonest John. For Clampett, Cecil embodied a multitude of emotions. "All the pains and pleasures, intense feelings . . . of my own adolescence are ingrained in Cecil," he confessed. "When you look at a Cecil gag, you might say, 'Oh, that's just funny.' But there's a tear to it, too." After more than twenty years, children still delight at the animated antics of these Clampett characters.

DONG KINGMAN......American-born artist who spent his childhood in Hong Kong. As a student at the Chan Sun-Wen School, Kingman did well in only two subjects—painting and calligraphy. Art became a permanent part of Kingman's life. Upon his return to America at the age of eighteen, he found himself painting everything, from "street scenes, waterfronts, parks, and skyscrapers" to "people, buses, bicycles, cars, lampposts, and stoplights." Kingman is responsible for promotional, advertising, or main title artwork for movies like "The World of Suzie Wong," "Flower Drum Song," and "The Sand Pebbles," and has illustrated children's books, like *The Bamboo Gate* by Vanya Oakes and *Johnny Hong of Chinatown* by Clyde Robert Bulla. The artist dismisses the labels "Occidental" and "Oriental" that are selectively applied to his work. "There is only my way of painting with watercolor," he asserts, "and I hope whoever sees my paintings will enjoy and understand them as such."

PHYLLIS McGINLEY......Pulitzer Prize-winning poet who described her childhood years in Colorado as "wild and wooly. . . . The nearest town . . . looked just like a scene from a TV western." She endured a sporadic education in a one-room schoolhouse only to be confronted by four years at a state university where she "seriously managed to learn nothing." On her own, McGinley patched the holes in her formal education, to her advantage. "[I] met Dickens, Austen, and Mark Twain," she recalled, "when I was capable of giving them the full court curtsy." McGinley firmly believed that "children are explorers by nature. They have to be in order to discover the world around them. . . . So they deserve brave books. They deserve the best that men and women of wit and talent can write for them. . . ." The best of McGinley can be found in her children's books like *The Plain Princess, All Around the Town, The Year without a Santa Claus,* and *Mince Pie and Mistletoe.*

WILLY POGÁNY......Hungarian-born artist who immigrated to America where he successfully worked as an illustrator, muralist, stage and costume designer, architect, and sculptor. Beginning in the late 1920s, Pogány made his mark in Hollywood as a scenic artist and art director for United Artists, Warner Brothers, Twentieth Century-Fox, and others. His prolific work included the illustrations for over 150 children's books, such as Lillian Gask's *Folk Tales from Many Lands,* H. de Vere Stacpoole's *The Blue Lagoon,* Phillis Garrard's *Running Away with Nebby,* and many of Padraic Colum's works. Pogány reveled in his chosen vocation. "There is scarcely anything in this world that rivals the pleasure and satisfaction of painting a picture," he declared.". . .The wonder world of the artist is open to all who feel the urge to paint."

MORDECAI RICHLER......author of the award-winning children's book, *Jacob Two-Two Meets the Hooded Fang.* Richler's success as a children's writer came as an aside to his already successful career as an adult novelist and screenwriter. *Jacob Two-Two,* in fact, was written so that Richler's younger offspring could read some of their father's writings. Other than "a few classics old and modern, and the incomparable Dr. Seuss," Richler admits he found the books he read aloud to his children "awfully boring or insufferably didactic." *Jacob Two-Two* was Richler's remedy. "Pure fun," he states, "not instruction, is what I had in mind."

These are only a few of the authors and illustrators that you'll find in this volume. We hope you find all the entries in *SATA* both interesting and useful.

Something about the Author Autobiography Series

You can complement the information in *SATA* with the *Something about the Author Autobiography Series (SAAS),* which provides autobiographical essays written by important current authors and illustrators of books for children and young adults. In every volume of *SAAS* you will find about twenty specially commissioned autobiographies, each accompanied by a selection of personal photographs supplied by the authors. The wide range of contemporary writers and artists who describe their lives and interests in the *Autobiography Series* includes Joan Aiken, Betsy Byers, Leonard Everett Fisher, Milton Meltzer, Maia Wojciechowska, and Jane Yolen. Though the information presented in the autobiographies is as varied and unique as the authors, you can learn about the people and events that influenced these writers' early lives, how they began their careers, what problems they faced in becoming established in their professions, what prompted them to write or illustrate particular books, what they now find most challenging or rewarding in their lives, and what advice they may have for young people interested in following in their footsteps, among many other subjects.

Autobiographies included in the *SATA Autobiography Series* can be located through both the *SATA* cumulative index and the *SAAS* cumulative index, which lists not only the authors' names but also the subjects mentioned in their essays, such as titles of works and geographical and personal names.

The *SATA Autobiography Series* gives you the opportunity to view "close up" some of the fascinating people who are included in the *SATA* parent series. The combined *SATA* series makes available to you an unequaled range of comprehensive and in-depth information about the authors and illustrators of young people's literature.

Please write and tell us if we can make *SATA* even more helpful to you.

Forthcoming Authors

A Partial List of Authors and Illustrators Who Will Appear in Forthcoming Volumes of *Something about the Author*

Abels, Harriette S.
Allen, Agnes B.   1898-1959
Allert, Kathy
Anders, Rebecca
Anderson, Leone C.   1923-
Andrist, Ralph K.   1914-
Appleby, Ellen
Atkinson, Allen
Austin, R. G.
Axeman, Lois
Ayme, Marcel   1902-1967
Bains, Rae
Baker, Olaf
Balderson, Margaret   1935-
Bartlett, Margaret F.   1896-
Bauer, Caroline Feller   1935-
Bauer, John Albert   1882-1918
Beckman, Delores
Beim, Jerrold   1910-1957
Beim, Lorraine   1909-1951
Bernheim, Evelyne   1935-
Bernheim, Marc   1924-
Birnbaum, Abe   1899-
Boegehold, Betty   1913-1985
Boning, Richard A.
Bonners, Susan
Bourke, Linda
Bowen, Gary
Bracken, Carolyn
Brewton, Sara W.
Bridgman, Elizabeth P.   1921-
Bromley, Dudley   1948-
Bronin, Andrew   1947-
Bronson, Wilfrid   1894-
Brooks, Ron(ald George)   1948-
Brown, Roy Frederick   1921-
Brownmiller, Susan   1935-
Buchanan, William   1930-
Buchenholz, Bruce
Budney, Blossom   1921-
Burchard, Marshall
Burke, David   1927-
Burstein, Chaya M.
Butler, Dorothy   1925-
Butler, Hal   1913-
Calvert, Patricia
Camps, Luis   1928-
Carley, Wayne
Carlson, Nancy L.
Carrie, Christopher
Carroll, Ruth R.   1899-
Chambliss, Maxie
Chang, Florence C.

Charles, Carole
Charles, Donald   1929-
Chartier, Normand
Chase, Catherine
Clarke, Bob
Cline, Linda   1941-
Cohen, Joel H.
Cole, Brock
Cooper, Elizabeth Keyser   1910-
Cooper, Paulette   1944-
Cosgrove, Margaret   1926-
Coutant, Helen
Croll, Carolyn
Dabcovich, Lydia
Daniel, Alan   1939-
D'Aulnoy, Marie Catherine   1650(?)-1705
David, Jay   1929-
Davies, Peter   1937-
Davis, Maggie S.   1942-
Dawson, Diane
Dean, Leigh
Degens, T.
Deguine, Jean-Claude   1943-
Dentinger, Don
Deweese, Gene   1934-
Ditmars, Raymond   1876-1942
Drescher, Henrik
Dumas, Philippe   1940-
Dunn, Phoebe
East, Ben
Edelson, Edward   1932-
Edens, Cooper
Eisenberg, Lisa
Elder, Lauren
Elwood, Roger   1943-
Endres, Helen
Enik, Ted
Epstein, Len
Eriksson, Eva
Erwin, Betty K.
Estes, Rose
Etter, Les   1904-
Everett-Green, Evelyn   1856-1932
Ewers, Joe
Falkner, John Meade   1858-1932
Feczko, Kathy
Felix, Monique
Fender, Kay
Filson, Brent
Fischer, Hans Erich   1909-1958
Flanagan, Geraldine Lux
Flint, Russ

Folch-Ribas, Jacques   1928-
Foley, Louise M.   1933-
Fox, Thomas C.
Freschet, Berniece   1927-
Frevert, Patricia D(endtler)   1943-
Funai, Mamoru R.   1932-
Gans, Roma   1894-
Garcia Sanchez, J(ose) L(uis)
Garrison, Christian   1942-
Gathje, Curtis
Gelman, Rita G.   1937-
Gemme, Leila Boyle   1942-
Gerber, Dan   1940-
Goldstein, Nathan   1927-
Gorbaty, Norman
Gould, Chester   1900-1985
Gray, J.M.L.
Gusman, Annie
Hakes, Thomas L.
Halverson, Lydia
Harris, Marilyn   1931-
Hayman, LeRoy   1916-
Heine, Helme   1941-
Henty, George Alfred   1832-1902
Herzig, Alison Cragin
Hicks, Clifford B.   1920-
Higashi, Sandra
Hockerman, Dennis
Hollander, Zander   1923-
Hood, Thomas   1779-1845
Howell, Troy
Hull, Jessie Redding
Hunt, Clara Whitehill   1871-1958
Hunt, Robert
Inderieden, Nancy
Irvine, Georgeanne
Isaak, Betty
Iwamura, Kazuo   1939-
Jackson, Anita
Jackson, Kathryn   1907-
Jackson, Robert   1941-
Jameson, Cynthia
Janssen, Pierre
Jenkins, Jean
Johnson, Maud
Johnson, Sylvia A.
Kahn, Joan   1914-
Kalan, Robert
Kantrowitz, Mildred
Kasuya, Masahiro   1937-
Keith, Eros   1942-
Kiedrowski, Priscilla
Kirn, Ann (Minette)   1910-

Koenig, Marion
Kohl, Herbert   1937-
Kohl, Judith
Kredenser, Gail   1936-
Kurland, Michael   1938-
Lawson, Annetta
Leach, Christopher   1925-
Lebrun, Claude
Leckie, Robert   1920-
Leder, Dora
Le-Tan, Pierre   1950-
Lewis, Naomi
Lindgren, Barbro
Lines, Kathleen
Livermore, Elaine
Lye, Keith
Madsen, Lorna
Mahany, Patricia
Marcus, Elizabeth
Marks, Rita   1938-
Marron, Carol A.
Marryat, Frederick   1792-1848
Marsh, Carole
Marxhausen, Joanne G.   1935-
May, Dorothy
Mayakovsky, Vladimir   1894-1930
McKim, Audrey Margaret   1909-
McLoughlin, John C.   1949-
McReynolds, Ginny
Melcher, Frederic G.   1879-1963
Meyer, Kathleen Allan
Miller, J(ohn) P.   1919-
Milone, Karen
Molesworth, Mary L.   1839(?)-1921
Molly, Anne S.   1907-
Morris, Neil
Morris, Ting
Moskowitz, Stewart
Muntean, Michaela
Murdocca, Sal
Nickl, Peter
Nicoll, Helen
Obligado, Lillian Isabel   1931-
O'Brien, John   1953-
Oppenheim, Shulamith (Levey)   1930-
Orr, Frank   1936-
Orton, Helen Fuller   1872-1955
Overbeck, Cynthia
Owens, Gail   1939-

Packard, Edward   1931-
Parker, Robert Andrew   1927-
Paterson, A(ndrew) B(arton)   1864-1941
Patterson, Sarah   1959-
Pavey, Peter
Pelgrom, Els
Peretz, Isaac Loeb   1851-1915
Perkins, Lucy Fitch   1865-1937
Phillips, Betty Lou
Plowden, David   1932-
Poignant, Axel
Pollard, Nan
Pollock, Bruce   1945-
Polushkin, Maria
Porter, Eleanor Hodgman   1868-1920
Poulsson, Emilie   1853-1939
Powers, Richard M.   1921-
Prather, Ray
Pursell, Margaret S.
Pursell, Thomas F.
Pyle, Katharine   1863-1938
Rabinowitz, Solomon   1859-1916
Randall, E.T.
Rappoport, Ken   1935-
Reese, Bob
Reich, Hanns
Reid, Alistair   1926-
Reidel, Marlene
Reiff, Tana
Reiss, Elayne
Reynolds, Marjorie   1903-
Rhodes, J.H.
Richards, Dorothy Fay   1915-
Rippon, Angela
Robert, Adrian
Rohmer, Harriet
Rosier, Lydia
Ross, Pat
Roy, Cal
Rudstrom, Lennart
Sadler, Marilyn
Sallis, Susan
Satchwell, John
Schindler, Regine
Schneider, Leo   1916-
Sealy, Adrienne V.
Seidler, Rosalie
Shelton, Ingrid
Silbert, Linda P.

Slepian, Jan(ice B.)
Smith, Alison
Smith, Catriona (Mary)   1948-
Smith, Ray(mond Kenneth)   1949-
Smollin, Michael J.
Sorenson, Jane
Steiner, Charlotte
Stevens, Leonard A.   1920-
Stine, R. Conrad   1937-
Stubbs, Joanna   1940-
Sullivan, Mary Beth
Suteev, Vladimir Grigor'evich
Sutherland, Robert D.   1937-
Sweet, Ozzie
Tarrant, Graham
Thaler, Mike
Timmermans, Gommaar   1930-
Todd, Ruthven   1914-
Tourneur, Dina K.   1934-
Treadgold, Mary   1910-
Velthuijs, Max   1923-
Villiard, Paul   1910-1974
Vincent, Gabrielle
Wagner, Jenny
Walker, Charles W.
Walsh, Anne Batterberry
Walter, Mildred P.
Watts, Franklin   1904-1978
Wayne, Bennett
Weston, Martha
Whelen, Gloria   1923-
White, Wallace   1930-
Wild, Jocelyn
Wild, Robin
Winter, Paula   1929-
Winterfeld, Henry   1901-
Wolde, Gunilla   1939-
Wong, Herbert H.
Woolfolk, Dorothy
Wormser, Richard   1908-
Wright, Betty R.
Wright, Bob
Yabuuchi, Masayuki   1940-
Yagawa, Sumiko
Youldon, Gillian
Zaslow, David
Zistel, Era
Zwerger, Lisbeth

In the interest of making *Something about the Author* as responsive as possible to the needs of its readers, the editor welcomes your suggestions for additional authors and illustrators to be included in the series.

Acknowledgments

Grateful acknowledgment is made to the following publishers, authors, and artists
for their kind permission to reproduce copyrighted material.

AMERICAN LIBRARY ASSOCIATION. Sidelight excerpts from an article "Where Do You Get Your Ideas?" by H. M. Hoover, fall, 1982 in *Top of the News.* Copyright © 1982 by American Library Association./ Sidelight excerpts from *British Children's Authors: Interviews at Home,* edited by Cornelia Jones and Olivia R. Way. Copyright © 1976 by American Library Association. Both reprinted by permission of American Library Association.

ANANSI. Sidelight excerpts from *Eleven Canadian Novelists* by Graeme Gibson. Reprinted by permission of Anansi.

ATHENEUM PUBLISHERS. Jacket illustration by Leslie Morrill from *Bring to a Boil and Separate* by Hadley Irwin. Copyright © 1980 by Lee Hadley and Ann Irwin./ Jacket illustration by Richard Williams from *Moon and Me* by Hadley Irwin. Copyright © 1981 by Lee Hadley and Ann Irwin./ Illustration by Pat Marriott from *The Strangers* by Ann Schlee. Copyright © 1971 by Ann Schlee. All reprinted by permission of Atheneum Publishers.

BANTAM BOOKS, INC. Illustration by Dong Kingman from *The Effect of Gamma Rays on Man-in-the-Moon Marigolds* by Paul Zindel. Copyright © 1970, 1971 by Paul Zindel. Reprinted by permission of Bantam Books, Inc.

A. & C. BLACK LTD. Illustration by Willy Pogány from *The Blue Lagoon* by H. de Vere Stacpoole. Reprinted by permission of A. & C. Black Ltd.

BOWMAR NATURE SERIES. Illustration by Albert John Pucci and lettering by Paul Taylor from *Tail Twisters* by Aileen Fisher. Text copyright © 1973 by Aileen Fisher. Illustrations copyright © 1973 by Bowmar. Reprinted by permission of Bowmar Nature Series.

JONATHAN CAPE LTD. Illustration by Mike Wilks from *Pile: Petals from St. Klaed's Computer* by Brian W. Aldiss. Text copyright © 1979 by Brian W. Aldiss. Illustrations copyright © 1979 by Mike Wilks./ Sidelight excerpts from the introduction and photograph from *Masquerade: The Complete Book with Answers and Clues Explained* by Kit Williams./ Illustrations by Kit Williams from *Masquerade* by Kit Williams. Copyright © 1979 by Kit Williams. All reprinted by permission of Jonathan Cape Ltd.

CELESTIAL ARTS. Illustration by Barbara Reinertson from *Grandma and Grandpa Are Special People* by Barbara Kay Polland. Text copyright © 1982 by Barbara Kay Polland. Illustrations copyright © 1982 by Barbara Reinertson. Reprinted by permission of Celestial Arts.

THOMAS Y. CROWELL, INC. Illustration by Harper Johnson from "A Tulip for Tony" by Marietta Moskin in *Round about the City: Stories You Can Read to Yourself,* selected by the Child Study Association of America. Copyright © 1966 by Thomas Y. Crowell, Inc. Reprinted by permission of Thomas Y. Crowell, Inc.

CROWN PUBLISHERS, INC. Jacket illustration by Michael Garland from *Secret Lies* by Sarah Sargent. Copyright © 1981 by Sarah Sargent. Reprinted by permission of Crown Publishers, Inc.

DELACORTE PRESS. Jacket illustration by Joe Cstari from *It's No Crush, I'm in Love!* by June Foley. Text copyright © 1982 by June Foley. Jacket illustration copyright © 1982 by Joe Cstari. Reprinted by permission of Delacorte Press.

T. S. DENISON & CO., INC. Sidelight excerpts from *Minnesota Writers,* edited by Carmen Richards. Reprinted by permission of T. S. Denison & Co., Inc.

DODD, MEAD & CO. Sidelight excerpts from *Arna Bontemps-Langston Hughes Letters: 1925-1967,* edited by Charles H. Nichols./ Jacket illustration by Eileen McKeating from *A Place for Allie* by Mary Carey. Copyright © 1985 by Mary Carey. Both reprinted by permission of Dodd, Mead & Co.

DOUBLEDAY PUBLISHING CO. Illustration by Willy Pogány from "The House with Nobody in It" by Joyce Kilmer in *My Poetry Book: An Anthology of Modern Verse for Boys and Girls,* selected by Grace Thompson Huffard and Laura Mae Carlisle. Copyright 1934 by The John C. Winston Co. Reprinted by permission of Doubleday Publishing Co.

E. P. DUTTON, INC. Jacket illustration by Michael Eagle from *Blood Feud* by Rosemary Sutcliff. Copyright © 1976 by Rosemary Sutcliff./ Illustration by Victor Ambrus from *A Crown of Wild Olive* by Rosemary Sutcliff. Text copyright © 1971 by Rosemary Sutcliff. Illustrations copyright © 1971 by Victor Ambrus./ Illustration by Charles Keeping from *Beowulf,* retold by Rosemary Sutcliff. Text copyright © 1961 by Rosemary Sutcliff. Illustrations copyright © 1961 by The Bodley Head Ltd. All reprinted by permission of E. P. Dutton, Inc.

ENSLOW PUBLISHERS. Illustration from *Mister President: The Story of Ronald Reagan* by Mary Virginia Fox. Copyright © 1982 by Mary Virginia Fox. Reprinted by permission of Enslow Publishers.

FARRAR, STRAUS & GIROUX, INC. Illustration from *Astrophel; or, The Life and Death of the Renowned Sir Philip Sidney* by Alfred H. Bill. Copyright 1937 by Alfred H. Bill. Reprinted by permission of Farrar, Straus & Giroux, Inc.

GARRARD PUBLISHING CO. Illustration by Paul Frame from *Kidnapped on Astarr* by Joan Lowery Nixon. Copyright © 1981 by Joan Lowery Nixon. Reprinted by permission of Garrard Publishing Co.

GROSSET & DUNLAP, INC. Illustration by Harper Johnson from *The Story of George Washington Carver* by Arna Bontemps. Copyright 1954 by Arna Bontemps. Reprinted by permission of Grosset & Dunlap, Inc.

HAMISH HAMILTON LTD. Illustration by John Lawrence from *A Christmas Card* by Paul Theroux. Copyright © 1978 by Paul Theroux. Reprinted by permission of Hamish Hamilton Ltd.

HARCOURT BRACE JOVANOVICH, INC. Illustration by Doris Lee from *The Great Quillow* by James Thurber. Copyright 1944 by James Thurber. Copyright © 1972 by Helen Thurber./ Illustration by Nora S. Unwin from *The White Ring* by Enys Tregarthen. Edited by Elizabeth Yates. Text copyright 1949 by Elizabeth Yates. Illustrations copyright 1949 by Nora S. Unwin./ Illustration by Sonia O. Lisker from *Two Special Cards* by Sonia O. Lisker and Leigh Dean. All reprinted by permission of Harcourt Brace Jovanovich, Inc.

HARPER & ROW, PUBLISHERS, INC. Illustration by Philip Smith from *Delbert, the Plainclothes Detective* by Joan Lowery Nixon. Copyright © 1971 by Joan Lowery Nixon./ Illustration by Nora S. Unwin from *The Doll Who Came Alive* by Enys Tregarthen. Edited by Elizabeth Yates. Copyright 1942 by Elizabeth Yates, copyright renewed © 1969. New text copyright © 1972 by Elizabeth Yates. Illustrations copyright © 1972 by Nora S. Unwin./ Illustration by Maurice Sendak from *The Bee-Man of Orn* by Frank R. Stockton. Illustrations copyright © 1964 by Maurice Sendak./ Illustration by Dong Kingman from "Dong Kingman" by June M. Omura in *Wings and Wishes.* Copyright © 1977 by Harper & Row, Publishers, Inc. All reprinted by permission of Harper & Row, Publishers, Inc.

HASTINGS HOUSE, PUBLISHERS, INC. Jacket illustration by Janet Scabrini from *Auras and Other Rainbow Secrets* by Lila McGinnis. Reprinted by permission of Hastings House, Publishers, Inc.

WILLIAM HEINEMANN LTD. Sidelight excerpts from *Daguerreotypes and Other Essays* by Isak Dinesen. Copyright © 1979 by The University of Chicago Press. Reprinted by permission of William Heinemann Ltd.

LAWRENCE HILL & CO., PUBLISHERS, INC. Photograph by Norma Holt from *The Blue Rose* by Gerda Klein. Text copyright © 1974 by Gerda Klein. Photographs copyright by Norma Holt. Reprinted by permission of Lawrence Hill & Co., Publishers, Inc.

HOLIDAY HOUSE, INC. Illustration by Blanche Sims from *Me and Katie (the Pest)* by Ann M. Martin. Text copyright © 1985 by Ann M. Martin. Illustrations copyright © 1985 by Blanche Sims. Reprinted by permission of Holiday House, Inc.

HOLT, RINEHART & WINSTON GENERAL BOOK. Illustration by Willy Pogány from "In the Nursery" in *The Home Book of Verse for Young Folks,* selected and arranged by Burton Egbert Stevenson. Copyright 1915, 1929 by Henry Holt & Co./ Illustration by Willy Pogány from "The Happy Warrior" in *The Home Book of Verse for Young Folks,* selected and arranged by Burton Egbert Stevenson. Copyright 1915, 1929 by Henry Holt & Co./ Illustration by Maurice Sendak from *The Griffin and the Minor Canon* by Frank R. Stockton. Illustrations copyright © 1963 by Maurice Sendak./ Illustration by Cyrus Leroy Baldridge from *Chariot in the Sky* by Arna Bontemps. Copyright 1951 by Arna Bontemps. All reprinted by permission of Holt, Rinehart & Winston General Book.

THE HORN BOOK, INC. Sidelight excerpts from *Illustrators of Children's Books: 1946-1956* by Bertha Mahony Miller and others. Copyright © 1958 by The Horn Book, Inc./ Sidelight excerpts from an article "Enys Tregarthen" by Elizabeth Yates, May, 1949 in *Horn Book*. Both reprinted by permission of The Horn Book, Inc.

HOUGHTON MIFFLIN CO. Illustration by Virginia Lee Burton from *Sad-Faced Boy* by Arna Bontemps. Copyright 1937 by Arna Bontemps./ Illustration by Ursula Koering from *Slappy Hooper, the Wonderful Sign Painter* by Arna Bontemps and Jack Conroy. Copyright 1946 by Arna Bontemps and Jack Conroy./ Illustration by Feliks Topolski from *Lonesome Boy* by Arna Bontemps. Text copyright 1955 by Arna Bontemps. Illustrations copyright 1955 by Feliks Topolski./ Illustration by Virginia Lee Burton from *The Fast Sooner Hound* by Arna Bontemps and Jack Conroy. Copyright 1942 by Houghton Mifflin Co./ Frontispiece wood engraving by John Lawrence from *London Snow: A Christmas Story* by Paul Theroux. Copyright © 1979 by Paul Theroux./ Illustration by John Lawrence from *A Christmas Card* by Paul Theroux. Copyright © 1978 by Paul Theroux./ Sidelight excerpts from *The Great Railway Bazaar: By Train through Asia* by Paul Theroux./ Jacket illustration by Jerry Pinkney from *Fong and the Indians* by Paul Theroux. Copyright © 1968 by Paul Theroux. All reprinted by permission of Houghton Mifflin Co.

ALFRED A. KNOPF, INC. Illustration courtesy of the *Illustrated London News* from *The Beleaguered City: Richmond, 1861-1865* by Alfred Hoyt Bill. Copyright 1946 by Alfred A. Knopf, Inc./ Illustration by Raymond Lufkin from *Story of the Negro* by Arna Bontemps. Copyright 1948, 1955, © 1969 by Arna Bontemps./ Sidelight excerpts from *Home Sweet Home: My Canadian Album* by Mordecai Richler. Copyright © 1984 by Mordecai Richler./ Illustrations by Kit Williams from *Book without a Name* by Kit Williams. Copyright © 1984 by Kit Williams./ Illustration by Frederick T. Chapman from *The Ring of Danger: A Tale of Elizabethan England* by Alfred H. Bill. Copyright 1948 by Alfred H. Bill./ Illustration by Harper Johnson from *Frederick Douglass: Slave, Fighter, Freeman* by Arna Bontemps. Copyright © 1959 by Arna Bontemps. All reprinted by permission of Alfred A. Knopf, Inc.

J. B. LIPPINCOTT CO. Illustration by Len Ebert from *Mr. Kelso's Lion* by Arna Bontemps. Copyright © 1970 by Arna Bontemps./ Illustration by Carol Newsom from *When the Boys Ran the House* by Joan Carris. Text copyright © 1982 by Joan Carris. Illustrations copyright © 1982 by Carol Newsom./ Illustration by Harold Berson from *Mince Pie and Mistletoe* by Phyllis McGinley. Copyright © 1959, 1961 by Phyllis McGinley./ Illustration by Helen Stone from *Lucy McLockett* by Phyllis McGinley. Copyright © 1958, 1959 by Phyllis McGinley./ Illustration by Helen Stone from *The Horse Who Lived Upstairs* by Phyllis McGinley. Text copyright 1944 by Phyllis McGinley. Illustrations copyright 1944 by Helen Stone./ Illustration by Helen Stone from *The Most Wonderful Doll in the World* by Phyllis McGinley. Text copyright 1950 by Phyllis McGinley. Illustrations copyright 1950 by Helen Stone./ Illustration by John Alcorn from *Wonderful Time* by Phyllis McGinley. Text copyright © 1965, 1966 by Phyllis McGinley. Illustrations copyright © 1966 by John Alcorn. All reprinted by permission of J. B. Lippincott Co.

LITTLE, BROWN & CO. Illustration by John Larrecq from *Just the Thing for Geraldine* by Ellen Conford. Text copyright © 1974 by Ellen Conford. Illustrations copyright © 1974 by John Larrecq. Reprinted by permission of Little, Brown & Co.

LOTHROP, LEE & SHEPARD BOOKS. Illustration by Consuelo Joerns from *The Midnight Castle* by Consuelo Joerns. Copyright © 1983 by Consuelo Joerns. Reprinted by permission of Lothrop, Lee & Shepard Books.

MACMILLAN, INC. Jacket illustration by Richard Cuffari from *The Lion's Cub* by H. M. Hoover. Copyright © 1974 by H. M. Hoover./ Illustration by Leonard Kessler from *Grandma Witch and the Magic Doobelator* by Ethel and Leonard Kessler. Copyright © 1981 by Ethel Kessler and Leonard Kessler./ Illustration by Leonard Weisgard from *A Wreath of Christmas Legends* by Phyllis McGinley. Text copyright © 1964, 1966, 1967 by Phyllis McGinley. Illustrations copyright © 1967 by Leonard Weisgard./ Illustration by Andrew Glass from *The Gift* by Joan Lowery Nixon. Text copyright © 1983 by Joan Lowery Nixon. Illustrations copyright © 1983 by Andrew Glass./ Illustration by Willy Pogány from "The Story of the Fairy Rowan Tree" in *The King of Ireland's Son* by Padraic Colum. Copyright 1916 by The Macmillan Co. Copyright renewed 1944 by Padraic Colum./ Illustration by Willy Pogány from "The Voyage to Colchis" in *The Golden Fleece and the Heroes Who Lived before Achilles* by Padraic Colum. Copyright 1921 by The Macmillan Co./ Jacket illustration by Susan Stillman from *At the Back of the Woods* by Claudia Mills. Copyright © 1982 by Claudia Mills./ Illustration by Dong Kingman from "Di-Di—The New Scholar in the Old Temple" in *The Bamboo Gate Stories of Children of Modern China* by Vanya Oakes. Copyright 1946 by The Macmillan Co. All reprinted by permission of Macmillan, Inc.

McCLELLAND & STEWART LTD. Illustration by Fritz Wegner from *Jacob Two-Two Meets the Hooded Fang* by Mordecai Richler. Text copyright © 1975 by Mordecai Richler.

Carnival: Entertainments and Posthumous Tales by Isak Dinesen. Copyright © 1975 by Rungstedlundfonden. Copyright © 1977 by The University of Chicago Press./ Sidelight excerpts from *Daguerreotypes and Other Essays* by Isak Dinesen. Copyright © 1979 by The University of Chicago Press./ Photographs from *The Life and Destiny of Isak Dinesen*, collected and edited by Frans Lasson. Text by Clara Svendsen. Copyright © 1970 by Random House, Inc. All reprinted by permission of The University of Chicago Press.

UNIVERSITY OF PENNSYLVANIA PRESS. Sidelight excerpts from *Frank R. Stockton: A Critical Biography* by Martin Griffin. Reprinted by permission of University of Pennsylvania Press.

THE VIKING PRESS. Jacket illustration by Derek James from *The Shepherd Moon: A Novel of the Future* by H. M. Hoover. Copyright © 1984 by Viking Penguin, Inc./ Jacket illustration by Charles Mikolaycak from *The Rains of Eridan* by H. M. Hoover. Copyright © 1977 by H. M. Hoover./ Illustration by Jerry Lazare from *Queenie Peavy* by Robert Burch. Copyright © 1966 by Robert Burch./ Sidelight excerpts from *The Province of the Heart* by Phyllis McGinley. Copyright 1953, © 1959 by Phyllis McGinley. All reprinted by permission of The Viking Press.

HENRY Z. WALCK, INC. Illustration by Charles Keeping from *The Silver Branch* by Rosemary Sutcliff./ Illustration by Richard Cuffari from *The Capricorn Bracelet* by Rosemary Sutcliff. Copyright © 1973 by Rosemary Sutcliff./ Illustration by Richard Lebenson from *The Witch's Brat* by Rosemary Sutcliff. Copyright © 1970 by Rosemary Sutcliff. All reprinted by permission of Henry Z. Walck, Inc.

WALKER & CO. Illustration by Sonia O. Lisker from *Captain Hook, That's Me* by Ada B. Litchfield. Reprinted by permission of Walker & Co.

FREDERICK WARNE AND CO., INC. Illustration by Lorinda Bryan Cauley from *If You Say So, Claude* by Joan Lowery Nixon. Text copyright © 1980 by Joan Lowery Nixon. Illustrations copyright © 1980 by Lorinda Bryan Cauley. Reprinted by permission of Frederick Warne and Co., Inc.

WATSON-GUPTILL PUBLICATIONS. Photograph, illustrations, and Sidelight excerpts from *Dong Kingman's Watercolors* by Dong Kingman and Helena Kuo Kingman. All reprinted by permission of Watson-Guptill Publications.

FRANKLIN WATTS, INC. Illustration by Steven Assel from *World War II Resistance Stories* by Arthur Prager and Emily Prager. Text copyright © 1979 by Arthur Prager and Emily Prager. Illustrations copyright © 1979 by Franklin Watts, Inc./ Illustration by Ellen Weiss from *Millicent Maybe* by Ellen Weiss. Copyright © 1979 by Ellen Weiss. Both reprinted by permission of Franklin Watts, Inc.

FRANKLIN WATTS LTD. Photograph by Gwynneth Ashby from *Take a Trip to Japan* by Gwynneth Ashby. Copyright © 1980 by Franklin Watts Ltd. Reprinted by permission of Franklin Watts Ltd.

WRITER'S HOUSE. Photograph by Arlene Alda from *Sonya's Mommy Works* by Arlene Alda. Copyright © 1982 by Arlene Alda. Reprinted by permission of Writer's House.

Sidelight excerpts from *The Great Railway Bazaar: By Train through Asia* by Paul Theroux. Reprinted by permission of Gillon Aitken Ltd./ Illustration by Rex Schneider from *Ain't We Got Fun?* by Rex Schneider. Reprinted by permission of Blue Mouse Studio./ Sidelight excerpts from *More Books by More People* by Lee Bennett Hopkins. Reprinted by permission of Curtis Brown Ltd./ Cover photograph by Julie Thompson from the album cover of *Malvina and Friends Sing Magical Songs*. Words and music by Malvina Reynolds. Copyright © 1978 by Cassandra Records. Reprinted by permission of Cassandra Records./ Illustration by Willy Pogány from "A Christmas Folk Song" by Lizette Woodworth Reese in *My Poetry Book: An Anthology of Modern Verse for Boys and Girls*, selected by Grace Thompson Huffard and Laura Mae Carlisle. Copyright 1934 by The John C. Winston Co. Reprinted by permission of Edward Dietrich./ Sidelight excerpts from an article "My Father's Life," by Mordecai Richler, August, 1982 in *Esquire*. Reprinted by permission of *Esquire*./ Sidelight excerpts from an article "Bob Clampett: An Interview with a Master Cartoon Maker and Puppeteer" by Mike Barrier, summer, 1970 in *Funnyworld*. Reprinted by permission of *Funnyworld*./ Sidelight excerpts from an article "Why I Returned" by Arna Bontemps, April, 1965 in *Harper's*. Reprinted by permission of *Harper's*.

Sidelight excerpts from an article "There's No Secret to Water Color" by Dong Kingman, May, 1950 in *Design*. Reprinted by permission of Dong Kingman./ Sidelight excerpts from "The Man of Masquerade" by Susan Raven, June 20, 1982 in *London Sunday Times*. Reprinted by permission of *London Sunday Times*./ Sidelight excerpts from an article "Malvina Reynolds: Time to Sing Her Praises" by Amie Hill, June, 1975 in *Ms*. Reprinted by permission of *Ms*./ Sidelight excerpts from an article "A Song of San Francisco Bay" by Malvina Reynolds, January, 1968 in *Natural History*, Volume 77. Copyright © 1968 by American Museum of Natural History. Reprinted by permission of American Museum of Natural History./ Sidelight excerpts from "Willy Pogány and Film Art," January 1, 1928 in the *New York Times*. Copyright 1928 by The New York Times Co. Reprinted by permission of The New York Times Co./ Sidelight excerpts from an article "Mordecai Richler Then and Now" by Thomas R. Edwards, June 22, 1980 in *New York Times Book Review*. Copyright © 1980 by The New York Times Co. Reprinted by permission of The New York Times Co./ Sidelight excerpts from *Arna Bontemps-Langston Hughes Letters: 1925-1967*, edited by Charles H. Nichols. Reprinted by permission of Harold Ober Associates.

Sidelight excerpts from an article "Writing Jacob Two-Two" by Mordecai Richler, autumn, 1978 in *Canadian Literature*. Reprinted by permission of Mordecai Richler./ Illustration by Jodi Robbin from *Tweedles and Foodles for Young Noodles*. Words and music by Malvina Reynolds. Copyright © 1961 by Schroder Music Co. Reprinted by permission of Jodi Robbin./ Sidelight excerpts from "Songster Malvina Reynolds Dies," March 18, 1978 in *San Francisco Chronicle*. Reprinted by permission of *San Francisco Chronicle*./ Sidelight excerpts from an article "Paul Theroux" by Anthony Weller, November, 1983 in *GEO*. Reprinted by permission of Paul Theroux./ Sidelight excerpts from an article "Wit, Wisdom and Phyllis McGinley," November, 1965 in *Reader's Digest*. Reprinted by permission of Time, Inc./ Cover painting of Phyllis McGinley, June 18, 1965 in *Time*. Reprinted by permission of Time Inc./ Sidelight excerpts from an article "I Sell More Books in the United States, but I'm Understood in England" by Paul Theroux, December 17, 1979 in *U. S. News & World Report*. Reprinted by permission of *U. S. News & World Report*./ Sidelight excerpts from an article "Letters" by Phyllis McGinley, February, 1963 in *Wilson Library Bulletin*. Copyright © 1963 by The H. W. Wilson Co. Reprinted by permission of *Wilson Library Bulletin*.

Sidelight excerpts from an article "Talking Down" by Phyllis McGinley, April, 1962 in *Wilson Library Bulletin*, Volume 36, number 8. Copyright © 1962 by The H. W. Wilson Co. Reprinted by permission of *Wilson Library Bulletin*./ Sidelight excerpts from an article "The Reward at the End of the Read" by Kit Williams, July 6, 1984 in *Publishers Weekly*. Copyright © 1984 by Xerox Corp. Reprinted by permission of Xerox Corp.

Appreciation also to the Performing Arts Research Center of the New York Public Library at Lincoln Center for permission to reprint the theater stills "The Lady, or the Tiger?" and "The Apple Tree."

PHOTOGRAPH CREDITS

Arlene Alda: Copyright © 1982 by Stephanie Cohen; Gwynneth Ashby: Roland Adams, A.B.I. P.P.; Arna Bntemps: Frank O. Roberts Studio; Mary Carey: Glen-Tone Photo; Mary Virginia Fox: Olan Mills; H. M. Hoover: Altman-Pach-Studio; Ann Irwin and Lee Hadley: Shirley Walrod; Ethel and Leonard Kessler: Parents' Magazine Enterprises, Inc.; Phyllis McGinley (alone, and with husband): David Gahr; Claudia Mills: Diane Kaufmann; Dinah L. Moché: William Russ; Malvina Reynolds: Eleanor M. Lawrence; Paul Theroux: Jerry Bauer; Paul Theroux: Terry Smith; Kit Williams: (with inlaid box) Sophie Baker.

SOMETHING ABOUT THE AUTHOR

ALDA, Arlene   1933-

PERSONAL: Born March 12, 1933, in Bronx, N.Y.; daughter of Simon (a lithographer) and Jeanette (a seamstress; maiden name, Kelman) Weiss; married Alan Alda (an actor, writer, and director), March 15, 1957; children: Eve, Elizabeth, Beatrice. *Education:* Received degree from Hunter College (now of the City University of New York), 1954. *Home:* Los Angeles, Calif. *Office:* New York. *Agent:* Amy Berkower, Writers House Inc., 21 West 26th St., New York, N.Y. 10010.

CAREER; Houston Symphony, Houston, Tex., assistant first clarinetist, 1956-57; photographer, 1967—; writer, 1980—. Performed with National Orchestral Association in New York City, and with suburban orchestras. Taught orchestral music in Manhattan; worked as private clarinet instructor. Photographs exhibited at Nikon House, New York City. *Member:* Phi Beta Kappa. *Awards, honors:* Fulbright scholarship for music study in Germany, 1954-55.

WRITINGS—All self-illustrated with photographs: *Arlene Alda's ABC Book* (juvenile), Celestial Arts, 1981; *On Set: A Personal Story in Photographs and Words,* Simon & Schuster, 1981; *Sonya's Mommy Works* (juvenile), Messner, 1982; (contributor) *Women of Vision: Photographic Statements of Twenty Women Photographers,* Unicorn Publishing, 1982; *Matthew and His Dad* (juvenile), Simon & Schuster, 1983; (with husband, Alan Alda) *M*A*S*H*: The Final Days,* Unicorn Publishing, 1983.

Contributor of photographs to periodicals, including *Vogue, Saturday Evening Post, People,* and *Good Housekeeping.*

SIDELIGHTS: Before marrying Alan Alda in 1957, Arlene Alda was an accomplished clarinetist who began playing in high school, studied music in Europe, and then joined the Houston Symphony. Although she essentially gave up her professional music career to raise her children, she supported her struggling young husband in his early days of acting by giving private clarinet lessons and playing in obscure suburban orchestras.

According to *McCall's,* both Aldas also believe that "for a relationship to work happily, you need two whole, self-fulfilled people." In 1967 Arlene Alda took a couse in photography, and the venture proved successful. Since her fist efforts in the medium, Alda has gone on to hold exhibitions of her work, contribute photographs to national magazines, and write books containing her own photographs. In one instance, the talents of the entire Alda family united in a professional project, the film "The Four Seasons." Alan Alda wrote, directed, and starred in it, the two younger girls acted in it and, with the assistance of the eldest daughter, Arlene Alda supplied wacky vegetable photographs to appear as the work of an obsessive photographer. She remained on the set during the film's shooting and snapped pictures documenting its making. She eventually published her behind-the-scenes observations as *On Set: A Personal Story in Photographs and Words.*

For all the changes marriage has brought to her life and career, Alda expresses no regrets. In 1981 she told the *New York Times:* "I am so happy at this point in my life, I can't imagine how I could be any happier. If I were still playing the clarinet, I would never have gotten into photography, which I love. In music you rise and fall by virtue of the group; it's a group

ARLENE ALDA

"I still don't want Mommy to go." ■ (From *Sonya's Mommy Works* by Arlene Alda. Photograph by the author.)

experience. But photography is so expressive because it's *you.* You control everything, and I like that.''

FOR MORE INFORMATION SEE: McCall's, January, 1976; *New York Times,* May 31, 1981; *People,* June 15, 1981, November 15, 1982; *New York Times Book Review,* November 22, 1981; *Instructor,* September, 1982; *Ms.,* December, 1982; *Los Angeles Times Book Review,* December 5, 1982.

ASHBY, Gwynneth 1922-

PERSONAL: Born May 1, 1922, in England; daughter of Sydney Thomas (an engineer) and Dorothy (Bevan) Ashby. *Education:* Hereford Training College, teaching certificate, 1942. *Politics:* Conservative. *Religion:* Church of England. *Home:* 12D Blenheim Dr., Christchurch, Dorset BH23 3JE, England.

CAREER: Teacher in girls' schools in Newcastle-upon-Tyne, England, 1943-45, and London, England, 1945-47; A. & C. Black Ltd. (publishers), London, member of editorial staff (educational section), 1948-50; teacher in Australia and Fiji Islands, 1950-52, with one period as head of school for aborigines in North Queensland, Australia; writer for young people. Past member of Commonwealth Institute lecturing panel, speaking on Fiji, aboriginal children of the Australian Outback, and life on an Australian cattle station. Lecturer on Japan to schools. *Member:* Royal Geographical Society (fellow), Society of Authors (member of educational executive committee), World Expeditionary Association, Society of Women Writers and Journalists, Tunbridge Wells Writers Circle.

WRITINGS: Mystery of Coveside House, Hodder & Stoughton, 1946; *The Secret Ring,* Hodder & Stoughton, 1948; *Cruise of the Silver Spray,* Hodder & Stoughton, 1951; *The Land and People of Sweden,* A. & C. Black, 1951; *The Land and People of Belgium,* A. & C. Black, 1955; (with Jean Gadsby and David Gadsby) *Looking at the World Today,* Book 4, A. & C. Black, 1960, 3rd edition, 1965; *Let's Look at Austria,* Museum Press, 1966; *Looking at Norway,* Lippincott, 1967, 3rd edition, 1971; *Looking at Japan,* Lippincott, 1969, revised edition, 1971; *Let's Go to Japan,* F. Watts (England), 1980, published in America as *Take a Trip to Japan,* F. Watts, 1981.

Author of two television plays for children, ''Adventure at Cow Crossing'' and ''The Friendly Bandit,'' and scripts for British Broadcasting Corp. school radio programs, ''Fiji and Its Capital Suva,'' ''Norway-Winter Leisure,'' and ''Giant's Causeway.'' Contributor to *Lady, Guide, Wildlife Observer, Autocar, Animals,* and *Christian Science Monitor.*

WORK IN PROGRESS: Book about Korea for eight-year-olds.

SIDELIGHTS: ''My writing career really took-off when I was at teacher training college. I caught chicken pox and was banished to the sick room. I wasn't allowed to study so to keep myself occupied, I removed all the lining paper from the room's drawers and cupboards, sharpened an old pencil on my cutlery and started writing a children's adventure story. During the long [recuperative period], I bullied my father into buying me an ancient typewriter and took a course of typing lessons. The resulting typescript was peppered with errors, but to my amazement (and even more to my family's), Hodder & Stoughton accepted the book, *The Mystery of Coveside House,* and gave me a contract for two further books—*The Secret Ring* and *The Cruise of the Silver Spray.*''

GWYNNETH ASHBY

1950. ''Although I enjoyed writing fiction, my love of travel, of seeing new countries and meeting people of different races took me on a two-year working holiday round the world. My starting point was Australia, where I alternated teaching with travelling. With billy cans and a mosquito net, I hitch-hiked with a friend up the eastern seaboard from Sydney to Cairns, moving on to a remote cattle station and mission on the Cape York Aboriginal Reserve. For three months, on a bush settlement known as Mitchell River, I taught a group of Aboriginal children. Once a week, on Thursday's 'Cattle Stations' Hop' Plane, we received a bundle of old magazines, and from one of these I snipped out a few lines—'Cattle station owners in North Queensland are warned to be on the look-out for crocodile shooters, hunting out of season and using old wartime airstrips to fly out the skins.' Later, back home, I wrote a children's TV play based on the incident and called *Adventure at Cow Crossing.* My travels also took me to Thursday Island on an old pearling lugger, and to the Fiji Islands where I taught in a delightful boarding school for Fijian girls.

''After my travels, life in England seemed rather tame. For several years I travelled round the country lecturing for the Commonwealth Institute on Australia and the South Pacific. The tours were exhilarating but very exhausting. In a single day I might have a group of infants in the morning, a Sixth Form College in the afternoon and perhaps an adult group or a prison meeting in the evening.

''Everything I write about in my junior travel books is based on first-hand experience. I cycled round Belgium to gather material for *The Land and People of Belgium,* and for *Looking at Norway* walked with a rucksack using youth hostels and mountain huts.''

They wear white masks so that they will not breathe germs over the food. ■ (From *Take a Trip to Japan* by Gwynneth Ashby. Photograph by the author.)

1970. "I made a return trip to Norway as the Bergen Library Service had offered me a week's trip on their library boat. During the winter months the *Epos* travels around the outer skerries bringing library books to the scattered settlements; in summer the shelves are removed and it reverts to a pleasure boat taking visitors on the fjords. Besides a captain, a mate and cook, the *Epos* also carried two librarians and a Swedish folk singer who gave concerts each evening when the boat moored for the night at some snowy, storm-tossed island. Out of this trip I wrote a program for BBC Schools' Radio: 'Norway-Winter Leisure.' The following year I was commissioned to write a semi-dramatised script about the Giant's Causeway. Once again I dug out boots and rucksack, flew to Northern Island, and walked along the wild and beautiful Giant's Causeway path which snakes along the cliffs, dipping and climbing beneath the weird rock formations of the northern coastline.

"One of my most exciting assignments was a trip to Japan to gather text and photographs for *Looking at Japan.* I travelled from the northern island of Hokkaido, where an American missionary introduced me to the chief of the *Ainu*, to the off-shore islands of southern Kyushu. This trip was a stimulating experience although at times language problems caused difficulties—particularly when I bathed by mistake in the communal men's bath, and the local judo team burst in upon me!"

1984. "I spent the summer and autumn in the Republic of Korea, travelling extensively on the excellent network of trains and buses, compiling a book about the country and its people.

"What next? Who knows? I have many exciting projects in mind—perhaps a trip to China by the Trans Siberian Railway, something I have wanted to do for many years. Whatever turns up, there is one thing which I always promise my readers, everything I write about in my junior travel books I have seen and experienced. I have lived with the families mentioned in the text, eaten the food described, and visited the places written about."

HOBBIES AND OTHER INTERESTS: Color photography, swimming.

FOR MORE INFORMATION SEE: Royal Commnwealth Society Journal, summer, 1959; *Bournemouth Evening Echo* (England), May 7, 1966, November 24, 1967.

BARRETT, Ethel

BRIEF ENTRY: Widely known as an inspirational lecturer at dinner clubs and conferences as well as on radio and television, Barrett is the author of more than forty books, most of them published by Regal Books. She presents a unique view of Biblical characters in her easy-to-read biographies for young readers, including *Abraham: God's Faithful Pilgrim, Moses: Mission Impossible!, Peter: The Story of a Deserter Who Became a Forceful Leader,* and *David: The Giantslayer* (all 1982). Barrett focuses on the troublesome years of adolescence in *"Sometimes I Feel Like a Blob"* (1977) as she attempts to aid teenagers in their quest for self-identity. At the other end of the age spectrum, she promotes Christian values to preschool and primary-grade children in stories like *Quacky and Wacky* (1978), *Buzz Bee* (1978), *Cracker, the Horse Who Lost His Temper* (1979), and *Sylvester the Three-Spined Tickleback* (1980). Her works also include adult writings such as *Peace and Quiet and Other Hazards* (Revell, 1980), described by *Library Journal* as "a sort of Bombeckian memoir of bumpy spots Barrett has encountered along her personal Christian path."

BAYER, Jane E. (?)-1985

OBITUARY NOTICE: Died February 3, 1985, after a long illness. Library worker, project director, and author. Associated with the children's book program at the Wells River Library in Vermont, Bayer was also the co-director of special projects at a women's center in St. Johnsbury, Vermont. For her achievements, Bayer was posthumously awarded the Susan B. Anthony Award for outstanding service to women by the Vermont Young Women's Christian Association (YWCA). She wrote *A, My Name Is Alice,* a children's alphabet book.

FOR MORE INFORMATION SEE—Obituaries: *School Library Journal,* May, 1985.

BILL, Alfred Hoyt 1879-1964

PERSONAL: Born May 5, 1879, in Rochester, N.Y.; died August 10, 1964, in Princeton, N.J.; buried at All Saints Cemetery, Princeton, N.J.; son of Edward Clark (an Episcopal clergyman and a teacher) and Eliza Huline (Hoyt) Bill; married Florence Dorothy Reid, June 30, 1903; children: Alfred Reid (deceased), Florence Dorothy (Mrs. Gregory P. Tschebotarioff), Edward Clark. *Education:* Yale University, A.B., 1903. *Politics:* Republican. *Religion:* Episcopalian. *Residence:* Princeton, N.J.

CAREER: Seabury Divinity School, Faribault, Minn., instructor of English, 1910-13; Bishop Seabury Mission and Shattuck School, Faribault, treasurer and teacher, 1916-21; began writing full time, about 1922. *Military service:* National Guard, 1910-16; became captain and was regimental adjutant of the 2nd Infantry; American Red Cross, captain and division representative, attached to the 91st Division of American Expeditionary Forces, 1918. *Member:* American Historical Association, Society of American Historians, Minnesota Historical Society, Zeta Psi, Yale Club, Players Club (both New York City), Nassau Club (Princeton, N.J.).

WRITINGS—For young readers: *The Clutch of the Corsican: A Tale of the Days of the Downfall of the Great Napolean,* Atlantic Monthly Press, 1925; *Highroads of Peril: Being the Adventures of Franklin Darlington, American, among the Secret Agents of the Exiled Louis XVIII, King of France,* Little, Brown, 1926; *The Red Prior's Legacy: The Story of the Adventures of an American Boy in the French Revolution* (illustrated by Henry Pitz), Longmans, Green, 1929; *The Ring of Danger: A Tale of Elizabethan England* (illustrated by Frederick T. Chapman), Knopf, 1948.

Other: *Alas, Poor Yorick!: Being Three Hitherto Unrecorded Adventures in the Life of the Reverend Laurence Sterne,* Little, Brown, 1927, reprinted, Books for Libraries, 1970; *The Wolf in the Garden,* Longmans, Green, 1931; *Astrophel; or, The Life and Death of the Renowned Sir Philip Sidney* (biography), Farrar & Rinehart, 1937, reprinted, Arden Library, 1979; *The Beleaguered City: Richmond, 1861-1865,* Knopf, 1946, reprinted, Greenwood Press, 1980; *Rehearsal for Conflict: The War with Mexico, 1846-1848* (history), Knopf, 1947, reprinted, Cooper Square, 1970; *The Campaign of Princeton, 1776-1777* (history), Princeton University Press, 1948, reprinted, 1976.

Valley Forge: The Making of an Army (history), Harper, 1952; (with Walter E. Edge) *A House Called Morven: Its Role in American History, 1701-1954* (history), Princeton University Press, 1954, new edition revised by Constance M. Greiff, 1978; *One Hundred Years of Fellowship and Service, 1856-1956: The Story of the Saint Paul Young Men's Christian Association,* privately printed, 1956; (with James Ralph Johnson) *Horsemen, Blue and Gray: A Pictorial History* (illustrated by

ALFRED HOYT BILL

Backward he sprang, whirling the naked blade in a flashing semicircle of steel in front of him. . . . ■ (From *The Ring of Danger: A Tale of Elizabethan England* by Alfred H. Bill. Illustrated by Frederick T. Chapman.)

Hirst D. Milhollen), Oxford University Press, 1906; *New Jersey and the Revolutionary War,* Van Nostrand, 1965.

Contributor of articles to periodicals, including *American Heritage.*

SIDELIGHTS: **May 5, 1879.** Born in Rochester, New York; moved to Faribault, Minnesota when he was five months old. "There used to be Indians around Faribault in the times that I can first remember. On Sunday morning they used to tramp in from a little reservation up Straight River and sit around the font in the Cathedral, very decently dressed, with strong, patient faces filled with religious devotion. It seemed to me hardly possible that they were of the same race as those who had spread ruin and massacre through the settlements only a little more than twenty years before.

"My father had come out to Minnesota from Brooklyn, New York, to become one of Bishop Whipple's clergymen, but his work did not take him among the Indians. Mostly he taught

at Seabury Divinity School. But he made many journeys among the struggling missionary stations in the southern part of the state, often by sleigh in the depth of winter, and I still remember his humorous accounts of being dug out of snowdrifts, sleeping in his clothes in the unheated guest rooms of the more prosperous farmers, and of the kindly hospitality of settlers who made him welcome in the single room in which the whole family slept, cooked, and ate during the coldest weather because the cook-stove was the only stove they had.

"The small cities were centers of civilization in my boyhood as they cannot be in these days of motor highways, radios, and chain stores. Life in Faribault was anything but dull. Shattuck School with its corps of uniformed cadets, the flock of pretty girls at St. Mary's Hall, the professors at Seabury, whose embroidered stoles and academic hoods gave color and interest to the Cathedral services, all united to present a sort of microcosm to a small boy whose family life was naturally bound up in the ecclesiastical and scholastic activities of the place.

"Perhaps it is owing to this that I have always been moved to write about the romantic side of life, of brilliant historical periods like the Napoleonic and the Elizabethan, and of figures bizarre and chivalrous, such as Lawrence Sterne and Sir Philip Sidney, and to treat them in a romantic and somewhat old-fashioned way. It has always been what Sir Watler Scott called 'the big Bow-Wow strain' which attracted me; and though I have more than once tried my hand at the 'ordinary commonplace things and characters interesting from the truth of the description and the sentiment,' I have never succeeded in getting past a publisher's second reader with such efforts." [Carmen Richards, editor, *Minnesota Writers,* Denison, 1961.[1]]

Queen Elizabeth on a picnic. ■ (From *Astrophel; or, The Life and Death of the Renowned Sir Philip Sidney* by Alfred H. Bill.)

A slave auction in Virginia. ■ (From *The Beleaguered City: Richmond, 1861-1865* by Alfred Hoyt Bill. Illustration courtesy of the *Illustrated London News.*)

1903. After receiving a bachelor of arts degree from Yale University, Bill returned to Faribault to teach, and to act as treasurer for the Bishop Seabury Mission and Shattuck School.

1918. During World War I, he served as captain and division representative of the American Red Cross and was attached to the Ninety-First Division of the American Expeditionary Force. "... I have been fortunate in traveling widely among historic scenes both in America and abroad, in being present on some historic occasions, and in bearing a humble part—though only a Red Cross man—in one of the decisive battles of history.

"It was my painful privilege to see ... [patriotic men] in France in the battle of the Meuse-Argonne in World War I: thousands of them streaming forward on three parallel roads toward the all but impregnable German positions with such a unanimous courage that a man would have had to be more courageous to turn back than to go forward with them. Next day I saw the platoon columns of a regiment of them plod steadily across a bare hilltop with the German shell-fire exploding above them; and a night or two later in the great field hospital tents which were crammed shoulder to shoulder with prostrate men too dangerously wounded to be carried farther to the rear, I heard them sing 'Good-bye, Broadway! Hello, France!' And in the circumstances 'The Battle Hymn of the Republic' could not have been more moving than that gay ditty.

"As memorable, though in a different way, of course, was the state entry of President Wilson into London in the December of that year. With the history of the small beginnings of our coutnry well in mind, our struggles against the arrogance and tyranny of England, it was a fine thing to see the President of the United States welcomed by the English king with all the royal pageantry at his command as a most valued friend; to see the great statue of old George III covered with United States bluejackets from his shoulders to his prancing horse's ears; to hear the roaring British cheers as if those people saw before them the savior of a civilization all but lost. But there was pathos in that cheering, too, for one like me, who even then foresaw that the people of the United States of America would turn aside from the sacrifices which would be entailed by following their leader's vision of a United States of the World."[1]

1922. Began full-time writing. Bill's books were about events in world history. He wrote historical fiction, weaving his characters and tales against a background of authentic history. "Quite often, to be sure, characteristics of people whom I have known or seen have turned up in my books, to give, I hope verisimilitude to what would have been otherwise a paper-stuffed Napoleonic uniform or the richly upholstered lay figure of a young lady in the toils of the French Revolution. But it is the heart-stopping event against a brilliant, even a violent background, that makes my fingers itch to describe it. I would still walk a mile to see a small-town Decoration Day parade; and though I adore Jane Austen and all her works, I could choose only one way if 'Pride and Prejudice' and 'Foreign Correspondent' were at the movies on the only night when I could go.

"Visits to Wolfe's Cove below the heights of Quebec, to Ticonderoga, and Gettysburg, to the Tower of London, the Martyr's Monument at Oxford, the farm of Hugomont at Waterloo, and the forts around Verdun are a few of many similar high points in my experience. Nor do I believe that any one with a knowledge of the past can stand in such surroundings without being uplifted by the memory of men who believed so profoundly in the righteousness of their cause or in the obligation of their duty that they gave their lives for their faith.

"If I were asked how all these things have helped me to write, I would have to answer that I hardly know how, but that I know they did help. Sometimes they gave me incidents and characters, to be sure, which I was able to use. They showed me what similar events in the past must have been like. But, of course, such picturesque experiences are in no way essential to writing. Good factual accounts of them might have given me as much, provided—it is a great proviso, however—provided that I had been moved to think deeply upon them. For that is the essential of all creative writing, it seems to me— the ability and the perseverance to delve deeply into one's subject matter until one has discovered at least some part of the true inwardness of it.''[1]

Throughout his long writing career, Bill wrote several books of United States and European historical events and eras. He was also a contributor to *American Heritage.*

1930s. Moved to Princeton, New Jersey, where he continued to write his historical books. For adults, he also wrote a biography on Sir Philip Sidney. From the writer's viewpoint, Bill believed that it was not the material (events and people) that made a good book, but the ability of the writer to communicate his material to the reader. "It is such ability and perseverance at their height which make for great writing, which place Jane Austen's novels on a higher plane than Walter Scott's and make *David Copperfield* a finer book than *A Tale of Two Cities.* It is not the event, but what the writer is able to discover in the event which gives the account of it its importance. I would not be misunderstood from this, however. I do not mean that any dull chronicle of clodhopperdom is better than a fine romance, as some of our critics of the baser sort would have us believe today. If in a tale of commonplace people and everyday happenings, characters and events seem commonplace, the truth is not in that tale. 'There is one glory of the sun and another glory of the moon.' A fine moonlight night is better than a drizzly day; and *The Three Musketeers* is a better book than the best of William Dean Howells'.''[1]

August 10, 1964. Died at Princeton Hospital in New Jersey at the age of eighty-five.

FOR MORE INFORMATION SEE: Stanley J. Kunitz and Howard Haycraft, editors, *Junior Book of Authors,* H. W. Wilson, 1934, 2nd edition, 1951; *Saturday Review of Literature,* January 31, 1948; *American Historical Review,* April, 1948, January, 1953; *Political Science Quarterly,* September, 1948; *New York Herald Tribune Weekly Book Review,* November 14, 1948; *Social Education,* January, 1949; *Christian Science Monitor,* July 22, 1954; Carmen Richards, editor, *Minnesota Writers,* Denison, 1961. Obituaries: *New York Times,* August 11, 1964.

BLIXEN, Karen (Christentze Dinesen) 1885-1962
(Isak Dinesen; other pseudonyms: Pierre Andrézel, Tania B., Osceola)

PERSONAL: Born April 17, 1885, in Rungsted, Denmark; died September 7, 1962, in Rungsted, Denmark; daughter of Wilhelm (an army officer and writer under his own name and his Indian name Boganis) and Ingeborg (Westenholz) Dinesen; married Baron Bror Blixen-Finecke (a big-game hunter and writer), January 14, 1914 (divorced, 1921). *Education:* Studied English at Oxford University, 1904; studied painting at Royal Academy in Copenhagen, in Paris, 1910, and in Rome. *Home:* Rungstedlund, Rungsted Kyst, Denmark.

CAREER: Writer from 1907 to 1962, from 1934 writing in English and translating her own work into Danish. With her husband Baron Blixen, she managed a coffee plantation in British East Africa (now Nairobi, Kenya), 1913-21, then took over the management herself until failing coffee prices forced her to give up the farm in 1931. Commissioned by three Scandinavian newspapers to write a series of twelve articles on wartime Berlin, Paris, and London, 1940. *Member:* American Academy of Arts and Letters (honorary member), National Institute of Arts and Letters (honorary member), Bayerische Akademie der Schoenen Kuenste (corresponding member), Danish Academy, Cosmopolitan Club (New York). *Awards,*

Karen Blixen as a young woman.

Wilhelm and Ingeborg Dinesen with their three daughters: Inger, called Ea; Karen, called Tanne (with fingers in her mouth); and Ellen, called Elle, in 1888.

honors: Ingenio et Arti Medal from King Frederick IX of Denmark, 1950; The Golden Laurels, 1952; Hans Christian Andersen Prize, 1955; Danish Critics' Prize, 1957; Henri Nathansen Memorial Fund award, 1957.

WRITINGS—Published in Danish under name Karen Blixen, except as noted, and in English under pseudonym Isak Dinesen: *Sandhedens Haevn* (play; title means "The Revenge of Truth"; first produced at Royal Theatre, Copenhagen, 1936), [Tilskueren], 1926, Gyldendal (Copenhagen), 1960; *Seven Gothic Tales* (Book-of-the-Month Club selection; contains "The Deluge at Norderney," "The Old Chevalier," "The Monkey," "The Roads Round Pisa," "The Supper at Elsinore," "The Dreamers," and "The Poet"), Smith & Haas, 1934, reissued with new introduction, Modern Library, 1961, Danish translation published as *Syv Fantastiske Fortaellinger*, Reitzels, 1935, reprinted, Gyldendal, 1968; *Out of Africa* (Book-of-the-Month Club selection), Putnam (London), 1937, Random House, 1938, reprinted, 1970, Danish translation published as *Den Afrikanske Farm*, Gyldendal, 1937, reprinted, 1964; *Winter's Tales* (Book-of-the-Month Club selection), Random House, 1942, reprinted, Books for Libraries, 1971, Danish translation published as *Vinter-Eventyr*, Gyldendal, 1942; (under pseudnoym Pierre Andrezel) *Gengaeldelsens Veje* (title means "The Ways of Retribution"), Danish translation by

Clara Svendsen, Gyldendal, 1944, published as *The Angelic Avengers* (Book-of-the-Month Club selection), Putnam, 1946, Random House, 1947; *Om revtskrivning 23-24 marts 1938*, Gyldendal, 1949.

Farah, Wivel (Copenhagen), 1950; *Daguerreotypier* (two radio talks presented January, 1951), Gyldendal, 1951; *Babettes Gaestebud* (title means "Babette's Feast"), Fremad (Copenhagen), 1952; *Omkring den Nye Lov om Dyreforsoeg*, Politikens Forlag (Copenhagen), 1952; *Kardinalens tredie Historie* (title means "The Cardinal's Third Tale"), Gyldendal, 1952; *En Baaltale med 14 Aars Forsinkelse* (title means "Bonfire Speech 14 Years Delayed"), Berlingske Forlag (Copenhagen), 1953; *Spoegelseshestene*, Fremad, 1955; *Last Tales*, Random House, 1957, Danish translation published as *Sidste Fortaellinger*, Gyldendal, 1957; *Anecdotes of Destiny* (contains "The Diver," "Babette's Feast," "Tempests," "The Immortal Story," and "The Ring"), Random House, 1958, reprinted, 1974, Danish translation published as *Skaebne-Anekdoter*, Gyldendal, 1958.

Skygger paa Graesset, Gyldendal, 1960, published as *Shadows on the Grass* (Book-of-the-Month Club selection), Random House, 1961; (author of introduction) Truman Capote, *Holly* (an edition of *Breakfast at Tiffany's*), Gyldendal, 1960;

(author of introduction) Olive Schreiner, *The Story of An African Farm*, Limited Editions Club, 1961; *On Mottoes of My Life* (originally published under name Isak Dinesen in *Proceedings of the American Academy of Arts and Letters and The National Institute of Arts and Letters*, Second Series, Number 10, 1960), Ministry of Foreign Affairs (Copenhagen), 1962; (author of introduction) Hans Christian Andersen, *Thumbelina, and Other Stories*, Macmillan, 1962; *Osceola* (posthumously published collection of early stories and poems), Gyldendal, 1962; (author of introduction) Basil Davidson, *Det Genfundne Africa*, Gyldendal, 1962; *Ehrengard* (posthumously published), Random House, 1963, Danish translation by Clara Svendsen, Gyldendal, 1963; *Karen Blixen* (memorial edition of principal works), Gyldendal, 1964; *Essays*, Gyldendal, 1965; *Efterladte Fortallinger*, Gyldendal, 1975.

Contributor of short stories, articles, and reviews to *Ladies' Home Journal, Saturday Evening Post, Atlantic, Harper's Bazaar, Vogue, Botteghe Oscure,* and *Heretica*. She has recorded excerpts from her books for Gyldendal, and has made two films, consisting of readings, for *Encyclopaedia Britannica*.

ADAPTATIONS—Films: "The Immortal Story," adapted by Orson Welles, Altura, 1968; "Out of Africa," starring Meryl Streep and Robert Redford, Universal, 1985.

SIDELIGHTS: **April 17, 1885.** Born in Rungsted, Denmark. Blixen's family home, Rungstedlund, previously Rungsted Inn, was situated on the sea near Copenhagen. The greatest lyric poet of Denmark, Johannes Ewald, had lived and worked at the historic inn. "A hundred years later, another young man came from foreign lands and established himself at Rungstedlund. He was Wilhelm Dinesen, my father, who as a seventeen-year-old lieutenant had been at Danevirke and Dybbol; then as a French officer had served in the Franco-Prussian War and who, during the Paris Commune, had seen barricades built and French blood flow in French streets. He had turned away from Europe and its civilization and for three years had lived among the Indians in North America without seeing another white man. He had been a competent and fortunate hunter of pelts, but the money he earned he spent on his Indian friends. . . . He married the lovely young Ingeborg Westenholtz, my mother, [who] told me that when they returned from their honeymoon and walked beneath the trees in through the fields, he said to her, 'Whatever may happen in the future, please remember we came here on the last day of May and it was beautiful and you were happy.' " [Karen Blixen, *Daguerrotypes, and Other Essays*, University of Chicago Press, 1979.[1]]

Blixen's maternal grandmother, Mary Westenholtz (called "Mama" by her children and grandchildren) and her two unmarried daughters, Lidda and Bess, moved to the nearby manor of Folehave. Blixen's Aunt Bess, a prominent member of Denmark's Unitarian church, and an outspoken feminist, spent the next sixty years at Folehave. Though Bess Westenholtz and her niece Karen Blixen loved each other deeply, they had a difficult and tempestuous relationship. While in Africa, Blixen wrote her brother Thomas about her mixed feelings concerning Aunt Bess. "I always have a feeling of ingratitude where she is concerned,—for in a way she has given us her all, and we cannot repay her with what she desires from us. She wanted to teach us all her ideas and thoughts about life, and most of what she taught us was negative: in order that we should avoid a destiny like hers. And yet in a way she is one of the warmest hearted people I have ever known and a highly talented person,—how can that be? I believe that life demands of us that we love it, not merely certain sides of it and not only one's own ideas and ideals, but life itself in all its forms before it will give us anything in return, and when you mention my

philosophy of life, I have no other than that . . . I wish so much that I could be something to Aunt Bess and repay her a little for her great love; but she would have to reconcile herself to so much in my life and my ideas before she could get any joy from me, and that she cannot or will not do. . . ." [*Isak Dinesen: Letters from Africa, 1914-1931*, edited by Frans Lasson, The University of Chicago Press, 1981.[2]]

Blixen's family called her "Tanne," which was her own mispronunciation of Karen. She had one elder sister, Inger ("Ea"), a younger sister, Ellen ("Elle"), and two younger brothers, Thomas—with whom she was very close as an adult—and Anders. The family legend has it that when Blixen's elder sister Ea was born, the women in the family crowded so possessively around her cradle that Wilhelm Dinesen, feeling completely "useless and shunted aside," went out with his rifle and promised himself that the next child (which was Karen) would be "his." [Judith Thurman, *Isak Dinesen*, St. Martin's Press, 1982.[3]]

". . . I think I was his favorite child, and I know he thought I resembled him. He took me with him when he walked over the fields, when he troated for a roebuck in the woods, or searched through the marsh for a snipe with his two French griffon hounds. . . . I remember clearly how he taught me to distinguish among the various kinds of birds and told me about migratory birds—and his quick, happy reaction at the sight of a rare bird, the kite with a notched tail, like other people's happiness over a glass of good wine."[1]

1895. Blixen's father committed suicide by hanging himself in the Copenhagen boardinghouse where he routinely stayed while Parliament was in session. At the time, the Dinesen children were told only that their father had been ill and had suddenly died. Years later, the twelve-year-old Thomas, upon asking his mother whether his father had killed himself, was told, "You must understand, a man like Father, a soldier and an outdoorsman, could not live with the thought that he would have to continue to exist, throughout many years, as a wreck, a helpless relic of what he once was."[2]

Thomas Dinesen later believed that it was likely his father had suffered from syphilis, contracted many years earlier and never cured. While visiting Africa, Thomas shared his conclusions with his sister and she accepted them as logical and even probable. "I was ten years old when Father died. His death was for me a great sorrow, of a kind which probably only children feel."[1]

"It was as if part of oneself had also died . . . the desolate feeling that there was no one to remember the talks on Ewald's Hill . . . suddenly one was pushed out into the foremost row of life, bereft of the joy and irresponsibility of childhood." [Parmenia Migel, *Titania: The Biography of Isak Dinesen*, Random House, 1967.[4]]

After Wilhelm Dinesen's death, Ingeborg Dinesen and her children were given a great deal of support from her sister at nearby Folehave, who felt the best thing for the Dinesen children was to keep them to their routine and to speak as little of their father as possible. Blixen recalled they were admonished that "a widow's children must behave better than other children."[3]

Blixen and her sisters were not sent to school, but were taught at home by governesses. She showed artistic talent and filled numerous notebooks with poems, plays, stories and drawings. "Children of my day, even in great houses, had very little in the way of toys. Toy shops were almost unknown; modern

Blixen with three of her Scotch deerhounds, known in the colony as "the Lioness' dogs."

mechanical playthings, which furnish their own activity, had hardly come into existence. One might, of course, buy oneself a hobbyhorse, but generally speaking, an individually selected knotty stick from the woods, upon which imagination might work freely, was dearer to the heart. We were not observers, as childen today seem to be from birth, of their own accord;

and not utilizers, as they are brought up to be; we were creators.

"I . . . was taught by governesses at home, to which circumstances I owe, I think, the fact that I am totally ignorant of many things that are common knowledge to other people. Still

Blixen with the tame owl that liked to sit on her shoulder.

these young or elderly women were ambitious persons; at the age of twelve we were called upon to write an essay on Racine, a task that I should fear to undertake today, and to translate Walter Scott's 'The Lady of the Lake' into Danish verse, passages of which were frequently on the lips of my sisters and myself years later.''[1]

1899. After a fire destroyed their home at Rungsted, Blixen and her mother and sisters spent nine months in Switzerland, where Blixen attended a French school and studied drawing, painting and languages.

1900. Returned to Denmark. Though her family opposed the idea, she expressed her strong desire to study art in Copenhagen at the Royal Academy.

1902. Enrolled in the private drawing school of Charlotte Sode and Julie Meldahl in Copenhagen, a prerequisite for all women who hoped to enter the Royal Academy, as women were excluded from the academy's own preparatory classes.

1903. Passed the entrance exam at the Royal Academy of Fine Arts and was accepted. Her first year ''exposed a new and beautiful side of the world to me . . . [I was] enchanted by the unshakable justice and regularity in the laws of perspective. If I myself acted correctly the outcome could not fail to be correct—but if I permitted myself the least negligence it invariably, and with frightening power, took revenge at the conclusion of the assignment.''[3]

Writing of the sexist environment at the Academy, which she attended for five semesters, Blixen noted that the students at the men's division ''worked with an enthusiasm which we did not know in our school, and I understood that the responsibility of the true teacher is not first and foremost to 'instruct' but to inspire.

"[I owe painting] . . . for revealing the nature of reality to me. I have always had difficulty seeing how a landscape looked, if I had not first got the key to it from a great painter. I have experienced and recognized a land's particular character where a painter has interpreted it to me. Constable, Gainsborough and Turner showed me England. When I travelled to Holland as a young girl, I understood all that the landscape and the cities said because the old Dutch painters did me the kind service of interpreting it. . . ."[3]

Blixen was inspired by the writings of the famous Scandinavian intellectual, Georg Brandes, with whom her father had been friends. While he was hospitalized in 1904, she sent him a bouquet of flowers with a note of deeply felt homage and respect. "I had done this with all the fervent enthusiasm of a young heart for what was to me the first revelation of intellectual genius; I had been immersed in Brandes's books for a long time and I can say that it was he who revealed literature to me. My first *personal* enthusiasm for books,—for Shakespeare, Shelly, Heine,—came to me through him. From a purely objective point of view, Brandes was of course one of the greatest minds of my country, and a sick old man. I took this step without the least element of bad conscience, but I was of course aware that it would not be approved of,—and after all, that is the kind of infatuation and romantic action that a young girl keeps secret from her family."[2]

Touched by the gesture, Brandes visited Runstedlund to thank her. Blixen's mother, shocked by her daughter's bold action (aside from his literary notoriety, Brandes had a reputation as a seducer of women), politely told Brandes that her daughter was not at home. Writing to her Aunt Bess from Africa in 1924, Blixen lamented the great lost opportunity for his friendship and encouragement. "This was a great grief to me then and now I consider it to have been a great misfortune. It would have been a chance for my youthful fervor for 'intellect,' which was after all rather 'starved' in my everyday life; it is the only time in my life when there has been a possibility for personal contact with one of the great minds of Denmark, and I believe that Brandes might have made a writer or artist of me, as he did with so many—indeed, probably none of the artists and writers of Denmark during the last fifty years have been without his influence to a greater or lesser extent,—and my youth might have been blessed with intellectual work and enthusiasm for art and 'genius.' If I had realized at that time how much was at stake I would probably, if I had not the strength to carry it through openly, have had strength enough to deceive you, and I wish that I had had it."[4]

1904-08. Dropped out of the Royal Academy. Wrote first draft of play, *The Revenge of Truth* and a series of tales which she titled "Likely Stories." Mario Krohn, an art historian, whom Blixen had met while studying at the Academy, read her work and urged her to take herself seriously as a writer. Krohn arranged to have some of her tales read by Valdemar Vedel, editor of *Tilskueren,* Denmark's most distinguished literary magazine. Vedel wrote to Krohn that one of Blixen's tales, "The Hermits," was "so original . . . and so well made that I would like to take it for *Tilskueren* . . . there is certainly talent in this author." The tale was published in 1907, under the pseudonym Osceola. Mario Krohn later became editor of *Tilskueren,* and accepted Blixen's story, "The de Cats Family" in 1909.

During these years, Blixen spent much of her time in the company of her upper-class paternal relatives, the Frijes, and her Swedish cousins, the twin barons Bror and Hans von Blixen-Finecke. Her cousin, Daisy Frijs, who was three years younger, became her closest friend. During this time, Blixen fell deeply

but unhappily in love with her second cousin, Baron Hans Blixen-Finecke, twin brother to her future husband. "More than anything else, a deep, unrequited love left its mark on my early youth."[3]

1910. Blixen was bridesmaid to her cousin Daisy, who married Chamberlain Henrik Grevenkop-Castenskiold, a Danish ambassador twenty-six years her senior. The marriage disturbed Blixen, as she knew Daisy was not in love with Grevenkop-Castenskiold. Thinking of her friend's marriage, Blixen wrote, "is it not wonderful how easily we betray ourselves, and turn aside from the path we have ourselves chosen, and wander off? . . . What frail timber people are made of."[3]

Blixen, in an extremely depressed state of mind over Hans Blixen, left for Paris with her sister Ea to attend a new college of art. In her Paris diary, she wrote, "I shall never again have the happiness to feel as if I stood high and looked out over the whole, great beautiful world.

"Monday, April 4. How tired, tired, tired I am. How trivial it all is. Perhaps I should have moved to another place, here it is so stuffy. I shall certainly go to art school, although one has the feeling that it is not any use. . . ."[3]

Mario Krohn visited Blixen in Paris. When he asked about her literary ambitions, Blixen replied that she wanted "all things in life more than to be a writer—travel, dancing, living, the freedom to paint."[3]

Her return to Rungstedlund gave her "something of the same feeling, moral and intellectual, that one encounters physically in a crowded compartment or waiting room, where the windows are kept closed: the air has been consumed."[3]

1911. Continued writing fiction including several early versions of her tales "Carnival," "Peter and Rosa," and her play

Blixen in a Pierrot costume from her youth. Photograph by Rie Nissen.

The Revenge of Truth. Still obsessed with her unrequited love for Hans Blixen, she wrote in her 1911 diary, "Perhaps Destiny will see its way to making good its debts to me." In July 1911, she resolved not to go to Frijsenborg, stating, "The circumstances will be too little in harmony with my feelings for [Hans]. What I experienced the last time I was with him . . . I shall never go through again."[3]

1912. Visited Rome with her cousin, Daisy. "[We were] almost perfectly happy together."[3] Returned to Rungstedlund. Announced her engagement to Hans Blixen's twin brother, Bror. The engagement shocked and dismayed Karen Blixen's family, who felt she was acting on impulse. Blixen convinced her fiancé that they should live in "some distant country with prospects not yet realized."[3]

1913. Discussing their future prospects with mutual uncles, the engaged couple decided to go to Africa, which was recommended as the land of the future for young people of initiative. Bror Blixen traveled to British East Africa. The newly established family limited corporation in Denmark and a considerable capital deposit, mainly provided by Karen Blixen's maternal relatives, made it possible for Bror Blixen to acquire a coffee farm. Despite his limited knowledge of both agriculture and accounting, the company appointed him manager of the farm. Years later, Bror Blixen conjectured that he might have become a "well-to-do farmer" had he not become engaged to "the girl I called Tanne but whom the world was to know many years later as Isak Dinesen. . . . The human imagination is a curious thing. If it is properly fertilized it can shoot up like a fakir's tree in the twinkling of an eye. Tanne knew the trick and between us we built a future in our imagination in which everything but the impossible had a place."[3] Although the acreage Blixen acquired seemed to be at an ideal altitude for coffee, Blixen did not know at the time of purchase that the soil was in fact too acidic and the rainfall insufficient to ever grow coffee successfully.

December 2, 1913. Karen Blixen left Denmark to travel, via Naples, to her new life in Africa.

January 14, 1914. Blixen sailed into the port of Mombasa and was married the same day to Bror Blixen. She was met by Bror's Somali steward, Farah, who was to share her daily life

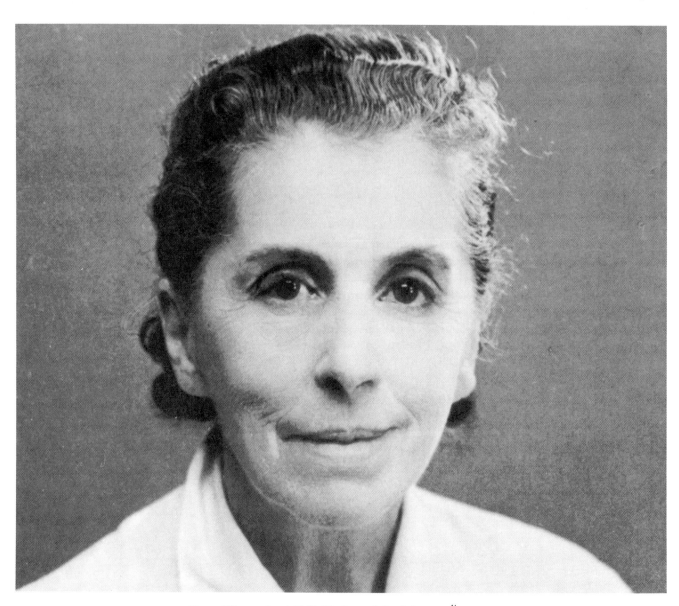

Karen Blixen, about 1940. Photograph by Johannes Övereng.

The main house of Blixen's plantation in Kenya. Photograph by Thomas Dinesen.

on the farm, mediate her relations with the Africans, and relieve her of many practical burdens. Farah also became Blixen's closest confidant. "I talked to him about my worries as about my successes, and he knew all that I did or thought.

"There was a time, when Farah and my other people and all things in Africa and Africa itself said one and the same thing to me: 'Trust in us and we shall protect you.'"[3]

Though it would be many years before Blixen returned to writing fiction, the year 1914 marks the beginning of Blixen's correspondence to her friends and family, collected in the volume, *Letters from Africa,* published posthumously.

"Now I'll begin at the beginning.—Bror was in Mombasa to meet me and it was wonderful to be with someone one feels one belongs with again, but Mombasa is a fiery hothouse and the sun blazing down on your head almost makes you unconscious. We went up to look at a very attractive old fort, and at eleven o'clock we were married . . . it was very easy and simple and only took ten minutes at most. Then we drove out by ricksha to have lunch with Hobely, who had married us . . . and from there to the train . . . there is no sleeping car, but Bror had brought sheets and blankets. By the following morning the landscape had completely changed and then it was the real Africa, vast grass plains and the mountains in the

distance and then an incredible wealth of game, huge flocks of zebra and gnu and antelope right beside the train, and although when you hear about that you don't attach much importance to it, when you see it for yourself you find it really impressive.—"[2]

Arrived at her new home just outside the government town of Nairobi in British East Africa. "In Nairobi there was an official reception and luncheon with the Govenor at his charming house—I had the Govenor on my right and the Vice-Govenor on my left and everyone called me Baroness every other word; to start with I didn't realize they were addressing me. . . .—Immediately after lunch, Bror and I drove out by car to our own farm. It is the most enchanting road you can imagine, like our own Deer Park, and the long blue range of Ngong Hills stretching out beyond it. There are so many flowering trees and shrubs, and a scent rather like bog myrtle, or pine trees, pervades everything. Out here it is not too hot at all, the air is so soft and lovely, and one feels so light and free and happy.

"There was a surprise in store for me when we arrived at the farm. All the thousand boys were drawn up in ranks and after a really earsplitting welcome they closed ranks and came up to the house with us, surrounded us when we got out of the car and insisted on touching us,—and all those black heads

(From the movie "Out of Africa," starring Meryl Streep and Robert Redford. Copyright © 1984/1985 by Universal City Studios, Inc.)

right in front of one's gaze were quite overwhelming. You have no idea how delightful the farm was and how beautifully everything had been done up.

"The *natives* . . . are my greatest interest out here; but I think that I,—and Bror,—are about the only people here who really do have this interest. Where the natives are concerned the English are remarkably narrow-minded; it never occurs to them to regard them as human beings, and when I talk to English ladies on racial differences and such matters, they laugh patronizingly, touched by my eccentricity. Of course, the natives, who in many ways are more intelligent than they are, take advantage of this, but there will never be any understanding and cooperation. . . . When I observe the various races here I feel that the superiority of the white race is an illusion . . . when it comes to character I think they surpass us. When I think that we have 1200 young men on the farm here, who live ten or twelve to a wretched little grass hut, and that I have never seen an angry face or heard quarreling, that everything is always done with a song and a smile, that from what I have heard, coarseness or impertinence are completely unknown concepts, that they are constantly seen with their arms about each other and pulling thorns out of each other's feet,—and think what trouble there would be with 1200 white workmen, I think they are better people than we are."[2]

Looking back on her first encounters with the Africans, for whom she felt an immediate affinity, Blixen wrote in her later years. "They came into my life, as a kind of answer to some call in my own nature, to dreams of childhood perhaps, or to

poetry read and cherished long ago, or to emotions and instincts deep down in the mind. . . ."[3]

Blixen learned to hunt and frequently accompanied her husband on safari. "I have spent four weeks in the happy hunting grounds and have just emerged from the depths of the great wide open spaces, from the life of prehistoric times, today just as it was a thousand years ago, from meeting with the great beasts of prey, which enthrall one, which obsess one so that one feels that lions are all that one lives for—strengthened by the air of the high mountain region, tanned by its sun, filled with its wild, free, magnificent beauty in heat-dazzling days, in great clear moonlit nights. I must humbly apologize to those hunters whose delight in the chase I failed to understand. There is nothing in the world to equal it.—"[2]

August 1, 1914. Outbreak of World War I. The Blixens contributed to the Allied war effort, acting as leaders of the dispatch service and provision transports. Despite these courageous efforts, the Blixens were for a time accused without cause of being pro-German because of their affiliation to the Swedish colony in British East Africa.

Blixen began to suffer from an illness which she first assumed to be malaria. After consulting a physician, she learned that her husband had infected her with syphilis. Many years later, she told her secretary Clara Svendsen: "There are two things you can do in such a situation: shoot a man, or accept it."[3] Blixen was treated with mercury tablets, which proved ineffective.

"My father's destiny has, curiously enough, to a great extent been repeated in my own."[3]

1915. Advised by her doctor, Blixen traveled to France to seek treatment. When French experts in the treatment of venereal disease told her that she would need long and painful treatment if she was ever to be cured permanently, Blixen left Paris for Denmark and entered the National Hospital in Copenhagen, under the care of two of Denmark's leading venereologists. Blixen kept her condition a secret from the family and insisted on taking a bed in the general ward while she underwent a three-month course of therapy. Though the primary symptoms of syphilis retreated after the administration of an arsenic-based medication, the disease had irreversibly progressed to its secondary stage and continued to affect her throughout her lifetime.

During her hospital stay Blixen wrote a poem, "Ex Africa," which was published in *Tilskueren* ten years later. "As I lay in the hospital in Copenhagen I yearned for Africa and was afraid the difficulties of a journey out would be so great that I could never get back."[3]

September 7, 1915. Blixen's maternal grandmother, Mary Westenholz, died at the age of eighty-three.

Released from the National Hospital after her three-month stay, Blixen returned to Rungstedlund to live with her mother.

1916. Blixen's sister, Elle, married a rich lawyer, Knud Dahl, who later published the first Danish edition of Blixen's *Seven Gothic Tales*. Her sister, Ea, married Viggo de Neergaard, a Sealand land owner. Blixen spent the summer in Denmark with her husband returning to Africa with him in November. During their stay in Denmark, the family expressed their assurance in the future success of the farm, now incorporated as The Karen Coffee Company. Shares were sold to the family and friends, a bank loan was raised and the corporation purchased a larger farm for the Blixens outside Nairobi.

January 29, 1917. Arrived at the farm after a long voyage home to Africa. "At last we are home again! It seems like a dream to be here, and like a dream to walk around and look at everything again. . . . I have been over to see [the new farm], and the house there is so beautifully cool, the rooms so high and airy and there will be the most wonderful view. . . .

"I do so much want to start painting again and hope I will have time when I get everything in order at home. . . . I think that one must have a certain amount of experience before one can assimilate one's personality in some kind of art, but I think that later one can then transform it again into the art; I believe that I have much more feeling for color and line now than a few years ago. . . ."[2]

Blixen's cousin, Daisy, died suddenly in London. "—I have only just received the news of Daisy's death. . . . I feel that

Denys Finch Hatton, probably during his time at Oxford.

Blixen at Rungstedlund. Photograph by Pierre Boulat for *Life* magazine.

so much color and radiance has gone from life with her passing, and for me so much of my youth. . . . I find it impossible to comprehend that I will never see her again. . . . There are so few people who can lift life out of the mundane run and give it poetry. . . . I believe what one feels most for them is gratitude.—''[2]

Began to paint again at her new home, Mbogani, or ''house in the woods,'' frequently using her African and Somali friends and workers as models. Her sister, Ea, gave birth to a daughter. After graduating from the Polytechnic Institute in Denmark, Thomas Dinesen joined the Canadian Army as a volunteer to fight against the Germans. ''I believe that Tommy is so clearly aware of his own faults and failings, of his difficulty in getting started on anything and making a success of it, and probably he can only escape from this by being carried away, not merely by an idea but through 'the baptism of action.' . . . Perhaps he will be fulfilling the destiny of his talents and abilities and will make something complete of his life.—''[2]

1918. Went on safari with her husband. ''There is something about safari life that makes you forget all your sorrows and feel the whole time as if you had drunk half a bottle of champagne,—bubbling over with heartfelt gratitude for being alive. It seems right that human beings should live in the nomad fashion and unnatural to have one's home always in the same place; one only feels really free when one can go in whatever direction one pleases. . . .''

''Unfortunately we are experiencing a drought here that exceeds anything one can imagine at home. The whole country will perish if it goes on much longer. . . . Everyone is saying that '*the long rains*' will fail this year just like '*the short,*' but I don't know what they base this on. . . .''[2]

April 5, 1918. Met the English Army pilot Denys Finch Hatton at a dinner in Nairobi. Finch Hatton was to become her lover and companion as well as the first audience to hear her tales. ''I think it is extremely rare . . . at my sorry age to meet one's ideal personified.

''It is seldom one meets someone one is immediately in sympathy with and gets along so well with, and what a marvelous thing is talent and intelligence. . . .''[3]

Thomas Dinesen was awarded both the British Victoria Cross and the French Croix de Guerre for heroism during the Allied offensive on the French Front. ''My heart rejoices when I think of you. How proud Father would have been of you; how much I feel myself that you have lent us luster . . . there are many great and beautiful arts in the world, but the greatest of all is the art of living. Go on living beautifully!!''[2]

As a result of the drought in East Africa, The Karen Coffee Company suffered tremendous financial setbacks.

1919. Blixen and her husband sailed to England and on to Denmark. Blixen spent the following year with her mother at Rungstedlund while receiving treatment for both Spanish flu and blood poisoning contracted after she injured her leg in a fall. During her stay at home, Blixen confided her marital problems to her mother and brother who urged divorce.

November 1920. Returned to Africa with brother, Thomas; as the representative of the family company he was to assess the situation and assist in sorting out the finances of the farm, which were now in a completely chaotic state. Shortly after their arrival, Bror Blixen left the farm. During the next few

months the economic position of the farm deteriorated still further.

1921. Blixen's maternal uncle visited Kenya to make a decision on the future of the farm. His inspection resulted in the dismissal of Bror Blixen as manager and the appointment of Karen Blixen to run the farm, with the provision that Bror Blixen was to have nothing more to do with the plantation or The Karen Coffee Company. Much against her wishes, Blixen and her husband separated, but she refused to consider the divorce which her family urged. ''I am going to beg you, dearest Mother not to write to me any more concerning my marriage to Bror. . . . I really think it is a unique situation when a whole family tries with all its might to persuade, almost force one of its members into divorcing. . . . Even in the unhappiest marriage . . . you yourself must realize that this is an unreasonable interference in private affairs, which *cannot be judged by others.*''[2]

''I would never demand a divorce or try to push it through against Bror's will. I do not know how anyone can do that unless one is quite frenzied; and even though I have occasionally been angry with Bror or, rather, perhaps, in despair over his behavior, there is far, far too much binding us together from all the years of difficulties we have shared here, for me to be able to take the initiative in putting an end to what, if nothing else, was a most intimate companionship. . . . I am quite unable to comprehend the state of mind of anyone who can cancel such a relationship. . . . In any case, it is my heartfelt hope that he will be happy . . . I feel for Bror, and will until I die, the greatest friendship or the deepest tenderness that I am capable of feeling.''[2] In the end, however, Bror Blixen requested a divorce, which was granted.

Blixen's eldest sister, Ea, died after giving birth to a stillborn child. ''. . . We have all lost so indescribably much; I cannot understand that we have been bereft of so much richness and beauty, so much warmth and love, and it is such an infinite loss . . .''[2]

1923. Thomas Dinesen returned to Denmark convinced that The Karen Coffee Company was past hope of recovery. Inspired by the conflict between her brother and mother concerning sexual morality, Blixen worked on a long essay on the institution of marriage past and present, entitled *Modern Marriage and Other Considerations,* her first formal effort at writing in years. Denys Finch Hatton frequently visited Africa and always stayed with Blixen on her farm on these occasions. ''That such a person as Denys does exist,—something I have indeed guessed at before, but hardly dared to believe,—and that I have been lucky enough to meet him in this life and been so close to him,—even though there have been long periods of missing him in between,—compensates for everything else in the world, and other things cease to have any significance.''[3]

1924. Mother, Ingeborg Dinesen, visited Kenya with Thomas and stayed with her daughter on the farm for over two months.

1925. Traveled with brother, Thomas, to Europe and then on alone to Denmark where she stayed with her mother at Rungstedlund for eight months. During this time, Blixen attempted to arrange a meeting with George Brandes, who responded graciously. After their meeting, Blixen resubmitted *The Revenge of Truth* to *Tilskueren* and it was accepted for publication the following year. ''With regard to 'The Revenge of Truth,' I don't want anything in it changed; but I imagine there is little chance of it ever being published. I don't think there

(Detail of jacket illustration by Virgil Burnett from *Carnival: Entertainments and Posthumous Tales* by Isak Dinesen.)

is anything blasphemous in it, simply that it is written from an atheist's viewpoint. I believe it would be impossible to write if one gave consideration to who is going to read one's work,—but for that matter I don't think I will be writing anything in the near future. On the whole I don't think there is room for so many considerations in life, or the world. . . . Life here is more brutal and would probably upset you more than the worst revelations from life at home; I, for one, prefer it like that, but still I well understand the happiness,—and charm,—of a quiet and peaceful spot that shuts its eyes and doors against all brutality. There is, naturally, only one choice possible, and the test of whether one has chosen rightly can never be made by considering what is best, only by whether one has rightly judged what made one happy. . . .''[2]

1926. Returned to Africa. Brother, Thomas, married Jonna Lindhardt. Blixen resumed fiction writing after many long years, drafting the first *Gothic Tales* in English, which she preferred to her native Danish. In *Out of Africa* she relates, ''I began in the evenings to write stories, fairy tales and romances, that would take my mind a long way off, to other countries and times. I had been telling some of these stories to a friend [Finch Hatton] when he came to stay on the farm.''

1927. Ingeborg Dinesen visited the farm for the second time, staying three months.

1929. Mother fell seriously ill in Denmark. Blixen returned to Rungstedlund at once and stayed seven months.

1930-1931. After years of financial crisis, Blixen's farm was sold by the company at a forced auction and she prepared for her departure to Denmark.

May 14, 1931. Denys Finch Hatton killed when his private plane crashed in Tanganyika. Blixen returned to her family in Denmark.

''During my last months in Africa, as it became clear to me that I could not keep the farm, I had started writing at night, to get my mind off the things which in the daytime it had gone over a hundred times, and on to a new track. My squatters on the farm, by then, had got into the habit of coming up to my house and sitting around it for hours in silence, as if just

waiting to see how things would develop. I felt their presence there more like a friendly gesture than a reproach, but all the same of sufficient weight to make it difficult for me to start any undertaking of my own. But they would go away, back to their huts, at nightfall. And as I sat there, in the house, alone, or perhaps with Farah, the infallibly loyal, standing motionless in his long white Arab robe with his back to the wall, figures, voices and colors from far away or from nowhere began to swarm around my paraffin lamp. I wrote two of my *Seven Gothic Tales* there.

''Now I was back again in my old home, with my mother, who received the prodigal daughter with all the warmth of her heart, but who never quite realized that I was more than fifteen years old and accustomed, for the past eighteen years, to a life of exceptional freedom. My home is a lovely place; I might have lived on there from day to day in a kind of sweet idyl; but I could not see any kind of future before me. And I had no money; my dowry, so to say, had gone with the farm. I owed it to the people on whom I was dependent to try to make some kind of existence for myself. Those Gothic Tales began to demand to be written . . .''[1]

1934. *Seven Gothic Tales* published in English and chosen as a Book-of-the-Month Club selection. For a pseudonym, Blixen used her maiden name, Dinesen, and preceded it with a man's name, Isak, which in Hebrew means ''one who laughs.'' Her true identity was not revealed until after the success of *Seven Gothic Tales*. When asked in an interview whether she planned to stay in Denmark permanently, Blixen replied, ''Out there I longed for Denmark, now I suffer homesickness for Africa, and think how can I ever sink roots here? One cannot possibly live on the basis that one has written a talked about book, one becomes a kind of museum-piece, a strange thing that is contemplated but not a person, with relations to the world. If I shall lie here it can only be if I establish my life so that I come into relation with the people in their daily life, as I did in Kenya. One must grow if one shall live, one cannot float free in the air.''[3]

1935. *Seven Gothic Tales*, which had first been published in English, published in Denmark, translated by the author. Traveled to Geneva to attend meetings at the League of Nations.

1936. Worked on English version of *Out of Africa*. Blixen continued to suffer from tertiary syphilis and spent two brief stays in the hospital. *The Revenge of Truth* performed at the Royal Theatre in Copenhagen.

1937. Completed English and Danish versions of *Out of Africa*, which has been said to have made Blixen's name as a modern classical writer.

January 27, 1939. Mother died at the age of eighty-five, making Blixen mistress of Rungstedlund. "When my mother died, and I sat vigil through the night at her bedside, I saw then not only the old woman, but the lovely young wife, and the girl, and I grasped much I had not understood before."[3]

1940. Commissioned by the Copenhagen daily newspaper, *Politiken,* to spend a month in London, a month in Paris, and a month in Berlin to write four articles about each city. The German occupation of Denmark took place immediately after her return from Berlin, and the other visits were cancelled on account of the war. Her articles on Hitler's Germany, entitled "Letters from a Land at War," were published in a Danish periodical after the war, and later in her collection, *Daguerrotypes and Other Essays.*

Began work on a new collection of stories, but the completion was delayed owing to long spells of illness.

1942. *Winter's Tales* published in America, England and Denmark. During the war years, Dinesen helped many Jews escape the Nazis by opening the family home at Rungstedlund as a runaway station. "There were Jews in the kitchen and Nazis in the garden. The hair-raising problem was to keep them from meeting."[4]

1945. Clara Svendsen began work as secretary to Blixen at Rungstedlund. Their collaboration continued until Blixen's death, after which Svendsen as literary executor in association with the Rungstedlund Foundation administered the artistic and financial rights of Blixen's writings.

February, 1946. Blixen successfully underwent a spine operation which relieved some of her frequent and severe attacks of pain.

1950. First in a series of radio broadcasts for Danish radio featured Blixen reading a description of her African Somali servant, Farah.

Arthur Miller, Marilyn Monroe, Carson McCullers and Karen Blixen, in McCullers' home.

1951. Traveled to Greece and Rome with writer and publisher Knud W. Jensen and his wife.

1955. Blixen celebrated her seventieth birthday which was universally feted. In August, a new operation became necessary in which several spinal nerves were severed. Blixen also had an extensive operation for a stomach ulcer. After the surgery, she became an invalid, never again ate normally, and never weighed more than eighty-five pounds. "This past eight months have been more horrible than I can really describe to others—such continuous, insufferable pains, under which I howled like a wolf, are something one cannot fully comprehend. I feel that I have been in an Underworld. . . . The problem for me now is how I shall manage to come back into the world of human beings. It sometimes feels practically insoluable, though I believe that if I find something to look forward to, it could be possible."³

1958. *Anecdotes of Destiny* published in America and in Denmark. Extremely ill, she wrote: "I have been terribly ill ever since Christmas, on my back in bed, feeling weaker with every day. I cannot eat anything but oysters, and I cannot get my weight above 35 kilos [77 lbs.]. I am up a little now, but I am really only longing to get back in a horizontal position, I am still unsteady on my legs and sway about from right to left. . . .

"All the same, I still cling to my plan of going to the States in September or October. I should like to stay in New York for about three weeks, then our Ambassador has asked me to stay with him in Washington for a fortnight, then again I should go south to a really nice place, and sit down there quietly with a few trips and excursions, and people to come and talk to me if they care to. . . . If only I can get my strength back."⁴

Blixen was hailed as a major literary figure of the century and, although she never won, was nominated for the Nobel Prize several times during her lifetime.

1958. Her desire to secure the future of the family home, Rungstedlund, resulted in the establishment of the Rungstedlund Foundation, a private institution which purchased the historical building, and the sixty hectares of garden and woodland, to be preserved as a bird reserve. The Foundation also secured the rights of Blixen's works.

July 6, 1958. Blixen gave a radio talk on the future of Rungstedlund and asked her listening audience to support the cause by sending one Danish crown to the Foundation. Over 80,000 listeners complied with her request.

1959. Made her only trip to the United States, staying three months. "I . . . left part of my heart in New York. People had told me before I went there that it was a unique and magnificent place, but that in some way it had no heart. Now as I look back on the time I spent there, although I am well aware that it is in a way an awe-inspiring, even a demonic city, the chief impression that I have brought back with me is that of a most wonderful generosity. I have always loved demons, I am yearning for the particular New York demon. I do not think that I could ever fall in love with anything demon-free. I am in love with New York. . . ."⁴

While in New York, Blixen gave a public reading of her stories which was widely acclaimed. Her extreme fragility and her deeply lined, wrinkled face made interesting subject material for famous artists. She was constantly photographed and painted by such notable artists as Carl Van Vechten, Richard Avedon, Cecil Beaton, Brofferio, and Rene Bouche. She preferred to describe herself as a storyteller, not a writer. "I belong to an ancient, idle, wild and useless tribe, perhaps I am even one of the last members of it, who, for many thousands of years, in all countries and parts of the world, has, now and again, stayed for a time among the hard-working honest people in real life, and sometimes has thus been fortunate enough to create another sort of reality for them, which in some way or another, has satisfied them. I am a storyteller." [Donald Hannah, *'Isak Dinesen' and Karen Blixen: The Mask and the Reality*, Putnam, 1971.⁵]

Sister Ellen died.

November 28, 1960. Became one of the founding members of the Danish Academy.

September 7, 1962. Died from emaciation at her home in Rungsted, Denmark. "And by the time I had nothing left, I myself was the lightest thing of all, for fate to get rid of." [Isak Dinesen, *Out of Africa*, Random House, 1938.⁶]

FOR MORE INFORMATION SEE: Seven Gothic Tales, introduction by Dorothy Canfield Fisher, Modern Library, 1961; *Time,* January 6, 1961, September 27, 1968; Eric O. Johannesson, *The World of Isak Dinesen,* University of Washington, 1961; *Saturday Review,* March 16, 1963; Clara Svendsen, editor, *Isak Dinesen: A Memorial,* Random House, 1964; Robert Langbaum, *The Gayety of Vision: A Study of Isak Dinesen's Art,* Random House, 1965, published as *The Life and Destiny of Isak Dinesen,* University of Chicago Press, 1976; Parmenia Migel, *Titania: The Biography of Isak Dinesen,* Random House, 1967; *Books and Bookmen,* February, 1968; *New Yorker,* November 9, 1968; *Virginia Quarterly Review,* autumn, 1968; C. Svendsen, editor, *The Life and Destiny of Isak Dinesen,* Random House, 1970; Donald Hannah, *'Isak Dinesen' and Karen Blixen: The Mask and the Reality,* Putnam, 1971; Thorkild Bjørnvig, *The Pact: My Friendship with Isak Dinesen,* Louisiana State University Press, 1974; Errol Trzebinski, *Silence Will Speak,* University of Chicago Press, 1977; Liselotte Henricksen, *Isak Dinesen, A Bibliography,* University of Chicago Press, 1977; Isak Dinesen, *Daguerreotypes and Other Essays,* University of Chicago Press, 1979; *Isak Dinesen: Letters from Africa 1914-1931,* edited by Frans Lasson, University of Chicago Press, 1981; Judith Thurman, *Isak Dinesen: The Life of a Storyteller,* St. Martin's Press, 1982.

BLOCKSMA, Mary

BRIEF ENTRY: Now a free-lance writer, Blocksma's past career positions included those as peace corps volunteer and teacher in high schools and colleges. With her brother, Dewey Blocksma, she has written two handicraft books of interest to middle-grade readers. *Easy-to-Make Spaceships That Really Fly* (Prentice-Hall, 1983) was described by *Booklist* as "a competent execution of a terrific concept that gives readers concrete guidance while allowing ample room for creative innovation." Using materials like paper plates, styrofoam cups, and straws, children are guided through the necessary steps to construct fourteen different models. "[The author's] instructions are so simple and clearly presented," observed *School Library Journal,* ". . . that there is no need for adult supervision." The sister-and-brother team employ the same successful format in *Easy-to-Make Water Toys That Really Work* (Prentice-Hall, 1985).

For older readers, Blocksma is the author of *The Marvelous Music Machine: A History of the Piano* (Prentice-Hall, 1984).

Reviewers praised the enthusiasm generated as she delves into the background and physical construction of the instrument. *Horn Book* called this book "a grab bag of fascinating piano lore," adding that "by the end . . . more than one reader may be moved to go tickle the ivories." Writing for yet another level of the juvenile reading audience, Blocksma has produced six books in the "Just One More" series published by Childrens Press. These books are aimed at the very early beginning reader and feature a controlled vocabulary accompanied by word lists in each volume. As *School Library Journal* noted, the stories "competently fill the need for picture books that children can read independently." Among the titles are *Apple Tree! Apple Tree!* (1983), *Grandma Dragon's Birthday* (1983), *The Best-Dressed Bear* (1984), and *Rub-a-Dub-Dub: What's in the Tub?* (1984). Blocksma also designs greeting cards and is a contributor to magazines and newspapers. *Residence:* Fort Collins, Colo.

BONTEMPS, Arna   1902-1973

PERSONAL: Born October 13, 1902, in Alexandria, La.; died of a heart attack, at his home in Nashville, Tenn., June 4, 1973; son of Paul Bismark (a brick mason) and Marie Caroline (a teacher; maiden name, Pembrooke) Bontemps; married Alberta Johnson, August 26, 1926; children: Joan Marie Bontemps Williams, Paul Bismark, Poppy Alberta Bontemps Booker, Camille Ruby Bontemps Graves, Constance Rebecca Bontemps Thomas, Arna Alex. *Education:* Pacific Union College, B.A., 1923; University of Chicago, M.A., 1943. *Residence:* Nashville, Tenn.

CAREER: Teacher in New York, N.Y., Huntsville, Ala., and Chicago, Ill., 1923-38; Fisk University, Nashville, Tenn., librarian, 1943-65; University of Illinois at Chicago Circle, professor, 1966-69; Yale University, New Haven, Conn., visiting professor and curator of James Weldon Johnson Collection, 1969; Fisk University, writer-in-residence, 1970-73. *Member:* National Association for the Advancement of Colored People, P.E.N., Authors League of America, Dramatists Guild, American Library Association, Sigma Pi Phi, Omega Psi Phi. *Awards, honors: Crisis* (magazine) poetry prize, 1926; Alexander Pushkin Poetry Prize, 1926, 1927; *Opportunity* (journal) short story prize, 1932; Julius Rosenwald fellow, 1938-39, 1942-43; Guggenheim fellowship for creative writing, 1949-50; Newbery Honor Book, 1949, and Jane Addams Children's Book Award, 1956, both for *Story of the Negro;* Dow Award, Society of Midland Authors, 1967, for *Anyplace But Here;* L.H.D., Morgan State College, 1969.

WRITINGS: God Sends Sunday (adult novel), Harcourt, 1931; (with Langston Hughes) *Popo and Fifina: Children of Haiti* (juvenile; illustrated by E. Simms Campbell), Macmillan, 1932; *You Can't Pet a Possum* (illustrated by Ilse Bischoff), Morrow, 1934; *Black Thunder* (adult historical novel), Macmillan, 1936, 3rd edition, Beacon Press, 1968; *Sad-Faced Boy* (juvenile; illustrated by Virginia Lee Burton), Houghton, 1937; *Drums at Dusk* (novel), Macmillan, 1939.

(Compiler) *Golden Slippers: An Anthology of Negro Poetry for Young Readers* (illustrated by Henrietta Bruce Sharon), Harper, 1941; (editor) W. C. Handy, *Father of the Blues: An Autobiography,* Macmillan, 1941; (with Jack Conroy) *The Fast Sooner Hound* (juvenile; illustrated by V. L. Burton), Houghton, 1942; (with J. Conroy) *They Seek a City* (history), Doubleday, 1945, revised edition published as *Anyplace But Here,* Hill & Wang, 1966; *We Have Tomorrow* (history; illustrated with photographs by Marian Palfi), Houghton, 1945; (with J.

ARNA BONTEMPS

Conroy) *Slappy Hooper, the Wonderful Sign Painter* (juvenile; illustrated by Ursula Koering), Houghton, 1946; *Story of the Negro* (illustrated by Raymond Lufkin; ALA Notable Book), Knopf, 1948, 5th edition, 1969; (editor with L. Hughes) *The Poetry of the Negro: 1746-1949,* Doubleday, 1949, revised edition published as *The Poetry of the Negro: 1746-1970,* 1970.

George Washington Carver (illustrated by Cleveland L. Woodward), Row, Peterson, 1950; (with J. Conroy) *Sam Patch, the High, Wide and Handsome Jumper* (juvenile; illustrated by Paul Brown), Houghton, 1951; *Chariot in the Sky: A Story of the Jubilee Singers* (juvenile; illustrated by Cyrus L. Baldridge), Winston, 1951, new edition, Holt, 1971; *The Story of George Washington Carver* (juvenile biography; illustrated by Harper Johnson), Grosset, 1954; *Lonesome Boy* (juvenile; illustrated by Feliks Topolski), Houghton, 1955; *Frederick Douglass: Slave, Fighter, Freeman* (illustrated by H. Johnson), Knopf, 1958; (editor with L. Hughes) *The Book of Negro Folklore,* Dodd, 1958.

One Hundred Years of Negro Freedom (history), Dodd, 1961; (editor) *American Negro Poetry,* Hill & Wang, 1963, revised edition, 1974; *Personals,* Paul Breman, 1963, 2nd edition, 1973; *Famous Negro Athletes* (juvenile), Dodd, 1964; (editor with others) *American Negro Heritage,* Century Schoolbooks Press, 1965; (compiler and author of introduction) *Great Slave Narratives,* Beacon Press, 1969; (compiler) *Hold Fast to Dreams: Poems Old and New* (ALA Notable Book), Follett, 1969; (author of introduction) L. Hughes, *Don't You Turn Back: Poems,* Knopf, 1969.

Mr. Kelso's Lion, Lippincott, 1970; *Free at Last: The Life of Frederick Douglass*, Dodd, 1971; (editor with others) *Five Black Lives: The Autobiographies of Venture Smith, James Mars, William Grimes, G. W. Offley, and James L. Smith*, Wesleyan University Press, 1971; *Young Booker: Booker T. Washington's Early Days*, Dodd, 1972; (editor) *The Harlem Renaissance Remembered* (essays), Dodd, 1972; *The Old South: A Summer Tragedy and Other Stories of the Thirties*, Dodd, 1973; *Arna Bontemps-Langston Hughes Letters, 1925-1967*, edited by Charles H. Nichols, Dodd, 1980.

Author of plays, including (with Countee Cullen) "St. Louis Woman" (adapted from his novel, *God Sends Sunday*), starring Pearl Bailey, first produced at the Martin Beck Theatre, New York, N.Y., March 30, 1946; "Creole"; "Careless Love"; and (with C. Cullen) "Free and Easy," 1949. Fiction included in numerous anthologies, including *Grandma Moses' Story Book*, Random House, 1961. Contributor to *Harper's* and other national magazines.

SIDELIGHTS: **October 13, 1902.** Born in Alexandria, Louisiana. "Mine had not been a varmint-infested childhood so often the hallmark of Negro American autobiography. My parents and grandparents had been well-fed, well-clothed, and well-housed, although in my earliest recollections of the corner at Ninth and Winn in Alexandria both streets were rutted and sloppy. On Winn there was an abominable ditch where water settled for weeks at a time. I can remember Crazy George, the town idiot, following a flock of geese with the bough of a tree in his hand, standing in slush while the geese paddled about or probed into the muck. So fascinated was I, in fact, I did not hear my grandmother calling from the kitchen door. It was after I felt her hand on my shoulder shaking me out of my daydream that I said something that made her laugh. 'You called me Arna,' I protested, when she insisted on knowing

One old lady who carried a basket of clothes on her head was about to walk on. Suddenly she stopped. ■
(From *The Story of George Washington Carver* by Arna Bontemps. Illustrated by Harper Johnson.)

why I had not answered. 'My name is George.' But I became Arna for the rest of her years.

"I had already become aware of nicknames among the people we regarded as members of the family. Teel, Mousie, Buddy, Pinkie, Ya-ya, Mat, and Pig all had other names which one heard occasionally. I got the impression that to be loved intensely one needed a nickname. I was glad my grandmother, whose love mattered so much, had found one she liked for me.

"As I recall, my hand was in my grandmother's a good part of the time. If we were not standing outside the picket gate waiting for my young uncles to come home from school, we were under the tree in the front yard picking up pecans after one of the boys had climbed up and shaken the branches. If we were not decorating a backyard bush with eggshells, we were driving in our buggy across the bridge to Pineville on the other side of the Red River.

"This idyll came to a sudden, senseless end at a time when everything about it seemed flawless. One afternoon my mother and her several sisters had come out of their sewing room with thimbles still on their fingers, needles and thread stuck to their tiny aprons, to fill their pockets with pecans. Next, it seemed, we were at the railroad station catching a train to California, my mother, sister, and I, with a young woman named Susy.

"The story behind it, I learned, concerned my father. When he was not away working at brick or stone construction, other things occupied his time. He had come from a family of builders. His oldest brother had married into the Metoyer family on Cane River, descendants of the free Negroes who were the original builders of the famous Melrose plantation mansion. Another brother older than my father went down to New Orleans, where his daughter married one of the prominent jazzmen. My father was a bandman himself and, when he was not working too far away, the chances were he would be blowing his horn under the direction of Claiborne Williams, whose passion for band music awakened the impulse that worked its way up the river and helped to quicken American popular music.

"My father was one of those dark Negroes with 'good' hair, meaning almost straight. This did not bother anybody in Avoyelles Parish, where the type was common and 'broken French' accents expected, but later in California people who had traveled in the Far East wondered if he were not a Ceylonese or something equally exotic. In Alexandria his looks, good clothes, and hauteur were something of a disadvantage in the first decade of this century.

"He was walking on Lee Street one night when two white men wavered out of a saloon and blocked his path. One of them muttered, 'Let's walk over the big nigger.' My father was capable of fury, and he might have reasoned differently at another time, but that night he calmly stepped aside, allowing the pair to have the walk to themselves. The decision he made as he walked on home changed everything for all of us.

"My first clear memory of my father as a person is of him waiting for us outside the Southern Pacific Depot in Los Angeles. He was shy about showing emotion, and he greeted us quickly on our arrival and let us know this was the place he had chosen for us to end our journey. We had tickets to San Francisco and were prepared to continue beyond if necessary.

"We moved into a house in a neighborhood where we were the only colored family. The people next door and up and

When they did finally see something moving in the moonlight, it was not running and it was not Grandpa. ■ (From *Mr. Kelso's Lion* by Arna Bontemps. Illustrated by Len Ebert.)

down the block were friendly and talkative, the weather was perfect, there wasn't a mud puddle anywhere, and my mother seemed to float about on the clean air. When my grandmother and a host of others followed us to this refreshing new country, I began to pick up comment about the place we had left, comment which had been withheld from me while we were still in Louisiana.

When Bubber first learned to play the trumpet, his old grandpa winked his eye and laughed. ■ (From *Lonesome Boy* by Arna Bontemps. Illustrated by Feliks Topolski.)

"They talked mainly about my grandmother's younger brother, nicknamed Buddy. I could not remember seeing him in Louisiana, and I now learned he had been down at the Keeley Institute in New Orleans taking a cure for alcoholism. A framed portrait of Uncle Buddy was placed in my grandmother's living room in California, a young mulatto dandy in elegant cravat and jeweled stickpin. All the talk about him gave me an impression of style, grace, éclat.

"That impression vanished a few years later, however, when we gathered to wait for him in my grandmother's house; he entered wearing a detachable collar without a tie. His clothes did not fit. They had been slept in for nearly a week on the train. His shoes had come unlaced. His face was pockmarked. Nothing resembled the picture in the living room.

"Two things redeemed the occasion, however. He opened his makeshift luggage and brought out jars of syrup, bags of candy my grandmother had said in her letters that she missed, pecans, and filé for making gumbo. He had stuffed his suitcase with these instead of clothes; he had not brought an overcoat or a change of underwear. As we ate the sweets, he began to talk. He was not trying to impress or even entertain us. He was just telling how things were down home, how he had not taken a drink or been locked up since he came back from Keeley the last time, how the family of his employer and benefactor had been scattered or died, how the school-teacher friend of the family was getting along, how high the Red River had risen along the levee, and such things.

"When my mother became ill, a year or so after Buddy's arrival, we went to live with my grandmother in the country for a time. Buddy was there. He had acquired a rusticity wholly foreign to his upbringing. He had never before worked out of doors. Smoking a corncob pipe and wearing oversized clothes provided by my uncles, he resembled a scarecrow in the garden, but the dry air and the smell of green vegetables seemed to be good for him. I promptly became his companion and confidant in the corn rows.

"At mealtime we were occasionally joined by my father, home from his bricklaying. The two men eyed each other with sus-

The road that Frederick Douglass took to freedom was also followed by many other slaves. ■ (From *Story of the Negro* by Arna Bontemps. Illustrated by Raymond Lufkin.)

And when the dog trotted into the Roadmaster's office a mile ahead of the train, the Roadmaster got angry. ■ (From *Fast Sooner Hound* by Arna Bontemps and Jack Conroy. Illustrated by Virginia Lee Burton.)

picion, but they did not quarrel immediately. Mostly they reminisced about Louisiana. My father would say, 'Sometimes I miss all that. If I was just thinking about myself, I might want to go back and try it again. But I've got the children to think about—their education.'

"'Folks talk a lot about California,' Buddy would reply thoughtfully, 'but I'd a heap rather be down home than here, if it wasn't for the *conditions*.'

"Obviously their remarks made sense to each other, but they left me with a deepening question. Why was this exchange repeated after so many of their conversations? What was it that made the South—excusing what Buddy called the *conditions*—so appealing for them?

"There was less accord between them in the attitudes they revealed when each of the men talked to me privately. My father respected Buddy's ability to quote the whole of Thomas Hood's 'The Vision of Eugene Aram,' praised his reading and spelling ability, but he was concerned, almost troubled, about the possibility of my adopting the old derelict as an example. He was horrified by Buddy's casual and frequent use of the word *nigger*. Buddy even forgot and used it in the presence of white people once or twice that year, and was soundly

criticized for it. Buddy's new friends, moreover, were sometimes below the level of polite respect. They were not bad people. They were what my father described as don't-care folk. To top it all, Buddy was still crazy about the minstrel shows and minstrel talk that had been the joy of his young manhood. He loved dialect stories, preacher stories, ghost stories, slave and master stories. He half-believed in signs and charms and mumbo-jumbo, and he believed whole-heartedly in ghosts.

"I took it that my father was still endeavoring to counter Buddy's baneful influence when he sent me away to a white boarding school during my high school years, after my mother had died. 'Now don't go up there acting colored,' he cautioned. I believe I carried out his wish. He sometimes threatened to pull me out of school and let me scuttle for myself the minute I fell short in any one of several ways he indicated. Before I finished college, I had begun to feel that in some large and important areas I was being miseducated, and that perhaps I should have rebelled.

"In their opposing attitudes toward roots my father and my great uncle made me aware of a conflict in which every educated American Negro, and some who are not educated, must somehow take sides. By implication at least, one group ad-

Caleb saw nothing distinctly in the dark palmetto grove, but he knew he was being followed. ■ (From *Chariot in the Sky* by Arna Bontemps. Illustrated by Cyrus Leroy Baldridge.)

vocates embracing the riches of the folk heritage; their opposites demand a clean break with the past and all it represents. Had I not gone home summers and hobnobbed with Negroes, I would have finished college without knowing that any Negro other than Paul Laurence Dunbar ever wrote a poem. I would have come out imagining that the story of the Negro could be told in two short paragraphs: a statement about jungle people in Africa and an equally brief account of the slavery issue in American history.'' [Arna Bontemps, "Why I Returned," *Harper's*, April, 1965.[1]]

1923. Graduated from Pacific Union College. Went to New York City, where he taught at the Harlem Academy. "So what did one do after concluding that for him a break with the past and the shedding of his Negro-ness were not only impossible but unthinkable? First, perhaps, like myself, he went to New York in the 'twenties, met young Negro writers and intellectuals who were similarly searching, learned poems like Claude McKay's 'Harlem Dancer' and Jean Toomer's 'Song of the Son,' and started writing and publishing things in this vein himself.''[1]

Bontemps became a contributor to the Harlem Renaissance, a period in the 1920s when young black writers, such as Langston Hughes, Countee Cullen, and Jean Toomer, flocked to Harlem to explore black culture. "The Harlem Renaissance, so called, was publicly recognized in March of 1924. Much that had gone before can now be seen as part of the awakening, but still another year was to pass before those personally involved could make themselves believe that they were, or had been, a part of something memorable.'' [Arna Bontemps, editor, *The Harlem Renaissance Remembered*, Dodd, 1972.[2]]

1926. Married Alberta Johnson. Won the Alexander Pushkin Poetry prize.

1931. First novel, *God Sends Sunday*, published. "My first book was published just after the Depression struck. . . . Alfred Harcourt, Sr. was my publisher. When he invited me to the office, I found that he was also to be my editor. He explained with a smile that he was back on the job doing editorial work because of the hard times. I soon found out what he meant. Book business appeared to be as bad as every other kind, and the lively and talented young people I had met in Harlem were

scurrying to whatever brier patches they could find. I found one in Alabama.

"It was the best of times and the worst of times to run to that state for refuge. Best, because the summer air was so laden with honeysuckle and spiraea it almost drugged the senses at night. I have occasionally returned since then but never at a time when the green of trees, of countryside, or even of swamps seemed so wanton. While paying jobs were harder to find here than in New York, indeed scarcely existed, one did not see evidences of hunger. Negro girls worked in kitchens not for wages but for the toting privilege—permission to take home leftovers.

"It was also the worst times to be in Northern Alabama. That was the year, 1931, of the nine Scottsboro boys and their trials in nearby Decatur. Instead of chasing possums at night and swimming in creeks in the daytime, this group of kids without jobs and nothing else to do had taken to riding empty boxcars. When they found themselves in a boxcar with two white girls wearing overalls and traveling the same way, they knew they were in bad trouble. The charge against them was rape, and the usual finding in Alabama, when a Negro man was so much as remotely suspected, was guilty; the usual penalty, death.

Nobody in the boat paid any attention to him, of course, because he was too far away, but that did not stop Fred from waving. ■ (From *Frederick Douglass: Slave, Fighter, Freeman* by Arna Bontemps. Illustrated by Harper Johnson.)

"To relieve the tension, as we hoped, we drove to Athens one night and listened to a program of music by young people from Negro high schools and colleges in the area. A visitor arrived from Decatur during the intermission and reported shocking developments at the trial that day.... The rumor that reached Athens was that crowds were spilling along the highway, lurking in unseemly places, threatening to vent their anger. After the music was over, someone suggested nervously that those of us from around Huntsville leave at the same time, keep our cars close together as we drove home, be prepared to stand by, possibly help, if anyone met with mischief.

"We readily agreed. Though the drive home was actually uneventful, the tension remained, and I began to take stock with a seriousness comparable to my father's when he stepped aside for the Saturday night bullies on Lee Street in Alexandria. I was younger than he had been when he made his move, but my family was already larger by one. Moreover, I had weathered a Northern as well as a Southern exposure. My education was different, and what I was reading in newspapers differed greatly from anything he could have found in the Alexandria *Town Talk* in the first decade of this century.

"With Gandhi making world news in India while the Scottsboro case inflamed passions in Alabama and awakened consciences elsewhere, I thought I could sense something beginning to shape up, possibly something on a wide scale.

"Even so, deliverance did not yet seem imminent, and it was becoming plain that an able-bodied young Negro with a healthy

[He] went to the pump in the back yard to wash his dirty hands and face. ■ (From *You Can't Pet a Possum* by Arna Bontemps. Illustrated by Ilse Bischoff.)

family could not continue to keep friends in that community if he sat around trifling with a typewriter on the shady side of his house when he should have been working or at least trying to raise something for the table. So we moved on to Chicago."[1]

Taught school in Chicago. "Crime seemed to be the principal occupation of the South Side at the time of our arrival. The openness of it so startled us we could scarcely believe what we saw. Twice our small apartment was burglarized. Nearly every week we witnessed a stickup, a purse-snatching, or something equally dismaying on the street. Once I saw two men get out of a car, enter one of those blinded shops around the corner from us, return dragging a resisting victim, slam him into the back seat of the car, and speed away. We had fled from the jungle of Alabama's Scottsboro era to the jungle of Chicago's crime-ridden South Side, and one was as terrifying as the other.

"Despite literary encouragement, and the heartiness of a writing clan that adopted me and bolstered my courage, I never felt that I could settle permanently with my family in Chicago. I could not accept the ghetto, and ironclad residential restrictions against Negroes situated as we were made escape impossible, confining us to neighborhoods where we had to fly home each evening before darkness fell and honest people abandoned the streets to predators. Garbage was dumped in alleys around us. Police protection was regarded as a farce. Corruption was everywhere.

"When I inquired about transfers for two of our children to integrated schools which were actually more accessible to our address, I was referred to a person not connected with the school system or the city government. He assured me he could arrange the transfers—at an outrageous price. This represented ways in which Negro leadership was operating in the community at that time and by which it had been reduced to impotence.

SLUMBER WAS POUNDING THE BIG OLD DRUM

(From *Sad-Faced Boy* by Arna Bontemps. Illustrated by Virginia Lee Burton.)

"I did not consider exchanging this way of life for the insitutionalized assault on Negro personality one encountered in the Alabama of the Scottsboro trials, but suddenly the campus of a Negro college I had twice visited in Tennessee began to seem attractive. A measure of isolation, a degree of security seemed possible there. If a refuge for the harassed Negro could be found anywhere in the 1930s, it had to be in such a setting."[1]

1932. Collaborated with Langston Hughes on a children's book, *Popo and Fifina: Children of Haiti.* "Langston had the story and told it to me; I had the children! So we worked together." [Lee Bennett Hopkins, *More Books by More People,* Citation, 1974.[3]]

1936. Wrote an adult historical novel, *Black Thunder.*

1937. Wrote *Sad-Faced Boy,* a children's book. When asked why he wrote stories for children, Bontemps responded: "As a child I read a great deal and never forgot the books I had enjoyed most, and secondly, by the time I started writing as a man, I had children of my own and wanted them to read *my* books—as well as other people's, of course!"[3]

1938. Awarded a Rosenwald Fellowship for writing and travel in the Caribbean.

1942. Wrote *The Fast Sooner Hound,* the first of several children's books written with Jack Conroy.

1943. Began long career as librarian at Fisk University in Tennessee. "Fisk University, since its beginnings in surplus barracks provided by a general of the occupying army six months after the close of the Civil War, had always striven to exemplify racial concord. Integration started immediately with children of white teachers and continued till state laws forced segregation after the turn of the century. Even then, a mixed faculty was retained, together with a liberal environment, and these eventually won a truce from an outside community that gradually changed from hostility to indifference to acceptance and perhaps a certain pride. Its founders helped fight the battle for public schools in Nashville, and donated part of the college's property for this purpose. Its students first introduced Negro spirituals to the musical world. The college provided a setting for a continuing dialogue between scholars across barriers and brought to the city before 1943 a pioneering Institute of Race Relations and a Program of African Studies, both firsts in the region."[1]

1946. Collaborated with Countee Cullen on the musical play, "St. Louis Woman."

1948. Wrote history book entitled *Story of the Negro.* Wrote to Langston Hughes: "Knopf just wired to congratulate me on the fact that *Story of the Negro* was mentioned as runner-up for the Newbery Medal (the Pulitzer of the juveniles), but near misses don't make me happy. I'd like a jackpot, a bullseye, or something—*sometime.*" [Charles H. Nichols, editor, *Arna Bontemps-Langston Hughes Letters: 1925-1967,* Dodd, 1980.[4]]

1949. Collaborated with Langston Hughes on anthology *The Poetry of the Negro: 1746-1949.*

1950. Received the Guggenheim Foundation Award. ". . . Now I can start dreaming again about that sabbatical perhaps to begin about January '50. And if that car I ordered arrives, I might even drive around a little. . . .

"One thing I've decided already: to take a two-year truce on little chicken-feed assignments, to concentrate on clearing up outstanding commitments by the end of the year so as to concentrate on the dynasty of Negro leadership during the period of the leave and the fellowship. Since notification of the award reached me on April 1st, perhaps this can be taken as an April Fool's Resolution."[4]

1953. Play, "St. Louis Woman," was contracted by M-G-M to be adapted into a movie. "The MGM contracts and related papers for 'St. Loo' arrived, and the parcel weighs several pounds, I'd estimate. There are 9 separate sets of documents, containing from 5 to 7 copies each. I'll have to sign or initial over 100 times! Of these, 20 will have to be notarized. There are even two sets of documents to be signed by every member of my family. Alex will have to make his 8-year-old signature 12 times. These two sets, of course, had to be sent to Bennett College for Poppy and Camille [two of his children] to sign first. I am now waiting for their return. I gather Loews Inc. (MGM) wants to make sure it leaves no stone unturned. . . . It goes without saying that most of the wording is Greek to me."[4] The project was later shelved.

1955. Wrote another juvenile book, *Lonesome Boy.* "Some people have found *Lonesome Boy* puzzling. (I get the impression that some adults who work with children have felt that with young people you should leave no uncertainty, no vagueness.) Some have wondered whether or not it is a folk tale. It is not, but it is told somewhat in the manner of a folk tale because I thought that style suited the material. Was Bubber dreaming when all the last part happened?

"A difficult question. Coming back to autobiography, I can remember instances in my own childhood when I was not sure whether I had experienced or dreamed certain things. That is as much as I can say about the mystery of the story. . . . [Arna Bontemps, "The *Lonesome Boy* Theme," *Horn Book,* December, 1966.[5]]

1959. On his 57th birthday, wrote to Langston Hughes: "I celebrated my birthday by cancelling three lecture engagements. . . . All for the week before Thanksgiving. Can't afford the time, now that the literary pot is boiling again. But I do plan to fill the engagement in Philadelphia on the 27th of this month, and I hope to get up to NYC right after, if not before. *Free and Easy* is calling rehearsals on the 26th. . . .''[4]

1960. Invited to Makerere College in Uganda, Africa.

1964. *Famous Negro Athletes* published. Commenting on his diverse writing activities, Bontemps said: "I have never had to worry about ideas. My problem is finding enough time to write them down. So many things happened while I was growing up, and I have seen and participated in so many activities; I keep a full storeroom of ideas."[3]

1966. Professor of English at the University of Illinois at Chicago Circle. "Some of my students are writing beautifully (better than anyone before them) on the Renaissance [Harlem Renaissance], etc. They perk me up. And my classes for next quarter are already FULL. . . .''[4]

1967. Friend and collaborator, Langston Hughes, died.

1969. Edited the poetry anthology, *Hold Fast to Dreams.* "Sometime during my childhood I heard it said that old-time bakers would save a little of the dough they mixed each day. The following day they would mix a little of the dough saved from yesterday with today's dough and then bake them to-

When Mike Flint came along, he found a crowd of people standing about on the sidewalk watching a tall man painting a billboard sign with swift and sure strokes. ■ (From *Slappy Hooper, the Wonderful Sign Painter* by Arna Bontemps and Jack Conroy. Illustrated by Ursula Koering.)

gether. I asked my old great uncle about this. He was a retired baker in my school days, and he assured me that this was right. I liked the idea of mixing a little of the old with the new in this way. So when I became a teacher in Chicago, an editor at Follett, Ms. Bertha Jenkinson, asked me if I had in the back of my mind some book that I had always wanted to do. I told her that I would like to collect a book of poems old and new that seemed to go well together. I said I thought all poems could be divided two ways—the poems we remember and the ones we forget. Mine would be a collection of the poems I remembered well, and some would be old, some new. The result was *Hold Fast to Dreams*.''[3]

June 4, 1973. Died at his home in Nashville, Tennessee.

HOBBIES AND OTHER INTERESTS: Literature, theatre, and sports.

FOR MORE INFORMATION SEE: Stanley Kunitz and Howard Haycraft, editors, *Junior Book of Authors,* 2nd edition, H. W. Wilson, 1951; Harry R. Warfel, *American Novelists of Today,* American Book, 1951; Huck and Young, *Children's Literature in the Elementary School,* Holt, 1961; *Negro Digest,* September, 1963, August, 1967; May Hill Arbuthnot, *Children and Books,* 3rd edition, Scott, Foresman, 1964; Arna Bontemps, "Why I Returned," *Harper's,* April, 1965; Robert A. Bone, *The Negro Novel in America,* Yale University Press, 1965; A. Bontemps, "The *Lonesome Boy* Theme," *Horn Book,* December, 1966; Nancy Larrick, *A Teacher's Guide to Children's Books,* Merrill, 1966; *Best Sellers,* January 1, 1968; *New York Times,* January 21, 1969, April 25, 1969; *Book World,* September 7, 1969; N. Larrick, *A Parent's Guide to Children's Reading,* 3rd edition, Doubleday, 1969; Virginia Haviland and William Jay Smith, compilers, *Children and Poetry,* Library of Congress, 1969.

Martha E. Ward and Dorothy A. Marquardt, *Authors of Books for Young People,* 2nd edition, Scarecrow, 1971; Houston A. Baker, Jr., *Black Literature in America,* McGraw, 1971; Jacqueline S. Weiss, "Arna Bontemps" (videocassette; interview), *Profiles in Literature,* Temple University, 1971; *National Review,* September 15, 1972; *New Republic,* November 4, 1972, January 14, 1974; A. Bontemps, editor, *The Harlem Renaissance Remembered,* Dodd, 1972; *Library Journal,* July, 1973; *Black World,* September, 1973; *New York Times Book Review,* December 23, 1973; Dorothy M. Broderick, *Image of the Black in Children's Fiction,* Bowker, 1973; Lee Bennett Hopkins, *More Books by More People,* Citation, 1974; Rush, Myers, and Arata, *Black American Writers Past and Present,* Scarecrow, 1975; Michael Popkin, editor, *Modern Black Writers,* Ungar, 1978; Charles H. Nichols, editor, *Arna Bontemps-Langston Hughes Letters, 1925-1967,* Dodd, 1980.

Obituaries: *New York Times,* June 6, 1973; *Time,* June 18, 1973; *Library Journal,* July, 1973; *Publishers Weekly,* July 9, 1973; *AB Bookman's Weekly,* October 1, 1973; *Wilson Library Bulletin,* October, 1973; *Current Biography,* H. W. Wilson, 1973.

BROWN, Joe David 1915-1976

PERSONAL: Born May 12, 1915, in East Lake, Ala.; died April 22, 1976, of a heart attack at his home, Covey Rise Farm, in Mayfield, Ga.; son of William Samuel (a newspaper publisher) and Lucille (Lokey) Brown; married Mildred Harbour, October 24, 1935 (divorced, 1943); married Frances O'Reilly, June 30, 1945; children: Joe David, Jr., Tedd H., Gilbreth. *Education:* Attended University of Alabama. *Politics:* Independent. *Religion:* Protestant. *Agent:* Curtis Brown Ltd., 60 East 56h St., New York, N.Y. 10022.

CAREER: Worked on newspapers in Alabama and Missouri, 1935-39; *New York Daily News,* New York, N.Y., feature writer, 1939-46; *Time* and *Life,* New York, N.Y., foreign correspondent in New Delhi, Paris, London, Moscow, 1949-57; free-lance writer, beginning 1957. *Military service:* U.S Army, parachutist with 517th Combat Team, 1942-45; became second lieutenant; received battlefield commission, Purple Heart, and Croix de Guerre with palm (France).

*WRITINGS—*Novels: *Stars in My Crown,* Morrow, 1946 (also author of film adaptation); *The Freeholder,* Morrow, 1949; *Kings Go Forth,* Morrow, 1956; *Glimpse of a Stranger,* Mor-

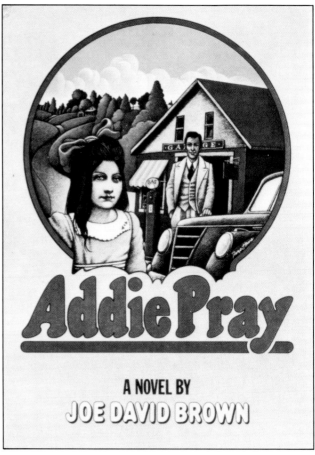

(Jacket illustration by Roger Hane from *Addie Pray* by Joe David Brown.)

row, 1968; *Addie Pray* (Literary Guild selection), Simon & Schuster, 1971, published as *Paper Moon,* New American Library, 1972.

Nonfiction: (With the editors of *Life*) *India,* Time-Life, 1961, revised edition, 1969.

Editor; all published by Time-Life: *The Hippies,* 1967; *Can Christianity Survive?,* 1967; *Sex in the 60s,* 1967.

Short stories anthologized in *Best Post Stories, Literature in America,* and *This Is Your War.* Contributor of short stories and articles to most national magazines, including *Saturday Evening Post, Sports Illustrated,* and *Colliers.*

*ADAPTATIONS—*Motion Pictures: "Stars in My Crown," starring Joel McCrea and Ellen Drew, Metro-Goldwyn-Mayer, 1949; "Kings Go Forth," starring Frank Sinatra, Tony Curtis, and Natalie Wood, United Artists, 1958; "Paper Moon," starring Ryan O'Neal and Tatum O'Neal, Paramount, 1973.

Television: "Paper Moon," ABC-TV, 1974-75, weekly half-hour comedy series, starring Christopher Connelly and Jodie Foster.

SIDELIGHTS: Brown was born in the Birmingham, Alabama suburb of East Lake in 1915. He attended local schools and the University of Alabama. During the Depression, he was forced to abandon college to go to work as a reporter for the Birmingham *Post.* He subsequently worked on several Southern newspapers before joining the *New York Daily News.*

JOE DAVID BROWN

(From the movie "Paper Moon," based on the novel *Addie Pray* by Joe David Brown, starring Ryan O'Neal and his daughter, Tatum. Miss O'Neal won the Academy Award for Best Supporting Actress that year. Copyright © 1973 by Paramount Pictures.)

In 1943 Brown joined the U.S. Army where he became a paratrooper, even though, at twenty-eight, he was considered a bit old to be accepted. During World War II, he was one of the first twenty men to parachute into France in advance of D-Day, June 6, 1944. Wounded in battle, he was awarded the Purple Heart, three battle stars, and the French Croix de Guerre. After spending months in hospitals in France and England recuperating from battle wounds, he was sent back to the States, where he returned to the *New York Daily News* as a feature writer.

One of his editors at the *Daily News* urged Brown to write short stories about his Southern family. His short story, "Grandpa and the Miracle Grindstone," was published in March, 1946 by the *Saturday Evening Post*. The central character of that story became the hero in Brown's first novel, *Stars in My Crown* (1946). This novel, written about the South during the Depression, was vaguely autobiographical. It became a movie, as did two later novels, *Kings Go Forth* and *Paper Moon* (first published as *Addie Pray*).

From 1949 to 1957 Brown was a *Time* and *Life* magazine correspondent in New York, Paris, New Delhi, London, and Moscow, quitting three times in sixteen years to write three more novels. In 1957 he quit reporting, moved to Atlanta,

Georgia, and began free-lance writing. He wrote several novels and edited or co-edited several volumes for Time-Life Books.

Brown's last book, *Addie Pray,* earned the author $400,000 before it was published. The book, about an eleven-year-old con girl, was a bestseller and a Literary Guild selection. Reissued in 1972 as *Paper Moon,* the book was made into a movie with the same title, starring Ryan O'Neal and Tatum O'Neal. It was nominated for an Academy Award.

Six months before his death, Brown and his wife Frances moved from Atlanta to their 100-year-old country home near Augusta, Georgia. He died on April 22, 1976, of a heart attack at his home, Covey Rise Farm, at the age of sixty.

HOBBIES AND OTHER INTERESTS: Hunting and fishing.

FOR MORE INFORMATION SEE—Obituaries: *New York Times,* April 24, 1976; *Washington Post,* April 24, 1976; *Newsweek,* May 3, 1976; *Time,* May 3, 1976; *Variety,* May 5, 1976; *AB Bookman's Weekly,* June 28, 1976.

A good tale is none the worse for being twice told.
—Proverb

BROWNE, Anthony (Edward Tudor) 1946-

BRIEF ENTRY: Born September 11, 1946, in Sheffield, England. Greeting card designer, author, and illustrator. Browne graduated with honors from Leeds College of Art in 1967. He went on to become a medical artist at the Royal Infirmary at Victoria University of Manchester and, since 1971, has been a designer at Gordon Fraser Greeting Cards. He is also the author and illustrator of several children's books, including *Gorilla* (Julia MacRae Books, 1983) for which he won the 1983 Kurt Maschler Award and the 1985 Kate Greenaway Medal. Browne has been praised by reviewers for his use of surrealism. In a review of *Look What I've Got!* (F. Watts, 1980), *School Library Journal* stated that "... the surreal art, with its absurd visual wit, makes very real the minimal text that details a familiar childhood situation." The same magazine also applauded his adaptation of *Hansel and Gretel* by the Brothers Grimm (Julia MacRae Books, 1981), noting that "the contemporary setting and slightly surreal style ... underscore the timelessness of this tale...."

Humor is also evident in Browne's work. In *Willy the Wimp* (Knopf, 1984), a chimpanzee grows tired of being bullied by a gang of apes and commits himself to a regimen of diet and exercise to build up his muscles. *Horn Book* described it as "a hilarious picture book," while *Booklist* mentioned the book's "riotous pictures" and "delicious tongue-in-cheek humor." Browne also wrote and illustrated *Bear Hunt* (Atheneum, 1980), in which a white bear being hunted by humans draws his way out of various traps with a magic pencil. *Publishers Weekly* called it an "unusually diverting picture book, with an understated story that maximizes the chuckles." Other books by Browne are *A Walk in the Park* (Hamish Hamilton, 1977), *Bear Goes to Town* (Hamish Hamilton, 1982), and *Willy the Champ* (Julia MacRae Books [London], 1985). He also illustrated *The Visitors Who Came to Stay* by Annalena McAffee and *Knock Knock! Who's There?* by Sally Grindley. *Home and office:* 4 Prospect Pl., Down Barton Rd., St. Nicholas-at-Wade, Kent, England.

FOR MORE INFORMATION SEE: Contemporary Authors, Volumes 97-100, Gale, 1981.

BUBA, Joy Flinsch 1904-

PERSONAL: Surname is pronounced "Boo-ba." Born July 25, 1904, in Lloyd's Neck, N.Y.; married Dr. Henry Buba. *Education:* Studied at Eberle Studio, New York, N.Y., Staedel Kunst Institute, Frankfurt, Germany, and Art Academy, Munich, Germany. Also studied privately with Theodor Kaerner, Angelo Yank, Rosenthal Porcelaine, and Philippe Berard. *Home:* 8 Wagon Trail, Black Mountain, N.C. 28711.

CAREER: Sculptor, book and magazine illustrator. Work is represented at various locations, including Metropolitan Museum of Art, New York, N.Y.; Statuary Hall, Capitol Building, Washington, D.C.; National Portrait Gallery, Washington, D.C.; Rockefeller Plaza, New York City; Palais Schaumburg, Bonn, Germany; Vatican Museum, Vatican City, Italy; and Yale University, New Haven, Conn. *Member:* National Sculpture Society (fellow).

ILLUSTRATOR—All for children, except as indicated: (Contributor) Henry Fairfield Osborn, *Proboscidea Memoir* (adult; monograph), two volumes, American Museum of Natural His-

(From *Rabbits* by Herbert S. Zim. Illustrated by Joy Buba.)

tory, 1936-42; Josephine Young Case, *Written in Sand* (adult fiction), Houghton, 1945; Herbert S. Zim, *Elephants,* Morrow, 1946, reprinted, 1982; H. S. Zim, *Goldfish,* Morrow, 1947, reprinted, 1982; H. S. Zim, *Rabbits,* Morrow, 1948, reprinted, 1982; H. S. Zim, *Frogs and Toads,* Morrow, 1950, reprinted, 1982; Elizabeth Vincent Foster, *Lyrico: The Only Horse of His Kind,* Gambit, 1970. Contributor of illustrations to periodicals, including *Illustrated London News, Audubon, Natur und Volk,* and *New Yorker.*

SIDELIGHTS: "I grew up on the land and salt water off Long Island, resenting eight months' annual schooling in New York, revelling in the wilderness around our farm on Lloyd's Neck where all birds and beasts and plants and livestock, including bees, were sketched and studied during summers. In nature we caught the 'phrenzy' as John James Audubon called it, my four brothers and I, and could hardly be dragged into civilization from our chosen haunts among the wild or from tending horses and creatures of the farm, or from sailing and fishing, and puttering along [the] shore. My lifelong interest in birds and animals, abetted by both parents, took root in childhood. When I was sixteen our habitat became Europe. Town life and art courses were spiked with hiking tours in France, skiing and mountaineering in Germany, Austria and Italy. I illustrated several professors' lectures and articles at Senckenberg Museum in Frankfurt. After eight years I returned to New York and illustrated Professor Henry Fairfield Osborn's studies on prehistoric elephants, being one of the artists of his *Proboscidea Memoir.*" [Bertha Mahony Miller and others, compilers, *Illustrators of Children's Books: 1946-1956,* Horn Book, 1958.]

Buba has also illustrated several of Herbert S. Zim's books and did illustrations for magazines.

FOR MORE INFORMATION SEE: Bertha Mahony Miller and others, compilers, *Illustrators of Children's Books: 1946-1956,* Horn Book, 1958; *National Sculpture Review,* winter, 1975; Martha E. Ward and Dorothy A. Marquardt, *Illustrators of Books for Young People,* 2nd edition, Scarecrow, 1975.

CAMPBELL, Rod 1945-

BRIEF ENTRY: Born May 5, 1945, in Scotland. Free-lance artist, and author and illustrator of children's books. Campbell received a B.Sc. and M.Phil. from the University College of Rhodesia and Nyasaland (now the University of Zimbabwe) and a Ph.D. from the University of Nottingham. He began his career doing postdoctoral research at the University of Rhodesia (now the University of Zimbabwe), but in 1972 left the field of science to pursue his interest in drawing and painting. He was a full-time painter until 1981 and supported himself with picture sales and part-time jobs framing pictures, working for an art gallery, painting, and decorating. Since then he has worked as a free-lance artist and has written and illustrated numerous books for preschoolers. Among Campbell's books are a number of "flap books." These contain cardboard or paper flaps built into the illustrations which, when opened, reveal an object underneath. In Campbell's view, ". . . flap books . . . are an important type of book for young children, especially those who can't yet read. The flaps appeal to children's curiosity and affords an element of physical participation. . . ."

The first of Campbell's flap books is *Dear Zoo* (Four Winds Press, 1982), for which he received an American Institute of Graphic Arts Certificate of Excellence in 1983. In the book, an unseen narrator describes the experience of acquiring a pet from the zoo. The first pet the zoo sends the child is "too Big!," as the reader discovers when opening the flap. It's an elephant. This animal is returned to the zoo, which later sends a giraffe ("too tall"), a lion ("too fierce"), and so on. Finally the zoo sends a puppy, which the narrator describes as "perfect" and keeps. Other flap books by Campbell include *Look Inside! All Kinds of Places* (Abelard-Schuman, 1983), *Look Inside! Land, Sea, Air* (Abelard-Schuman, 1983), and *Oh. Dear!* (Scholastic, 1983). In addition, Campbell created "play-slots" books with figures that may be pressed out and tucked into slots in the illustrations. Among these are *Toy Soldiers, Baby Animals,* and *Pet Shop* (all published by Scholastic, 1984). Other toy books by Campbell include *Rod Campbell's Magic Circus* (Abelard-Schuman, 1983), *Rod Campbell's Magic Fairground* (Abelard-Schuman, 1983), and *Take the Wheel* (Blackie & Son, 1984). *Home and office:* 19 Hazeldon Rd., London SE4, England.

CAREY, Mary (Virginia) 1925-
(M. V. Carey)

PERSONAL: Born May 19, 1925, in New Brighton, England; came to the United States in 1925, naturalized citizen, 1955; daughter of John Cornelius (an engineer) and Mary (Hughes) Carey. *Education:* College of Mount St. Vincent, B.S., 1946. *Religion:* Roman Catholic. *Home and office:* 645 Hampshire Rd., Apt. 137, Westlake Village, Calif. 91361.

CAREER: Coronet, New York, N.Y., editorial associate, 1948-55; Walt Disney Productions, Burbank, Calif., assistant editor

MARY CAREY

of publications, 1955-69; free-lance writer, 1969—. *Member:* PEN, Society of Children's Book Writers.

WRITINGS—Novelizations of Walt Disney motion pictures; juvenile: (With George Sherman) *Walt Disney's Babes in Toyland,* Golden Press, 1961; *Walt Disney's The Sword in the Stone,* Whitman Publishing, 1963; *The Story of Walt Disney's Motion Picture Mary Poppins,* Whitman Publishing, 1964; *Walt Disney's The Misadventures of Merlin Jones,* Whitman Publishing, 1964; *Walt Disney's Donald Duck and the Lost Mesa Ranch,* Whitman Publishing, 1966; *The Story of Walt Disney's Motion Picture Jungle Book,* Whitman Publishing, 1967; *The Story of Walt Disney's Motion Picture Blackbeard's Ghost,* Whitman Publishing, 1968; *Walt Disney's Peter Pan and Captain Hook,* Random House, 1973; *Walt Disney's Pooh Sleepytime Stories,* Golden Books, 1979; *Walt Disney's The Return of Oz Storybook,* Golden Books, 1985.

"Alfred Hitchcock and the Three Investigators" series; juvenile; all published by Random House: *Alfred Hitchcock and the Three Investigators in the Mystery of the Flaming Footprints,* 1971; . . . *in the Mystery of the Singing Serpent,* 1972; . . . *in the Mystery of Monster Mountain,* 1973; . . . *in the Secret of the Haunted Mirror* (illustrated by Jack Hearne), 1974; . . . *in the Mystery of the Invisible Dog* (illustrated by J. Hearne), 1975; . . . *in the Mystery of Death Trap Mine* (illustrated by J. Hearne), 1976; . . . *in the Mystery of the Magic Circle* (illustrated by J. Hearne), 1978; . . . *in the Mystery of the Sinister Scarecrow,* 1980; . . . *in the Mystery of the Scar-Faced Beggar,* 1981; . . . *in the Mystery of the Blazing*

(Jacket illustration by Eileen McKeating from *A Place for Allie* by Mary Carey.)

Cliffs, 1981; . . . *in the Mystery of the Wandering Cave Man,* 1982; . . . *in the Mystery of the Missing Mermaid,* 1983; . . . *in the Mystery of the Trail of Terror,* 1984; . . . *in the Mystery of the Creepshow Crooks,* 1985.

Other: *Step-by-Step Candlemaking,* Golden Press, 1972; *Raggedy Ann and the Glad and Sad Day* (juvenile; illustrated by June Goldsborough), Golden Press, 1972; *Step-by-Step Winemaking,* Golden Press, 1973; *The Tawny Scrawny Lion and the Clever Monkey* (juvenile), Golden Press, 1974; *Alonzo Purr, the Seagoing Cat* (juvenile; illustrated by Marilyn Hefner), Western Publishing, 1974; *Love Is Forever* (collection of prose and poetry), C. R. Gibson, 1975; (with George Sherman) *A Compendium of Bunk,* C. C Thomas, 1976; (adapter) L. Frank Baum, *Wizard of Oz* (juvenile; illustrated by Don Turner), Western Publishing, 1976; (editor) *Grandmothers Are Very Special People,* C. R. Gibson, 1977; *The Owl Who Loved Sunshine* (juvenile), Golden Press, 1977; *Mrs. Brisby's Important Package* (juvenile; adapted from the animated film "The Secret of Nimh"; illustrated by A. O. Williams), Western Publishing, 1982; *Caverns of Fear* (juvenile; illustrated by Alden McWilliams), Golden Books, 1983; *The Gremlins Storybook* (juvenile; adapted from the motion picture), Western Publishing, 1984; *A Place for Allie* (juvenile), Dodd, 1985.

SIDELIGHTS: "Young people ask why I became a writer, as if it were something I decided. I didn't decide; it grew on me like ivy. When I was a child I liked to read to my friends, or to tell them stories. When I grew up I had several false starts before I found a job on a magazine and discovered that people who read and write are more fun than people who don't.

"I first wrote for profit at the Disney Studio. I worked on the *Mickey Mouse Club* magazine there. Suddenly I felt that I was ten again, sitting on the front porch telling stories to the other kids.

"Now that I am a free-lance writer, the sensation of reliving younger days is even stronger. I remember how it was when my brothers and I were small. We had no money because of that thing called a depression, but we had freedom. If there were wicked people on Long Island in the 1930s—people who might harm kids—we did not know of it. On summer mornings my mother could open the door and send us out to wander through the neighborhood and she did not worry. So long as we came back in time for lunch—and relatively clean and undamaged—everything was fine. We explored all empty houses, and all empty houses were considered haunted. We went out on the sound in a tiny boat which my second brother had salvaged from the beach after a storm. We had clubs with secret passwords. We watched the older people of the community come and go and I think we knew quite a bit about what they were up to—probably including things we were not supposed to know.

"And we read. We read everything we were supposed to read, and much that we weren't supposed to know about. We fished pulp magazines out of the neighbor's trash and learned all about Dr. Fu Manchu and Tarzan of the Apes and other super heroes. We also plowed through Dickens and Jules Verne and the *Saturday Evening Post* and *Colliers* and everything the librarian would let us carry home from the library.

"Today all of the reading and the roaming stands me in good stead. So does my habit of being not especially practical or brisk. People ask if I work for a certain number of hours each day. I admire people who do, but I must admit that I don't. Some days it seems more important to wander and watch, or to read. There is only one brisk rule that I do observe; if I plan to write today, I do not leave the house until I've written. I know that once I go out, I will stay out until dark, and then I will come trailing home, tired and probably hungry. I will have lost the day.

"I think that writing should be honest and simple, and it should say something about what it means to be a person. When God is good to us, we write in such a way that the act of reading becomes a pleasure to those who buy our books. This experience doesn't happen all the time, but when it does it is at least as heady as winning the Irish sweepstakes. It makes mere competence seem dull. It is probably also what makes writing a compulsive occupation; some of us are uncomfortable when we are away from our typewriters for any length of time.

"The 'Three Investigator' books have always seemed so very special, in part because I remember my first encounter with detective stories. By the time I was eleven I had read my way through the children's section at our local library, and our librarian—a dear lady named Gertrude Foley—permitted me to come into the adult section. There was a whole corner devoted to mysteries. I was instantly hooked, and I think I was almost completely happy for about three years.

"I did not originate the 'Three Investigators.' The characters of the boys were developed by Robert Arthur, and when he passed away I was given a chance to work on the series. As time goes by I become more and more fascinated with the 'why' of criminal behavior. Not that the Investigators get into really heavy criminal detection; I don't think we've had any murderers in the series. However, I can see where the life-is-not-fair-so-I-think-I'll-hold-up-the-bank type of thinking can lead to murder.

"*A Place for Allie* is a complete departure from anything I've done previously. It is the story of a girl who loses her father, and of the changes in her life that take place following that loss. It was years in the writing, and I have great hopes that young people will read it and enjoy it.

"My lifelong ambition, aside from writing, is to finish exploring the American West. This should keep me busy for at least another thirty years, since there is a great deal of space here and we have always attracted great individualists."

HOBBIES AND OTHER INTERESTS: Walking on the beach.

CARRIS, Joan Davenport 1938-

PERSONAL: Born August 18, 1938, in Toledo, Ohio; daughter of Roy (a sales manager) and Elfrid (an artist; maiden name, Nichols) Davenport; married Barr Tupper Carris (in data processing), December 28, 1960; children: Mindy, Leigh Ann, Bradley. *Education:* Iowa State University, B.S., 1960; graduate study at Drake University, 1970-71. *Politics:* "Greek 'Golden Mean' group." *Religion:* Protestant. *Home and office address:* Box 231, 48 Princeton Ave., Rocky Hill, N.J. 08553. *Agent:* Dorothy Markinko, McIntosh & Otis, Inc., 475 Fifth Ave., New York, N.Y. 10017.

JOAN DAVENPORT CARRIS

CAREER: High school English teacher in Nevada, Iowa, 1960-61; high school teacher of French, speech, and English in Des Moines, Iowa, 1963-65; Franklin Convalescent Center, Princeton, N.J., occupational therapist, 1974; private English tutor in Princeton, 1974—; author of books for young people, 1977—. Member of New Jersey Council for Children's Literature. *Member:* National League of American Pen Women (president of Princeton, N.J., branch, 1980-84), Society of Children's Book Writers, Rocky Hill Community Group (member of executive board, 1974-78). *Awards, honors: Pets, Vets and Marty Howard* was selected for the "Outstanding Science Book of 1984" list in *Science and Children* magazine; *Witch-Cat* won a New York Readers Award from Ethical Culture School, 1985; *When the Boys Ran the House* won the Tennessee Readers Award, 1985.

WRITINGS—All for children, except as noted: *The Revolt of 10-X* (Junior Literary Guild selection), Harcourt, 1980; (co-author with Michael R. Crystal) *SAT Success* (young adult), Peterson's Guides, 1982; *When the Boys Ran the House,* Crowell, 1982; *Witch-Cat* (illustrated by Beth Peck), Lippincott, 1984; *Pets, Vets and Marty Howard* (Junior Literary Guild selection; illustrated by Carol Newsom), Lippincott, 1984; *Rusty Timmons' First Million* (illustrated by Kim Mulkey), Lippincott, 1985.

Author of "Tremendous Trifles," a humor column in the *Princeton Spectrum Trenton Times,* 1977-81. Contributor to magazines, including *Better Homes and Gardens, Think Magazine,* and newspapers.

"I haffa peepee," Gus said when he was standing up. ■ (From *When the Boys Ran the House* by
Joan Carris. Illustrated by Carol Newsom.)

ADAPTATIONS: ''Witch-Cat,'' CBS-TV Children's Special, 1985.

WORK IN PROGRESS: Two picture books; a third book about the Howard boys; collection of short stories for middle-level readers.

SIDELIGHTS: ''I discovered the vast number of things I couldn't do pretty early in life. I couldn't do a handstand, jump rope past 'pepper,' skate without bloodying my entire body, or dance. I thought I might have to take my mother to college with me so that she could continue doing my hair—a feat I'd never managed alone.

''Just as I was about to declare myself a washout, I discovered that I could understand literature, really understand it. I could diagram sentences and spell—of all things. Moreover, I could write an analytical essay in English class and some God-sent professor would read it aloud, or even publish it in a literary magazine. What a relief. Even my French was passable, and in a feeble way I can still communicate and read that sonorous language descended from Latin, my all-time favorite.

''Now that I am older, I am still involved with language, and my love for it grows, even though it *is* tricky to work those old spelling medals into a cocktail-party conversation.

''My impetus for writing was the glut of English teachers in the field at the time I wanted to return to teaching. There was no place for me—I'd been gone ten years (whomping up three children) and it was too long. In a snit, I plunked my typewriter on the dining room table and said I'd try my hand at the only other possibility: education through writing for young people. But I didn't want to lure people to reading in the traditional way. I wanted to do it through humor, with as much warmth as I could transfer to paper, with that always-difficult goal of making readers laugh and say 'ah, yes' at the same time.

''Trying to teach young people to love and use good English is behind everything I do. For that reason I began teaching Scholastic Aptitude Test (SAT) classes. In class we discuss old myths, the fascinating stories behind words, the power words have to take us anywhere we want to go. Out of this class has grown a book. I have a hunch it will be much like a house I would build—full of faults that get discovered only after I take possession.

''Writing children's books is my delight. If I can create even one character who truly comes to life, I'll feel immense satisfaction. And there will never be enough time for all the stories I want to tell about the kids who are like my kids, like the ones next door, like me when I was a kid. It is the hardest work I have ever done, the loneliest, the least rewarding financially, and the most frustrating.

''I wouldn't trade it for anything.''

HOBBIES AND OTHER INTERESTS: Walking, playing tennis and bridge.

There is more treasure in books than in all the pirates'
loot on Treasure Island. . .and best of all, you can
enjoy these riches every day of your life.
—Walt Disney

CAUDILL, Rebecca   1899-1985

OBITUARY NOTICE—See sketch in *SATA* Volume 1: Born February 2, 1899, in Harlan County, Ky.; died October 2, 1985, in Urbana, Ill. Educator, editor, and author. Born and raised in the Kentucky mountains, Caudill was noted for the Appalachian settings she created in her novels for young adults and stories for children. She graduated from Wesleyan College in 1920, the first woman to work her way through that institution, and received her M.A. in international relations from Vanderbilt University in 1922. Caudill then set out to see the world, working as a teacher and editor. She traveled to countries like Brazil and Canada and covered most of Europe, as well as the Scandinavian countries and Russia. It was in Turkey that she met her husband, editor James Ayars, whom she married in 1931. Caudill began her writing career with the publication of *Barrie and Daughter* in 1943 and through the years produced over twenty books. Among her numerous award-winning works are *Tree of Freedom,* runner-up for the 1949 Newbery Medal, *House of Fifers,* named an honor book by the *New York Herald-Tribune* in 1954, and *A Certain Small Shepherd,* winner of the 1966 Clara Ingram Judson Award. Other honors she received include the Wesleyan College Alumnae Award for Distinguished Achievement and the Chicago Children's Reading Round Table Award for distinguished service in the field of children's reading. *Residence:* Urbana, Ill.

FOR MORE INFORMATION SEE: More Junior Authors, H. W. Wilson, 1963; *Authors of Books for Young People,* 2nd edition, Scarecrow, 1971; *Contemporary Authors, New Revision Series,* Volume 2, Gale, 1981; *Twentieth-Century Children's Writers,* 2nd edition, Gale, 1983. Obituaries: *Publishers Weekly,* November 1, 1985; *School Library Journal,* December, 1985.

CLAMPETT, Robert   1914(?)-1984
(Bob Clampett)

PERSONAL: Born May 8, about 1914, in San Diego, Calif.; died of a heart attack May 2, 1984, in Detroit, Mich.; son of Robert C. and Joan (Merrifield) Clampett; married Sody Stone, June 25, 1955; children: Robert, Ruth Ann, Cheri. *Education:* Attended Otis Art Institute, early 1930s.

CAREER: King Features Syndicate, cartoonist, 1926-31; Walt Disney Productions, designer of first licensed Mickey Mouse dolls, 1929-30; Warner Bros., Inc., ''Merrie Melodies'' and ''Looney Tunes'' cartoons, animator, 1931-37, director of animation, 1937-46, writer, co-creator of cartoon characters ''Porky Pig,'' ''Beans,'' and ''Tweety Bird'' (other sources cite name as ''Tweetie Pie'' and ''Tweety Pie''), one of the creators of the cartoon characters ''Bugs Bunny,'' 1934-41, and ''Daffy Duck''; Bob Clampett Studio, Hollywood, Calif., owner and operator, beginning about 1938; worked for Screen Gems, beginning 1946; creator of productions for Columbia Pictures, Republic Studio, MCA, 1946-48; creator of ''Time for Beany'' television series, 1949-59 (other sources cite 1949-54); creator of ''Thunderbolt the Wonder Colt,'' ''William Shakespeare Wolf,'' and ''The Buffalo Billy Show'' television series, 1950-59; creator of ''The Beany and Cecil Show'' television series, beginning about 1962 to 1967; lecturer at universities, beginning about 1970, and film festivals throughout the world; guest speaker on television talk shows, beginning about 1970; operator of studio in Hollywood, with wife, Sody Clampett; host with Orson Welles of ''Bugs Bunny Superstar'' theatrical feature, 1975-78. Member of the President's People to People Committee, 1956.

In the early 1930s Walt Disney posed with Clampett-designed Mickey Mouse dolls.

MEMBER: Directors Guild of America, Academy of Television Arts and Sciences, ASCAP (American Society of Composers, Authors, and Publishers). *Awards, honors:* Grand Shorts award, 1939; Emmy award for best children's programming, from National Academy of Television Arts and Sciences, 1949, 1950, and 1952, for "Time for Beany"; government citation for film "Snafu for Signal Corps"; Billboard Award; Ink Pot Award, for achievement in comic art medium; PTA Award; honored by Cinematheque Francaise, Paris; Annie Award, from the Association Internationale du Film d'Animation; named one of the eight greatest animators by *Mediascene*.

FILMS—Selected works; all supervised by the author, all animated short subjects, all part of the Warner Bros. "Looney Tunes" cartoon series, all released by Vitaphone, except as indicated: (Animator with Chuck Jones) "Porky and Gabby," 1937; "Porky's Badtime Story," 1937; "Porky's Poppa," 1937; "Porky's Hero Agency," 1937; (animator with C. Jones) "Porky's Super Service," 1937; "Porky's Party," 1938; "Porky's Five and Ten," 1938; "Porky in Wackyland," 1938; "Porky in Egypt," 1938; "Porky's Naughty Nephew," 1938; "Porky and Daffy," 1938; "Porky's Movie Mystery," 1939; "Porky's Tire Trouble," 1939; "Porky's Picnic," 1939; (director) "Baby Bottleneck," 1945; (director) "Book Revue," 1945; (director) "Wagon Heels" ("Merrie Melodies" series),

1945; (director) "Bugs Bunny Superstar" (partially animated, feature length compilation and documentary), Hare Raising Films, 1975.

Also director of a cartoon sequence for feature-length film "When's Your Birthday?," 1936(?), and of animated film "Horton Hatches the Egg" (adapted from the book by Dr. Seuss [pseudonym of Theodor Seuss Geisel]), 1940(?); writer and director of "Snafu for Signal Corps."

TELEVISION: "Time for Beany," February, 1949 to 1959 (other sources cite 1949-54), Paramount, station KTTV, and CBS-TV, daily 15-minute puppet adventure series, with voices of Stan Freberg, Daws Butler, and Jerry Colona.

"The Buffalo Billy Show," 1950, CBS-TV, 30-minute western puppet-adventure series, with voices of Don Messick, B. Clampett, and Joan Gardiner.

"The Beany and Cecil Show" (animated cartoons, featuring "Beany Boy" and "Cecil, the Seasick Sea Serpent," that originally appeared on the television program "Matty's Funday Funnies," 1959-61, United Artists), beginning about 1962 to 1967, ABC-TV, 1968-76, distributed by ABC Films, 1977-

80, distributed by ICI, 30-minute animated cartoon series, with voices of D. Butler, D. Messick, and Joan Gerber.

Also creator of television series "Thunderbolt the Wonder Colt" and "William Shakespeare Wolf," aired on KTTV, Hollywood, Calif., and CBS-TV, New York, N.Y., in the 1950s.

ADAPTATIONS: Beany: Cecil Captured for the Zoo (story adapted by Barbara Hammer, illustrations adapted by Jack Bradbury and Gene Wolfe), A. Whitman, 1954; (videocassette) "Beany and Cecil" (animated cartoons), RCA/Columbia Pictures Home Video, Volumes I-V, 1984, Volume VI, 1985.

SIDELIGHTS: **May 8, 1914.** Born in San Diego, California, and raised in Hollywood. Throughout his childhood, Clampett was always interested in drawing, and his drawings were influenced by his environment. Growing up in Hollywood, he drew local characters and made up stories to go along with them. "That was when they shot the comedies in the streets. And one day I watched Valentino at Paramount.

"I saw a movie where there were these long-necked prehistoric creatures and I was so excited I went home and made drawings of long-necked characters. My mother helped me make the hand puppet out of the sock and I put on shows on my front porch. Cecil amused people from the beginning. My dad would often show some of my cartoons to his business friends." [Kathy Clarey, "He is 'Father' of Bugs, Tweety, and Porky," *Authors in the News,* Volume 1, Gale, 1976.[1]]

Upon graduation from high school, Clampett was offered a job with King Features at seventy-five dollars a week. "When I was in school, I drew a full page comic about the nocturnal adventures of a pussycat that was published in color in the Los Angeles Sunday *Times*. King Features saw this and offered me a cartoonist's contract. . . .

"They let me work in their L.A. art department on Saturdays and vacations. I had a drawing board between Webb Smith, who later became a key Disney gagman, the one who's credited with the classic Pluto flypaper sequence, and Robert Day, later of *The New Yorker* magazine. I learned a lot from those two fine craftsmen. And from time to time the paper published one of my cartoons for encouragement.

"They also paid my way through Otis Art Institute, where I learned to paint with oils and to sculpt." [Mike Barrier, "Bob Clampett: An Interview with a Master Cartoon Maker and Puppeteer," *Funnyworld* magazine, summer, 1970.[2]]

Mel Blanc, the voice of numerous cartoon characters, with Bob Clampett and "Cecil."

Bob Clampett with "Bugs."

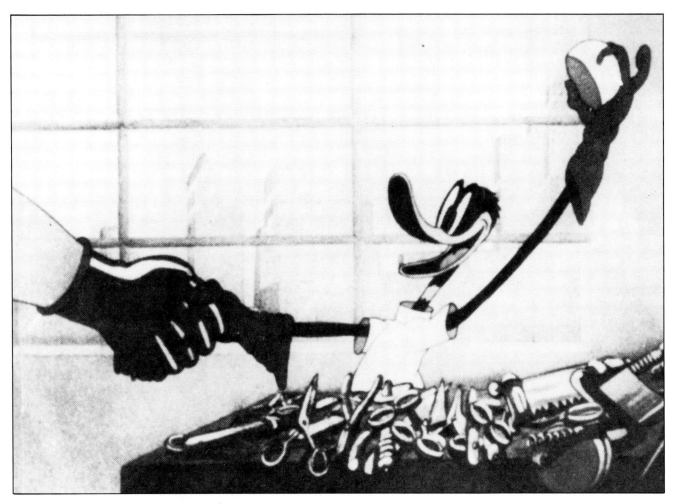

(From the animated cartoon "The Daffy Doc," directed by Bob Clampett and starring Daffy Duck. Released by Warner Bros., 1938.)

1929. Designed the first Mickey Mouse dolls. "The first time I ever met Walt Disney was when I walked into his studio . . . carrying the first felt Mickey Mouse doll, which my 'Aunt' Charlotte Clark and I had made. Mrs. Clark, who sold cookies from store to store, thought she could sell an appealing doll if I would design one.

"I suggested a doll based on the new mouse character that was beginning to be so popular in the movies. I couldn't find a drawing of him anywhere. The local theater, newspapers, stores—no one had a drawing of Mickey Mouse! So, I took my sketch pad to the theater, and sat through several shows. I came out with sketches of Mickey, and Charlotte and I used them when we made the first Mickey Mouse doll.

"My dad walked in and said, 'Wait just a darn minute! You can't sell that without permission from the copyright owner.' So he drove us to the Disney studio, which was then quite small.

"[Walt and Roy] Disney were delighted, and they set Charlotte up in business in a house near the studio. We turned out Meece by the gross.

"In my spare time, I went there and worked a kapok machine, a foot-operated machine that brushed the stuffing off the Mickey Mouse dolls. There were six young French girls who did the sewing. I used to put my hand in the unstuffed dolls and amuse them by talking in the Mickey falsetto.

"Walt Disney himself sometimes came over in an old car to pick up the dolls; he would give them out to visitors to the studio and at sales meetings. I helped him load the dolls in the car. One time his car, loaded with Mickeys, wouldn't start, and I pushed while Walt steered, until it caught, and he took off."[2]

1931. Relinquished his position with King Features to work at Warner Brothers, where he helped draw the "Merrie Melody" cartoons. "I became so enchanted with the new medium of sound cartoons that I gave up the seventy-five dollars a week to join Warner Brothers cartoons for ten dollars a week.

"When I started there, the rule was that we had to have a singing chorus in every Merrie Melodie. We'd have a great story going along, but then we'd have to stop and have the singing chorus.

"The first Looney Tune . . . made was 'Sinkin' in the Bathtub,' which featured Tiny Tim's favorite song, 'Tiptoe Through the Tulips.' After the first few Looney Tunes, the studio moved to a rather modern suite of offices, on Hollywood Boulevard, that was owned by Cecil B. DeMille. That was where I joined them.

"Tweety."

"Porky Pig."

"The first few Looney Tunes shown in 1930 made such a hit that [they] . . . started Merrie Melodies early in 1931, which was just as I joined them. And they gave me a number of secondary characters to animate in the very first Merrie Melodie, 'Lady Play Your Mandolin.'

"We made the Looney Tunes and Merrie Melodies at Harman-Ising until near mid-1933. . . .

"The first week I was at the studio, a meeting of the entire staff was called to shore up the story for Merrie Melodie No. 2. It revolved around a streetcar and they needed a fresh and novel way to gag up the usual singing chorus. Nothing much came out of the meeting. Riding home on the streetcar, I hit on an idea.

"I submitted a sequence in which the streetcar's advertising cards—the Smith Brothers, Dutch Cleanser girl, and other famous trademark figures—came to life and satirized the song. My idea was used, and made a tremendous hit in the theaters. A critic called it the first original Warner Brothers cartoon formula, as distinguished from Disney. We followed it with magazine covers, grocery store labels, and on and on."

"The funniest cartoons we drew at the studio were done just to amuse ourselves, and most of them never reached the screen. But a few of them did.

". . . Back in 1931 Rudy Ising went hunting one weekend. The following Monday, he told in all seriousness of how he tried to shoot this rabbit, and every time he got a bead on it, it would disappear, and then pop up behind him. And so on.

"The more he told of his troubles with this consarned rabbit, the more hilarious it became, perhaps because he was a boss. Several of us made caricatures of him in a hunter's outfit, tracking down the rabbit.

"During the ensuing month or two, I thought up a steady stream of 'wabbit' hunting jokes, some of which reached the screen seven years later in the first Bugs Bunny cartoon."[2]

In the early days of animation, animators were assigned to directors. "I can remember when around 1934, a director got ready to hand out a picture, and then we animators in the studio would go to him for scenes."

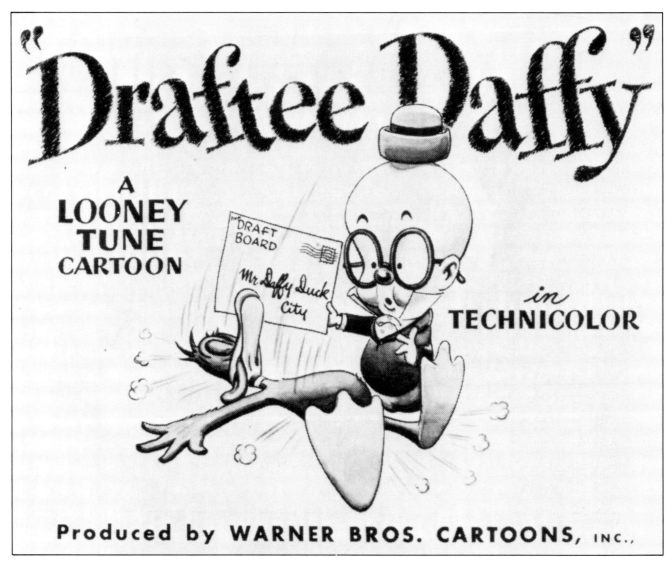

Promotional still for one of Warner Brothers' best "home front" wartime cartoons, starring Clampett's co-creation, Daffy Duck. Released in 1945.

"For the first several years Leon [Schlesinger] had a terrible time finding directors capable. . . . So, Leon was in there in his shirt sleeves, trying to find the right talent, promoting those who showed promise, and encouraging everyone to come up with funny ideas and characters. After five years of Looney Tunes, Leon still didn't have one well known cartoon character. And it was becoming a bit of a crisis.

"Then, Leon himself had an idea. He said, 'Look, Hal Roach has Our Gang, which is very popular. A bunch of little kids doing things together.' So, we had a big studio-wide drive to get ideas for our own animal Our Gang. In one of the sessions, I brought up the point that in Roach's Our Gang comedies there was always a little fat boy and a little black boy who was named after something to eat . . . Farina, or Buckwheat. So, somebody, I don't remember who, thought of two puppies called 'Ham and Ex.' That started me thinking. And after dinner one night, I thought of the name 'Porky and Beans.'

"I made a drawing of this fat little pig, which I named Porky, and a little black cat named Beans. Under the drawing, . . . I wrote 'Clampett's Porky and Beans,' and turned it in. Every-

one liked my idea and Porky and Beans were made members of the gang. . . ."[2]

Clampett's Porky Pig character quickly became the first "Looney Tunes" star at Warner Brothers. "At this time, Tex [Avery] came up wth the idea of Porky going on a duck hunt. . . . We thought of a ream of gags—they happened to come easy—and we had all these crazy ducks. After we boiled it down, we had two or three times as many gags as we needed. I asked Tex, 'What if instead of all these ducks being crazy, you consolidated most of them into one comic relief character?' Tex did that, and when he did, he created Daffy Duck, who turned out to be the second hit character that we had. That first Daffy Duck cartoon was called 'Porky's Duck Hunt.'

"As with all characters, the first Daffy didn't look or talk exactly like the later one, but that certain magic was there. Tex put a voice on him that was rather bombastic, with 'woo-woos' inspired by a Warner comedian, Hugh Herbert.

"Tex gave me the first scene of Daffy to animate. In this scene, Porky confronts Daffy, who in trying to explain he's harmless says, 'I'm just a crazy darn fool duck' and then was

Publicity still from the television cartoon series, "Beany and Cecil." (Copyright by Bob Clampett.)

(From the animated cartoon special "Bugs Bunny: All-American Hero," starring Bob Clampett's co-creation Bugs Bunny. Copyright © by Warner Bros., Inc.)

Tweety as he first appeared in Bob Clampett's cartoons. (Copyright © by Warner Bros., Inc.)

to swim off across the water. Tex told me, 'Make him exit funny.' I asked, 'Can I do anything I want?' And he said, 'Yes—anything.' So I had Daffy cross his eyes, do a Stan Laurel jump, and then do cartwheels, and do a ballet pirouette, and bounce off his head, and so forth.

"Now, at that time, audiences weren't accustomed to seeing a cartoon character do these things. And so, when it hit the theaters it was like an explosion. People would leave the theaters talking about this daffy duck.

"We had a bit of a problem finding just the right name for him. We were sure to get criticism from the public if we called somebody imbecilic. Porky's stuttering was criticized. One of the first names suggested for our duck was 'Dizzy,' after the famous baseball player, Dizzy Dean. But Leon said, 'No, you can't call him Dizzy—it sounds as if he's going to faint.' And then we thought of Dizzy Dean's brother who also played ball—Daffy Dean. And thus Daffy Duck was named. The name was used for the first time in the title, Tex's second duck-hunt picture, and the first in color, 'Daffy Duck and Egghead.' "[2]

1937. Became director of animation at Warner Brothers. "Ub Iwerks, who was famed for having done all the drawings in Walt's first Mickey Mouse cartoon, had a studio out in Beverly Hills, and he came to the end of his contract in late 1936. Leon needed more pictures, so he in effect said, 'Look, Ub,

make some Porkys for me in your own plant.' Then Leon called me in and said, 'You know our characters, Porky was your creation . . . and he sent me to help Ub make the Porkys. Leon's brother-in-law, Ray Katz, came along as the business manager.

"Ub made a couple of pictures, and then one Monday morning when I walked in they told me, 'Ub's gone. You're the director now.' I had to sit down at Ub's desk, in Ub's chair, with Ub's stopwatch, to make my first cartoon. All of Ub's old staff were looking at me like, 'What the blazes are you doing sitting in Ub's chair?' I felt the same way, because we all revered him.

"[The first cartoon] I called . . . 'Porky's Bedtime Story.' I originally titled this cartoon 'It Happened All Night,' after Capra's Oscar-winning movie 'It Happened One Night.' They said that sounded risque, and asked me to think up another title.

"On my next cartoon, I had no gag man. So I wrote and sketched the next Porky story 'by self,' and called it 'Get Rich Quick Porky.'

"I created a couple of new characters for this story. One of them was an oily villain named 'Honest John,' but the one who stole the picture was my little gopher, who came up out of a hole in the ground and did feats of magic.

Sylvester and Tweety, two of the many stars featured on "The Bugs Bunny/Road Runner Show." Its debut in 1968 marks it "the longest running cartoon series in the history of Saturday morning television."

''I used to perform a magic act when I was in school, and I was always fascinated with sleight of hand. So, in this cartoon, each time a dog tried to bury a bone in the ground, I'd have my gopher take the bone and perform sophisticated sleight-of-hand tricks with it—making it disappear and appear again, much to the dog's consternation.

''When this film played the theaters, my friends called me regarding the little magician character, whom they loved. But nobody quite knew what he was, referring to him as the ground hog, the prairie dog, and whatnot. So, for the follow-up story, I decided to transform my gopher into a magician's white rabbit, which gave me all the wonderful magician's props to work with. I started sketching a new story with just my dog and white rabbit—who came out of a silk hat instead of a hole in the ground—and again used his magic to outwit the dog. I didn't want to clutter up the situation with Porky, but Katz insisted he be the prime character in every Looney Tune, so I put my story aside for later use as a Merrie Melodie.''[2]

''During 1937, I became very enthused about the newest trend in feature film comedy, where, in place of comedians in baggy pants, normal-appearing actors were performing hilarious comedy in a more underplayed and sophisticated manner. But, when you least expected it, there would be a broad comedy breakout. These films, which began with 'My Man Godfrey,' were known in the trade as 'screwball' comedies.

''I was looking for a character with which to try and capture the brash but sophisticated spirit of this new comedy style.

''Then, in early 1938, one of Leon's units was having story trouble. They had started a story that covered a number of boards and had lots of characters in it. They had a lot of good material, but somehow it wasn't jelling. Leon called me into the office, and asked me if I had any two- or three-character story ideas that were very simple and could go into production quickly. I'm sure he asked the same thing of others. As I recall, there was only a week or so before it had to go to the animators.

''So I looked in my desk drawer, and among my other story sketches, I found this big pile of gags that we didn't use in 'Pork's Duck Hunt.'

''This was on a Friday afternoon. So I took these sketches with me, and driving home I mulled over what else I could do with these gags. Should I switch it into a quail hunt? Or a fox hunt? Or a . . .? And then, recalling some of my 1931 'wabbit' and hunter gags . . . I settled on making him a rabbit.

''After dinner, I began putting the duck sketches on my light board, intending to just draw the rabbit doing the duck's actions and gags. But, I found that the rabbit simply refused to do the same things that Daffy did. It just didn't feel right. And as my work progressed into the early morning hours the rabbit took on a personality of his own. I had found the character I was looking for. This was the birth of Bugs Bunny.

''I worked on the sketches all that weekend, showed them to my folks for their reaction, and delivered them to Leon Mon-

(From the animated cartoon "Bugs Bunny's 3rd Movie: 1001 Rabbit Tales," featuring two of Clampett's co-creations, Daffy Duck and Bugs Bunny. Copyright © by Warner Bros., Inc.)

day morning. He chuckled through it, thought it was pretty funny stuff, and assigned it to the Ben Hardaway-Cal Dalton unit to film.

"My story timed a little short, so the gag men added some material, such as Bugs spinning his ears and flying through the air like a helicopter, and a few other actions like that, which was off what I was attempting to do. They also added a new end gag. In the pell-mell rush to and through animation, many of the refinements in Bugs' appearance and actions were lost. But, there is one thing that all newly-born cartoon stars seem to have in common, and that is a certain indefinable 'magic' that endears them to the audience from the moment they first set foot on the screen. This first Bugs Bunny cartoon was a hit.

"The head of Warner Brothers' short-subject sales, Norm Moray, sent us word from the East that people were stopping on their way out of the theater to ask the manager when they could see the next rabbit cartoon. But, there wasn't any! It was then that Leon assigned Bugs to a second hare-hunt story, this time in color. For this film, a model-sheet maker was assigned to try and advance the design of the character. My first sketches were simple, but they were very close to what you saw finally in [the film]."[2]

1939. Awarded the Grand Shorts Award for best cartoon for "Lone Stranger and Porky," and third place for another Porky cartoon, "Injun Trouble." "That same year I made 'Porky in Wackyland,' which the critic on the L.A. *Herald* called 'a masterpiece of preposterous fantasy.' I designed the backgrounds in the manner of surrealistic, Picasso-like modern art, and it got all sorts of critical attention. This was the first of its kind. What we were trying to do, UPA did beautifully after us. . . .

"These black-and-white Porkys were popular, and it's interesting that I only had about three thousand dollars and three weeks to make each short.

"Ray Katz used to tell us, 'We don't want quality, and we don't want it in the worst way.' We were always trying to do something really good, but we were having to do it on a nickel-and-dime basis.

"Even though our budgets for a color Merrie Melodie and Bugs Bunny moved up, we were competing with Disney cartoons that we understood cost something like forty thousand dollars on up to even as much as sixty thousand dollars. So the only way we could top them was if we came up with cleverer ideas and characterizations."[2]

1940s. During World War II, Bugs Bunny reached the pinnacle of his popularity with movie-going audiences. "Just as America whistled the tune from Disney's 'Three Little Pigs,' 'Who's Afraid of the Big Bad Wolf?' in the dark days of the Depression . . . so, Bugs Bunny was a symbol of America's resistance to Hitler and the fascist powers. In both instances, we were in a battle for our lives, and it is most difficult now to comprehend the tremendous emotional impact Bugs Bunny exerted on the audience then. You must try to recapture the mood of a people who had seen the enemy murder millions of innocent people in gas ovens, blitzkrieg defenseless civilians, sink our fleet in a sneak attack, and threaten our very existence.

"Psychologists found that the public subconsciously identified the stupid little man with the gun and his counterparts with Hitler, and strongly identified the rabbit—unarmed except for his wits and will to win—with themselves. They further ad-

vised that justification was already established and that the sooner and more often that the audience's alter-ego (Bugs) could get back at the Hitler symbol, the greater the therapy. . . .

"In fact, . . . it was during those war years, from Pearl Harbor to January of 1945, that the Bugs Bunny cartoons, all of which were made by the other two directors and myself, passed Disney and MGM for the first time to become the No. 1 short subject. . . . But, of course, . . . when the war ended, we all looked upon any overt aggressiveness in an entirely different light.

"During those war years we all jumped in and made Private Snafu training films for Frank Capra's Army Signal Corps unit. . . . And one of mine, 'Booby Traps,' was credited with saving thousands of lives and was given a special government citation. My Snafu was the only one to be given a two-page spread in the history of wartime documentaries and training films, 'Movie Lot to Beachhead.'

"I also collaborated with Hank (Dennis the Menace) Ketcham on a Navy version of Snafu called Hook, for which Arthur Lake (Bumstead of the 'Blondie' series) did the lead voice for me. We also made technical training films for the government, and did a special Bugs Bunny bond-selling short for theaters, 'Any Bonds Today?'"[2]

During the early 1940s, Clampett created another cartoon character destined for popularity, "Tweety Bird." "My first Tweety was called 'The Tale of Two Kitties.' And then, I was the only one to make the Tweetys until such time as I left Warner Brothers.

"I started out to do a thing about the then tremendously popular comedians, Abbott and Costello, as pussycats named 'Babbitt and Cats-tello.' I introduced my little bird in the nest as the foil for the pussycats. But when I had Tweety say, 'I tot I taw a putty-tat! I did, I did, I taw a putty-tat!', he stole the picture from the pussycats.

"That was my first Tweety, and then in the second one, 'Birdy and the Beast,' I teamed Tweety with one black putty-tat, which was the first step towards the final putty-tat, Sylvester.

"All the time I was growing up, my mother insisted upon keeping out a baby picture of me . . . in the nude. I detested that picture all my life. So, when I was making the first sketches of Tweety in his nest, completely naked, I was actually satirizing my own baby picture."[2]

1946-1948. Created cartoon production for Columbia Pictures. "Much of the time [ideas come] from that 'wee small voice' in my cranium . . . that whispers endless ideas to me, the source of which I usually haven't the foggiest. I find that I am continually thinking of little individual ideas, like a piece of distinctive business, a prop, or a unique characteristic . . . or a funny name . . . a type of character I'd like to try . . . a catch line . . . or a funny pose, facial expression or attitude . . . and these many thoughts, like individual pieces of a jigsaw puzzle will remain with me, sometimes for years. . . and then, in one magical moment a number of these little individual pieces will suddenly fall into place, forming a new character concept. . . .

"And I get much inspiration from working with my gag men, or from reading the classics or the headlines, and from things I've observed in daily life, the theater or motion pictures. And I can usually trace these ideas back to their source."[2]

Wednesday, May 9, 1984   *VARIETY*   535

This full-page spread appeared in *Variety* the week after Clampett's death.

1949. Created 'Time for Beany,' a fifteen-minute television series, which ran daily for ten years and won three Emmys. "When I started my 'Time for Beany' puppet show with fifteen minutes a day to fill, it was just great! Because now I had sufficient screen time to use and develop all my ideas without slashing, pruning and compressing them.

"For 'Beany' on TV, I wrote and filmed more footage in one week, than a director at Warner's turned out in one year.

"I'd been at Warner's almost half my life, I'd gone as high up in the studio as was possible, and had proved to myself that I could create enormously popular characters for them— so, why not for myself?

"And, the decision proved right, for in a few years' time my weekly check rose from in the hundreds of dollars to into the thousands. And now my character creations remained my own property, not that of the Warners and the Harry Cohns.

"And Cecil the Sea Sick Serpent received the true mark of success in Hollywood . . . his caricature on the wall of the Brown Derby along with Gable, Bergen, McCarthy and Snerd, Groucho, Danny Thomas and Durante."[2]

1962. Created "The Beany and Cecil" television show, which was based on his earlier television puppet show, "Time for Beany." The show brought Clampett's favorite puppet, a lovable sea serpent named Cecil, to stardom. "All the pains and pleasures, intense feelings, and emotions of my own adolescence are ingrained in Cecil. So much of what I put into Cecil in my puppet show was deep-rooted emotions, which I am able to convey to other people. When you look at a Cecil gag you might say, 'Oh, that's just funny.' But there's a tear to it, too.

"In my daily puppet show I was able to develop Cecil's personality and changing moods much more slowly, and get the feeling of loneliness and sadness. And Cecil has great changes of pace. He is very slow to catch on to how Dishonest John is conning him. He is slow to anger, but when he finally realizes that little Beany boy is in trouble and D.J.'s got him, well, ol' Cece really tears the place apart. Then you feel better about it than if he'd gone into action the very first moment. And then, I'd have that wonderful warm feeling between Beany and Cecil, ending with a 'slurp kiss.'

"So, you see, Cecil was with me all those years, until the right time came along. Some felt he was actually my alter ego."[2]

In later years, Clampett and his wife operated a studio in Hollywood which made television commercials. Clampett did the "Mr. Clean," "Rinso Blue," and "Lifebuoy" soap commercials, to name a few.

1970s. Lectured at college campuses throughout the country. "It's a wonderful thing to hear these college kids laugh as hard and in the same places as people did when I made the cartoons. I really enjoy going around to the universities. I learn more from the students than they do from me."[1]

May 2, 1984. Died of a heart attack in Detroit, Michigan. "I've always done what I thought was exciting, even though it wasn't maybe as lucrative at the moment, and the things that I got into turned out to be wonderful. . . . I was making up to $5,000.00 a week on my own. But, I've never done something just to make money." [Tim Onosko, "Bob Clampett: Cartoonist," *The Velvet Light Trap,* fall, 1975.[3]]

FOR MORE INFORMATION SEE: Funnyworld, summer, 1970; *Sacramento Bee* (Sacramento, Calif.), November 15, 1974; *Film Comment,* January-February, 1957; Tim Onosko, "Bob Clampett: Cartoonist," *The Velvet Light Trap,* fall, 1975; *Authors in the News,* Volume 1, Gale, 1976; Carl Macek, "Bob Clampett on Mars," *Mediascene,* September/October, 1976; *New York Times Encyclopedia of Television,* New York Times Book Co., 1977; Patrick McGilligan, "Robert Clampett," in *The American Animated Cartoon: A Critical Anthology,* edited by Gerald Peary and Danny Peary, Dutton, 1980; Leonard Maltin, *Of Mice and Magic: A History of American Animated Cartoons,* McGraw, 1980; *World Encyclopedia of Cartoons,* Volume 1, Gale, 1980; Jeff Lenburg, *The Encyclopedia of Animated Cartoon Series,* Arlington House, 1981; *Art in America,* December, 1981; Harry S. McCracken, "The Animation of Bob Clampett," *Comics Buyer's Guide,* August 2, 1985.

Obituaries: *Los Angeles Times,* May 4, 1984; *Variety,* May 9, 1984; *Comics Buyer's Guide,* June 1, 1984; *Facts on File,* June 8, 1984; *Film Comment,* December, 1984.

CORBETT, W(illiam) J(esse) 1938-

BRIEF ENTRY: Born February 21, 1938, in Warwickshire, England. Now a full-time writer, Corbett's past jobs included those as factory worker, soldier, construction laborer, and dishwasher. He left school at the age of fifteen "having failed every examination placed before me." For a while he was a lathe worker, but soon tired of that and found himself at sea as a merchant seaman. Corbett describes his life, until quite recently, as "just a long series of dead-end jobs but with a life-long love of reading to ease the tedium." The turning point came when, in his forties, he was suddenly "thrown out of work with no chance of ever getting another job. So what to do . . .?" Corbett decided to write. He began with poems, proceeded to short stories, and eventually he "was writing about a harvest mouse called Pentecost. He, too, was in search of a better life. Together we re-discovered the Lickey Hills of my childhood."

Corbett's first novel, *The Song of Pentecost* (Dutton, 1983), winner of Britain's 1982 Whitbread Literary Award was hailed by critics as a new children's classic. *New York Times Book Review* called it "a rare tale, briskly written and rich with . . . enough meanings to satisfy readers of all ages." In the allegory, Corbett successfully creates a large cast of animal characters which includes the heroic young Pentecost, a self-serving Snake, a scheming Frog, the noble Fox of Furrowfield, and a gullible Owl. "[The] astonishing mix of broad comedy, pathos, subtlety and mystery," noted *Publishers Weekly,* "bring the actors and events vividly into the reader's mind." Ultimately, observed *Booklist,* "the quest for truth is the philosophical basis of the parable." *Times Literary Supplement* agreed. "The story, in a tremendous way," said the reviewer, "is about liars, and rogues of every kind. . . . And despite the echoing nature of the territory it treads, it is essentially unlike any other story I've read."

The Song of Pentecost was followed by *Pentecost and the Chosen One* (Methuen, 1984). *Books and Bookmen* described the latter as "a worthy sequel . . . written with humour, the same passion and the same brilliant characterisation." Currently, Corbett is completing *Pentecost of Lickey Top,* the third and final book in the trilogy. His most recent published work is *The End of the Tale* (Methuen, 1985), a story for children. *Home and office:* 6 Selborne Grove, Billesley, Birmingham 13, England.

CRAWFORD, Mel   1925-

PERSONAL: Born September 10, 1925, in Toronto, Ontario, Canada. *Education:* Attended Royal Ontario College of Art; studied watercolor painting with John Pike.

CAREER: Painter, author, and illustrator of more than 300 children's books, magazines, and calendars. Work has been exhibited at the Franklin Mint Gallery of American Art, Franklin Center, Pa.; Allied Artists of America, New York, N.Y.; American Watercolor Society, New York, N.Y.; Connecticut Watercolor Society, Hartford, Conn.; and Hudson Valley Art Association, White Plains, N.Y. Work is represented in the permanent collections at the Anchorage Museum, Anchorage, Alaska; Mattatuck Museum, Waterbury, Conn.; and the Stamford Museum, Stamford, Conn. *Member:* Allied Artists of America, Hudson Valley Art Association, Kent Art Association, Housatonic Art League (vice-president, 1972-74). *Awards, honors:* Salmagundi Award, American Watercolor Society, 1969; Thora M. Eriksen Award, Hudson Valley Art Association, 1971; Franklin Mint Gold Medal Award, Franklin Mint Gallery of American Art, 1973, for distinguished watercolor art.

WRITINGS—All for children; all published by Golden Press: *The Turtle Book* (nonfiction; self-illustrated), 1965; (adapter) *Walt Disney Presents: The Bambi Book* (fiction; self-illustrated, adapted from illustrations by Walt Disney Studio), 1966; *The Cowboy Book*, 1968; *The Smokey Bear Book*, 1970.

Illustrator; all for children; all fiction, except as indicated; all published by Golden Press, except as indicated: Gina Ingoglia Weiner, *Edgar Rice Burroughs' Tarzan*, 1964; *Golden Prize and Other Stories about Horses*, Whitman Publishing, 1965; *Old Macdonald Had a Farm*, 1967; Betty Hubka, *Where Is the Bear?* (poem), 1967; Annie North Bedford (pseudonym of Jane Werner Watson), reteller, *Walt Disney Presents Legends of America* (pictures adapted from those of Walt Disney Studio), 1969; Shirley Trammell, *Upside Over* (fantasy), 1969; Lawrence F. Lowery, *Looking for Animals* (nonfiction), Holt, 1969; *The Chuckle Book* (jokes and riddles), 1971; Naida Dickson, *The Story of Harmony Lane*, 1972; Addie, *Christopher for President*, 1973; Ruth Harley, *Andy Churchmouse and the Pastor*, C. R. Gibson, 1975; R. Harley, *Andy Churchmouse Tells about Prayer*, C. R. Gibson, 1975; (with others) Michael Frith and Sharon Lerner, editors, *Big Bird's Busy Book: Starring Jim Henson's Muppets* (collection), Random House, 1975; Daniel Wilcox, *I'm My Mommy; I'm My Daddy*, 1975; Mariellen Hanrahan, *Surprise at the Farm*, 1975.

Laura French, *Cats*, 1976; R. Harley, *Andy Churchmouse Tells about God's Rules*, C. R. Gibson, 1976; R. Harley, *Andy Churchmouse, What Shall I Be?*, C. R. Gibson, 1976; Irwin Shapiro, *Smokey Bear's Camping Book*, 1976; Emily Perl Kingsley, *Big Bird and Little Bird's Big and Little Book*, 1977; Peggy Parish, *Hush, Hush, It's Sleepytime*, 1977; (with others) M. Frith, and others, *The Sesame Street Library: With Jim Henson's Muppets* (collection), twelve volumes, Children's Television Workshop, 1978.

SIDELIGHTS: Crawford's works are included in the Kerlan Collection at the University of Minnesota.

DANK, Leonard D(ewey)   1929-

PERSONAL: Born December 21, 1929, in Birmingham, Ala.; son of George and Ellen (Balsam) Dank; married Beryl Eileen Jealous (president of an herb and horse farm), September 30, 1961; children: Amelia Theresa. *Education:* Cornell University, B.A., 1952; Massachusetts General Hospital School of Medical Illustration, certificate, 1955; additional study at Art Students League and Jules Laurents Studio. *Religion:* Roman Catholic. *Home:* 800 Cox Ln., Cutchogue, N.Y. 1935. *Office:* 736 West End Ave., New York, N.Y. 10025.

CAREER: Manhattan Eye, Ear, and Throat Hospital, New York, N.Y., staff medical artist in plastic surgery, 1955-57; Eye Bank for Sight Restoration, New York City, staff medical artist, 1957-59; Leonard D. Dank Medical Illustration Studio, New York City, proprietor, 1959-61; Medical Illustrations Co., New York City and Cutchogue, N.Y., proprietor, 1961—. Consulting medical illustrator for numerous organizations, including Home Library Press, 1960-70, St. Luke's Hospital, 1961-83, Woman's Hospital, 1963-83, H. S. Stuttman, Inc., 1964-80, Milprint, Inc., 1965-83, Synapse Communications, Inc., 1973-75. Has executed various commissions, including animated medical films. Work is represented in public collections, including those of McGraw-Hill Publishing Co., New York City; Stravon Educational Press, Inc., New York City; and Doubleday & Co., Inc., New York City. *Member:* Association of Medical Illustrators, Guild of Natural Science Illustrators, Columbia University Faculty Club. *Awards, honors:* First Prize Certificate of Merit from the American Medical Association, 1959; First Prize Citation of Merit in Motion Picture Program from the American College of Surgery, 1959 and 1962; Better Teller Award from the Association of Industrial Advertisers, 1973; *Space Colony: Frontier of the 21st Century* was chosen as an Outstanding Science and Trade Book for Children by the National Association of Science Teachers, 1982.

WRITINGS: (With Harold M. Tovell and others) *Gynecologic Operations: As Performed by Members of the Staff of the Woman's Hospital, St. Luke's Hospital Center, New York* (partially serialized in *Clinical Obstetrics and Gynecology*), Harper, 1978.

Illustrator; all for young adults, except as noted: Arthur N. Strahler, *The Story of Our Earth*, Home Library Press, 1963; Vicki Cobb, *Cells: The Basic Structure of Life*, F. Watts, 1970; Alfred Allen Lewis and others, *The Male: His Body, His Sex* (adult), Anchor Press, 1978; Franklyn M. Branley, *The Electromagnetic Spectrum: Key to the Universe*, Crowell, 1979; Morris Fishbein, *Dr. Fishbein's Popular Illustrated Medical Encyclopedia* (adult), Doubleday, 1979; F. M. Branley, *Jupiter: King of the Gods, Giant of the Planets*, Elsevier/Nelson, 1981; F. M. Branley, *Space Colony: Frontier of the 21st Century*, Elsevier/Nelson, 1982.

Contributor of medical illustrations to *Primary Cardiology, Hospital Physician, Physician Assistant*, and *Esquire*. Also contributor of articles to *Clinical Obstetrics and Gynecology*, Harper, 1973-76.

At Mr. Wackford Squeers' Academy, Dotheboys Hall . . . Youth are boarded, clothed, booked, furnished with pocket-money, provided with all necessaries, instructed in all languages living and dead . . . No extras, no vacations, and diet unparalleled.

—Charles Dickens
(From *Nicholas Nickleby*)

DARLING, David J.

BRIEF ENTRY: British astronomer, author of books on astronomy for young readers, and lecturer. Darling, who holds a doctorate of astronomy from the University of Manchester, spent some time in the United States as manager of applications software for Cray Research. He is the author of ten books in the "Discovering Our Universe" series, published by Dillon Press, which is designed to introduce students to the vast mysteries of the universe. As *Booklist* observed, "The texts address their topics succinctly . . . [while] many drawings and photographs, both black-and-white and full-color, are clear and helpful." In each volume, Darling includes ideas for possible experiments, a "Fast Facts" and question-and-answer section, lists of suggested reading, and a glossary. Among the titles are *The Sun: Our Neighborhood Star; Comets, Meteors, and Asteroids: Rocks in Space; Where Are We Going in Space?* (all 1984); *The Stars: From Birth to Black Hole; Other Worlds: Is There Life Out There?;* and *The New Astronomy: An Ever-Changing Universe* (all 1985). In addition to his science books, Darling wrote *Diana: The People's Princess* (Dillon, 1984), an illustrated biography of the Princess of Wales for children. He has also contributed numerous articles to *Astronomy* and *Odyssey* magazines. *Residence:* Northern England.

DEMAREST, Chris(topher) L(ynn) 1951-

BRIEF ENTRY: Born April 18, 1951, in Hartford, Conn. Cartoonist, author and illustrator of books for children. Although trained in fine arts at the University of Massachusetts, Demarest later discovered a more natural affinity for cartooning. He is the creator of a cerulean bluebird which became popular on a series of greeting cards and was eventually featured in his first self-illustrated children's book, *Benedict Finds a Home* (Lothrop, 1982). In this humorous story of a fledgling anxious to leave his crowded nest, Demarest's pictures reflect a cartoonlike style that emphasizes his use of visual gags. The same style continues in his second book, *Clemens' Kingdom* (Lothrop, 1983), a fantasy about a lion statue who decides to explore his "kingdom"—the library. *Publishers Weekly* called it "a gentle fable . . . with big, loose, gaily colored scenes."

Demarest's simple but amusing texts are examples of his philosophy regarding books for children. ". . . My motive is pure entertainment," he reveals. "It is fun to tell a story which makes the reader laugh, without having to sneak in some sort of message. . . ." Included among the books he has illustrated are Rose Greydanus's *Tree House Fun* (Troll Associates, 1980), Betty Jo Stanovich's *Hedgehog Adventures* (Lothrop, 1983), and *Hedgehog Surprises* (Lothrop, 1984), and Sue Alexander's *World Famous Muriel* (Little, Brown, 1984). He is currently working on a third self-illustrated book for children entitled *The Keeper of the Stars. Home and office:* 10 Sanborn St., Winchester, Mass. 01890.

FOR MORE INFORMATION SEE: Contemporary Authors, Volume 109, Gale, 1983.

Still sits the school-house by the road,
  A ragged beggar sleeping;
Around it still the sumachs grow
  And blackberry-vines are creeping.
          —John Greenleaf Whittier

DILLON, Barbara 1927-

PERSONAL: Born September 2, 1927, in Montclair, N.J.; daughter of George Rudolph (a sugar broker) and Janet (Quin) Dinkel; married Harold C. Dillon (an account executive for International Business Machines Corp.), November 22, 1952; children: Lisa Dillon Tullis, Brook, Nina. *Education:* Brown University, B.A., 1949. *Home:* 29 Harbor Rd., Darien, Conn. 06820.

CAREER: New Yorker, New York, N.Y., editorial assistant, 1949-57; writer, 1978—. Volunteer teacher at Mountaintop Day Care Center.

WRITINGS—For children: *The Good-Guy Cake* (illustrated by Alan Tiegreen), Morrow, 1980; *The Beast in the Bed* (illustrated by Chris Conover), Morrow, 1981; *Who Needs a Bear?* (illustrated by Diane De Groat), Morrow, 1981; *What's Happened to Harry?* (illustrated by C. Conover), Morrow, 1982; *The Teddy Bear Tree* (illustrated by David Rose), Morrow, 1982; *Mr. Chill,* Morrow, 1985.

WORK IN PROGRESS: The Disappearance of Danny Dinkel; The Key King Caper, a ghost story about a family that moves into a Victorian mansion in which another nineteenth-century ghost family is also in residence.

SIDELIGHTS: "The first time I can remember feeling a sense of achievement in school was in fourth grade. A somewhat

BARBARA DILLON

Everywhere she went, he went too. ■ (From *The Beast in the Bed* by Barbara Dillon. Illustrated by Chris Conover.)

flamboyant description I had written of a beach path in Ogunquit, Maine was lavishly praised by my teacher and by the principal of Jefferson Elementary, the school I attended in Maplewood, New Jersey. I don't think that incident marked the moment I decided to become a writer; I do think though that I had discovered my forte.

"At Brown University where I crammed in as many English courses as I could, it used to astound me to hear the other students discussing what they should major in. With me, there was never any question; English was the only academic subject I was truly ever interested in.

"Though I did little creative writing in college other than contributing a story or two to the Brown literary magazine (and editing my class yearbook), I drew renewed inspiration from *The New Yorker* magazine where I was fortunate enough to land a job after graduating. While at *The New Yorker* I sold a short story, 'The Grand Champion Peanut Racer,' to *Woman's*

Day. It concerned a small boy's triumph over shyness during the first week of school. I guess even then I had found the subject matter that was to interest me most: children.

"Looking back now with a heightened awareness of how swiftly time slips away, I am amazed to recall that although I always assumed I would one day write, I had no real urge to try my hand at it while my three daughters were growing up. Being a wife and mother seemed to satisfy any creative needs I had then. It was not until the girls were beginning to leave home that I thought seriously about picking up my pen. But by this time I knew what I wanted to write—children's books.

"John McCarten, a former movie critic at *The New Yorker,* once told me, 'Don't write right, just write.' So that is what I did. I began to write and throw out and rewrite as well as reread some of my favorite childhood books, hoping to learn the magic formula for success. I quickly learned there isn't one, other than just to keep trying. Although I certainly can't claim to have had immediate success with my work, I received enough encouragement from the editors to whom I sent my manuscripts to keep me going. After two years of rejections, albeit kindly ones, I had the good fortune to find an editor who was interested in my stories and who was willing and able to nurse me through the arduous task of writing and revising *The Beast in the Bed.*

"Writing is, as the author Colette said, 'a difficult metier.' But once one is hooked on it, there is no turning back. The shape and color of my day usually hinged on how well my well has gone that morning. Letters from young readers are a particular source of pleasure to me, and I shall keep writing for them till I've used up every idea in my head."

ERNST, Lisa Campbell   1957-

BRIEF ENTRY: Born March 13, 1957, in Bartlesville, Okla. Ernst graduated from the University of Oklahoma in 1978 and worked briefly in advertising before becoming a full-time writer, illustrator, and designer of books. After illustrating seven children's books written by others, she decided to write one of her own. Ernst chose turn-of-the-century America as the setting for *Sam Johnson and the Blue Ribbon Quilt* (Lothrop, 1983), the story of a farmer who sets out to prove that men, like women, are capable of creating a beautiful quilt. "Quaint pictures in gentled hues," observed *Publishers Weekly,* "bring an old-timey, buccolic scene to life." As *School Library Journal* noted, Ernst bordered each spread with "an actual quilt pattern that relates to the event in the illustration" and further described the traditional quilt designs in an addendum. Her second picture book, *The Prize Pig Surprise* (Lothrop, 1984), is set in the countryside of France and features a truffle-hunting pig named Emil. "It is *très gai,*" said *Publishers Weekly,* "an unusual fable . . . [with] imaginative, witty, yet realistic scenes of the terrain, people, and animals." Ernst is also author and illustrator of *Up to Ten and Down Again,* soon to be published by Lothrop. Among the books she has illustrated are *Kites for Kids* by Burton and Rita Marks, *It's a Girl's Game Too* by Alice Siegel and Margo McLoone, and *Mirror Magic* by Seymour Simon. *Office:* 41 Union Sq. W., No. 1228, New York, N.Y. 10003.

FOR MORE INFORMATION SEE: Contemporary Authors, Volume 114, Gale, 1985.

FISHER, Barbara   1940-
(Barbara Fisher Perry)

PERSONAL: Born December 10, 1940, in New York, N.Y.; daughter of David (an attorney) and Regina (Mandel) Fisher; married Ernest Perry, September 23, 1967 (divorced, 1980); married Richard Spiegel, June 21, 1983; children: Athelantis. *Education:* Hunter College of the City University of New York, B.A., 1962. *Home and office:* 799 Greenwich St., New York, N.Y. 10014. *Agent:* Philip G. Spitzer Literary Agency, 1465 Third Ave., New York, N.Y. 10028.

CAREER: Dauntless Books, Inc., New York City, editorial assistant, 1962-63; Academic Press, Inc., New York City, writer in promotion department, 1963-64; Chelsea Theater Center, New York City, director of research and development, 1966-68; Ten Penny Players, New York City, co-director and editor of publications, 1967—. Manager and fiscal director of

BARBARA FISHER

799 Greenwich Street Tenants Corp., 1972—; fundraiser for Institutes for the Achievement of Human Potential, 1974-76; fiscal director of New York Book Fair, 1978—; co-director of Waterways Project. Instructor at workshops; consultant to New York State Narcotics Control Commission, 1971-73. *Member:* Authors Guild. *Awards, honors:* Grants from New York State Council on the Arts, 1970, Rockefeller Brothers Fund, 1970, International Business Machines, 1971, and William C. Whitney Fund, 1972.

WRITINGS—For children; all self-illustrated; all published by Ten Penny Players, except as indicated: *Big Harold and Tiny Enid,* 1975; *Jud,* 1976; *Philpin's Tree,* 1976; *Car Boy,* 1977; *Linkups,* 1977; *Jolly Molly Molar,* 1979; *Harmony Hurricane Muldoon,* 1979; *Max St. Peter McBride and Theodora,* 1981; *Dan,* 1981; *Davy, Davy Dumpling,* SZ Press, 1985.

Editor; all with Richard Spiegel; all juvenile; all published by Ten Penny Players: *Poetry Hunter, No. 1,* 1981; *More Poetry Hunter,* 1981; *Still More Poetry Hunter,* 1981; *Subway Slams,* 1981; *In Search of a Song,* Volume 1: *PS-114,* 1981, Volume 2: *PS-276,* 1981, Volume 3: *Jefferson Market Library,* 1982, Volume 4, 1983, Volume 5, 1983, Volume 6, 1984, Volume 7, 1984, Volume 8, 1985; *Greenwich Village Lore and Chinatown Tales,* 1983; *Dolls,* 1984; *Yearning to Breathe Free,* 1984; *Fairies, Elves and Gnomes,* 1985.

Other: (Under name Barbara Fisher Perry) *Care Without Care,* Avon, 1970; (contributor) *More Than a Gathering of Dreamers,* Coordinating Council of Literary Magazines, 1981.

Author of "Noisy City Sam" (one-act play for children), first produced in New York City, at Clinton Park, July, 1970; and adapter and director of "Goblin Market" (juvenile play), first produced in New York City at Jefferson Market Library, April 7, 1984.

Contributor to magazines. Co-editor with R. Spiegel of *Foreward Face,* Cranio-Facial Unit of New York University Hospital. Also co-editor of "Nutrition Awareness Program," a series of books and materials; co-editor with R. Spiegel of a newsletter for Active New York City Committee on the Handicapped Parent, Educational Advocacy; and co-editor of *Waterways: Poetry in the Mainstream,* 1979.

WORK IN PROGRESS: Adah Isaacs Menken; revised edition of *Care Without Care,* with supplement on educational advocacy; a resource book for parents and professionals.

SIDELIGHTS: "I am a patients' rights and educational rights advocate and resource person for people who need help in these areas. When possible we do our own letterpress printing and are active in the small press movement and the populist poetry movement, believing books and poetry should be accessible to all. I am animal, child, and people oriented.

"Given education, training, and support systems people can exercise more control over their lives. Educational and health care decisions must be shared by the persons directly affected *and* by the professionals. Literature and arts similarly can be experienced by the laymen. The arts don't have to be elitist, almost mystical experiences removed from the everyday experience of 'ordinary' people. As an educational and health care advocate I help train, initiate programs for, and advocate for, when necessary, people who have yet to find their personal voice. As a publisher involved in the Populist Poetry movement I want to share with the reading public the dissimilar voices of people who care about extending themselves and their ideas through the printed and performed word. In my own writing (fiction, nonfiction, poetry or drama), I try to use English clearly and with rhythm and beauty so that the reader can understand what I am saying and empathize as well."

FOR MORE INFORMATION SEE: Human Behavior, May, 1978; *Tub,* Volume II, number 1, 1978.

FOLEY, June 1944-

PERSONAL: Born June 6, 1944, in Trenton, N.J.; daughter of William Patrick (a manager of a service station) and June (Gadsby) Foley; married Michael Lindenman, June 13, 1970 (divorced, 1976); children: Max. *Education:* Attended New York University, 1969-70; Montclair State College, B.A., 1974, teacher's certificate in social studies, 1976. *Agent:* Marilyn Marlow, Curtis Brown Ltd., 10 Astor Pl., New York, N.Y. 10003. *Office:* World Almanac, 200 Park Ave., New York, N.Y. 10166.

CAREER: World Almanac, New York, N.Y., assistant editor, 1978-84, senior assistant editor, 1984—.

WRITINGS: It's No Crush, I'm in Love! (young adult novel), Delacorte, 1982; *Love by Any Other Name* (young adult novel), Delacorte, 1983; *Falling in Love Is No Snap* (young adult novel), Delacorte, 1986.

ADAPTATIONS: "It's No Crush, I'm in Love," ABC After School Special, ABC-TV, September, 1983.

WORK IN PROGRESS: A young adult novel, *Susanna Siegelbaum Gives Up Guys.*

SIDELIGHTS: "I write about adolescence because I think it's the most awkward, exciting, and poignant time of life. It's like being pregnant for years and years—and the person you're going to give birth to is yourself. Adolescents are like everybody else, only more so; their feelings are more intense, they're more alive. Adolescents still have dreams, and they also have energy and time so that some of those dreams may indeed be fulfilled. I write about adolescents because I can give them happy endings—which are only the beginning.

"I became interested in writing through reading. All my life, my single favorite activity has been reading. Many photos of

June Foley with son, Max.

me when I was a child show my body, with my face hidden behind a book. One photo of my family at the Jersey shore shows everyone else swimming, splashing, frolicking in the ocean; I'm in a tube, reading.

"Although writing came naturally to me from reading so much, I never thought I could grow up to be a writer . . . because I lived in New Jersey. I thought all writers were British. After all, Shakespeare was, Jane Austen was. I thought all writers lived in mansions, wore silk dressing gowns, and had butlers to fetch their pens and paper. I thought every word writers put down on paper came out of their mouths in exactly the same form—as a perfect pearl of prose. I thought this prose had to sound sophisticated, for example, 'My darling, my beloved, I adore you.' Since the closest anybody in my family ever came to saying that was my father's saying to my mother, 'How about another baloney sandwich, honey?' I thought I could never be a writer. I'm so glad I was wrong.

"One of the good things about being a writer is that everything you experience—everything you think and feel and do, and also everything your family and friends tell you they think and feel and do—can go into your writing. For instance, my son Max is a teenager now, but one day when he was around eight, he came home from school and said, 'Rufus is always torturing me on the bus. He's always giving me Indian burns, knuckle rubs, and noogies.' Well, as a mother I responded by murmuring, 'Oh, poor Max.' But as a writer, I was grabbing a pencil and paper to write down what Max had said. I thought

(From the movie "It's No Crush, I'm in Love." Released by Learning Corporation of America, 1983.)

it would make a great opening sentence for a young adult or juvenile novel. I haven't written that book yet, and if I don't, I hope Max does.

"As for experiences I *have* used in books, I am all my heroines—the shy, bookish Annie Cassidy of *It's No Crush* . . . ; the insecure class clown Billie Quinn of *Love by Any Other Name;* the spunky Alexandra Susskind of *Falling in Love Is No Snap;* and the wacky, uninhibited Susanna Siegelbaum of *It's No Crush* . . . ; and also the book I'm writing now, *Susanna Siegelbaum Gives Up Guys.*

"Like Annie, I had a big crush when I was in high school. However, mine wasn't on my English teacher—probably because my high school English teachers were Sister Charlotte, Sister Paschal, Sister Dennis, and Sister Jacinta—it was on a classmate. The crush lasted through high school, college, and beyond; I loved him for about ten years, and he loved me for about ten minutes. No wonder I wrote about it!

"Like Billie, I had a father who wanted to be a jazz musician but instead worked in a relative's gas station; like her, I became interested in acting when I was in high school, and through acting got to know a sensitive, intellectual boy like Cameron. However, Cameron is also based on a man who's my friend right now, Aaron Kinne. His remarks about the tragedy of being a Boston Red Sox fan became Cameron's.

"There's a lot of me in Alexandra, but there's even more of my son, Max. In fact, Alexandra was first named Alexander. But I just couldn't seem to get inside a boy's head, so I was forced to change the character to a girl. There's also a lot of me in Alexandra's mother. Like Kate Malone, I'm of Irish descent and was raised a Catholic; I'm divorced; I work as an

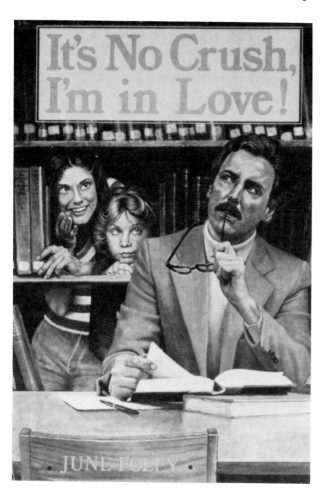

(Jacket illustration by Joe Cstari from *It's No Crush, I'm in Love!* by June Foley.)

editor for a publishing company; I live with my child in New York City; there have been times in the last few years when I've been accused of being a workaholic.

"Susanna is the crazy part of me; that's why she's so much fun to write about. But after I'm finished with the fourth book, I think I'll be ready to write about somebody shy and quiet. I already have her name—Lizzie Fitzgerald.

"Often readers ask me, 'Where do you get those names?' Evidently many people think the names of my characters— like Susanna Siegelbaum, David Angelucci, Bubba Umlauf, Cameron Ingersoll, Heracles Damaskinakis, and Nora Naka- mura—are unusual. They aren't to me, though. Most of the people I grew up with, my friends today, and my son Max's friends have names like those. Max's best friends today are Niko Kolodny and Ezra Pogorsky. Mine are Marie Attanasio, Diana Drake, Paula Danziger, Suzanne Nakamura, and Ruth Rothbart.

"Although I don't think the names are unusual, I do think I've gone about as far as I can go in length and foreignness when I call the hero of the third book Heracles Damaskinakis. That's why the hero of the fourth book is called Howard (nicknamed Hod) Green."

FOR MORE INFORMATION SEE: Trentonian, October 20, 1982.

FOX, Mary Virginia   1919-

PERSONAL: Born November 17, 1919, in Richmond, Va.; daughter of George Henry (a realtor) and Leila Virginia (Mer- rell) Foster; married Richard Earl Fox (a manufacturer); chil- dren: Phillip Richard, Thomas George, William Earl. _Edu- cation:_ Northwestern University, B.S. (with honors), 1940. _Politics:_ "Very flexible." _Religion:_ United Church of Christ. _Home:_ 2841 Century Harbor, Middleton, Wis. 53562.

MARY VIRGINIA FOX

Teenager Ronald Reagan worked as a lifeguard. ∎ (From _Mister President: The Story of Ronald Reagan_ by Mary Virginia Fox. Photograph courtesy of the Wisconsin Center for Film and Theater Research.)

CAREER: Writer. _Member:_ National League of American Pen Women, Council for Wisconsin Writers (board member, 1984- 86), Children's Reading Round Table of Chicago, American Society of Journalists and Authors, Alpha Phi. _Awards, hon- ors:_ Midwest Writers Award, 1960, for _Apprentice to Liberty;_ Juvenile Award from the Council for Wisconsin Writers, 1976, for _Lady for the Defense: A Biography of Belva Lockwood._

WRITINGS—All juvenile: *Apprentice to Liberty* (illustrated by Mel Silverman), Abingdon, 1960; *Treasure of the Revolution* (illustrated by Cary), Abingdon, 1961; *Ambush at Fort Dearborn* (illustrated by Lorence Bjorklund), St. Martin's, 1962; *Ethel Barrymore: A Portrait*, Reilly & Lee, 1970; *Pacifists: Adventures in Courage*, Reilly & Lee, 1971; *Lady for the Defense: A Biography of Belva Lockwood*, Harcourt, 1975; *Jane Fonda: Something to Fight For*, Dillon, 1980; *Barbara Walters: The News Her Way*, Dillon, 1980; *Janet Guthrie: Foot to the Floor*, Dillon, 1981; *Jane Goodall: Living Chimp Style* (illustrated by Nona Hengen), Dillon, 1981; *The Skating Heidens*, Enslow, 1981; *Mister President: The Story of Ronald Reagan*, Enslow, 1982; *Justice Sandra Day O'Connor*, Enslow, 1983; *Women Astronauts: Aboard the Shuttle*, Messner, 1985; *The Statue of Liberty*, Simon & Schuster, 1985; *Her Royal Highness, the Princess of Wales*, Enslow, 1986; *A Queen Named King*, Eakin, 1986; *A Life of Her Own*, Enslow, 1986.

Author of short fiction and articles for publishers, including Scott, Foresman, Harper, Science Research Associates, Lyons & Carnahan, Scholastic, and David C. Cook. Contributor to *Encyclopaedia Britannica* and of articles to newspapers and periodicals, including *Chicago Tribune, The Capital Times, Wisconsin State Journal, Milwaukee Sentinel, Exclusively Yours, Wisconsin Trails, Wanderlust,* and *Space World;* author of radio scripts.

SIDELIGHTS: "I sold a short story to *Wee Wisdom Magazine* when I was twelve years old. I've always been a compulsive writer, filling diaries and dashing off letters. I am almost always working on a manuscript with a query in the mail for the next project.

"I read a lot and am fascinated with space technology and the science of the future. Science fiction isn't half as exciting as history being written today for our world tomorrow."

Fox traveled with her husband, Richard Earl Fox, who was an adviser to industry in undeveloped countries, 1966-69, living in the Philippines, Iran, Colombia, and Tunisia.

FRANKEL, Edward 1910-

PERSONAL: Born June 4, 1910, in New York, N.Y.; son of Morris (a furrier) and Sara (Gelehrter) Frankel; married Helen Strawsky, May 26, 1939 (died, November, 1979); married Regina Rumstein (psychologist), December 6, 1981; children: (first marriage) Steven, Richard. *Education:* City College (now of the City University of New York), B.S., 1931; Columbia University, M.A., 1932; Yeshiva University, Ph.D., 1958. *Home and office:* 230 Hayward St., Yonkers, N.Y. 10704.

CAREER: Bronx High School of Science, Bronx, N.Y., science teacher and guidance counselor, 1940-58; New York City Board of Education, Bureau of Educational Research, New York City, research assistant, 1958-65; Herbert H. Lehman College of the City University of New York, Bronx, N.Y., associate professor, 1965-72, professor of science education and educational research, 1972-80, and 1984, director of institutional and educational research, 1968-74, professor emeritus, 1979—. Member of executive committee of Bronx River Restoration Project; New York Botanical Garden, Bronx, N.Y., instructor, 1976—; educational and environmental consultant. *Member:* National Science Teachers Association, American Fern Society, Torrey Botanical Club, New York Botanical Garden, Scarsdale Audubon Club (vice-president, 1978), Federated Conservationists of Westchester.

EDWARD FRANKEL

WRITINGS: DNA: Ladder of Life (illustrated by Anne Marie Jauss), McGraw, 1964, 2nd edition (illustrated by Radu Vero), 1979; *Ferns: A Natural History* (illustrated by Edgar M. Paulton), Stephen Greene, 1981. Contributor of about seventy-five articles to education and environmental studies journals and newspapers.

WORK IN PROGRESS: Poisonous Plants; Poison Ivy Family: Their Story.

SIDELIGHTS: "As a native New Yorker, born, bred, educated and educator in the schools, colleges and universities of this city, my discovery of the plant world was about the time I attained my majority and has grown into a passionate love affair spanning half a century.

"The first paper I wrote was entitled 'Flora of an "Empty" City Lot;' it listed the plants which my high school biology class and I found along an embankment of the Brighton subway line near James Madison High School in Flatbush, Brooklyn. Hundreds of papers later, I wrote 'A Floristic Survey of the Vascular Plants of the Bronx River Park in Westchester County, New York,' listing close to one thousand species found between Bronxville and Valhalla. Botanical surveys and ecological studies in the form of *environmental impact statements* have become a way of life for me. My interest includes rare and threatened species, introduced species, allergenic and poisonous plants, floral fables and folklore, and the history of common fruits and vegetables. My emphasis has been on local immigrant and indigenous plants.

"In my extensive travels on all four continents, camera and field guides are my constant companions. Photographic records of plant life are more important than eating and shopping, and certainly more rewarding.

"No high school or college student in my classes escaped my enthusiasm and love for plants and my concern about their preservation. Conserving green space locally, nationally and internationally has been my mission. My book *Ferns: A Natural History* carries my conservation message using ferns as the vehicle.

"Although Professor Emeritus from Lehman College in Bronx, New York, I have been unable to resist the lure of the classroom and students. I am sharing my interest in plants with prospective teachers who hopefully will pass on this information to their students. They are the citizens of the future who will face a world with shrinking green space and growing environmental problems.

"My association with Westchester Parks, Recreation and Conservation Department, Yonkers Shade Tree Commission, Torrey Botanical Club, American Fern Society, Scarsdale Audubon Society, New York Botanical Garden and various local nature centers keeps me busy writing, lecturing, photographing, leading field trips and doing research. For the past several years, I have been studying the poison ivy group, Anacardiaceae, with emphasis on the various species of poison ivy. Hopefully, this endeavor which is still in progress will become a book in which the virtues as well as the venom of these plants will be explained and extolled."

Frankel's book *DNA: Ladder of Life* has been translated into Spanish and Japanese.

FOR MORE INFORMATION SEE: Martha E. Ward and Dorothy A. Marquardt, *Authors of Books for Young People,* 2nd edition, Scarecrow, 1971; *New York Times,* November 27, 1977; *Review Press-Reporter* (Bronxville, N.Y.), December 24, 1981.

FREEMAN, Tony

BRIEF ENTRY: Educator, photographer, and author of books for children. A high school teacher of photography since 1962,

Freeman has also worked as a free-lance photographer for over fifteen years. During that time, he has provided thousands of photographs to publications nationwide. When editors began requesting words to accompany his photographs, Freeman found himself developing into a writer as well. He is now the author of nine books for children, all published by Childrens Press and illustrated with his own photographs. In these nonfiction works, Freeman explores a variety of topics. His interest in the world of flying machines is revealed in books like *Blimps* (1979), *An Introduction to Radio-Controlled Sailplanes* (1979), *Aircraft That Work for Us* (1981), and *Hot-Air Balloons* (1983). Both boys and girls are provided with simple introductions to sports in *Beginning Surfing* (1980), *Beginning Backpacking* (1980), *Baseball Is Our Game* (1982), and *Beginning Bicycle Motocross* (1983). Freeman has also written *Photography* (1983), in which he examines everything from how a camera works to possible careers in the field.

GARRETSON, Victoria Diane 1945- (Victoria Cox)

PERSONAL: Born November 12, 1945, in Roswell, N.M. *Education:* Principia College, B.A., 1967; attended Parsons School of Design, 1968, and School of Visual Arts. *Home:* 3929 East Camelback, Phoenix, Ariz. 85018.

CAREER: Artist, metaphysician, and writer. Work has been exhibited in one-woman shows, numerous juried shows, and at such places as the Detroit Institute of Arts, Memorial Art Gallery (Rochester, N.Y.), and the Flint Institute of Arts (Flint, Mich.). Works are included in permanent collections at Manufacturers Bank of Livonia, Michigan, Buffalo Bills Football Stadium, Buffalo, N.Y., and Xerox Corporation, Southfield, Mich.

WRITINGS—Under name Victoria Cox; all for children: (With Stan Applebaum) *A Not So Ugly Friend,* edited by L. C. Hunt,

VICTORIA DIANE GARRETSON

Holt, 1973; (with S. Applebaum) *Going My Way? Nature's Hitchhikers* (illustrated by Leonard Shortall), Harcourt, 1976.

Under name Victoria Cox; all for children; all with Stan Applebaum; "Nature's Sanitation Corps" series; published by Western Publishing, 1974: *The Knight in Crusty Armor* (illustrated by George Sandström); *The Laughing Garbage Disposal* (illustrated by Dorothea Barlowe); *Nature's Assistant* (illustrated by W. T. Mars); *Nature's Carpet Sweeper* (illustrated by G. Sandström); *Nature's Flying Janitor* (illustrated by Jo Polseno); *Nature's Smallest Gravedigger* (illustrated by D. Barlowe).

Also author of two metaphysical books, *In Silence I Hear the Most* and *A Lasting Relationship*, both self-published.

SIDELIGHTS: "I have not been writing children's books for the past six years. However, I may take up writing again soon, and this time I would like to combine art and metaphysics (inspirational writing to help people get in touch with their natural flow and purpose in life)."

GRAEBER, Charlotte Towner

BRIEF ENTRY: In her fictional works for children, Graeber reveals her affinity for animals of all kinds, particularly injured ones. Through the years her home has been a way station for a variety of maimed creatures, including a flying squirrel, a skunk, and a crow. Not surprisingly, her book *Grey Cloud* (Four Winds, 1979) focuses on an injured racing pigeon and the young boy who attempts to nurse it back to health. *School Library Journal* called it "a readable book dealing with friendship, responsibility, loss and compassion." In *Mustard* (Macmillan, 1982), Graeber deals with the death of a much loved family pet as seen through the eyes of eight-year-old Alex. According to *Horn Book,* the story "is all the more poignant for its restraint." *Publishers Weekly* agreed, noting that Graeber avoids "any uncalled-for happy endings" while symbolizing "the kind of love that makes sorrow endurable."

In her third book, *The Thing in Kat's Attic* (Dutton, 1984), Graeber touches on two themes: first, that a mother in a fatherless home is capable of handling a troublesome situation, and, second, that even unwanted squirrels in the attic deserve humane treatment at the hands of their evictors. "Younger readers," commented *Booklist,* "will find that the low-key story carries just enough tension to keep it lively." Graeber is the recipient of several awards, including the 1980 Friends of American Writers Award for *Grey Cloud* and the 1983 Irma Simonton Black Award for *Mustard.* She is also the author of two "I Love to Read" books published by Chariot Books—*Up, Down, and Around the Rain Tree* and *In, Out, and Beside the Catfish Pond* (both 1984). With Joe Boddy, she has written several books in Thomas Nelson's "Mr. T and Me" series, designed to help children learn right from wrong in everyday situations. *Residence:* Elgin, Ill.

GREENE, Carol

BRIEF ENTRY: Author of books for children. Greene graduated from Park College in Missouri with a B.A. in English literature and later received an M.A. in musicology from Indiana University. In addition to working as a children's editor, she has taught adult classes in writing for children. Greene has written over thirty children's books, including fictional works like *The Dancing Bear, and Other Stories* (Concordia,

1973), *The Super Snoops and the Missing Sleepers* (Childrens Press, 1976), *Hinny Winny Bunco* (Harper, 1982), and *The Insignificant Elephant* (Harcourt, 1985). Most of her numerous nonfictional works are part of several series published by Childrens Press. These include "New True Books" (*Language; Music; The United Nations; Astronauts; Robots*), "Enchantment of the World" (*England; Poland; Japan; Yugoslavia*), "Picture-Story Biographies" (*Mother Teresa: Friend of the Friendless; Sandra Day O'Connor: First Woman on the Supreme Court*), "Rookie Readers" (*Hi, Clouds; Please, Wind?; Ice Is . . . Whee!; Shine, Sun!*), and "Sing-Along Holiday Stories" (*A Computer Went A-Courting: A Love Song for Valentine's Day; The Thirteen Days of Halloween*). Aside from children's books, Greene also writes poems, songs, and filmstrips. *Residence:* St. Louis, Mo.

GUNDERSHEIMER, Karen

BRIEF ENTRY: Gundersheimer is the illustrator of nearly a dozen books for children, including three that she wrote herself. Although critics have consistently noted the similarity between her art work and that of Maurice Sendak's, she nonetheless has won praise for her illustrative style. As *School Library Journal* observed in a review of James Skofield's *Nightdances* (Harper, 1981): "The artist has not been able to escape the influence of Sendak . . . but her personality declares itself in the . . . falling leaves, ponds and rocks, rail fences and stone walls . . . [that] create a rural setting with character." In a review of Doris Schwerin's *The Tomorrow Book* (Pantheon, 1984), *Publishers Weekly* pointed out that "Gundersheimer's illustrations in gala colors are fetching, even if her capering tykes hint at . . . Sendak." Among the other books she has illustrated are Sally Whitman's *A Special Trade* (Harper, 1978), Jane Feder's *Beany* (Pantheon, 1979), and Edith Baer's *Words Are Like Faces* (Pantheon, 1980).

Gundersheimer provided both illustrations and text for *Happy Winter* (Harper, 1982) which describes, in rhyming couplets, the activities of two small sisters on a cold, winter day. *New York Times Book Review* called this work "a joyous catalogue," while *School Library Journal* found "the colorful, gentle pictures . . . as captivating as the verse." For preschool and primary-grade readers, Gundersheimer has produced *A B C Say with Me* and its companion volume, *1 2 3 Play with Me* (both Harper, 1984). "In addition to the educational content," *School Library Journal* again commented, "Gundersheimer's typically whimsical and cozy-looking illustrations will be very appealing to small children."

HAHN, Mary Downing   1937-

BRIEF ENTRY: Born December 9, 1937, in Washington, D.C. Writer, artist, teacher, and librarian. Hahn graduated from the University of Maryland in 1960 where she also received her M.A. in 1969. Since 1975 she has worked as a children's librarian in Prince George's County, Md. Prior to that time, she held positions as a junior high school teacher of art, part-time instructor in English at her alma mater, and free-lance artist for WETA public television in Virginia. The author of four novels for preadolescents, Hahn draws upon her own past experiences "to re-create real life. Like the people I know, I want my characters to be a mixture of strengths and weaknesses . . . to be a little confused and unsure of themselves." In a review of her first book, *The Sara Summer* (Clarion Books, 1979), *Publishers Weekly* labeled her an author with an "intimate knowledge of subteens and a well-tuned ear.'' The effectiveness of these qualities continued to sharpen in her succeeding works: *The Time of the Witch* (Clarion Books, 1982), *Daphne's Book* (Clarion Books, 1983), and *The Jellyfish Season* (Clarion Books, 1985).

Hahn is currently at work on a fifth novel, tentatively titled *Tallahassee Higgins*. Her plans for the near future include a ghost story, a teen novel, a mystery, and a fantasy. When she's not writing, Hahn paints "pictures of wizards, dragons, unicorns, elves and other magical creatures" which she sells at science fiction and fantasy conventions. She and her husband also enjoy taking long walks around the footpaths and lakes of their hometown, exploring flea markets and antique shops, and visiting museums. *Home:* 9746 Basket Ring Rd., Columbia, Md. 21045.

HASELEY, Dennis

BRIEF ENTRY: Born in Cleveland, Ohio. Haseley graduated from Oberlin College and received his master's degree from New York University. In addition to pursuing a career in clinical social work, he is the author of four books for children. In *The Old Banjo* (Macmillan, 1983), the setting is a Depression-era farm where a collection of battered and forgotten musical instruments suddenly break forth in music as they remember much happier past days. Illustrated by Stephen Gammell, this free verse poem was described by *Booklist* as "a mystical, musical fantasy." *New York Times Book Review* added: "The combo of Mr. Haseley on words and Mr. Gammell on pencil . . . will strike a responsive chord in most readers." *The Pirate Who Tried to Capture the Moon* (Harper, 1983), another fantasy, tells the tale of a fierce pirate who sets out to trap all the things loved by the moon but, in the end, finds himself the moon's willing captive.

Haseley explores the world of native American Indians in *The Scared One* (F. Warne, 1983), the story of a timid little Indian boy whose encounter with a wounded eagle gives him the courage to fulfill tribal rites of manhood. "[This] tale," observed *Publishers Weekly*, "resonates with the cadences of heroic legends." The setting of the *Soap Bandit* (F. Warne, 1984), is the turn-of-the-century Victorian period. In what *Publishers Weekly* again noted as a "gentle allegory," seven-year-old Jesse is the only dirty spot in a seaside town of very pristine adults—until the mysterious Soap Bandit appears. According to *New York Times Book Review*, Haseley injects "imaginative and humorous touches" into this most recent work. *Residence:* Brooklyn, N.Y.

HEALEY, Larry 1927-

PERSONAL: Born November 10, 1927, in Boston, Mass.; son of William J. (an attorney) and Katherine (Sullivan) Healey; married Rose Million (a writer), 1958. *Education:* Harvard College, B.A., 1949. *Politics:* Democrat. *Home:* 68 Fifth Ave., New York, N.Y. 10011. *Agent:* McIntosh and Otis, Inc., 475 Fifth Ave., New York, N.Y. 10017.

CAREER: L'Aigon Apparel, Inc., Philadelphia, Pa., salesman, 1952-63; Nelly Don, Inc., Kansas City, Mo., sales manager, 1963-66; Hahne and Co., Newark, N.J., buyer, 1966-71; Hearn's Department Store, New York City, buyer, 1972-77. *Member:* Mystery Writers of America.

LARRY HEALEY

WRITINGS—Novels for young adults: *The Claw of the Bear,* F. Watts, 1978; *The Town Is on Fire,* F. Watts, 1979; *The Hoard of the Himalayas,* Dodd, 1980; *Angry Mountain,* Dodd, 1983.

WORK IN PROGRESS: The Marble Pawn, a mystery on counterfeit classic sculpture.

HEUER, Kenneth John 1927-

PERSONAL: Born January 30, 1927, in Yonkers, N.Y.; son of Lester Frederick and Ida Antoinette (Fechner) Heuer. *Education:* Attended Amherst College, 1945-48; New School for Social Research, B.A., 1961. *Home:* 451 West 21st St., New York, N.Y. 10011.

CAREER: Head of science department at boys' preparatory school in New York City, 1948; American Museum, Hayden Planetarium, New York City, lecturer, 1948-53; Viking Press, Inc., New York City, science editor, 1953-60; Thomas Y. Crowell Co., New York City, science editor, 1960-61; Macmillan Publishing Co., Inc., New York City, editor in chief of trade science department, 1961-63; Charles Scribner's Sons, New York City, director of science book department, 1963-76, vice-president, 1974—. New York editor of Cornell University Press, 1980—. *Member:* American Museum of Natural History (associate benefactor), Royal Astronomical Society (fellow), Explorers Club. *Awards, honors:* Science book award from National Science Teachers Association, 1978, for *Rainbows, Halos, and Other Wonders.*

WRITINGS: Men of Other Planets, Pellegrin & Cudahy, 1951; *The Next Fifty Billion Years: An Astronomer's Glimpse into the Future,* Gollancz, 1951, Viking, 1954; *The End of the World: Scientific Inquiry,* Rinehart, 1953; *Wonders of the Heavens,* Dodd, 1954; *An Adventure in Astronomy,* Viking, 1958; *City of the Stargazers,* Scribner, 1972; *Rainbows, Halos, and Other Wonders: Light and Color in the Atmosphere,* Dodd, 1978; *Thunder, Singing Sands, and Other Wonders: Sound in the Atmosphere,* Dodd, 1981.

Due to atmospheric turbulence, the city lights sparkle like diamonds. ■ (From *Rainbows, Halos, and Other Wonders: Lights and Color in the Atmosphere* by Kenneth Heuer. Photograph courtesy of Wide World Photos.)

Also co-author with George Seldon of play, "The Genie of Sutton Place," televised on Studio One, 1956 (included in *All the World's a Stage: Modern Plays for Young People,* edited by Lowell Swortzell, Delacorte, 1972). Contributor to magazines.

WORK IN PROGRESS: Editing the nature notebooks of the late Loren Eiseley, to be published by Little, Brown.

FOR MORE INFORMATION SEE: Sky and Telescope, February, 1973, April, 1973, August, 1978; *English Journal,* April, 1973, November, 1978; *Science Books and Films,* May, 1973, May, 1979; *Scientific American,* December, 1978.

HOOPES, Lyn Littlefield 1953-

BRIEF ENTRY: Born July 14, 1953, in New York, N.Y. Editor, writer, and children's book reviewer. Hoopes received her A.B. from Stanford University in 1975, graduating with honors in English literature. For the following two years, she worked as an editorial assistant at Harper & Row in New York City. In 1977 she moved to Boston where she was employed as an assistant editor at Atlantic Monthly Press before becoming editor of children's books at Houghton Mifflin from 1980 to 1982. Hoopes now spends her time writing and reviewing children's books and raising her four-year-old son, Nathaniel Lowry. She finds that being with her child, "seeing and feeling through him, connects me to my own childhood directly. Not in a reminiscing way, but in a present, active way."

Hoopes emphasizes a small child's personal relationships in her three picture books, aimed at preschool and early primary-grade readers. *Nana* (Harper, 1981) reveals the thoughts of a young girl the day after her grandmother's death. *School Library Journal* described it as "quiet, reflective, pensive. . . . Moving from house to garden, images of new life from old in nature help convey a comforting feeling." In *When I Was Little* (Unicorn Books, 1983), another girl finds reassurance of her mother's love through a question-and-answer dialogue set against a wintry landscape. "A personal creation," *Horn Book* stated, "ideal for initiating those special moments when families discuss what is really important: the meaning of love, the continuity of life, and the joy of belonging." The love between a toddler and his parents is evident in *Daddy's Coming Home* (Harper, 1984), the simple story of a mother and son who walk down their farmyard lane to meet Daddy. *School Library Journal* again noted the book's "artless, repetitive style of a two year old's rhythmic chant," adding that it should be especially appealing to "under threes." Hoopes has completed her fourth picture book, entitled *Mommy, Daddy, Me,* with publication expected by Harper. *Home:* 2989 Rivermeade Dr. N.W., Atlanta, Ga. 30327.

HOOVER, H(elen) M(ary) 1935-

PERSONAL: Born April 5, 1935, in Stark County, Ohio; daughter of Edward Lehr (a teacher) and Sadie (a teacher; maiden name, Schandel) Hoover. *Education:* Attended Mount Union College, Los Angeles City College, and Los Angeles County School of Nursing. *Religion:* Protestant. *Residence:* Alexandria, Va. *Agent:* Russell & Volkening, Inc., 50 West 29th St., New York, N.Y. 10001.

CAREER: Writer. *Member:* Authors Guild, Smithsonian Institution, New York Museum of Natural History. *Awards,*

honors: The Lion's Cub was selected as a Children's Book of the Year, 1974, by the Child Study Association of America; Ohioana Award, 1982, for *Another Heaven, Another Earth,* which also was selected one of American Library Association's "Best Books for Young Adults," 1982; Central Missouri State College Award for Children's Literature, 1984, for "Outstanding Contribution to Children's Literature."

WRITINGS—For young people: *Children of Morrow,* Four Winds Press, 1973; *The Lion's Cub,* Four Winds Press, 1974; *Treasures of Morrow,* Four Winds Press, 1976; *The Delikon,* Viking, 1977; *The Rains of Eridan,* Viking, 1977; *The Lost Star,* Viking, 1979; *Return to Earth: A Novel of the Future,* Viking, 1980; *This Time of Darkness,* Viking, 1980; *Another Heaven, Another Earth,* Viking, 1981; *The Bell Tree,* Viking, 1982; *The Shepherd Moon: A Novel of the Future* (Junior Literary Guild selection), Viking, 1984. Contributor to *Language Arts.*

WORK IN PROGRESS: A science-fiction book for young adults to be published by Viking; a historical fiction for adults.

SIDELIGHTS: ". . . I grew up in an old country house in northeastern Ohio with fields and woods for roaming, orchards and ponds and creeks. Pets and children were left unleashed. There was no litter. There were few strangers. On still nights you could hear train whistles on the Pennsylvania tracks four miles south and see the glow of Pittsburgh's lights reflected by the smoke that hung above it then, ninety miles to the east. I took for granted that most people could walk a mile and still be on family property or a neighbor's land across the fence." [H. M. Hoover, "Where Do You Get Your Ideas?," *Top of the News,* fall, 1982.']

H. M. HOOVER

(Jacket illustration by Charles Mikolaycak from *The Rains of Eridan* by H. M. Hoover.)

"My parents were both amateur naturalists. They could identify most plants, birds, and animals. Their books reflected their interest in human history and natural history. . . . My parents were good teachers. They gave my imagination something to work on. They gave me a sense of time and wonder. . . ." [*Language Arts,* April, 1980.[2]]

"Perhaps because my parents were teachers, my finding an arrowhead washed from the sandy track of the back lane could mean learning what tribe made it, what nation the tribe belonged to, why they had fled Ohio Territory long before my father's people cleared this farm, while eagles, bears, and wolves still remained. All that led to the facts that even earlier people had lived here, hunter-gatherers following the glacier's retreat north, while tribes to the south built mounds and followed overland trade routes to Central America, for found in those mounds were Guatemalan jade pipes and seashells from the Gulf. Information kept pouring out until one almost regretted finding the arrowhead. But later I would think about it, and imagine walking to Mexico, and walking back, and wonder how they crossed the rivers and if there were ferry-canoes, and how the country must have looked when forest stretched from horizon to horizon, and how old the land was and who would come after we, in turn, had gone.

"My parents were great readers. So were their four children, either by choice or in self-defense. I don't really remember a time when I couldn't read, or was read to. I do recall that the reading texts in school came as a distinct shock. I couldn't believe I was being asked to waste my time with *Dick and Jane* after reading 'The Relief of Lucknow' in the *McGuffey's Fifth* in our attic. (Teachers in the family had stored readers up there that went back through *McGuffey* to *Webster's* and earlier, wonderful sewn books on heavy paper, books with wavy covers and onionskin over the prints.)

"It always struck me as odd that few of our friends or neighbors had any books in their houses. Ours was overrun with reading material. I slowly decided that if people's first exposure to reading was *Dick and Jane,* it was possible that for the rest of their lives the very sight of a book might induce giddiness and the mad urge to cry, 'Run, Self! Run! Run!'

"For me the high spot in the school week was Wednesday morning, when the Stark County Library truck arrived. I read anything, juvenile or adult, junk or classic. Junk books affected me like junk food; when my stomach turned I switched to more solid stuff. I had a preference for natural history, biographies and history, books of fact, and ghost stories. Books of social significance bored me, aside from Dickens and some old Jack London books—worlds so remote from my life that I read them as tragic fantasy. Now when I write, it's not for 'children or young adults.' Remembering my own reading, I can't possibly imagine a stranger's wants or try to satisfy them. I can only hope that what pleases and interests me has the same appeal for some of those strangers."[1]

"I began writing the sort of stories I write for the simple reason that they are the type of stories I liked best when I was a child—that I still like best."[2]

"When I decided to write, I took four years off to teach myself the craft. It was a time of high anxiety and self-doubt. My first short story sold to *Scholastic* magazine. Thus encouraged, I promptly wrote two books which never sold. At the end of four years, *Children of Morrow* sold to Four Winds Press—and I breathed a big sigh of relief and went out and found a job. . . . Ten books later, I'm still learning how to write.

"If I waited for inspiration I'd get nothing published. Books are a matter of discipline, of working at a book each day, of thinking about it in the bathtub, or while reading or watching TV—but never when driving or cooking. (I once found a lost coffeepot in the freezer—absentmindedly put there when I was plotting.) Some days it's fun to write; other days it's not. Halfway through each book I'm sure it will never be finished, and when it is, I'm always surprised and a bit puzzled.

"Writing a book is like making a quilt and just as tedious. You cut and stitch small pieces of thought together to form a pattern in the mind. When it's done you often see you've botched it. Seams may have to be picked out stitch by stitch, pieces recut, other colors or shades chosen, and the whole put back together. With luck the finished piece will be pleasing and will fare well in the critical wash.

"Sometimes a story just isn't ready when you are. *The Rains of Eridan* began as four pages about a little boy named Roger.

It wasn't quite right but I put it away and a year later dug it out, got rid of Roger, added sixty-four more pages and then stored it away again until one day at the office I was reading a chemical encyclopedia's entry under 'virus' . . . and then I knew the rest of the story.

"*The Lion's Cub* was a result of reading old journals and diaries. My only historical fiction, it's the story of Jemal Edin Shamyl, a little boy used as a pawn by his father, the Imam of Daghestan, and Nicholas I during the long-forgotten Wars of the Caucasus. I enjoyed writing and researching the book. . . .

"*Another Heaven, Another Earth* also began as a result of reading, in this case the fragments of a diary and letters of a Virginia colonist who died waiting for a ship from the Old World that never came. Forest reclaimed the site and all records of the colony remained 'lost in the files' in England for three hundred and fifty years.

"*Children of Morrow* began with moonsnails on a beach near a New York landfill where rain oozed through garbage and leeched into the ocean. The snails were three to four times their normal size from feeding on garbage; their shells gray, friable, completely lacking nacre. But the animals inside were alive and foul. Nearby was a gull with three eyes, two on the right side, one on the left, and a tern with an extra miniature leg growing out of its breast. Great flocks of gulls fed on the

(Jacket illustration by Derek James from *The Shepherd Moon: A Novel of the Future* by H. M. Hoover.)

Cossacks! The word drove other thoughts from his mind. Although he had never seen one, from infancy he had been taught to hate them. ■ (Jacket illustration by Richard Cuffari from *The Lions Cub* by H. M. Hoover.)

landfill, rising and swirling when trucks arrived to dump more garbage. A sign labeled the site a 'development area'; I wondered if anyone in charge knew just what we were developing and how the children of tomorrow would appreciate our stupidity, or if they would merely match it.

"It's always seemed to me that there is more lasting truth in fantasy than in fiction. Legend or myth, fairy tale or fable, all contain truth we sometimes can't articulate, but intuitively understand. We have all lived or worked on *Animal Farm* and know pigs who feel 'some animals are more equal than others.' We can see the Great Oz in any humbugging politician, complete with tears on command or feigned rage, projected in power by media coverage. Sometimes the wizard is parent or professor or boss; the Dark Lord of Mordor is still with us and orcs do stalk suburban malls.

"All fiction writers create singular worlds if they try, but in some respects fantastic worlds must be more real, more logically detailed and specific than straight fiction. When one writes about an alien world, it is just that to the reader. He or she must be told how and why it functions, and the telling must have consistency or all is lost. It must also be part of the story and not an inventory of facts. As a child I resented authors who ignored known fact (or facts *they* established within their fantasy) to make their plots work. I suspected them at first of ignorance and, later, of contempt for their readers. It is still done and I still have those suspicions.

"If the story takes place on an alien world, the reader must be able to believe humans can walk there. Everything, from gravity and atmosphere, geology and life forms, must fit and be a part of that world if it is to ring true. If, for example, the author says the planet's gravity is three times that of Earth, then everything alive there must conform to that gravity, including earthlings if they arrive. Living things must eat and food must be provided. Animals must be built to physically function in their world. If not, somewhere a bright child will say 'baloney' or a less polite equivalent, and toss the book aside. Children may be gullible from lack of time to learn, but they're not stupid, and they remember details.

"Where do I get my ideas? From watching a scorpion walk, from listening to music that triggers a memory, from a face on the street, an overheard remark. But mostly from memory, from the past. And each idea adds to those already formed, or wells up out of them in dreams. Watching writers work is about as fascinating as watching a scoreless ball game. You know something is going on—but who cares at the time?

"No matter how hard one tries, there's always a haunting gap between what you want to create and what you finally manage. . . . Sometimes I think the most truly creative aspect of anything is knowing when to stop."[1]

HOBBIES AND OTHER INTERESTS: Reading, long walks, rock hounding, gardening, music, cars—especially antique vehicles, ancient history, natural history.

FOR MORE INFORMATION SEE: Language Arts, April, 1980, September, 1982; H. M. Hoover, "Where Do You Get Your Ideas?," *Top of the News,* fall, 1982.

IRWIN, Ann(abelle Bowen)   1915- (Hadley Irwin, a joint pseudonym)

PERSONAL: Born October 8, 1915, in Peterson, Iowa; daughter of Benjamin (a farmer) and Mary (a teacher; maiden name, Rees) Bowen; married Keith C. Irwin (in business), May 29,

Ann Irwin with co-author Lee Hadley.

"Moon, you read too much. Don't you ever play like other kids your age?"

"I've never been my age." His voice was flat. ■ (Jacket illustration by Richard Williams from *Moon and Me* by Hadley Irwin.)

1943; children: Jane Irwin Croll, Ann Irwin Bauer, Rees, Sara. *Education:* Morningside College, B.A., 1937; University of Iowa, M.A., 1967. *Residence:* Lake View, Iowa. *Office:* Department of English, Iowa State University, Ross Hall, Ames, Iowa 50011.

CAREER: High school English teacher in Iowa, 1937-67; Buena Vista College, Storm Lake, Iowa, instructor in English, 1967-68; Midwestern College, Denison, Iowa, instructor in English, 1968-70; Iowa State University, Ames, associate professor of English, 1970-85; writer. *Awards, honors:* One Bite at a Time was selected one of Child Study Association's "Children's Books of the Year," 1973; Society of Midland Authors Award, 1982, for *Moon and Me; What about Grandma?* was chosen one of the Best Young Adult Books of 1982, by the American Library Association.

WRITINGS—Juvenile: (With Bernice Reida) *Hawkeye Adventure,* Graphic Publishing, 1966; (with B. Reida) *Hawkeye Lore,* Graphic Publishing, 1968; *One Bite at a Time,* F. Watts, 1973; (with B. Reida) *Moon of the Red Strawberry,* Aurora, 1977; (with B. Reida) *Until We Reach the Valley,* Avon, 1979.

Novels; with Lee Hadley, under joint pseudonym Hadley Irwin: *The Lilith Summer,* Feminist Press, 1979; *We Are Mes-*

quakie, *We Are One,* Feminist Press, 1980; *Bring to Boil and Separate,* Atheneum, 1980; *Moon and Me,* Atheneum, 1981; *What about Grandma?,* Atheneum, 1982; *I Be Somebody,* Atheneum, 1984; *Abby, My Love,* Atheneum, 1985.

Author of one-act plays, *And the Fullness Thereof,* Pioneer, 1962, and *Pieces of Silver,* Eldridge Publishing, 1963.

WORK IN PROGRESS: With Lee Hadley, under joint pseudonym Hadley Irwin, *Kim, Kimi.*

SIDELIGHTS: Irwin and Hadley wrote: "Hadley Irwin is one writer even though she is two people. The name was never meant as a pseudonym, but rather as a means of identifying an entity who is, in some ways, separate from us.

"Lee Hadley and Ann Irwin [have] taught in the English Department of Iowa State University. The academic year offers little time for writing so, in the summer, Hadley Irwin comes alive, and books get written. One of us sits at the typewriter; the other lurks nearby and we talk the words of the novel onto the page. Often one of us begins a sentence and the other finishes it; occasionally we say the same words at the same time. The result is that a given line or paragraph does not belong to either Lee or Ann, but to someone who is a better writer than either of us. There is another advantage—no ego involvement in chopping out the bad lines that inevitably appear.

(Jacket illustration by Leslie Morrill from *Bring to a Boil and Separate* by Hadley Irwin.)

"Hadley Irwin combines two very different kinds of lives, although those lives began in something of the same way. Each of us was born on an Iowa farm, one of four children (two boys and two girls). We were both educated in Iowa and both taught junior high, high school, and college there, but after that things changed. Ann married and had four children; Lee didn't. Ann stayed in Iowa; Lee spent ten years on the Jersey shore. We met when the head of our English department appointed us to the same committee and asked us to write a report.

"Writing together is a fascinating experience and we've often discussed why it works so easily for us. Lee says it's because we're Libras; Ann says it's because we share the sense of humor of a twelve-year-old. Both of our lives are filled with words, whether it's teaching composition courses, doing crossword puzzles, or fighting our on-going Scrabble battle. Probably more important, we genuinely like and respect each other; there has never been a sense of competition in our relationship. In each other we have an instant editor; if we disagree, which is seldom, there's a standard response: 'Put it in parentheses with a question mark.' We're considering that for an epitaph. Best of all, when one of us would rather do almost anything else—make coffee, water plants, fix lunch—than confront the blank page in the typewriter, the other flicks the whip and the writing goes on.

"We have often been asked, 'When are you going to write an adult novel?' We do not see a major distinction between the adult novel and what we write. We have spent most of our lives working with people younger than ourselves, and if we've learned anything it is that the concerns, problems, and emotions of the young are basically the same as those of the adult. We respect this audience of young adults and try to write with honesty, humor, and understanding. Ann says it helps to have raised four children. Lee says it helps to have survived one's own adolescence. What is certain is that Hadley Irwin has become very real to us. We hope she's just as real to the readers of her books."

The Lilith Summer, We Are Mesquakie, What about Grandma? and *I Be Somebody* have been published in foreign countries, including Denmark, Holland, Sweden, Canada, Great Britain and France.

Pouf was wide awake. ■ (From *The Midnight Castle* by Consuelo Joerns. Illustrated by the author.)

JOERNS, Consuelo

PERSONAL—Education: Attended Chicago Art Institute, Mills College, Columbia University, and School of Visual Arts.

CAREER: Artist, author and illustrator of books for children.

WRITINGS—Fiction for children; all self-illustrated: *The Forgotten Bear,* Four Winds, 1978; *The Lost and Found House,* Four Winds, 1979; *The Foggy Rescue,* Four Winds, 1980; *Oliver's Escape,* Four Winds, 1981; *The Midnight Castle,* Lothrop, 1983.

Illustrator: Janet Adam Smith, compiler, *The Looking Glass Book of Verse,* Looking Glass Library, 1959; Sorche Nic Leodhas (pseudonym of Leclaire Alger), editor, *Heather and Broom: Tales of the Scottish Highlands,* Holt, 1960; Polly Cameron, *The Green Machine,* Coward, 1969; William Corbin, *The Everywhere Cat* (Junior Literary Guild selection), Coward, 1970; Carla Stevens, *Rabbit on Bear Mountain,* Scholastic Book Services, 1980; Robert Bahr, *Blizzard at the Zoo,* Lothrop, 1982.

JOHNSON, E(ugene) Harper
(Harper Johnson)

PERSONAL: Born in Birmingham, Ala.; married; children: Eileen, Iona, Eugene Harper, Jr. *Education:* Attended Académie Julian, Paris, France; American Academy of Art; Chicago Art Institute; National Academy School of Fine Arts; and Pratt Institute.

CAREER: Artist, illustrator, author. Early career as a concert violinist was cut short by a broken wrist; turned to career as an artist, supporting himself at a number of odd jobs, including dishwashing, newspaper reporting, and steel working; book illustrator, beginning 1949. *Exhibitions:* South Side Community Art Center, 1945. Paintings hang in many art galleries and private collections. *Military service:* U.S. Army, Special Services, during World War II.

WRITINGS—All for children; all self-illustrated: *Kenny,* Holt, 1957; *Piankhy the Great,* Thomas Nelson, 1962.

Illustrator; all for children; all under name E. Harper Johnson: Marie McSwigan, *All Aboard for Freedom!,* Dutton, 1954; Miriam Schlein, *Home: The Tale of a Mouse,* Abelard, 1958; Esma Booth, *Kalena,* Longmans, Green, 1958; Beatrix T. Moore, *Swim for It, Bridget!,* Morrow, 1958; B. T. Moore, *Kerry,* Morrow, 1959; Mary C. Rose, *Clara Barton: Soldier of Mercy,* Garrard, 1960; Katharine E. Wilkie, *Daniel Boone: Taming the Wilds,* Garrard, 1960; Laura Zirbes, *How Many Bears?,* Putnam, 1960; Marian Rumsey, *The Seal of Frog Island,* Morrow, 1961; Jane Collier (pseudonym of Zena Shumsky) *The Year of the Dream,* Funk, 1962; Edward Dolch and Marguerite P. Dolch, *More Dog Stories,* Garrard, 1962; Bernice Kohn, *Marvelous Mammals: Monotremes and Marsupials,* Prentice-Hall, 1964; Duane Bradley, *Meeting with a Stranger,* Lippincott, 1964; Burl Ives, *Albad the Oaf,* Abelard, 1965; Margaret G. Clark, *Mystery at Star Lake,* Funk, 1965; Sheldon N. Ripley, *Matthew Henson, Arctic Hero,* Houghton, 1966.

Illustrator; all for children; all under name Harper Johnson: Arna W. Bontemps, *The Story of George Washington Carver,* Grosset, 1954; Louise A. Stinetorf, *Elephant Outlaw,* Lippincott, 1956; Donald E. Worcester, *Lone Hunter's Gray Pony,*

Next thing I knew, Uncle Mose was picking me up in the dark and starting down the ladder with me. ■ (From *The Story of George Washington Carver* by Arna Bontemps. Illustrated by Harper Johnson.)

Oxford University Press (New York), 1956; D. E. Worcester, *Lone Hunter and the Cheyennes,* Oxford University Press (New York), 1957; D. E. Worcester, *Lone Hunter's First Buffalo Hunt,* Walck, 1958; Willis Lindquist, *The Red Drum's Warning,* Whittlesey House, 1958; A. W. Bontemps, *Frederick Douglass: Slave, Fighter, Freeman,* Knopf, 1959; Ruth F. Chandler, *Ladder to the Sky,* Abelard, 1959; Elsie Archer, *Let's Face It: A Guide to Good Grooming for Negro Girls,* Lippincott, 1959, revised edition published as *Let's Face It: The Guide to Good Grooming for Girls of Color,* 1968; D. E. Worcester, *Lone Hunter and the Wild Horses,* Walck, 1959; L. A. Stinetorf, *Musa, the Shoemaker,* Lippincott, 1959; Elizabeth J. Coatsworth, *Desert Dan,* Viking, 1960; Patricia M. Martin, *The Little Brown Hen,* Crowell, 1960; Eilis Dillon, *The Fort of Gold,* Funk, 1961; D. E. Worcester, *War Pony,* Walck, 1961; Andrée Clair, *Bemba: An African Adventure,* translated by Marie Ponsot, Harcourt, 1962; Joseph Kessel, *The Lion,* Knopf, 1962; Weyman B. Jones, *The Talking Leaf,* Dial, 1965; Child Study Association of America, *Round about the City: Stories You Can Read to Yourself,* Crowell, 1966.

Also illustrator of over 150 additional books. Contributor of articles to periodicals, including *Ebony, Collier's, Liberty,* and *Argosy.*

SIDELIGHTS: Johnson was born and raised in Birmingham, Alabama. He showed exceptional talent in a number of fields, including painting, singing, playing the violin, and writing. When he was not yet twelve years old, Johnson was encouraged by an artist and teacher, Professor D'launey, to travel to France and work in D'launey's studio.

During his time spent in France, young Johnson concentrated his efforts equally in the art and music fields. At this time he had hoped to become a violinist. He was fortunate enough to have a successful, albeit brief, career as a violinist touring

Europe and Africa. Unfortunately, a fall from a horse broke his wrist, ending that career. Unable to finger the violin, Johnson turned to painting.

Johnson studied art first in Paris at the Académie Julian, and later at the American Academy of Art and the Chicago Art Institute, the National Academy School of Fine Arts in New York, and the Pratt Institute in Brooklyn, New York. After three years of struggle, Johnson broke into the field of book illustration. Since 1949, Johnson has illustrated numerous children's books, including *The Story of George Washington Carver*

Once he started to talk, Tony forgot the staring eyes of the other children. ■ (From "A Tulip for Tony," by Marietta Moskin in *Round about the City: Stories You Can Read to Yourself,* selected by the Child Study Association of America. Illustrated by Harper Johnson.)

and *Frederick Douglass: Slave, Fighter, Freeman,* both by Arna W. Bontemps.

Besides book illustration, Johnson wrote two children's books, *Kenny,* based on a 1955 tour of North and East Africa, and *Piankhy the Great,* who once ruled Egypt.

FOR MORE INFORMATION SEE: Lee Kingman and others, compilers, *Illustrators of Children's Books: 1957-1966,* Horn Book, 1968.

KESSLER, Ethel 1922-

PERSONAL: Born January 7, 1922, in Pittsburgh, Pa.; daughter of J. Karney (a mining engineer) and Rachel (Basin) Gerson; married Leonard Kessler (an author and illustrator of books for children), January 23, 1946; children: Paul, Kim. *Education:* Carnegie-Mellon University, B.A., 1944; graduate study, Bank Street College of Education, 1955-56; teacher certification, 1960. *Home:* New City, N.Y. *Office:* 6 Stoneham Lane, New City, N.Y. 10956.

CAREER: Author of books for children. Has worked as a social worker, program director of summer camps for children, and kindergarten/primary grade schoolteacher. *Awards, honors: Big Red Bus* was one of *New York Times* choice of best illustrated children's books of the year, 1957; *What Do You Play on a Summer Day?* and *Night Story* were selected by the Child Study Association as "Children's Books of the Year," 1977 and 1982, respectively.

Ethel Kessler with husband, Leonard.

Grandpa Witch sat in his soft chair. ■ (From *Grandpa Witch and the Magic Doobelator* by Ethel and Leonard Kessler. Illustrated by Leonard Kessler.)

WRITINGS—All for children; all written with husband, Leonard Kessler; all illustrated by L. Kessler, except as noted: *Plink, Plink! Goes the Water in My Sink,* Doubleday, 1954; *Crunch, Crunch,* Doubleday, 1955; *Peek-a-Boo: A Child's First Book* (Junior Literary Guild selection), Doubleday, 1956; *Big Red Bus,* Doubleday, 1957; *The Day Daddy Stayed Home,* Doubleday, 1959; *I Have Twenty Teeth—Do You? A First Visit to the Dentist,* Dodd, 1959; *Kim and Me,* Doubleday, 1960; *Do Baby Bears Sit in Chairs?,* Doubleday, 1961; *All Aboard the Train* (Junior Literary Guild selection), Doubleday, 1964; *Are You Square?,* Doubleday, 1966.

Our Tooth Story: A Tale of Twenty Teeth, Dodd, 1972; *Slush, Slush!,* Parents Magazine Press, 1973; *Splish, Splash,* Parents Magazine Press, 1973; *All for Fall,* Parents Magazine Press, 1974; *What's Inside the Box?,* Dodd, 1976; *What Do You Play on a Summer Day?,* Parents Magazine Press, 1977; *Two, Four, Six, Eight: A Book about Legs,* Dodd, 1980; *Baby-Sitter, Duck* (illustrated by Pat Paris), Garrard, 1981; *The Big Fight* (illustrated by P. Paris), Garrard, 1981; *Grandpa Witch and the Magic Doobelator,* Macmillan, 1981; *Night Story,* Macmillan, 1981; *Pig's New Hat* (illustrated by P. Paris), Garrard, 1981; *Pig's Orange House* (illustrated by P. Paris), Garrard, 1981; *The Sweeneys from 9D,* Macmillan, 1984.

WORK IN PROGRESS: Books for toddlers and preschoolers; untitled series.

SIDELIGHTS: "I am a most fortunate woman. I have had three careers—all of them related to working with children under seven years of age. After my marriage, I worked at a family camp, planning the children's activities. Later, after completing my requirements for certification, I taught kindergarten and first grade. When our children were infants, I discovered that there were few books for the very young. My studies in early childhood motivated me to extend that interest into writing for an age group that was neglected.

"The encouragement that I received from Leonard, my author/ illustrator husband, resulted in a happy collaboration of . . . books for the young listener and reader. The most important thing I learned while working on these books was the need to condense words and trim down the story to the bone.

"My pleasure and interest in children has led to an additional but related activity. Leonard and I have been visiting elementary schools to talk to children about books, to answer their questions about writing, and to share the pleasure of book making with them."

Kessler's works are included in the de Grummond Collection at the University of Southern Mississippi.

HOBBIES AND OTHER INTERESTS: Visiting art galleries and museums, herb gardening, swimming, tennis, walking.

FOR MORE INFORMATION SEE: Sally Holmes Holtze, editor, *Fifth Book of Junior Authors and Illustrators,* H. W. Wilson, 1983.

KIKUKAWA, Cecily H.   1919-

PERSONAL: Surname is pronounced Key-koo-kah-wah; born October 23, 1919, in Connecticut; daughter of Albert J. (an educator) and Marion (Gebhardt) Harder; married Arthur M. Kikukawa (a restaurant owner and manager), March 22, 1947; children: Sr. Marion F., Mrs. Frank Capalare, John A., Phillip T. *Education:* New Haven State Teachers College (now Southern Connecticut State College), B.S., 1941; Yale University, M.A., 1944; attended University of Hawaii, Manoa and Maui. *Religion:* Roman Catholic. *Home and office:* P.O. Box 352, Kaunakakai, Hawaii 95748.

CAREER: Teacher, Milford, Conn., 1941-43, Trumbull, Conn., 1943-44, Grosse Pointe, Mich., 1944-46, schools on Molokai, Hawaii, 1946-79; retired, 1979—. Member, Maui County Charter Commission, 1981-82; member, Maui County Humane Concerns Commission. *Member:* Hawaii State Teachers Association, Molokai Teachers Association. *Awards, honors:* Woman of the Year, State of Hawaii Business and Professional Women's Clubs, 1967.

WRITINGS: Ka Mea Ho'ala, the Awakener: The Story of Henry Obookiah, Once Called Opukaha'ia (juvenile paperback; illustrated by Robin Burningham), Bess Press, 1982.

WORK IN PROGRESS: Biography for children about Prince Jonah Kuhio Kalaniana'ole.

SIDELIGHTS: "Through my teaching of grades 4-6 and cultural activities within the community, I have developed a deep interest in the history of Hawaii. Recognizing the dearth of books for children on the subject of Hawaii's history, I decided to use my years of retirement to filling this need. I want to concentrate especially on biographies of historic Hawaiian figures.

"My first, and so far only published, biography is about Henry Obookiah who as a teenager in the early 1800's shipped out on a Yankee vessel to New England. Here he learned the English language from students at Yale and was converted to Christianity. He was being trained to return to Hawaii as a missionary when he became ill and died. I have visited his grave in Cromwell, Conn. both before coming to Hawaii and after. His memoirs were published after his death and they excited great interest in the missionary effort in Hawaii, so that he became an important link connecting the Hawaiian Kingdom with the United States.

"My current research is on a more recent figure, Prince Kuhio, or Prince Cupid as he was affectionately known. A member of the Alii of Hawaii, he was involved in the aborted counter-revolution which tried to restore Queen Liliuokalani to her throne. He later came to terms with the realities of annexation and served for twenty years as the Hawaiian delegate to the U.S. Congress.

"I insist that my work be historically accurate, but I do my best to also make it interesting and readable for today's children. I write mainly for our children here in Hawaii, but hope that the books will interest children throughout the country.

"My own childhood and youth in Milford and New Haven, Conn. provides a strong contrast to growing up on Molokai. Our island is very small and rural and we have a large number of Hawaiian children living on Hawaiian Homes Commission homesteads. Many of them were my pupils and it is for them that I write, so that they will know and appreciate their important Hawaiian historic personages."

KINGMAN, Dong (Moy Shu)   1911-

PERSONAL: Born March 31, 1911, in Oakland, Calif.; raised in Hong Kong; returned to U.S., 1929; son of Chuan-Fee (a dry goods merchant) and Lew She Dong; married Wong Shee,

DONG KINGMAN

September, 1929 (died June, 1954); married Helena Kuo (a journalist and author), September, 1956; children: (first marriage) Eddie, Dong, Jr. *Education:* Studied art privately in Hong Kong and at the Fox and Morgan Art School, Oakland, Calif. *Religion:* Episcopalian. *Address:* 21 West 58th St., New York, N.Y. 10019. *Agent:* (Paintings) Conacher Gallery, 134 Maiden Lane, San Francisco, Calif. 94108.

CAREER: Artist, muralist, and educator. Project artist, Works Progress Administration, 1936-41; San Diego Art Gallery, San Diego, Calif., art instructor, 1941-43; Columbia University, New York City, instructor in art, 1946-58; Hunter College (now of the City University of New York), New York City, instructor in watercolor and the history of Chinese art, 1948-53; Famous Artists School, Westport, Conn., faculty member, 1953—; Hewitt Travelling Painting Workshops, member of faculty, 1957—. Lecturer, Academy of Advertising Art, 1938; visiting lecturer, University of Wyoming, summer, 1944, Mills College, summers, 1945 and 1952; world lecture tour, International Cultural Exchange Program, U.S. Department of State, 1954; treasurer, Living Artist Production, beginning 1954; summer painting tours to Mexico, beginning 1957; assisted in production and promotion of the film, "The World of Suzie Wong," Paramount, 1960; executive vice-president, Twenty-Second Century Films, Inc., beginning 1968; art director, *Great Amusement* (magazine), 1968—; producer and director, short subject film, "Hongkong Dong," 1975. Has executed numerous commissions, including murals for Hilton Hotel, New York City, 1963, Bank of California, San Francisco, 1968, Boca Raton Hotel, Boca Raton, Fla., 1970, tapestry for Ambassador Hotel, Hong Kong, 1974, and Lincoln Savings Bank, New York City, 1977.

EXHIBITIONS: Work has appeared in various exhibits, including San Francisco Art Association Annual, San Francisco Museum, San Francisco, Calif., 1933; Vallejo Library (one-man show), San Francisco, 1933; Art Center (one-man show), San Francisco, 1936; Metropolitan Museum of Art, New York City, 1940; Midtown Gallery (one-man show), New York City, 1942; Manhattan Gallery, New York City, ten-year retrospective, 1951; watercolor exhibition, Whitney Museum of American Art Annual, New York City; China Art Gallery, Peking, China, May, 1981. Work is represented in numerous permanent collections, including those of Metropolitan Museum of Art, New York City, Museum of Modern Art, New York City, San Francisco Museum of Art, San Francisco, Calif., Boston Museum of Fine Arts, Boston, Mass., M. H. De Young Museum, San Francisco, Calif., Whitney Museum of Art, New York City, Hirshhorn Museum, Washington, D.C., Art Institute of Chicago, Chicago, Ill., and many private collections. *Military service:* U.S. Army, 1945-46; served in office of Strategic Services.

MEMBER: American Watercolor Society, National Academy of Design, West Coast Watercolor Society, Audubon Society, Dutch Treat Club. *Awards, honors:* Recipient of numerous

Kingman likes to work on location. Above, in the 1960s he painted one of his favorite sites—the Hong Kong waterfront.

Kingman with television personality, Garry Moore.

prizes, including those from Pennsylvania Academy, Philadelphia, 1933, San Francisco Art Association Annual Exhibition, 1936, Chicago International Watercolor Exhibition, 1944, Metropolitan Museum of Art Special Watercolor Exhibition, 1952, and American Watercolor Society, 1956, 1960, 1962, 1964, 1965, 1967, 1972, 1973, 1976, 1978, 1979; Guggenheim fellowships, 1942-44; Oakland Art Gallery Award, 1943 and 1944; Audubon Artists Medal of Honor, 1946; Joseph Pennell Memorial Medal, Pennsylvania Academy of Fine Arts, 1955; Audubon Artists Award, 1958; National Academy of Design Award, 1963, 1971, 1975, 1977; San Diego Art Gallery Award, 1968; Philadelphia Watercolor Club Award, 1968, for advancement of watercolor art; San Diego Watercolor Society Prize, 1984.

WRITINGS: (With wife, Helena Kuo Kingman) _Dong Kingman's Watercolors,_ Watson-Guptill, 1980. Contributor of articles to _New York Times, Woman's Day_ and others.

Illustrator: Enid La Monte Meadowcroft, _China's Story_ (illustrated with Weda Yap and Georgi Helma), Crowell, 1946; Vanya Oakes, _The Bamboo Gate: Stories of Children of Modern China_ (juvenile), Macmillan, 1946; Hans Christian Andersen, _Nightingale_ (juvenile), Once-Upon-a-Time Press, 1948; Clyde Robert Bulla, _Johnny Hong of Chinatown_ (juvenile), Crowell, 1952; Herbert E. Caen, _City on the Golden Hill,_ Doubleday, 1967; Paul Zindel, _The Effect of Gamma Rays on Man-in-the-Moon Marigolds_ (two-act play), Harper, 1971.

Contributor of artwork to motion pictures, including "The World of Suzie Wong," Paramount, 1960, "Flower Drum Song," Universal, 1961, "Fifty-Five Days at Peking," Allied Artists, 1963, "Circus World," Paramount, 1964, "King Rat," Columbia, 1965, "The Sand Pebbles," Twentieth Century-Fox,

1966, "The Desperados," Columbia, 1969, and "Lost Horizon," Columbia, 1973. Contributed illustrations to _Wings and Wishes_ (a school reader), Harper, 1977. Illustrations have appeared in various magazines, including _Life, Fortune, Holiday, McCall's, Time,_ and _This Week._

WORK IN PROGRESS: Preparing for exhibitions in Rome, Italy and at Conacher Gallery, San Francisco.

SIDELIGHTS: **March 31, 1911.** Born in Oakland, California.

1916. Moved with his parents to China. ". . . Europe was raging with war, and my father, who was running a dry-goods store in Oakland, California, at the time, was afraid America might get involved in the war. So he decided to sell his business and move the entire family to Hong Kong.

"We traveled steerage class, which provided the cheapest passenger accommodations. During our thirty-five-day voyage from San Francisco, rumors kept popping up that our ship might be torpedoed by German submarines. Though I was just a child, I could sense the excitement on people's faces and observe their fascinating responses. There were many interesting characters aboard, so I began to sketch them day after day to break the monotony of life aboard ship. It was then that I first realized it would be fun to be an artist." [Dong Kingman and Helena Kuo Kingman, _Don Kingman's Watercolors,_ Watson-Guptill, 1980.']

Kingman's father was a farmer turned merchant, and his mother, who was an artist, found time to paint while raising eight children. "My mother was an amateur painter. She never had the opportunity to receive formal training, but in her youth, she enjoyed copying birds, trees, and still-life subjects from

(From _The Effect of Gamma Rays on Man-in-the-Moon Marigolds_ by Paul Zindel. Illustrated by Dong Kingman.)

Kingman's sketch of Somerset Maugham's home in Pango Pango.

Chinese paintings. One of her most memorable paintings, which hangs in my home, has two ducks swimming among lotus lilies in a pond. She also designed jewelry for her friends.

"When I became interested in art, my family was very happy. My parents never particularly encouraged me to continue, but they didn't discourage me either. I had a feeling they always kept an eye on me."[1]

Like his mother, Kingman loved drawing, and used to draw in chalk on the pavement outside his father's dry goods store in Hong Kong in an effort to lure customers inside. "I remember a picture I painted for my rich uncle, who was a banker in Hong Kong and whom we called Yee Bark, which means 'Second Elder Uncle.' He had great confidence in me and predicted that someday I would have a great future as an artist. I was only nine years old at the time.

"My uncle was building a huge mansion on Yee Ma Lo (Second Boulevard), and he asked me to paint a picture of it. I was too young to understand how to use color, so I did a large black-and-white charcoal painting for him. He was so happy and so proud of me that when he gave a large banquet for the opening he placed my painting in the center of the hall and introduced me to all his rich friends."[1]

Attended school in Hong Kong. "In my early years in Hong Kong, I went to the Chan Sun-Wen School, where I especially enjoyed the painting and calligraphy classes. I must confess I was not a good academic student. I was lucky to get an average grade in most subjects, except when it came to watercolor painting and calligraphy. Then I was always at the top of the class. Sometimes I wanted to paint all night to improve myself.

"I remember my teacher demonstrating in watercolor how to paint a bird, a tree, or an animal. Then we would all copy his pictures. In calligraphy class, we had to do various brush exercises for an hour at a time every day. This added up to many hours of practice, since it was generally understood that it took as long as ten years for a calligrapher to be any good.

"During my school years in Hong Kong, I studied the rich Chinese literature, including *Gu Wen* ('Ancient Classics'), *Lun Yu* ('Book of Confucious'), and Tang poems. Except for my art lessons, I was not a good academic student, though what I did learn still remains with me. Often, in nostalgic moments, I quietly recite lines from a Tang poem or an ancient classic to entertain myself. No music was taught in the old-fashioned Chinese schools, but I learned it anyhow. From the time I was ten years old, my father had taken me to see the Cantonese opera almost every night, and I knew its sounds and rhythms well. Later on, I also learned to play Chinese musical instruments.

"Hong Kong is a British colony, and even though 90 percent of the population was Chinese, English was required in every school. Chan Sun-Wen School, the first school I attended, was basically an old-fashioned school where they taught only Chinese classics, with just one hour of English lessons every day. The teacher would read each of the twenty-six letters of the alphabet out loud, one by one, and the students, some fifty strong, would simultaneously repeat after him. I don't think anyone who came out of that Chinese school in Hong Kong would know anything about English! . . ."[1]

1926. Attended Lingnan Grammar School. "The first and only art teacher who had a true influence on me was Szetu Wei, a devout Christian and the kindest, most friendly person you would ever wish to meet. Szetu had studied art in Paris in the early twenties and returned to become headmaster and art teacher of the Lingnan Branch School in Hong Kong.

". . . I went to Lingnan not only to study Chinese and English, but specifically to study art under Szetu. When he found out how anxious I was to study art, he took me under his wing and became my personal tutor. He took me sketching outdoors during the summer holidays. Our school was located in Happy

They were all seated behind the long wooden tables. . . . ■ (From "Di-Di—The New Scholar in the Old Temple" in *The Bamboo Gate: Stories of Children of Modern China* by Vanya Oakes. Illustrated by Dong Kingman.)

Valley near the race course, and one day he took me on a long hike up the side of the hill. From there, I could see young men playing soccer in the field down in the valley, and people and vehicles looked like moving toys. It was there that Szetu taught me to do oil painting in the Western style. He taught me how to simplify details as well as many basic theories of composition, brush techniques, rhythm, the use of color, etc."[1]

1929. Returned to the United States. ". . . I left my parents and was on my own for the first time in my life. I didn't know what to do with my future—but in the meantime, I had to eat, so during those first two years in Oakland I worked as a dishwasher, waiter, and newsboy, and found little time for painting.

"By **1931,** I had saved enough money to buy part ownership of a restaurant for $75. This gave me a little time to paint in the afternoon, and I began to study at the Fox & Morgan Art School, which was only a few blocks away. The school had life-drawing classes every Tuesday morning, and on Friday afternoons our teacher, Mr. Fox, took us out to sketch around the streets and parks of Oakland. It was these outdoor painting classes that I enjoyed the most. I was very happy painting with oil paints until one day Fox called me into his office. 'You will never make it as a painter,' he told me. 'You might as well quit painting and go back to your chop-suey house.'

"I was very upset, but it is my nature to never say die. Perhaps, I thought, I should change to another medium. I had learned how to work with watercolor in the Chinese schools in Hong Kong. So I put away my oil-painting equipment—and the following Friday, when I went to my outdoor sketch class, I began to paint in watercolor. Fox took one look at my painting and said, 'You may make it after all.'"[1]

Adopted watercolor as his medium, rejecting other media. "Although I initially took up watercolor somewhat by accident, I had always considered it an important medium. In Europe, especially in the early days, artists treated watercolor as a minor medium, using it primarily to make studies for their major oil paintings. But for the Chinese, watercolor is and always has been their most important medium. They've been painting pictures in watercolor for more than four thousand years, having developed the technique simultaneously with calligraphy. I've always felt at home with watercolor, even at times when I was unsure of myself as an artist—and that's why I decided it was my medium.

"I find watercolor best for my temperament. It's a quick-drying medium, and you must think fast. I can create light, sensitive tones on my paper as well as rich, dark colors—yet watercolor always retains its transparent quality. I've tried other media, too, but not very successfully. It's possible that I didn't spend enough time on any of them to discover their beauty. In my opinion, both oil and pastel are opaque media. Acrylic and gouache, however, can be treated either opaquely or transparently, depending on how you use them. You can achieve different and interesting effects."[1]

1933. While working as a servant for a San Francisco family, Kingman painted his surroundings. The result was his first exhibition. ". . . On my half-day off every Sunday morning, I would gather up my painting gear and go sketching outdoors, sometimes in the San Francisco streets and at other times along the waterfront. I enjoyed painting the cityscape around me. This included street scenes, waterfronts, parks, and skyscrapers; and of course, there were always people, buses, bicycles, cars, lampposts, and stoplights in these bustling city scenes.

This watercolor, painted in the 1950s, was done in a style quite different from Kingman's later work.

"Over the next year I painted enough pictures to give an exhibition at the San Francisco Art Center. Some critics who saw the show referred to my paintings as a cross between Oriental and Occidental because of my heritage. And I guess this was partly true: I am Oriental when I paint trees and landscapes, but Occidental when I paint buildings, ships, or three-dimensional subjects with sunlight and shadow.

"Today, however, my thinking is different, and I no longer worry about these distinctions. For me, there is no such thing as Oriental or Occidental. There is only my way of painting with watercolor, and I hope whoever sees my paintings will enjoy and understand them as such."[1]

Kingman's prices for his paintings at the time were based on the size of the picture. "My top figure was $12.50. I don't recall making any sales that first time, but I did receive a flattering commentary; a potential customer told the librarian he couldn't afford *any* of the pictures, but, if he could have, he said he would have bought the $12.50 one!

"Anyhow, it was the start for me. I exhibited some more at libraries and then at a large store named Gumps. It was here that I really started to establish myself as a serious artist. My early sales were modest enough, but I began to get newspaper notices, and this is what counts most for a beginner. Eventually I made more contacts and was able to start earning a decent living from my efforts." [Dong Kingman, "Going Professional," *Design*, May-June, 1956.[2]]

1936. "I was assigned to the Watercolor Division of the Works Progress Administration (WPA). I gave up my job, and for the next five years, I was able to concentrate on improving my watercolor technique, to think for myself, and to practice and develop my own style. And for the first time in my life, I had a studio of my own.

"During this period, other fortunate things began to happen. Albert Bender, a San Francisco art collector, bought some of my paintings and gave them to the permanent collections of several important museums, such as the Museum of Modern Art and the Metropolitan Museum of Art in New York City and the San Francisco Museum."[1]

1941. "The WPA Art Project came to an end . . . with America's involvement in World War II. I didn't know what I would do next. But my lucky star smiled again: I won a Guggenheim Fellowship—not for just one year, but for two—and it enabled me to travel across the U.S. to study and paint different cities and to come to New York, where I had a most exciting exhibition at the Midtown Gallery in 1942. The show, my first at the gallery, was very well received. Critics for magazines like *Time, Newsweek, The New Yorker, American Artist,* and *Fortune* all praised my work."[1]

1946. "I felt I had found my place at long last. After the war I moved to New York, set up a studio, and started teaching watercolor classes at Columbia University and Hunter College. Over the years, I've had some difficult times. But whenever I felt discouraged, I would stop and think of how something had always come along which enabled me to continue learning. I would tell myself to have faith and that with time and persistence I could overcome anything. And I did."[1]

Illustrated *The Bamboo Gate: Stories of Children of Modern China,* a children's story written by Vanya Oakes. Throughout his commercial art career, Kingman has illustrated several children's books and a play by Paul Zindel, *The Effect of Gamma Rays on Man-in-the-Moon Marigolds.*

1954. Went on a round-the-world sketching tour. ". . . I deliberately left my camera home because I was afraid I'd spend less time sketching if I took time out to photograph my subjects. But photos and tear sheets from magazines and newspapers, whether in color or black-and-white, are important reference materials. I think every artist should have a good file of these. . . ."[1]

1960. Assisted in production and promotion of the film, "The World of Suzie Wong." "It takes an exceptionally skilled fine artist to make a good commercial artist. One of the reasons there are so few good commercial artists today is due to the fact that many students do not spend enough time while in art school on Anatomy, expression in art, and composition. They become infatuated with a trick technique and place great dependency on the camera, enlarging machines and so forth. They are short-cut mechanics. Most of the commercial artists

(From "Dong Kingman" by June M. Omura in *Wings and Wishes.* Illustrated by Dong Kingman.)

I have known have proved to be alert and up-to-date on all of the arts. . . .

"There is little difference between fine art and commercial art. . . . A successful artist can never be one whose first thought is of financial remuneration. An artist's work will inevitably reveal whether or not there is a lively interest and positive joy in the work for its own sake. Just as surely, if the first thought is 'how much am I going to make out of this?' the artist's work will lack spontaneity and become dull and repetitious." [Dong Kingman, "There's No Secret to Water Color," *Design,* May, 1950.[3] Amended by the author.]

1965. Toured Venice for the first time. ". . . I was so intrigued by the colorful Venetian subjects that I decided the next time I went, I would take along my Thurman Hewitt Painting Workshop. When I did take the group to Venice, in 1971, it was October; most of the tourists had gone home, and the air was getting a little nippy. Most mornings, fog hung low over the canal, and the sun tried hard to break through all day. It reminded me of foggy San Francisco—perfect weather for outdoors sketching because you can see colors and form much better without sunlight and shadow."[1]

1978. Toured China with his wife. "My uncle once took me on an overnight trip to our ancestral village near Canton when I was a child. However, I had not been in mainland China since. . . . My wife and I finally made a trip to China for the first time and saw Peking, the Great Wall, Shanghai, Hangchow, Canton, and many other interesting places. The excitement of being there was beyond my expectations.

"As soon as we reached the base of the Great Wall, I immediately started sketching and let my wife and friends do the walking up the giant steps. . . . When I sketched in the figures, I was thinking of Rudyard Kipling. While the people of the People's Republic of China look east, all the foreigners look west."[1]

For outdoor sketching "I use three or four good, round sable watercolor brushes (small, medium, and large). Sometimes a Chinese brush works very well, too. I choose about nine tubes of the best made watercolors. I prefer it in the tube, as it keeps fresher that way. My palette of colors is composed of the following: cadmium yellow, orange; Winsor red, green; alizarin crimson; burnt sienna; sepia; and ivory black. With these pigments I can mix almost any color or shade I desire. I keep the brushes and tubes in a tin watercolor box. I carry a folding chair and a small water container which are both kept in a knapsack. I ordinarily paint on one of two sizes (15″ x 22″ or 22″ x 30″) of either a good thick watercolor paper or watercolor board, for they are both easy to handle.

"The actual working method that I like best is to complete about one-half of the painting at the scene of the subject. With the aid of sketches, the rest of the work is finished in the studio."[3]

Kingman draws largely on his surroundings for inspiration. "Since I've lived in cities all my life, it's only natural that I would be most familiar with busy urban scenes—street scenes, waterfronts, parks and picnic grounds, etc.—and the people, vehicles, and architecture within them. Amid the profusion of telephone poles, traffic signals, bicycles and cars, and new and old buildings is where I find the subjects that interest me the most. In fact, I've been living with these twentieth-century phenomena for so long that I often wonder if I could ever live without them!

"Sometimes I do run out of inspiration or ideas. But when this happens, I stop my work and just go for a walk down the street or sit for a while on a bench near Central Park, quietly observing the people and scenery before me. Slowly but surely, I become charged with excitement again, my inspiration returns, and I go back to my studio and continue my work."[1]

FOR MORE INFORMATION SEE: San Francisco News, April 4, 1936; *Life,* October 27, 1941, May 14, 1951, February 14, 1955; *American Artist,* February, 1943, September, 1947, February, 1955, June, 1958, September, 1961, April, 1969, January, 1982, February, 1983; *Design,* May, 1950, October, 1952, May-June, 1956; *Time,* May 28, 1951, January 25, 1960; Alan D. Gruskin, *The Watercolors of Dong Kingman,* introduction by William Saroyan, Studio, 1958; *New York Herald Tribune,* November 14, 1961; Dong Kingman and Helena Kuo Kingman, *Dong Kingman's Watercolors,* Watson-Guptill, 1980.

Motion pictures: "Dong Kingman Paints a Watercolor," Harmon Foundation, 1946; "Art in Action with Dong Kingman," Harmon Foundation, 1950; "Dong Kingman," Living Artists Productions, 1955; "The Scroll," U.S. Information Agency, 1956; "Hongkong Dong," Twenty-Second Century Films, 1975.

KLEIN, Gerda Weissmann 1924-

PERSONAL: Born May 8, 1924, in Bielsko, Poland; daughter of Julius (a business executive) and Helene (a homemaker; maiden name, Mueckenbrunn) Weissmann; married Kurt Klein (a printer), June 18, 1947; children: Vivian (Mrs. James Ullman), Leslie (Mrs. Roger Simon), James Arthur. *Education:*

GERDA WEISSMANN KLEIN

You see, Jenny is different. ■ (From *The Blue Rose* by Gerda Klein. Photograph by Norma Holt.)

Attended Notre Dame Gymnasium, Bielsko, Poland. *Religion:* Jewish. *Residence:* Kenmore, N.Y.

CAREER: Author and lecturer. Founder and honorary chairman of several educational, civic, and philanthropic organizations, including the Blue Rose Foundation and Silver Circle of Rosary Hill College; member of board, United Jewish Appeal, Holocaust Commission, and others. *Awards, honors:* Recipient of numerous public honors; Woman of the Year Award, Council of Jewish Women, 1974; D.H.L., Rosary Hill College and Our Lady of Holy Cross, both 1974; Homanitaria Citation from Trocaire College; special award for Year of the Child from D'Youville College.

WRITINGS—For children, except as indicated: *All But My Life* (adult autobiography), Hill & Wang, 1957; *The Blue Rose* (illustrated with photographs by Norma Holt), Lawrence Hill, 1974; *Promise of a New Spring: The Holocaust and Renewal* (illustrated by Vincent Tartaro), Rossel Books, 1981. Also author of television scripts and biographical booklets; author of weekly column "Stories for Young Readers" in *Buffalo Sunday News.*

WORK IN PROGRESS: A biography of Edith Rosenwald Stern.

SIDELIGHTS: Klein was fifteen years old when German Nazi forces invaded her native land of Poland during World War II. She and her family were among the millions of Jews deported to concentration camps. The bitter years of her struggle for survival are recounted in her first book, *All But My Life.* Published in 1957, the book was praised by critics who compared its sensitivity and compassion to *The Diary of Anne Frank.* The British War Museum utilizes Klein's autobiographical account as a reference work on European history, while parts of the book have appeared in a series of secondary school texts throughout the United States.

As a survivor of Hitler's concentration camps, Klein has assumed the task of explaining to children of succeeding generations this story of man's inhumanity to man. In *Promise of a New Spring,* she presents the horrors of the Holocaust to young readers by using the allegory of a forest fire that cruelly and completely destroys all in its path. With eloquent, poetic images, Klein describes how it is possible for life to renew itself in the aftermath of destruction—be it plant, animal, or the human soul.

Klein comments about her writing. "People always want to know about the Holocaust. My feeling is that most of the time it is told only in terms of its horror and not much about the humanity and friendship that prevailed.

"Having been where I've been and lost what I've lost, I see all of that and I must come to a certain awe. It is a question of why I have the privilege of being alive and what price that needs to be paid. When I think about all the things that I try to do I come to one important conclusion: I must make people see how great being alive really is!" ["Book Reviews," *Elul-Tishri,* September-October, 1982.]

KYTE, Kathy S. 1946-

BRIEF ENTRY: Born June 5, 1946, in Reno, Nev. Kyte graduated from Lewis and Clark College and earned her M.F.A. in creative writing at the University of Iowa. Now a full-time writer, she has worked briefly in college administration and public relations and devoted a large portion of her life to being a student/wife/mother. It was while she was preparing a college paper that Kyte became interested in the "latchkey kids" of America, those children who are left at home without supervision while their parents are at work. Discovering a lack of books or self-help guides on the subject, Kyte decided to write one of her own. The result was *In Charge: A Complete Handbook for Kids with Working Parents* (Knopf, 1983). *School Library Journal* called it "invaluable . . . a clear, brief, and witty handbook."

Although the book is intended for young adolescents, critics agree that people of all ages can find useful tips within its pages. Among the topics discussed by Kyte are organizing chores and jobs, safety measures, crime prevention, medical emergencies, meal planning, and doing the laundry. *Horn Book* observed that even though "many mothers might eye all this with weary cynicism . . . the ideas are practical and the implementation sensible." As a direct result of her research for *In Charge,* Kyte produced *Play It Safe: The Kids' Guide to Personal Safety and Crime Prevention* (Knopf, 1983) and *The Kids' Complete Guide to Money* (Knopf, 1984). According to Kyte, her books "all are concerned with giving kids more control over their lives in a world that is increasingly confusing and complex." Currently, she is at work on two nonfiction children's books and an adult novel. *Address:* P.O. Box 575, Iowa City, Iowa 52244.

LARRECQ, John M(aurice) 1926-1980

PERSONAL: Born April 10, 1926, in Santa Rosa, Calif.; died October 4, 1980; married; children: Andrea, Matthew. *Education:* California College of Arts and Crafts, B.A., 1952. *Residence:* Mill Valley, Calif.

CAREER: Staff artist, Kaiser Industries, 1953; free-lance illustrator and graphic designer, operator of own studio in San Francisco, Calif. Instructor, California College of Arts and Crafts and Academy of Art Institute of San Francisco. Work has been exhibited in shows in San Francisco, Calif., Los Angeles, Calif., and New York, N.Y. *Military service:* Served in the U.S. Air Force. *Awards, honors: Reasons and Raisins* was selected for the American Institute of Graphic Arts children's book show, 1971-72.

ILLUSTRATOR—All for children: Edward Ormondroyd, *Theodore* (ALA Notable Book; *Horn Book* honor list), Parnassus, 1966; Theodora Kroeber, *A Green Christmas* (*Horn Book* honor list), Parnassus, 1967; Crawford Kilian, *Wonders, Inc.,* Parnassus, 1968; E. Ormondroyd, *Broderick,* Parnassus, 1969; John Sparks, *Moe Takes the Cake,* Parnassus, 1970; E. Ormondroyd, *Theodore's Rival,* Parnassus, 1971; Josephine Aldridge and Richard Aldridge, *Reasons and Raisins,* Parnassus, 1972; Sonia Levitin, *Who Owns the Moon?,* Parnassus, 1973; Ellen Conford, *Just the Thing for Geraldine,* Little, Brown, 1974; S. Levitin, *A Single Speckled Egg,* Parnassus, 1976; E. Conford, *Eugene the Brave* (Junior Literary Guild selection), Little, Brown, 1978.

ADAPTATIONS—Filmstrips with record or cassette; produced by BFA Educational Media, 1976: "Theodore"; "Broderick."

SIDELIGHTS: An award-winning illustrator and graphic artist, Larrecq made his home throughout his lifetime in California. He was born in Santa Rosa, California, grew up in Santa Cruz, attended college in Oakland, and operated his own studio in San Francisco.

There was nothing Geraldine liked better than hanging by her tail from the branch of a tree and juggling a few acorns. ■ (From *Just the Thing for Geraldine* by Ellen Conford. Illustrated by John Larrecq.)

Larrecq's artistic talent led to travel in Japan, the Philippines, and Central America while he was an artist for the U.S. Air Force. Later, as a free-lance illustrator, he won awards for his illustrations in Art Directors' and Society of Illustrators' shows in both Los Angeles and San Francisco. In addition to free-lance illustration, Larrecq executed advertising designs, and was the designer of two overseas air mail stamps. He taught classes in book illustration at the Academy of Art Institute of San Francisco, and was an instructor at the College of Arts and Crafts in Oakland.

In the late 1960s and into the 1970s Larrecq illustrated books for children, thus gaining distinction in that field. He produced illustrations for a total of eleven popular children's books, many of which received awards. He died on October 4, 1980.

FOR MORE INFORMATION SEE: Martha E. Ward and Dorothy A. Marquardt, editors, *Illustrators of Books for Young People,* second edition, Scarecrow, 1975; Lee Kingman and others, compilers, *Illustrators of Children's Books: 1967-1976,* Horn Book, 1978. Obituaries: *School Library Journal,* March, 1981; *Horn Book,* April, 1981.

A three-year-old child is a being who gets almost as much fun out of a fifty-six dollar set of swings as it does out of finding a small green worm.

—Bill Vaughan

LAURÉ, Jason 1940-

BRIEF ENTRY: Born October 15, 1940, in Chehalis, Wash. Free-lance photojournalist and author of books for young people. Lauré attended Los Angeles City College, Columbia University, and Sorbonne, University of Paris. He began his career working as a copywriter for the *New York Times,* and since 1968 has been a free-lance photojournalist. During his career, he served as a photographer on a presidential mission to Latin America, accompanied UNICEF's mission among the nomads of the African Sahara, and was an official correspondent in Bangladesh. About 1972, Lauré was nominated for a Pulitzer Prize for photography for pictures of Bangladesh published in the *New York Times.*

All of Lauré's books are documentaries illustrated with his photographs and written with Ettagale Lauré. Each one focuses on the lives of individual young people trying to cope with difficult circumstances. In *Joi Bangla! The Children of Bangladesh* (Farrar, Straus, 1974), nine adolescents share their experiences of living in Bangladesh following the war that led to that country's independence. *Booklist* observed, "Remarkably emotive black-and-white photos . . . [add] visual impact to this arresting documentary." Similarly, *Best Sellers* found the text in *Jovem Portugal: After the Revolution* (Farrar, Straus, 1977) "accompanied by masterful photos." *Publishers Weekly* further remarked, ". . . This affecting document provides a rare glimpse of life in Portugal. . . ." Critics also praised Lauré's work in *South Africa: Coming of Age under Apartheid* (Farrar, Straus, 1980), named a notable book by the American Library Association. "... [The authors'] use of personal testimony," *Booklist* stated, "lends an immediacy historical treatments cannot duplicate." *School Library Journal* added, "The black-and-white photographs capture the brutality of the South African system; but also, overwhelmingly, the spiritedness and beauty of individual young people." Lauré is also the author of award-winning filmstrips, including "Bangladesh: Birth of a Nation," and "Zero Population Growth." *Home:* 8 West 13th St., New York, N.Y. 10011.

FOR MORE INFORMATION SEE: Contemporary Authors, Volume 104, Gale, 1982.

LAZARE, Gerald John 1927-
(Jerry Lazare)

PERSONAL: Born September 25, 1927, in Toronto, Ontario, Canada; children: a son. *Education:* Attended high school in Toronto; studied art in Paris and London, about 1952.

CAREER: Free-lance artist and illustrator, 1955—. Illustrator of comic strips during World War II. *Awards, honors:* Child Study Children's Book Award, 1967, and George G. Stone Center Recognition of Merit Award, 1974, both for *Queenie Peavy.*

ILLUSTRATOR—All for young people; all under name Jerry Lazare: Jean Little, *Home from Far*, Little, Brown, 1965; Robert Burch, *Queenie Peavy* (*Horn Book* honor list; ALA Notable Book; with record and cassette), Viking, 1966; Monica Dickens, *My Fair Lady*, Four Winds, 1967; Elinor Lyon, *Secret of Hermit's Bay*, Follett, 1967; Dorothy B. Francis, *Mystery of*

(From *Queenie Peavy* by Robert Burch. Illustrated by Jerry Lazare.)

the Forgotten Map, Follett, 1968; J. Little, *Take Wing* (Junior Literary Guild selection), Little, Brown, 1968; J. Little, *One to Grow On,* Little, Brown, 1969; William MacKellar, *Mystery of Mordach Castle,* Follett, 1970.

SIDELIGHTS: Lazare is a self-taught artist. "The only [art] training I received was at the age of twenty-one when I enrolled in the Famous Artists Course. I began professionally by illustrating comic strips during World War II when I was sixteen. The greatest impetus to my work came when I studied on my own for a year in Paris and London at the age of twenty-five." [Lee Kingman and others, compilers, *Illustrators of Children's Books: 1957-1966,* Horn Book, 1968.[1]]

A free-lance artist since 1955, Lazare works in advertising and magazine and book illustration. "A good book to illustrate is the most satisfying. The feeling of permanence that a book has is very rewarding. I spend most of my time working in my studio on the third floor of our house in Toronto. I like jazz, especially Duke Ellington, whose music I often play while working; and looking at any painting by Edgar Degas is my particular kind of heaven."[1]

FOR MORE INFORMATION SEE: Lee Kingman and others, compilers, *Illustrators of Children's Books: 1957-1966,* Horn Book, 1968; Martha E. Ward and Dorothy A. Marquardt, *Illustrators of Books for Young People,* 2nd edition, Scarecrow, 1975.

LEE, Doris (Emrick) 1905-1983

PERSONAL: Born February 1, 1905, in Aledo, Ill.; died June 16, 1983, in Clearwater, Fla.; daughter of Edward Everett (a merchant and banker) and Nancy May (a teacher; maiden name, Love) Emrick; married Russell Warner Lee, August 25, 1927 (divorced, 1939); married Arnold Blanch (an artist and teacher), 1941 (died, 1968). *Education:* Rockford College, A.B., 1927; graduate study at Kansas City Art Institute, 1928-29, in Europe with André Lhote, 1931, and with Arnold Blanch at California School of Fine Art, 1931. *Politics:* Democrat. *Religion:* Presbyterian. *Residence:* Woodstock, N.Y.

CAREER: Artist, 1929-83. Numerous commissioned works, including "Rural Postal Delivery" (mural) for the U.S. Post Office, 1936; scenes for Rogers' and Hammerstein's play "Oklahoma!," 1944; and pictorial essays for *Life* magazine, 1945, 1946, 1952. Guest lecturer at several institutions, including Colorado Springs Fine Art Center, Michigan State University, and the University of Hawaii. *Exhibitions:* Whitney Museum of American Art, New York, N.Y., 1932, 1934, 1936, 1937-40, 1960-61; Carnegie Museum, Pittsburgh, Penn., 1937-40. One-man shows: Walker Gallery, New York, N.Y., 1936, 1940; Association of American Artists, 1954; World House, New York, N.Y., 1965. Permanent collections: Metropolitan Museum of Art, Philipps Memorial Gallery, Art Institute of Chicago, Pennsylvania Academy of Fine Arts, Albright Museum, Providence School of Design, Mt. Holyoke Museum, University of Nebraska, Library of Congress, Smithsonian Museum, and others.

MEMBER: American Artists Congress, American Society of Painters, Sculptors, and Gravers, Woodstock Art Association (president, 1952). *Awards, honors:* First prize from the American annual exhibit at the Chicago Art Institute, 1935; Logan Gold Medal from the Chicago Art Institute, 1936, for the painting "Thanksgiving Dinner"; second prize from the Worcester (Mass.) Biennial Exhibit, 1937; *New York Herald*

Tribune's Children's Spring Book Festival Award, 1939, for *The Hired Man's Elephant;* Jennie Sesnan Landscape Medal from the Pennsylvania Academy of Fine Arts, 1943, for the painting "Shore Leave"; third prize from the Carnegie Art Institute, 1944, for the painting "Siesta"; New York Art Di-

rector Award of Merit, 1946, 1950; LL.D. from Rockford College, 1948; Lit.D. from Russell Sage College, 1954; Gold Medal from the Art Directors Club (New York), 1957; Berkshire Painting Prize from the New England Show, 1964; first prize in the Art and Science Exhibition, 1966.

DORIS LEE

(From *The Great Quillow* by James Thurber. Illustrated by Doris Lee.)

WRITINGS: (With husband, Arnold Blanch) *Methods and Techniques for Gouache Painting,* American Artists, 1946; (with A. Blanch) *Painting for Enjoyment,* Tudor, 1947, published as *It's Fun to Paint: Painting for Enjoyment,* c. 1961.

Illustrator: Philip D. Stong, *The Hired Man's Elephant* (juvenile), Dodd, 1939; James B. Cabell and A. J. Hanna, *The St. Johns: A Parade of Diversities,* Farrar, 1943; James Thurber, *The Great Quillow* (juvenile), Harcourt, 1944, reprinted, 1975; Walter D. Edmonds, *Mr. Benedict's Lion* (juvenile), Dodd, 1950; Richard Rodgers, *Rodgers and Hart Song Book,* Simon & Schuster, 1951; Dorothy Koch, *Gone Is My Goose* (juvenile), 1956; Lillian Morrison, editor, *Touch Blue* (juvenile), Crowell, 1958.

SIDELIGHTS: Lee's works are included in the Kerlan Collection at the University of Minnesota.

FOR MORE INFORMATION SEE: Life, May 12, 1947, November 10, 1952; Peyton Boswell, *Modern American Painting,* Dodd, 1948; *Current Biography,* January, 1954; "Studio Home of Arnold Blanch and Doris Lee," *American Artist,* April, 1955; Bertha E. Miller and others, compilers, *Illustrators of Children's Books: 1946-1956,* Horn Book, 1958; Mary Ann Guitar, *Twenty-Two Famous Painters and Illustrators Tell How They Work,* McKay, 1965; Hugo Munsterberg, *History of Women Artists,* Potter, 1975. Obituaries: *New York Times,* June 18, 1983.

When the first baby laughed for the first time, the laugh broke into a thousand pieces and they all went skipping about, and that was the beginning of fairies.

—Sir James Matthew Barrie
(From *Peter Pan*)

LISKER, Sonia O. 1933-

PERSONAL: Born March 22, 1933, in New York, N.Y.; daughter of Nat and Mrs. Olson; married Anthony Gargagliano (a commercial art studio owner), 1964; children: Shawn, Carla, Arlen, Emily, Peter. *Education:* Cooper Union, graduate, 1954. *Home and office:* 72 Cooper Lane, Larchmont, N.Y. 10538.

CAREER: Young & Rubicam, Inc. (advertising agency), New York, N.Y., television art director and writer, 1954-59; free-lance illustrator, 1959; writer; free-lance television art director, 1980—. Guest teacher at College of New Rochelle, 1971—; art consultant for Westchester, N.Y. public schools, 1982-83; guest teacher at University of Massachusetts, 1983. *Member:* Authors Guild. *Awards, honors:* Art Directors awards, 1957, 1958, for television commercials; *The Attic Witch* was chosen as a Children's Book of the Year, 1973, by the Child Study Association of America, and *The House on Pendleton Block* was chosen, 1975.

WRITINGS—For children; all self-illustrated: *I Can Be,* Hastings House, 1972; *The Attic Witch,* Four Winds, 1973; *I Am,* Hastings Hosue, 1973; *Lost,* Harcourt, 1975; (with Leigh Dean) *Two Special Cards,* Harcourt, 1976; *I Used To,* Four Winds, 1977.

Illustrator: Judy Blume, *Freckle Juice,* Four Winds, 1971; Seymour Simon, *Water on Your Street,* Holiday House, 1974; Ann Waldron, *The House on Pendleton Block,* Hastings House, 1975; (with Leo Summers) Margaret Davidson, *Seven True Horse Stories,* Hastings House, 1979; Ada B. Litchfield, *Captain Hook, That's Me,* Walker, 1982.

Illustrator of filmstrips including "Kneeknock Rise," 1977, "Noonday Friends," 1978, and "Mr. Popper's Penguins," 1979, all produced by Miller-Brody.

ADAPTATIONS: "Celebrate the Sky" (one-act musical play written by Mia Fazio Truxaw and Marilyn Weitz; based on books *I Can Be, I Am,* and *I Used To*), first produced at California State University Teenage Drama Workshop, 1985.

WORK IN PROGRESS: Grandpa Magic; The Not-So-Wicked Stepmother; That Monkey; School Day (a play).

SIDELIGHTS: "I was always interested in drawing and my parents, believing they were encouraging me, bought me coloring books. Probably an early disappointment to them, I refused to color within the lines, and drew pictures around the printed pictures, as well as my own designs on any white space available. I drew on the brown bags from the grocery store and the white papers that came with my mother's new stockings. I used up all the scratch pads that were kept near the telephone and eventually my parents realized that I needed more and more paper. They bought it and I filled pages with drawings and paintings.

"Fortunately my regional high school, Abraham Lincoln High School in Brooklyn, had a very strong arts program. My parents, having lived through a great depression, thought it best for me to take courses in bookkeeping, stenography and typing because they never imagined one could earn a living doing drawings, . . . but I was able to sit in on art classes during my free period and my lunch period and I joined the Art Squad

SONIA O. LISKER

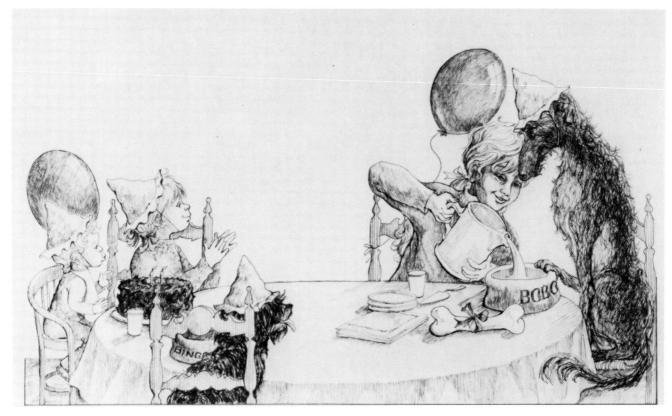

Back home, they all sang "Happy Birthday" to Bobo. ■ (From *Two Special Cards* by Sonia O. Lisker and Leigh Dean. Illustrated by Sonia O. Lisker.)

after school. With the encouragement of the art teacher, Leon Friend, I started entering contests and even winning some.

"One time I received an award for winning more 'Scholastic' medals than anyone in Brooklyn. I thought it was funny to get an award for getting other awards but all this notice helped convince my parents that I was serious about art and they let me stay up as late as I wanted to, to work on my drawings and paintings. They sent me to an art class at the Brooklyn Museum on Saturday mornings and I won a scholarship to an art class at the Museum of Modern Art on Saturday afternoons.

"Abraham Lincoln High School also afforded me the opportunity to take special English classes. One year the special class was 'poetry,' another year, 'creative writing.' I studied sculpture and did my first 'Mother and Child' in mahogany. I helped write the senior play and designed the sets. . . . But I failed bookkeeping and typing and stenography and almost didn't graduate.

"Through the help of some compassionate guidance people I was given 'credit' for all those extra classes I had taken and was able to squeeze out of high school. At graduation I received a medal for 'outstanding achievement in writing and art.'

"Once I was in Cooper Union, a merit scholarship school, I felt as if I had gone to heaven. I majored in advertising design but was able to take a basic foundation course where I studied architecture, sculpture, and painting. My confidence restored after those failures in high school, I was able to go out into the world and began to find out how many ways I could apply all that I had learned.

"My first career was in advertising. I became an assistant and then the first woman to be a television art director in an advertising agency. I've never really left advertising and still write and design television commercials.

"I started writing and illustrating books when my children were young and I was at home. After making a portfolio of illustrations, I took it around to various publishers. One of the first manuscripts I received to illustrate was *Freckle Juice* by Judy Blume. In one sequence I drew two children passing notes back and forth to each other until one reaches out too far and falls off his seat. It was drawn very much the way a storyboard is planned for a film and the sense of animation it gave the book was a favorite with my children, Judy Blume's children and others I've spoken to. That storyboard technique was used again in *The Attic Witch, Lost, Two Special Cards,* and *Captain Hook, That's Me.*

"The first book I wrote and illustrated, *I Can Be,* came out of listening to my own children play imagination games and remembering such games from my own childhood. I still didn't think of myself as a writer, and because I didn't expect to write any more books, I dedicated this one to all my five children.

"When I found out the doctor kit I wanted to buy for one of my daughters had a picture of a boy on it, and only the nurse's kit had a picture of a girl, I wrote a book which rebelled against old career boundaries. *I Am* showed both boys and girls (even alligators) as doctors and nurses, boys who diapered babies (and animals), girls who were astronauts, delivered mail or were milkwomen. All this has now come to pass, but in 1973 it was still pretty radical.

Some people say I'm handicapped. I suppose I am but I don't think about it much. I'm too busy.
■ (From *Captain Hook, That's Me* by Ada B. Litchfield. Illustrated by Sonia O. Lisker.)

"When we moved into a big old house, one of my daughters had a trap door on the ceiling of the closet in her room. We were all curious about what could be behind this mysterious door, so I stood up on a chair, got a strong wooden hanger and moved the door aside, but alas—there was only dust and wiring and insulation. We were all disappointed and we talked about what might have been behind the trap door. As a result, I wrote the wordless book, *The Attic Witch.*

"Later, I met a reading teacher who had seventy foster children in her school. She needed a book with a sad plot and no words. She wanted to use it as a tool to help them release some of the sadness within them. This interested me. I thought of how lost they must feel.

"Everyone has had the feeling of being lost in some way or other. One way of being lost could be in a large family. I used my own family and friends as the models for *Lost*, and even an old family toy, a monkey puppet, plays a key role in the book about the boy who gets lost in the zoo.

"Some books are easier to write and illustrate than others. The most difficult book I ever worked on was *Two Special Cards* which is about a little girl whose parents are getting a divorce. When a local librarian said she needed such a book, I thought about it and called a co-writer, Leigh Dean. It was a hard book for me to write because it brought back some unhappy memories. I had been divorced many years before when I had two little daughters. I tried to write the book *I* could have used at the time. According to the mail I receive, it has helped many

people. This book was used as a resource in a 'divorce workshop' given in the Westchester schools.

"In 1964 I married again—a wonderful man with two children. Combined with mine that gave us four, and a year later we had another child—a houseful of five children, and the pets followed. At one time we had hamsters, gerbils, a guinea pig, a rabbit and a tankful of tropical fish and a Scottish deer hound. They've all been my models at one time or another as have my husband, the children and our friends.

"As a suburban mother of many, I've driven my share of carpools and it was while doing this that I overheard five- and six-year-olds, mine and others, reminiscing about what they used to think and dream about when they were very young— way back then. *I Used To* was born.

"It was fascinating to do the research and illustrate the book *Captain Hook, That's Me* by Ada B. Litchfield. It's the story of a girl who had a steel hook instead of a left hand. In doing the research, I met a bio-engineer who makes devices for children who need artificial hands or legs and I met some very courageous children. It's this kind of experience that is one of the wonderful benefits of doing the work I do.

"Right now there are a couple of books in the works, a play for children, and a series of children's programs in the planning stage.

"Many people ask if I write for my children, and now for my grandchildren. I don't. I write for myself. I think most authors write for the children in themselves."

MacINNES, Helen   1907-1985
(Helen Highet)

OBITUARY NOTICE—See sketch in *SATA* Volume 22: Born October 7, 1907, in Glasgow, Scotland; came to the United States in 1937; became naturalized citizen in 1951; died September 30, 1985, in N.Y. Novelist. MacInnes was regarded as one of the masters of the suspense novel genre. Her best-selling novels of international espionage sold over twenty million copies in the United States alone and were translated into more than twenty-two languages. MacInnes gained immediate success with the publication of her first novel, *Above Suspicion,* in 1941. She became known for her complex plots of intrigue, romantic European settings, and the "ordinary" characters she created to resist oppression. MacInnes wrote a total of twenty-one novels during her career, including *Horizon, North from Rome, The Double Image, The Snare of the Hunter,* and *Cloak of Darkness.* Four of her works—*Above Suspicion, Assignment in Brittany, The Venetian Affair,* and *The Salzburg Connection*—were successfully adapted to film. With her husband, Gilbert Highet, she translated *Sexual Life in Ancient Rome* by Otto Kiefer. *Residence:* East Hampton, N.Y.

FOR MORE INFORMATION SEE: Contemporary Authors, New Revision Series, Volume 1, Gale, 1981; *Contemporary Literary Criticism,* Volume 27, Gale, 1984; *The Writers Directory: 1984-86,* St. James Press, 1984. Obituaries: *Publishers Weekly,* October 11, 1985.

MALI, Jane Lawrence   1937-

BRIEF ENTRY: Born June 2, 1937, in New York, N.Y. Co-author of books for children and homemaker. Mali and her co-author, Alison Cragin Herzig, met through their children at nursery school. Their joint writing career began following the unfortunate death of one of the young teachers. "Alison came to me with the suggestion that we try to make some kind of sense out of that tragedy," related Mali. "The resulting manuscript still lies at the bottom of a drawer, but after composing it we were hooked on writing." Their first published work was *A Word to the Wise* (Little, Brown, 1978), an amusing story about a group of middle-grade losers who discover a world of words in a pilfered thesaurus. Next came *Oh, Boy! Babies!* (Little, Brown, 1980), which earned them the 1981 National Book Award for children's nonfiction. *Oh, Boy! Babies!* records the events in an all boys' school where fifth and sixth graders learn infant care by using real babies. *Booklist* described it as an "amusing photojournal . . . [with] a fine sense of the eagerness and awkwardness the boys displayed," while *School Library Journal* noted that it "is sorely needed in a world of changing stereotypes." Mali and Herzig have collaborated on two additional works of fiction published by Little, Brown: *A Season of Secrets* (1982) and *Thaddeus* (1984). Although Mali has completed four children's books, she confesses, "I cannot say I always wanted to be a writer. . . . Even now I consider myself a writer only until my children come home, at which time I rather happily lapse back into being a homemaker." *Home and office:* 147 West 15th St., New York, N.Y. 10011.

FOR MORE INFORMATION SEE: Contemporary Authors, Volume 114, Gale, 1985.

A man's studies pass into his character.

—Proverb

MANSON, Beverlie   1945-

BRIEF ENTRY: Born June 10, 1945, in Manchester, England. Prior to becoming a free-lance writer and illustrator of children's books in 1969, Manson worked as a fashion artist as well as a book illustrator for World Distributors in Manchester. She began her free-lance career as illustrator of *My Little Book of Birthdays* (Tyndall Mitchell, 1969) and *The Storybook Annual* (Purnell, 1970). Her more recent works include three fairy books published in the United States by Doubleday. Manson supplied both texts and illustrations for *The Fairies' Alphabet Book* (1982) and *The Fairies' Nighttime Book* (1983), while her illustrations were used in *Fairy Poems for the Very Young* (1982). The latter is a collection of verse reprinted from children's books and magazines dating from the 1920s and 1930s. "I try to make books that make people smile, and even giggle, a little," revealed Manson. "My pictures have so much going on that the child will spend a long time finding new things." Among the books she has illustrated are Stella Lillian's *Sing a Song, Susie* (Lutterworth Press, 1972), Lornie Leete-Hodge's *The Big Golden Book of Fairy Tales* (Golden Press, 1981), and Mimi Khalvati's *I Know a Place* (Dent, 1985). In addition to children's books, Manson is an illustrator of greeting cards and textiles. *Home:* 11 Southwood Ave., London N.6, England.

FOR MORE INFORMATION SEE: Contemporary Authors, Volume 113, Gale, 1985.

MARTIN, Ann M(atthews)   1955-
(Ann Matthews)

PERSONAL: Born August 12, 1955, in Princeton, N.J.; daughter of Henry Read (an artist) and Edith (a teacher; maiden name, Matthews) Martin. *Education:* Smith College, A.B. (cum laude), 1977. *Politics:* Independent. *Home:* New York, N.Y. *Agent:* Amy Berkower, Writers House, Inc., 21 W. 23rd St., New York, N.Y. 10010.

CAREER: Plumfield School, Noroton, Conn., teacher, 1977-78; Pocket Books, Inc., New York City, editorial assistant for Archway Paperbacks, 1978-80; Scholastic Book Services, Teen Age Book Club, New York City, copywriter, 1980-81, associate editor, 1981-83, editor, 1983; Bantam Books, Inc., New York City, senior editor, Books for Young Readers, 1983-85; writer and free-lance editor, 1985—. *Member:* Authors Guild, Society of Children's Book Writers.

WRITINGS—For children: *Bummer Summer,* Holiday House, 1983; *Just You and Me,* Scholastic Book Services, 1983; (with Betsy Ryan) *My Puppy Scrapbook: Featuring Fenwick* (illustrated by Henry Martin), Scholastic Book Services, 1983; *Inside Out,* Holiday House, 1984; *Stage Fright* (illustrated by Blanche Sims), Holiday House, 1984; *Me and Katie (the Pest),* Holiday House, 1985; *With You, Without You,* Holiday House, 1986; *Missing Since Monday,* Holiday House, 1986.

WORK IN PROGRESS: The Babysitters Club for Scholastic Book Services, about four twelve-year-old girls who form a babysitting service and survive the ups and downs of friendship and partnership in a lighthearted mini-series.

SIDELIGHTS: "I grew up in a very imaginative family. My mother was a preschool teacher and my father, an artist. Both liked fantasy and children's literature, so my world was one of circuses, animals, Beatrix Potter, *Winnie-the-Pooh, The Wizard of Oz,* elves and gnomes and fairies. It was a lot of

I stood in front of the bathroom mirror and decided I looked like a real horsewoman. I looked professional. ■ (From *Me and Katie (the Pest)* by Ann M. Martin. Illustrated by Blanche Sims.)

ANN M. MARTIN

fun, and it stayed with me. I'm often off in some other world, and all my daydreaming goes into my books. Someday I'd like to write a fantasy.

"One of the most important tools I use in my writing is my memory. It is very clear. I can remember what that first day of kindergarten was like—the way the room looked, the children, how I felt when my mother left. And I remember my senior prom and my tenth birthday and vacations at the shore and junior high graduation just as clearly. Little things, too—making a bulletin board display in sixth grade and making doll clothes and playing statue after dinner on hot summer nights. It's just as important to be able to transport oneself back to childhood as it is to have a vivid imagination, in order to write believable children's books.

"When I speak through my young characters, I am remembering and reliving: redoing all those things one is never supposed to be able to redo, having a chance to play out the 'if onlys.'

"Some of my books are based on actual experiences; others are based more on imagination, and memories of feelings. *Inside Out* was based on my experiences working with autistic children. *Me and Katie (the Pest)* is loosely based on riding lessons I took in third grade. On the other hand, *Bummer Summer* is about a first overnight camp experience, and I never went to camp. (I was afraid to go.) *With You, Without You* is about the death of a parent, and my parents are still living.

"I turned to writing as an outlet for both my emotions and humor. I feel I'm more articulate and funnier on paper, but the more I write, the more comfortable I become speaking. It's a delightfully vicious cycle. The marriage of my love for children's literature with this cycle makes for a continually gratifying creative process.

"My hobbies are reading and needlework, especially smocking and knitting. I like being with people, but I am very happy alone, and prefer quiet and solitude to noise and excitement. I love animals and have one cat, a marmalade tabby named Mouse, who likes water and sometimes curls up for a nap in the bathroom sink. I usually put cats in my books, and plan to write a book from a cat's point of view."

McGINLEY, Phyllis 1905-1978

PERSONAL: Born March 21, 1905, in Ontario, Ore.; died of a stroke, February 22, 1978, in New York, N.Y.; daughter of Daniel (a land speculator) and Julia (Kiesel) McGinley; married Charles L. Hayden (a New York Telephone Co. executive), June 25, 1937 (died, 1972); children: Julia Elizabeth, Phyllis Louise. *Education:* University of Utah, graduate, 1927; attended University of California. *Religion:* Roman Catholic.

CAREER: Poet, essayist and author of children's books. Taught school in Utah for one year; before marriage held an assort-

PHYLLIS McGINLEY

ment of jobs in New York, including copywriter for an advertising agency, teacher in New Rochelle, and staff writer for *Town and Country*. *Member:* National Institute of Arts and Letters, Poetry Society of America, P.E.N., Catholic Poetry Society, Kappa Kappa Gamma, Cosmopolitan Club of New York City.

AWARDS, HONORS: All Around the Town, 1949, and *The Most Wonderful Doll in the World*, 1951, were selected as Caldecott Honor Books; Christopher Book Award, and Edna St. Vincent Millay Memorial Award, both 1955, both for *The Love Letters of Phyllis McGinley;* Catholic Writers Guild Award, 1955; St. Catherine of Sienna Medal, 1956; D.Litt., Wheaton College (Norton, Mass.), 1956, St. Mary's College (Notre Dame, Ind.), 1958, Marquette University, 1960, Dartmouth College, 1961, Boston College, 1962, Wilson College, 1964, Smith College, 1964, and St. John's University, 1964; Catholic Institute of the Press Award, 1960; Pulitzer Prize, 1961, and National Association of Independent Schools Award, 1961, both for *Times Three: Selected Verse from Three Decades;* Golden Book Award; Spirit Gold Medal, Catholic Poetry Society of America, 1962; Laetare Medal from University of Notre Dame, 1964; *Wonderful Time* was selected as one of *New York Times* Best Illustrated Books of the Year, 1966; Campion Award, 1967; *Wonders and Surprises: A Collection of Poems* was selected one of Child Study Association's Children's Books of the Year, 1968.

WRITINGS—Juvenile: *The Horse Who Lived Upstairs* (illustrated by Helen Stone), Lippincott, 1944; *The Plain Princess* (ALA Notable Book; illustrated by H. Stone), Lippincott, 1945; *All Around the Town* (illustrated by H. Stone), Lippincott, 1948; *A Name for Kitty* (illustrated by Feodor Rojankovsky), Simon & Schuster, 1948; *The Most Wonderful Doll in the World* (illustrated by H. Stone), Lippincott, 1950; *The Horse Who Had His Picture in the Paper* (illustrated by H. Stone), Lippincott, 1951; *Blunderbus* (illustrated by William Wiesner), Lippincott, 1951; *The Make-Believe Twins* (illustrated by Roberta MacDonald), Lippincott, 1953.

The Year without a Santa Claus (illustrated by Kurt Werth), Lippincott, 1957; *Lucy McLockett* (illustrated by H. Stone), Lippincott, 1959; *Sugar and Spice: The ABC of Being a Girl* (illustrated by Colleen Browning), Watts, 1960; *Mince Pie and Mistletoe* (illustrated by Harold Berson), Lippincott, 1961; *The B Book*, (illustrated by Robert Jones) Crowell-Collier, 1962, new edition illustrated by John E. Johnson, 1968; *Boys Are Awful* (illustrated by Ati Forberg), Watts, 1962; *How Mrs. Santa Claus Saved Christmas* (illustrated by K. Werth), Lippincott, 1963; *A Girl and Her Room* (illustrated by A. Forberg), Watts, 1963; *Wonderful Time* (illustrated by John Alcorn), Lippincott, 1966; *A Wreath of Christmas Legends* (illustrated by Leonard Weisgard), Macmillan, 1967; (compiler) *Wonders and Surprises: A Collection of Poems*, Lippincott, 1968.

Verse: *On the Contrary,* Doubleday, Doran, 1934; *One More Manhattan,* Harcourt, 1937; *A Pocketful of Wry,* Duell, Sloan & Pearce, 1940, revised edition, Grosset, 1959; *Husbands Are Difficult; or, The Book of Oliver Ames,* Duell, Sloan & Pearce, 1941; *Stones from a Glass House: New Poems,* Viking, 1946; *A Short Walk from the Station,* Viking, 1951; *The Love Letters of Phyllis McGinley,* Viking, 1954; *Merry Christmas, Happy New Year,* Viking, 1958; *Times Three: Selected Verse from Three Decades,* foreword by W. H. Auden, Viking, 1960, published in England as *Times Three: Selected Verse from Three Decades with Seventy New Poems,* Secker & Warburg, 1961; *Christmas Con and Pro,* Hart Press, 1971; *Confessions of a Reluctant Optimist,* Hallmark, 1973.

Essays: *The Province of the Heart,* Viking, 1959; *Sixpence in Her Shoe,* Macmillan, 1964; *Saint-Watching,* Viking, 1969, published as *Saint-Watching: A Personal View of Several Saints,* 1971.

Author of lyrics for "Small Wonder," a Broadway revue, 1948; and narration for film, "The Emperor's Nightingale," 1951. Member of advisory board, *American Scholar.* Contributor to *New Yorker, Good Housekeeping, Reader's Digest, Ladies' Home Journal, McCall's, Vogue, America, Atlantic,* and other publications.

ADAPTATIONS: "Holiday for Santa" (musical; based on *The Year without a Santa Claus*), produced at the Colony Square in Atlanta, Georgia, December, 1970.

SIDELIGHTS: **March 21, 1905.** Born in Ontario, Oregon. The family moved to Colorado when McGinley was quite young. "I had a wild and wooly childhood. We had a couple of sections of land east of Denver. The nearest town, about six miles away, looked just like a scene from a TV western—muddy Main Street, hitching posts, false-fronted stores and all. My brother and I rode ponies to school about three miles from home. On Sunday afternoons, instead of watching baseball games, we watched bronco-busting."

McGinley grew up in Colorado as the daughter of an unsuccessful land speculator. ". . . As a child I lived on a ranch in Colorado with the nearest one-room schoolhouse four miles away and the roads nearly impassable in winter. Sometimes there was no teacher for the school; sometimes my brother and I were the only pupils. If there was a public library within practical distance I never learned of it. We were a reading family but my father's library ran chiefly to history and law and the collected works of Bulwer-Lytton. I wolfed down what I could but found a good deal of it indigestible. In my teens neither the public high school of a very small Western town nor the decorous boarding school I later attended made much effort to mend the damage. It seems to me now that we were always having to make reports on *Ivanhoe* or repeat from memory passages from Burke's *Speech on Conciliation.* I think in two separate English classes we spent most of the year parsing 'Snowbound.'" [Phyllis McGinley, *The Province of the Heart,* Viking, 1959.[1]]

Composed her first poem at the age of six. "From then on it never occurred to me that I wasn't going to be a poet." ["The Telltale Hearth," *Time,* June 18, 1965.[2]]

1917. Father died. "We went back to Ogden, Utah to my mother's home. My aunt was a widow, too, so we lived in a sort of communal home—we never had a home, and to have a real home, after I got married, was just marvelous."[2]

1927. Graduated from the University of Utah. "I knew I was bright, but I also knew that in that period and in that environment, brainy women were not appreciated. I made myself over into a giddy prom trotter."[2]

"There is something to be said for a bad education. By any standards mine was deplorable; and I deplored it for years, in private and in public. I flaunted it as if it were a medal, a kind of cultural Purple-Heart which both excused my deficiencies and lent luster to my mild achievements. But as time goes on I murmur against it less. I find that even ignorance has its brighter side.

"For if I grew up no better instructed about the world of books than was Columbus about global geography, I had in store for me, as he did, the splendors of discovery. There is such a thing as a literary landscape; to that, to nearly the whole length and breadth of classic English writing, I came as an astonished stranger. No one who first enters that country on a conducted tour can have any notion what it is like to travel it alone, on foot, and at his own pace.

"I am not exaggerating. My education really was bad. . . . However, it was at college I seriously managed to learn nothing. My alma mater was one of those universities founded and supplied by the state which in the West everybody attends as automatically as kindergarten. There are—or were then—no entrance examinations. Anybody could come and everybody did, for the proms and the football games; and they sat under a faculty which for relentless mediocrity must have outstripped any in the land. So, by putting my mind to it, I was able to emerge from four years there quite uncorrupted by knowledge. Let me amend that to literary knowledge. Somewhere along

Phyllis McGinley, age six.

**We hadn't always Santa Claus
Or garlands in the hall.**

■ (From *Mince Pie and Mistletoe* by Phyllis McGinley. Illustrated by Harold Berson.)

the line, out of a jumble of courses in Sociology, Household Chemistry, Hygiene, Beginner's German, I remember picking up bits and pieces of learning designed to enrich my life: the Theory of Refrigeration; the fact that Old German and Anglo-Saxon were two languages balefully akin and equally revolting; and the law about no offspring's having eyes darker than the eyes of the darker of his two parents. I had also, in one semester, been made to bolt Shakespeare entire, including the sonnets; and the result of such forced feeding had left me with an acute allergy to the Bard I was years getting over. Otherwise, few Great Books had impinged on my life. Through a complicated system of juggling credits and wheedling heads of departments, I had been able to evade even the Standard General Survey of English Literature.

"I had read things, of course. I was even considered quite a bookworm by my sorority sisters, who had given up going to the library after polishing off *The Wizard of Oz*. But it was the contemporaries who occupied me. I had read Mencken but not Marlowe, Atherton but not Austen, Hoffenstein but not Herrick, Shaw but not Swift, Kipling but not Keats, Millay but not Marvell. Unbelievable as it may seem to an undergraduate, I had never even read A. E. Housman. Although I had scribbled verses in my notebooks during geology lectures, I had not so much as heard of Herbert or Donne or Gay or Prior or Hopkins. I had shunned Chaucer and avoided Dryden. Oliver Goldsmith I knew by hearsay as the author of a dull novel called *The Vicar of Wakefield*. Milton had written solely in order to plague the young with 'Il Penseroso.' I hadn't read *Vanity Fair* or *Ethan Frome* or 'Essay on Man' or *Anna Karenina* or 'The Hound of Heaven' or *Dubliners*. (Joyce was a contemporary but the furore over *Ulysses* was a mist that obscured his younger work.) Almost none of the alleged classics, under whose burden the student is supposed to bow, had I peered into either for pleasure or for credit.

"As a consequence, although I came to them late, I came to them without prejudice. We met on a basis completely friendly; and I do not think the well-educated can always claim as much.

"There is still much to deplore about my education. I shall never read Latin verse in the original or have a taste for the Brontës, and those are crippling lacks. But all handicaps have compensations, and I have learned to accept both cheerfully. To have first met Dickens, Austen, and Mark Twain when I was capable of giving them the full court curtsy is beatitude enough for any reader. Blessed are the illiterate, for they shall inherit the Word!'"[1]

1929. Taught English in New Rochelle, New York; began publishing poetry. "I got a job teaching high school English in New Rochelle, New York. I kept the job for four and a half years, teaching all day and writing at night, mailing my efforts to New York papers and magazines. Finally, when *The New Yorker* magazine started to accept my poems regularly, I gave up teaching and moved into Manhattan."

1937. Married Charles L. Hayden, an employee of the Bell Telephone Co. and a jazz musician. "The men I met were either divorced or they drank or they didn't have money. It wasn't so easy to find the right man."[2]

McGinley had some misgivings about Hayden's stability. "I thought somehow he wouldn't stay home. . . . Then, without telling me, he called on the pastor at St. Joseph's and arranged to have the banns read. When I went to church on Sunday and heard them, I almost swooned in the aisle. It was the only really brash, rash, adventurous thing Bill Hayden ever did."[2]

When Lucy McLockett
Was five years old,
She was plump
And curly
And good as gold—

■ (From *Lucy McLockett* by Phyllis McGinley. Illustrated by Helen Stone.)

"When we had been married only a few months, my husband (moved by God knows what private and loving impulse) paid me the supreme compliment in his power.

"'You know, dear,' he remarked fondly, 'you're a wonderful girl. You think like a man.'

"I can remember refuting him passionately. 'But I don't! I *don't*. What a horrid thing to say!'

"My outburst took us both by surprise. We laughed then and we laugh still when we recall it. But my denial, if overheated, was still the expression of a truth I had not until then really considered. I was, I am, a member of the nation of women. And in spite of our new freedoms, of all our recent skills and strengths and talents, we do not wish to belong to a different tribe. We do not want to think like men or feel like men or act like men—only like women and human beings.'"[1]

Three years later first daughter, Julie, was born. "I have never felt so divine in my life as the time before she was born. I was so full of euphoria, I was practically immune to all human illnesses!"[2]

1944. The first of McGinley's books for children, *The Horse Who Lived Upstairs,* was published. "Helen Stone, an artist friend, brought over a portfolio of horse pictures to my house one evening. She thought they might inspire a poem or two. I put them aside on a table in the living room and there they sat for two whole years. The passage of time finally shamed me into doing something about them.

"My girls read so early in life by themselves that I was completely out of touch with juvenile fiction. I went over to the library and read and read and read—every good juvenile title that was on the shelves. [Then] I went down to the Village in New York and watched how city horses live. It was quite a revelation. I discovered one stable that cried out for story-telling. The horses all were kept on the upper floors of the building and they surveyed the world from their second-story windows as calmly as though they were standing in country pastures. When I noticed that their watering trough was an old cast-off bathtub, I knew I had a book."

Writing for children was very rewarding for McGinley, who believed that the formula for juvenile writing was threefold: leanness, rhythm, and repetition. "The pity is that most first-rate authors do not write for children. They have done so in other eras without apology. Dickens was generous to the young and so were Thackeray and Browning and Mark Twain. Lang and Ruskin and Belloc and Lear never disdained to amuse their juniors. . . .

"But the majority of distinguished literary figures of the present seem not to have entertained a thought that children are the finest audience in the world. For that is what they are—enormous in numbers, avid for fulfillment, and immensely loyal. Children consider one perusal of a book only the *apéritif* before the meal. No wonder a cliché for a juvenile is 'dog-eared.' The well-loved book in a child's library is invariably that, worn, used, carried to bed, fetched to the table, even nostalgically borne off to college, years after it was first purchased.

"Children are also something better than loyal—they are adventurous. Something rich and strange delights them. One of my daughters was recovering, at five, from chicken pox when I first realized how little hazard one runs in letting children stretch the muscles of their minds. As a convalescent she demanded the right to be read to. At hand was *The Wind in the Willows* and I started in on the adventures of Mr. Toad. After a chapter or two, though, I began to have misgivings. The adventures were satisfactory but Kenneth Grahame had not been tutored in the new school of talking down to children. His vocabulary, his wit, his plotting gave no quarter to limited comprehension.

"'Look, dear,' I said, preparing to shut the pages. 'These are awfully hard words. I think the book is too old for you.'

"The patient was not only firm, she was distraught.

"'I don't care,' she cried. 'I don't *care* if it's too hard for me. I don't care if I can't understand the words. I just want to hear that story.'

"Children are explorers by nature. They have to be in order to discover the world around them. What kind of an expedition is it and to what dreary climates must they plod if their fiction contains nothing new and strange and mysterious—not even new and strange and mysterious words?

"If ever I had time and courage enough, I'd write a children's book stuck plum-pudding-rich with great jawbreakers of words. I would use 'egregious.' I would work in 'monstriferous.' I would use 'sepicolous' and 'ubiquitous' and 'antidisestablishmentarianism' and 'nictate' and 'supernumerary' and 'internecine' and a hundred glorious others. And I think children would get the joke and flock to it—if, that is, the story were good enough. They are a braver generation than we suppose.

"So they deserve brave books. They deserve the best that men and women of wit and talent can write for them. . . ." [Phyllis McGinley, "Talking Down," *Wilson Library Bulletin,* April, 1962.[3]]

1961. Awarded the Pulitzer Prize for poetry for *Times Three: Selected Verse from Three Decades.* Robert Frost, on hearing of her award, said: "She is very rhymey, and you know I like rhyme." Although McGinley was renowned for her poetry and her books for children, she considered herself first a homemaker, wife, and mother of two girls. She once described herself as primarily a "nest builder." "Of course, women have a right to work if they can do so without stinting the family. By and large, though, the world runs better when men and women keep to their own spheres. We who belong to the profession of housewife hold the fate of the world in our hands. It is our influence which will determine the culture of coming generations.

Up he went to his stall on the fourth floor of the big brick building. ■ (From *The Horse Who Lived Upstairs* by Phyllis McGinley. Illustrated by Helen Stone.)

McGinley with husband, Bill, at the pool of their Connecticut home.

THIRTY-FIVE CENTS

JUNE 18, 1965

"*I rise to defend
The quite possible She.*"

TIME
THE WEEKLY MAGAZINE

PHYLLIS McGINLEY

VOL. 85 NO. 25
(REG. U.S. PAT. OFF.)

McGinley made the cover of *Time* the week she read one of her poems at the White House Arts Festival.

"I have one facet of genius, and only one. I have an infinite capacity for taking pains. My passion is for lucidity. I do think, at a time when poetry has become the property of the universities and not the common people, I have kept the door open and perhaps led my readers into greater poetry.

"I realize I have been fulfilled, and I don't want my readers to think that I'm saying you can all be poets. All I'm saying is that if you really like being a wife and mother, don't be upset by characters who say you have to get out and do something. Because I think *you* hold the future in your hands." ["Wit, Wisdom and Phyllis McGinley," *Reader's Digest*, November, 1965.[4]]

1962. *Boys Are Awful* and *The B Book* were published. About *The B Book*, McGinley said: ". . . After having written against the trend toward a restricted vocabulary for children's books, I now appear to have turned around and committed one, myself. The book in question is *The B Book* published by Crowell-Collier in a series called, unblushingly, 'Modern Masters.'

"It is quite true, I am the author of *The B Book*. True again, it contains only 262 different words (79 of them beginning with B) as against the 364 which the cover says; somebody's computer must have run amok. *The B Book* is a story for very young children and, naturally, the vocabulary I used was restrained by intuition and what I hope is art, not by a list imposed on me.

"When Mr. Untermeyer as general editor of this series asked me to contribute to it, he did at first mention a vocabulary taboo. I told him I could not, in conscience, follow it.

"'Very well, then,' he said. 'Write anything you like. I'll just send over the list for your amusement.'

"When it arrived, I looked at it desultorily, caught sight of certain nouns beginning with B, and thought, 'It might be fun to do something with phonetics.' Then the idea occurred to me of the pun on 'B' and 'Bee'—a mild joke which, I thought, children just learning their letters might appreciate. I then completely discarded the list and gave the story its head. I jotted down my own list of B words—Balloon, Bold Brass Band, Bicycle, Bantam-hen, Butterfly, Black Bird, Birch trees, Bushes, etc., and let them go Bouncing and Buzzing and Bumping and Booming and Bounding along with Bumble the small Brown Bee.

"But authors are a naïve race. I did not see the book's jacket before it was published; and I was . . . shocked . . . to have my story classified as one which conformed 'to a restricted vocabulary.' There wasn't much to be done by then, so I made no public protest. But perhaps the time has come for me to do just that.

"I do not believe in limiting anything in books for children—not language or plot or imagery or construction. *The B Book* is no masterpiece. But it was written with pleasure to give pleasure and I followed no party line." [Phyllis McGinley, "Letters," *Wilson Library Bulletin*, February, 1963.[5]]

1965. Invited to read at the White House Arts Festival. Noted for her humorously-worded verses, McGinley was often compared to Ogden Nash and Dorothy Parker. "The line between light verse and poetry is very thin. In fact, the line is practically not there at all. I think, though, I've arrived at a distinction: the appeal of light verse is to the intellect and the appeal of serious verse is to the emotions. . . . A light-verse writer is a kind of critic. A critic's stock-in-trade is his ability

**The Cat by too much glory overcome
Could not withdraw her gaze. . . .**

■ (From *A Wreath of Christmas Legends* by Phyllis McGinley. Illustrated by Leonard Weisgard.)

to be angry at injustice, stupidity and pompousness. But today the critic and light-verse writer find it increasingly difficult to express social anger. The whole world is angry. All of us are deflated. In times of ease it is the duty of such a writer to deflate, but in times of unrest and fear it is perhaps his duty to celebrate, to single out some of the values we can cherish, to talk about some of the few warm things we know in a cold world."

McGinley described the process of poetry writing as long and arduous. "There is such a thing as inspiration (lower case), but it is no miracle. It is the reward handed to a writer for hard work and good conduct. It is the felicitous word sliding, after hours of evasion, obediently into place. It is a sudden comprehension of how to manufacture an effect, finish off a line or a stanza. At the triumphant moment this gift may seem like magic, but actually it is the result of effort, practice, and the slight temperature a sulky brain is apt to run when it is pushed beyond its usual exertions.

"As a basketball player after long practice does not need to measure his shots from the floor but knows by coordination of eye and muscle just how the ball will best enter the basket, so a poet achieves effects subconsciously—and, again, after long practice." [Linda Welshimer Wagner, *Phyllis McGinley*, Twayne, 1971.[6]]

1972. Husband died. McGinley's daughters persuaded her to move from her large house in Larchmont, New York to an apartment in Manhattan.

February 22, 1978. Died of a stroke in Manhattan. "An unillusioned acquaintance of mine once said the good life was what other people seemed to live. I used to think in youth that it consisted of a constant explosion of joys, a succession of ecstasies, prizes, and great rewards. Now I realize all life is made up merely of days. And a good day is the most I dare define." [Phyllis McGinley, "The Good Life on Earth," *McCall's*, January, 1970.[7]]

HOBBIES AND OTHER INTERESTS: Reading history, cooking, gardening, and "sticking pins into the smugger aspects of the social scene."

FOR MORE INFORMATION SEE: Scholastic, March 27, 1944, September 29, 1947; *Harper's,* December, 1949, November 1, 1964; Stanley Kunitz and Howard Haycraft, editors, *Junior Book of Authors,* H. W. Wilson, 1951; *Saturday Review,* August 1, 1953, September 18, 1954, December 10, 1960; *Good Housekeeping,* August, 1954, September, 1956; Harvey Breit, *The Writer Observed,* World Publishing, 1956; *Catholic World,* September, 1957, August, 1970; *Life,* May 12, 1958, December 28, 1959; *Ladies' Home Journal,* September, 1959, January, 1960, July, 1961, December, 1966; Phyllis McGinley, *The Province of the Heart,* Viking, 1959; *New York Herald Tribune,* September 25, 1960; *Newsweek,* September 26, 1960; *Commonweal,* December 9, 1960, March 31, 1978; *Current Biography,* H. W. Wilson, 1961; *Vogue,* April 1, 1962; *Wilson Library Bulletin,* April, 1962, February, 1963; *Time,* June 18, 1965, March 31, 1975; *Popular Gardening,* September, 1965; *American Scholar,* autumn, 1965; "Wit, Wisdom and Phyllis McGinley," *Reader's Digest,* November, 1965.

Writer's Digest, February, 1966; Everett S. Allen, *Famous American Humorous Poets,* Dodd, 1968; *Horn Book,* December, 1969; *Christian Century,* December 17, 1969; Lee Bennett Hopkins, *Books Are by People,* Citation Press, 1969; Nancy Larrick, *A Parent's Guide to Children's Reading,* 3rd edition, Doubleday, 1969; P. McGinley, "The Good Life on Earth," *McCall's,* January, 1970; *Variety,* December 2, 1970; Linda Welshimer Wagner, *Phyllis McGinley,* Twayne, 1971; Martha E. Ward and Dorothy A. Marquardt, *Authors of Books for Young People,* 2nd edition, Scarecrow, 1971; Donnarae MacCann & Olga Richard, *The Child's First Books,* H. W. Wilson, 1973; D. L. Kirkpatrick, *Twentieth-Century Children's Writers,* St. Martin's Press, 1978.

Obituaries: *New York Times,* February 23, 1978; *Washington Post,* February 24, 1978; *Newsweek,* March 6, 1978; *Time,* March 6, 1978; *Publishers Weekly,* March 20, 1978; *America,* March 25, 1978; *School Library Journal,* April, 1978; *AB Bookman's Weekly,* May 8, 1978.

She took out Miss Abernathy and Mary Alicia and Jack and Jill and Tosca and the Skater and the Ballerina and the rest of the family who had been so patient there through the long dark months. ■ (From *The Most Wonderful Doll in the World* by Phyllis McGinley. Illustrated by Helen Stone.)

**The Grandfather's Clock
Stands stiff and tall
Against the staircase
In the hall.**

■ (From *Wonderful Time* by Phyllis McGinley. Illustrated by John Alcorn.)

McGINNIS, Lila S(prague) 1924-

PERSONAL: Born May 29, 1924, in Ashtabula Harbor, Ohio; daughter of Lynn A. (a teacher) and Florence (White) Sprague; married Richard W. McGinnis (a regional planner), June 1, 1944; children: Richard, Ralph, Leslie, Benjamin. *Education:* Attended Kent State University, 1941-43; Ohio State University, B.Sc., 1948. *Religion:* Episcopal. *Home:* 359 Cornell Ave., Elyria, Ohio 44035. *Office:* Elyria Public Library, 320 Washington Ave., Elyria, Ohio 44035.

CAREER: Elementary school teacher in Orwell, Ohio, 1943-45, in Columbus, Ohio, 1949, and Interlaken, N.Y., 1949-50; Elyria Public Library, Elyria, Ohio, children's librarian, 1973—.

WRITINGS: What Will Simon Say? (adult), Logos International, 1974; *Secret of the Porcelain Cats* (juvenile; illustrated by Larry Frederick), A. Whitman, 1978; *The Ghost Upstairs* (juvenile; illustrated by Amy Rowen), Hastings House, 1982; *Auras and Other Rainbow Secrets* (juvenile), Hastings House, 1984. Contributor of over sixty stories to magazines, including *Co-ed* and *Good Housekeeping.*

WORK IN PROGRESS: A sequel to *The Ghost Upstairs* entitled *The Ghost Alarm.*

SIDELIGHTS: "I write because I enjoy it and feel more alive doing it. When I am working on a story or a book I am sure I am easier to live with—perhaps that is why I have such a supportive family!

"I like the short story form and have done most of my writing in that form, but the market for it is small. The last few years I have tried writing for children and enjoy it immensely. Working with children each day as a children's librarian brings me

(Jacket illustration by Janet Scabrini from *Auras and Other Rainbow Secrets* by Lila McGinnis.)

much pleasure too, and probably accounts for my turning to the juvenile field.

"The children who come into the library frequently want to know *why* an author wrote a particular book. The why for me is that I thought it would be fun. And I am right, it always is.

"It was great fun writing about a boy ghost who finds himself in the modern world, with thousands of new things like television and radios to learn about. It was fun to write about a girl who saw colors.

"My oldest son gave me a reprint of the 1902 Sears Roebuck catalog for Christmas one year, and in browsing through this it occured to me that a child who lived then would certainly be surprised at the kind of things children today take for granted. Then I remembered the two lovely old homes that were torn down to make room for our modern library, and *The Ghost Upstairs* began to come alive for me.

"As for *Auras,* I think that more children than we realize are able to see colors. And I think it would be fascinating to have this ability, and not lose it in the process of growing up. I wrote about Nora's auras, then, to find out how that would feel, and, I hoped, to remove some of the fear that children might have in connection with such things.

LILA S. McGINNIS

"But mostly, I believe, I wrote those books because they were fun to write and I hoped they would be fun to read. Many children today have worries and concerns far removed from those that childhood ought to have—I wrote the books for them.''

McHUGH, (Berit) Elisabet 1941-

BRIEF ENTRY: Born January 26, 1941, in Stoede, Sweden; came to the United States in 1971; became a naturalized citizen in 1982. Author of children's books. McHugh graduated from the Royal Naval College in Stockholm, Sweden in 1961. For twelve years she was a radio officer, during which time she traveled around the world and worked in East Africa and Australia. A writer since 1979, she is the author of three children's books featuring Karen Bergman, a Korean orphan adopted by a single woman. Similar to the character she created, McHugh is the single mother of four adopted Korean children.

In *Raising a Mother Isn't Easy* (Greenwillow Books, 1983), eleven-year-old Karen decides that her loving but disorganized mother needs a husband. Karen eventually receives more than one surprise when she learns that her mother is capable of handling her own life. *Bulletin of the Center for Children's Books* noted the book's "lively, informal style that has good dialogue, humor, and warmth." Its sequel, *Karen's Sister* (Greenwillow Books, 1983), was praised by *School Library Journal* for "the volatile relationships between three generations of mothers and daughters [that] are humorously and lovingly portrayed." The third book in the series, *Karen and Vicki* (Greenwillow Books, 1984), finds Karen adjusting to her new family after her mother marries a widower with three children. *Voice of Youth Advocates* stated, "Karen and [her stepsister] Vicki are well-drawn and their problems would be universal." *School Library Journal* observed, "As in the earlier books, much of the appeal stems from the amusing realistic descriptions of ordinary family situations. . . ." McHugh's anticipated works are another book for young people and an adult humor book. *Home:* 611 South Pine St., Troy, Idaho 83871.

FOR MORE INFORMATION SEE: Contemporary Authors, Volume 113, Gale, 1985.

MILLS, Claudia 1954-

PERSONAL: Born August 21, 1954, in New York, N.Y.; daughter of Charles Howard (a safety engineer) and Helen (a teacher; maiden name, Lederleitner) Mills. *Education:* Wellesley College, B.A., 1976; Princeton University, M.A., 1979. *Home:* 7302 Birch Ave., Takoma Park, Md. 20912. *Office:* Center for Philosophy and Public Policy, University of Maryland, College Park, Md. 20742.

CAREER: Four Winds Press, New York, N.Y., editorial secretary and production assistant, 1979-80; University of Maryland, College Park, editor of *QQ: Report From the Center for Philosophy and Public Policy,* 1980—. *Member:* Society of Children's Book Writers, Children's Book Guild of Washington, D.C., Phi Beta Kappa.

WRITINGS: Luisa's American Dream (juvenile), Four Winds, 1981; *At the Back of the Woods* (juvenile), Four Winds, 1982; *The Secret Carousel* (juvenile), Four Winds, 1983; (editor with Douglas MacLean) *Liberalism Reconsidered,* Rowman & Allanheld, 1983; *All the Living* (juvenile), Macmillan, 1983; *What*

CLAUDIA MILLS

about Annie (juvenile), Walker, 1985; *Boardwalk with Hotel* (juvenile), Macmillan, 1985.

SIDELIGHTS: "I have been writing books for children and teenagers since I was a child and a teenager. My autobiographical manuscript, *T Is for Tarzan,* written when I was fourteen, was widely circulated through my junior high school, as adolescent friends and foes waited turns to see how they were slandered.

"I didn't begin serious professional writing, however, until I left graduate school impulsively in mid-year to take a secretarial job at Four Winds Press. I occupied myself during the four-hour round-trip commute from Princeton by writing picturebook and novel manuscripts, which I submitted to Four Winds Press under various pseudonyms. It was very easy—but so disheartening—to slip a rejected manuscript unobtrusively into my book bag.

"Finally a manuscript proved promising enough on a first skim for the editor to hand it over to me, her secretary, for a reader's report. I took the challenge and wrote an objective, candid report on my own manuscript, including suggestions for needed revisions. The editor forwarded to the author (me) her 'excellent reader's report' and then I dutifully took my own suggestions in rewriting. I finally confessed my duplicity when the manuscript was completed. Fortunately, the editor had a keen sense of humor, and the manuscript was published as *At the Back of the Woods.*''

(Jacket illustration by Susan Stillman from *At the Back of the Woods* by Claudia Mills.)

MOCHÉ, Dinah (Rachel) L(evine) 1936-

PERSONAL: Born October 24, 1936, in New York, N.Y.; daughter of Bertram A. (a lawyer) and Mollie (Last) Levine; married I. Robert Rozen, September 5, 1955 (died November 17, 1966); children: Elizabeth Karen, Rebecca Ann. *Education:* Radcliffe College, B.A. (magna cum laude), 1958; Columbia University, M.A., 1961, Ph.D., 1976. *Residence:* Mamaroneck, N.Y. *Office:* Department of Physics, Queensborough Community College of the City University of New York, Bayside, N.Y. 11364.

CAREER: Columbia University, Radiation Laboratory, New York, N.Y., research assistant in physics, 1961-62; Bronx Community College of the City University of New York, Bronx, N.Y., instructor of physics, 1963-64; Fashion Institute of Technology, New York, N.Y., instructor in physics, 1964-65; Queensborough Community College of the City University of New York, Bayside, N.Y., lecturer, 1965-66, instructor, 1966-69, assistant professor, 1969-77, associate professor of physics, 1977-79, full professor of physics and astronomy, 1979—. Participant in (and sometimes director of) national meetings; lecturer; guest on numerous national television and radio programs. Regional resource person for National Air and Space Museum, Smithsonian Institution, 1980—.

MEMBER: American Physical Society, American Association of Physics Teachers, New York State Association of Two-Year College Physics Teachers, National Science Teachers Association, Astronomical Society of the Pacific, Phi Beta Kappa, Sigma Xi. *Awards, honors:* National Science Foundation grant, 1974-75, and 1978-80, and faculty fellowship, 1976; *The Astronauts* and *The Star Wars Question and Answer Book about Space* were both selected as an Outstanding Science Trade Book for Children by the National Science Teachers Association and Children's Book Council, 1979, and *Astronomy Today: Planets, Stars, Space Exploration,* was selected in 1982.

WRITINGS—For young readers, unless otherwise indicated: *What's Up There? Questions and Answers about Stars and Space,* Scholastic Book Services, 1975; *Magic Science Tricks,* Scholastic Book Services, 1977; *Astronomy* (adult), Wiley, 1978, 7th edition, 1986; *Mars,* F. Watts, 1978; *Search for Life Beyond Earth* (young adult), F. Watts, 1978; *The Astronauts,* Random House, 1979; *The Star Wars Question and Answer Book about Space* (illustrated by David Kawami), Random House, 1979; *Radiation: Benefits/Dangers* (young adult), F. Watts, 1979; *Life in Space* (adult), Ridge Press, 1979.

More Magic Science Tricks, Scholastic Book Services, 1980; (editor and co-author) *Laboratory Manual for Introductory Astronomy,* Queensborough Community College Press, 1980; *We're Taking an Airplane Trip* (illustrated by Carolyn Bracken), Western Publishing, 1982; *My First Book about Space,* West-

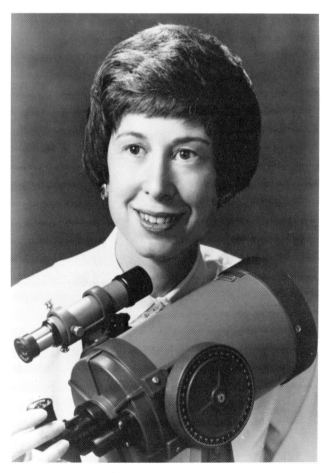

DINAH L. MOCHÉ

ern Publishing, 1982; *Astronomy Today: Planets, Stars, Space Exploration* (illustrated by Harry McNaught), Random House, 1982, revised edition, 1986; *Physics in Your Future,* American Physical Society, 1983; *What's Down There? Questions and Answers about the Ocean,* Scholastic Book Services, 1984; *If You Were an Astronaut,* Golden Books, 1985.

Author of multi-media presentation, "Women in Science," American Association of Physics Teachers and National Science Teachers Association, 1975. Contributor of articles and reviews to professional journals and popular magazines. Contributing editor of *Science World,* 1976-77; member of editorial board of *Physics Teacher,* 1974-77, and of review board of *American Journal of Physics,* 1977—.

SIDELIGHTS: "I aim to make science accessible, interesting, and exciting for people of all ages. I want my books to be accurate and enjoyable. To me, science and writing are fun."

FOR MORE INFORMATION SEE: Physics Teacher, September, 1976, February, 1979; *American Journal of Physics,* October, 1976; *Daily News* (New York), May 11, 1979, December 2, 1979; *New York Times,* July 22, 1979, December 4, 1979; *Sun Times* (Chicago), February 12, 1980; *Spotlight* (Westchester, N.Y.), February, 1981; *Physics Today,* December, 1981; *Education,* August, 1984.

NIXON, Joan Lowery 1927-

PERSONAL: Born February 3, 1927, in Los Angeles, Calif.; daughter of Joseph Michael (an accountant) and Margaret (Meyer) Lowery; married Hershell H. Nixon (a petroleum geologist), August 6, 1949; children: Kathleen Nixon Brush, Maureen Nixon Quinlan, Joseph Michael, Eileen Marie. *Education:* University of Southern California, A.B., 1947; California State College, certificate in elementary education, 1949. *Religion:* Roman Catholic. *Home:* 10215 Cedar Creek Dr., Houston, Tex. 77042. *Agent:* Amy Berkower, Writers House, Inc., 21 West 26th St., New York, N.Y. 10010.

CAREER: Elementary school teacher in Los Angeles, Calif., 1947-50; Midland College, Midland, Tex., instructor in creative writing, 1971-73; University of Houston, Houston, Tex., instructor in creative writing, 1974-78. Member of committee, Southwest Writers Conference, University of Houston. *Member:* Authors Guild, Authors League of America, Society of Children's Book Writers (former member of board of directors), Mystery Writers of America (regional vice-president, Southwest chapter), Kappa Delta Alumnae Association.

AWARDS, HONORS: Edgar Scroll, Mystery Writers of America, 1975, for *The Mysterious Red Tape Gang;* Steck-Vaughn Award, Texas Institute of Letters, 1975, for *The Alligator under the Bed; Volcanoes: Nature's Fireworks* was chosen as an Outstanding Science Trade Book for Children, 1979, by the National Science Teachers Association and Children's Book Council Joint Committee, *Glaciers: Nature's Frozen Rivers,* was chosen in 1980, and *Earthquakes: Nature in Motion,* was chosen in 1981; Edgar Allan Poe Award, Mystery Writers of America, 1980, for *The Kidnapping of Christina Lattimore,* and 1981, for *The Séance;* Crabbery Award from Oxon Hill branch of Prince George's County Library (Md.), 1984, for *Magnolia's Mixed-Up Magic.*

WRITINGS: The Alligator under the Bed (illustrated by Jan Hughes), Putnam, 1974; *The Secret Box Mystery* (illustrated by Leigh Grant; Junior Literary Guild selection), Putnam, 1974;

The Mysterious Red Tape Gang (illustrated by Joan Sandin), Putnam, 1974, paperback edition, published as *The Adventures of the Red Tape Gang* (illustrated by Steven H. Stroud), Scholastic, 1983; (with others) *People and Me,* Benefic, 1975; (with others) *This I Can Be,* Benefic, 1975; *The Mysterious Prowler* (illustrated by Berthe Amoss), Harcourt, 1976; *Who Is My Neighbor?,* Concordia, 1976; *Five Loaves and Two Fishes,* Concordia, 1976.

(With husband, Hershell H. Nixon) *Oil and Gas: From Fossils to Fuels* (illustrated by Jean Day Zallinger), Harcourt, 1977; *The Son Who Came Home Again,* Concordia, 1977; *Writing Mysteries for Young People,* Writer, Inc., 1977; *The Boy Who Could Find Anything* (illustrated by Syd Hoff), Harcourt, 1978; *Danger in Dinosaur Valley* (illustrated by Marc Simont; Junior Literary Guild selection), Putnam, 1978; (with H. H. Nixon) *Volcanoes: Nature's Fireworks,* Dodd, 1978; *Muffie Mouse and the Busy Birthday* (illustrated by Geoffrey Hayes; Junior Literary Guild selection), Seabury, 1978; *When God Speaks,* Our Sunday Visitor, 1978; *When God Listens,* Our Sunday Visitor, 1978; *The Kidnapping of Christina Lattimore,* Harcourt, 1979; *The Grandmother's Book,* Abingdon, 1979; *The Butterfly Tree,* Our Sunday Visitor, 1979; *Bigfoot Makes a Movie* (illustrated by S. Hoff), Putnam, 1979.

The Séance, Harcourt, 1980; *Before You Were Born* (illustrated by James McIlrath), Our Sunday Visitor, 1980; *Gloria Chipmunk, Star!* (illustrated by Diane Dawson), Houghton, 1980, paperback edition (illustrated by G. Hayes), Scholastic, 1980; *If You Say So, Claude* (illustrated by Lorinda Bryan

JOAN LOWERY NIXON

Cauley), Warne, 1980; (with H. H. Nixon) *Glaciers: Nature's Frozen Rivers*, Dodd, 1980; *Casey and the Great Idea* (illustrated by Amy Rowen), Dutton, 1980; (With H. H. Nixon) *Earthquakes: Nature in Motion*, Dodd, 1981; *The Specter*, Delacorte, 1982; *The Gift* (illustrated by Andrew Glass), Macmillan, 1983; *Magnolia's Mixed Up Magic* (illustrated by Linda Bucholtz-Ross), Putnam 1983; *Days of Fear* (photographs by Joan Menschenfreund), Dutton, 1983; *A Deadly Game of Magic*, Harcourt, 1983.

The Ghosts of Now: A Novel of Psychological Suspense, Delacorte, 1984; *The Horror on Hackman's Hill*, Scholastic, 1985; *The Stalker* (illustrated by Wendy Popp), Delacorte, 1985; (with H. H. Nixon), *Land under the Sea*, Dodd, 1985; *Maggie Too* (illustrated by Darrell Millsap), Harcourt, 1985; *The Other Side of Dark*, Delacorte, 1986; *Beats Me, Claude*, Viking, 1986; *And Maggie Makes Three*, Harcourt, 1986; *The Ghost with the Fiery Eyes*, Scholastic, 1986.

Published by Criterion: *The Mystery of Hurricane Castle*, 1964; *The Mystery of the Grinning Idol*, 1965; *The Mystery of the Hidden Cockatoo* (illustrated by Richard Lewis), 1966; *The Mystery of the Haunted Woods*, 1967; *The Mystery of the Secret Stowaway*, 1968; *Delbert, the Plainclothes Detective* (illustrated by Philip Smith), 1971.

"Holiday Mystery" series; all illustrated by Jim Cummins; all published by A. Whitman: *The New Year's Day Mystery*, 1979; *The Halloween Mystery*, 1979; *The Valentine's Day Mystery*, 1979; *The Happy Birthday Mystery*, 1979; *The Thanksgiving Day Mystery*, 1980; *The April Fool Mystery*, 1980; *The Easter Mystery*, 1981; *The Christmas Eve Mystery*, 1981.

"Kleep: Space Detective" series; all illustrated by Paul Frame; all published by Garrard, 1981: *Kidnapped on Astarr; Mysterious Queen of Magic; Mystery Dolls from Planet Urd*.

Contributor to magazines, including *West Coast Review of Books, The Writer, American Home, Parents, Woman's Day*, and *Ms*.

WORK IN PROGRESS: Fat Chance, Claude, for Viking; *If You Were a Writer*, for Macmillan; *The Dark and Deadly Pool*, for Delacorte; *Maggie Forever*, for Harcourt.

SIDELIGHTS: **February 3, 1927.** Born in Los Angeles, California. "I grew up in Hollywood. We lived in Laughlin Park, a small hill just under Griffith Park Observatory. My mother was a very creative person. When we were quite young, she began a puppet show with us as a family project. My father made a folding portable stage, which my mother embellished with some old, out of style red velvet drapes. With lots of help from Mother, we made our own fist puppets, decorated them, and wrote our own scripts, based on classic fairy tales such as *Peter Rabbit* and the traditional *Punch and Judy*. We took our shows to children's hospitals, orphanages, and schools for many years. We were amateurs, but entertainment wasn't quite as sophisticated back then. I particularly remember The Maryknoll Orphanage, where we put on our old standard *Punch and Judy* for a group of very young Japanese children, none of whom spoke English. This little audience, unable to understand the dialogue, responded to the puppets with remarkable enthusiasm as any audience we had ever met. I realized the power of story telling, of laughter, and of friendship.

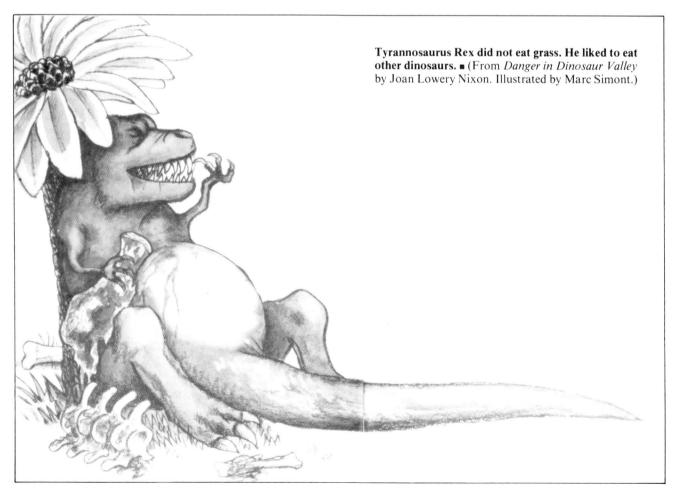

Tyrannosaurus Rex did not eat grass. He liked to eat other dinosaurs. ■ (From *Danger in Dinosaur Valley* by Joan Lowery Nixon. Illustrated by Marc Simont.)

Muffie Mouse wasn't old enough to know how to cook. "I'll make my mother a sandwich," she said. "I won't have to cook a sandwich." ■ (From *Muffie Mouse and the Busy Birthday* by Joan Lowery Nixon. Illustrated by Geoffrey Hayes.)

"I enjoyed living in Hollywood. I remember one time, a friend and I went for ice cream at a little shop called The Pig'n Whistle next to the Egyptian Theatre. Shirley Temple came in with a friend and sat down at the table next to us. Well, we refused to acknowledge that she was there at all. We didn't want anyone to think us so uncouth as to stare at a movie star.

"I wasn't the slightest bit interested in acting. I always wanted to become a writer. My mother told me that at the age of two, before I was old enough to read or write, I would come to her and say, 'Write this down. I have a poem.'

"In high school we were allowed to arrange our own schedules and choose our own teachers. I selected Miss Bertha Standfast for English for three years. I learned a great deal in her classes and was always encouraged by her. My mother advised me to pursue education in college as she had done, but Standfast insisted that I had the talent to become a writer. I followed her advice and majored in journalism. At that time you had to choose either a journalism or an English major, since creative writing courses were not offered. I published my first article in *Ford Times* when I was seventeen. Of course they didn't know how old I was! But I was delighted."

Nixon's decision to enter journalism was further fueled by the movies. "There were some really dreadful, low budget movies, featuring 'Torchy Blaine, Girl Reporter.' Torchy Blaine led about the most interesting life in the world, which inspired me to enter the field of journalism. The idea of being a reporter was exciting and glamorous. I saw Rosalind Russell, my favorite movie star, in 'His Girl Friday,' which further influenced me. Having received my inspiration from totally unrealistic situations, I've always maintained an interest in journalism and adventure."

Studied journalism at the University of Southern California. "My training in journalism taught me discipline. For one thing, I learned to create at the typewriter. We took our exams on the typewriter. Journalism taught me to focus because I had to sit down and *write*, whether I felt like it or not—no waiting for inspiration. I learned the skill of finding the important facts in a story, and how to isolate them from all of the unnecessary details.

"Journalistic skills proved helpful with my creative writing. Learning how to conduct interviews has been invaluable, as well. It taught good listening skills, and again, it taught me how to distill a lot of material. I use this technique when I'm working on an idea for a story. I begin with a situation, develop it a bit, and then find a main character. Along the way, all kinds of odds and ends creep into my mind, and I have to sort through them and discard what's not useful.

"When I graduated I discovered that jobs weren't available in journalism. Many of the war correspondents had returned to the States. There weren't many openings; most of the women in journalism ended up on women's pages. But there was a shortage of teachers in Los Angeles, so I applied for emergency credentials and found I enjoyed teaching so much that I went to night school for education classes. I didn't write much while I was teaching, but I still managed to publish some articles in *Parents* magazine and *American Home*.

She walked toward the door and Brian followed her, clutching the clothing to his chest so he wouldn't drop anything. ■ (From *The Gift* by Joan Lowery Nixon. Illustrated by Andrew Glass.)

Her shoulder was soft and warm and just right for hugging. ■ (From *Delbert, the Plainclothes Detective* by Joan Lowery Nixon. Illustrated by Philip Smith.)

"I met my husband, Hershell, while I was at the University of Southern California (U.S.C.). Hershell was in the Navy, and had signed up for a six year hitch. The Navy sent him to U.S.C. for the B-12 program and officer training. The war ended, but he had to finish his six-year stint with the service. We were engaged for two and a half years before we were married because he was overseas so much of the time.

"I had been writing nonfiction articles and short fiction for magazines for a number of years before I began writing for children. When we moved to Corpus Christi, Texas, I attended my first writers conference. I was quite excited about it, and felt especially inspired by two of the guest speakers who spoke to us about writing for children. It sounded so interesting I thought I'd like to try it. My two eldest daughters, who were in second and sixth grade, came to me and said, 'If you're going to write a book, it has to be for children, and it has to be a mystery, and you have to put us in it.' I did, and I enjoyed it so much that I kept writing books. I had a sense for mystery books because I had read so many to my children. That first book was *The Mystery of Hurricane Castle,* and the two main characters were named Kathy and Maureen. Our Eileen 'starred' in *The Mystery of the Grinning Idol,* and Joe was the main character in *The Mystery of the Secret Stowaway.*'' Two thirds of Nixon's books fall into the mystery category.

Nixon has also written many 'Easy-to-Read' mysteries. "Barbara Lucas, editor at Putnam called me up one day after she had bought my picture book, *The Alligator under the Bed* and asked whether I'd be interested in doing an 'Easy-to-Read' book. She sent me a book to look over. The local librarian helped me choose the best of the genre. I took a pile home and typed them up in manuscript form to get a feel for the length of the line, the structure, and the rhythm. I wrote *The Secret Box Mystery* and *The Mysterious Prowler* followed by several others.''

Gathering materials for one of her books is a subjective process "derived from places I have lived and visited, people I have known, and interesting things I have seen, with the deeper, underlying thoughts which are exclusively mine: my beliefs, my approach to life, my goals, even my own sense of what is humorous, right or good.

"My bulletin board serves as my idea bank. When an idea comes to me which I feel has possibilities, I jot it down in a paragraph or two, and then tack it on the bulletin board. Every now and then, I thumb through the ideas and find one that I'm ready to work on. It works for me. I like to be able to look at my ideas whenever I want, without having them tucked away somewhere.

"I do quite a bit of research for my books because I want them to be absolutely accurate. For *The Stalker,* I met with the head of public relations for the Corpus Christi police department. He showed me the homicide room and the place where the people are arraigned in court, took me through all the different steps of arraignment and brought me to the county jail. The Sheriff's Department didn't want to let me in at first, but I kept insisting I *had* to see what the women's jail looked like. I remember going through two doors, and then suddenly being locked in—a terrible feeling, to be locked inside—but I did get the information I wanted. I also research the locales of my books thoroughly familiarizing myself with street names.''

Nixon's children's books found a tremendous audience in her own children. "They would come home from school, sit down at my feet and say, 'O.K., now *read,*' and I'd read what I had written that day.''

Nixon noted several advantages in writing books for young people. "I believe that many books for young people are better written than adult books. Perhaps this is because the editors in the field will work hand in hand with authors to make certain everything is as perfect as it can be before it is published. This is not always true in the adult field. Books for young people stay in print much longer and have greater paperback and overseas sales possibilities. I'm more challenged when I write for young people. I've never felt constrained by it, because when you write for 'children' you write for everyone from a two-year-old to a teenager. There are so many, many different styles and forms for these age groups. Writing a young adult novel is very much like writing an adult novel. Your heroine has to be a little younger, however—eighteen instead of twenty-six.

"I write a book on two levels—my character has a problem to solve and my character has a mystery to solve. The two levels are so intertwined that toward the end of the book, near the climax, the character is able to weave the two levels together. Sometimes the mystery grows out of the problem, and sometimes the mystery and the problem are interrelated.

"As an author of books for young children, I try to remember my own childhood—how I felt, how I reacted, how I re-

This land has got the worst case of the uglies I've ever seen. ■ (From *If You Say So, Claude* by Joan Lowery Nixon. Illustrated by Lorinda Bryan Cauley.)

sponded to the emotions of happiness, sorrow, excitement, fear . . . so I can understand how a child of today would feel, how he would approach his problems, and how he would identify with the character in a book, who perhaps had the same problems to solve. My characters become a part of me and I feel with them.''

Writing, according to Nixon, can be a lonely experience. ''By lonely I mean it's a one person job. You work all by yourself without sharing the experience with others in a daily sense. You can't call people up and say, 'Let me read you what I wrote.' You have to be on your own with it. My loneliness disappears once I become totally absorbed by what I am doing. It's afterwards, when I close down my word processor that the house becomes a little quiet and I'm all alone again. I often wish I could sit down and talk to somebody about my day's work.

''It's important for writers to get together for moral support. I'm the regional vice-president of the Houston chapter of the Mystery Writers of America. Though we meet once a month in Houston, our chapter covers all of Texas, Oklahoma, Louisiana and Arkansas. It's very stimulating. We have speakers at the meetings, usually from one of the law enforcement professions. We've had policemen who specialize in police dogs, we've had a judge, the Guardian Angels, FBI agents, private eyes, a county coroner, and a medical examiner.'' Nixon

served on the board of directors of the Society of Children's Book Writers, as well.

''Because I enjoy writing for children, I also enjoy writing *with* children. It was my daughter Kathy who asked me to teach her how to write, and this began seven years of volunteer teaching of creative writing to junior high and high school age students. Eventually each of our children was in one of my classes and Kathy is now a professional writer.

''Although a teacher cannot bestow talent upon her students, she can give them certain basic rules of writing to follow which will help them develop their talents and writing skills. I emphasized description utilizing the five senses, use of strong action verbs which present a visual image, and opening sentences which are so interesting they reach out and firmly grasp a reader's attention. I had my students study their own feelings and the feelings of others. We worked on sensory perception and description, characterization, and plotting.

''I used exercises to get them writing—for example, looking at a situation or a problem from two different viewpoints. I provided them with settings, and asked them to write very short scenes. If I gave them a circus setting, I'd ask them to write something very sad; for hospital scenes, I'd ask them to write something funny and happy. This was to help them analyze their exact feelings, to help separate themselves emotion-

The shifting earth in the 1964 Alaska earthquake caused this section of a street in Anchorage to drop. ■ (From *Earthquakes: Nature in Motion* by Hershell H. Nixon and Joan Lowery Nixon. Photograph courtesy of the U.S. Army.)

Magnolia Possum opened her grandma's kitchen door and sniffed. ■ (From *Magnolia's Mixed-Up Magic* by Joan Lowery Nixon. Illustrated by Linda Bucholtz-Ross.)

ally from the environment or the setting of the scenes.

"I always encouraged new writers to find the character who was closest to the action and to use that character's viewpoint in telling the story. 'Mary Worth' or 'Dr. Watson' characters who tell the story from the sidelines of the action are not as effective in most fiction as characters who are involved in the story. My students entered a Scholastic writing contest in which a number of them won honorable mentions. It was very rewarding to see what they had achieved. Even students who were not interested or enthusiastic about writing improved greatly.

Hikers study a deep crevasse in the King's Glacier on West Spitsbergen Island, Norway. ■ (From *Glaciers: Nature's Frozen Rivers* by Hershell H. Nixon and Joan Lowery Nixon. Photograph courtesy of the Norwegian Information Service in the United States.)

"Grandfather! Arko! Come in! This is Kleep, and we need help!" ■ (From *Kidnapped on Astarr* by Joan Lowery Nixon. Illustrated by Paul Frame.)

"I never want to stop learning and it seems to me there is always something new to learn, and something new to try. I like to experiment when I'm writing. Lately I have been thinking about the different types of mysteries—the detective mystery versus the suspense mystery. I thought to myself, 'Why not try and combine the two forms? What would happen?' I wrote *The Stalker* which is suspenseful and which utilizes detection. A girl tries to find the killer of her friend's mother, with every other chapter from the point of view of the killer. There isn't any description, just the words and thoughts in the killer's head. He realizes at some point that this girl is looking for him and decides to 'take care' of the problem. These two characters find themselves on a collision course—the result being a mixture of detection and suspense. I think it worked out very well and is an example of what can happen when you try something a little bit different.

"I'm an optimist. I feel strongly that in books for children of any age there should be the element of hope. I have read some well written books, some beautifully written books which are very depressing—a shame because the writers are such fine writers. Adults can handle depressing or cynical fiction, but children lack the experience, at least with despair. And despair can even lead to suicide. We must be aware of the high suicide rate even in young children. We can give young people the feeling that although things may be tough *right now,* they will get better and that they have the power to make things get better."

Nixon collaborated with her geologist husband, Hershell H. Nixon, on many science books for young people. "One day, I heard my husband explaining to one of our children how the air cleans itself. I suggested taking notes for a children's book. We never found a publisher for the book, but we decided to collaborate. Hershell has a scientific mind, and I had always avoided science as a young person. Science was uninteresting to me, but I have learned so much from Hershell.

"Our first collaborative effort was a book about volcanoes. We were planning a trip to Hawaii and decided to do some research while we were there. I did a number of interviews by telephone, and visited volcano sites and universities talking with volcanologists and acquiring photographs. We then put everything together with Hershell's final opinion on its accu-

racy. Sometimes he wrote paragraphs, sometimes I did, and he always made suggestions about my approach to a certain section or structure of a chapter. Every book we work on goes through three or four drafts before it's ready for the publisher."

Nixon's habit is to "sit down in the morning and start writing. I work on a word processor, and as I write, I rewrite. I feel like a sculptor with a ball of clay which I pinch and poke and push and mold. Sometimes I even squash my 'clay' all together and start over again. I have to keep making changes as I go along. At the end of a morning of writing, I print out a copy of my work. I can think better about my work on paper rather than computer screen. In the afternoon, I go over the print out and make more changes. The next morning, I put those changes back into the computer, read the work over again, make more changes and then go on. The first hour of the morning is set aside for rewriting what I have written the day before.

"Before I write anything, I have to know how my story is going to begin and end, and approximately what I'm going to have in the middle. Towards the last third of the book I sometimes rely on 'progression.' I put various events I anticipate using in the book on file cards, and then put them in sequence. As I finish using each card, I toss it in the wastebasket. This system helps me remember what I want to include.

"If I'm writing a highly suspenseful story, I often like to use humor to break it up. You can't sustain a feeling of suspense throughout an entire book. Humor is often useful in relaxing the reader before he gets into the next suspenseful scene. It was my daughter Kathy, who as a child found one of my books too scary to read, who helped me reach this realization."

Nixon's advice to aspiring writers is to "read as much as you can, then practice writing. Don't think too much about getting published. Write for your own pleasure."

FOR MORE INFORMATION SEE: The Writer, September, 1972, February, 1977; *School Library Media Quarterly,* fall, 1982; Sally Holmes Holtze, editor, *Fifth Book of Junior Authors and Illustrators,* H. W. Wilson, 1983.

ODOR, Ruth Shannon 1926-

BRIEF ENTRY: Born September 22, 1926, in Corinth, Ky. Editor and author of over thirty books for children. Odor graduated magna cum laude from Georgetown College in 1947 and did graduate study at the University of Kentucky. After teaching high school for about five years, she began her career as an editor at Standard Publishing in Cincinnati, Ohio. Most of Odor's picture books are intended for preschool and early primary-grade readers, including *Cissy, the Pup, Lori's Day,* and *Sarah Lou's Untied Shoe* (all Children's Press, 1976). Revised editions of these three books were published by Child's World in 1979 under the titles *The Pup Who Did as She Pleased, Growing Up,* and *A Friend Is One Who Helps.* Odor has also written many books of a Christian nature, like *Baby in a Basket* (Child's World, 1979), the story of Moses; *The Baby Jesus: A Surprise Storybook* and *The Very Special Night* (both Standard Publishing, 1980); and *Bible Heroes* (Standard Publishing, 1982). Her most recent works include two books written with her husband, Harold Odor: *Becoming a Christian* and *Sharing Your Faith* (both Standard Publishing, 1985).

ORMEROD, Jan(ette Louise) 1946-

BRIEF ENTRY: Born September 23, 1946, in Bunbury, Western Australia. Now an author and illustrator of children's books, Ormerod previously worked as an art teacher and part-time lecturer in drawing and basic design. Critics have praised her ability to create meaningful stories using only pictures. "Without a single written word," observed *New York Times Book Review,* "her delicate watercolors plunge their readers into the middle of a family, letting them feel their love and their lives." In her first two books, *Sunshine* (Lothrop, 1981) and *Moonlight* (Lothrop, 1982), Ormerod used a strip cartoon format to wordlessly capture the beginning and end of a little girl's day. "Appealing pictures in color," noted *Publishers Weekly,* "make every happening quickly understood and enthralling."

In 1982 Ormerod received the Mother Goose Award and the Australian Picture Book of the Year award for *Sunshine,* also named a "highly commended" book by the Kate Greenaway Medal selection committee. She most recently produced the "Jan Ormerod Baby Book" series, a collection of four books that highlight the special relationship between a pre-toddler and his father. Intended for ages six to twenty-four months, the series consists of *Dad's Back, Messy Baby, Reading,* and *Sleeping* (all Lothrop, 1985). *Booklist* commented that "while the humor here definitely caters to an adult's rather than a child's perceptions, the books will still be useful in point-and-name situations." Ormerod's other works are *Be Brave, Billy* (Dent, 1983) and *101 Things to Do with a Baby* (Lothrop, 1984). She is also the illustrator of *Rhymes Around the Day* (Lothrop, 1983), a selection of nursery rhymes compiled by Pat Thompson. *Agent:* Laura Cecil, 17 Alwyne Villas, London N1 2HG, England.

FOR MORE INFORMATION SEE: Contemporary Authors, Volume 113, Gale, 1985.

PATTERSON, Geoffrey 1943-

BRIEF ENTRY: Born October 6, 1943, in Wimbledon, London, England. Author and illustrator of books for children. During the early 1960s, Patterson worked as a designer for John Siddeley in London; beginning in 1964, he was employed as a television set designer for the British Broadcasting Corp. A writer since 1977, Patterson also teaches visual and three-dimensional arts. He reveals that his children's books focus on "English country life as it used to be and is now. . . . Concerned about the changing landscape . . . in the name of progress and modern farming. . . , I try to make the next generation aware of what they will and are losing." To this end, Patterson blends fiction with historical fact in seven self-illustrated juvenile works, all published by Deutsch. *Growing Point* described *The Oak* (1979) as "a lively narrative . . . of the way a Tudor village grows into a modern town." Similarly, *Chestnut Farm, 1860* (1980) depicts the family tasks involved in maintaining a farm more than one hundred years ago. Patterson explores other facets of country life in *The Story of Hay* (1981), *A Pig's Tale* (1982), and *Dairy Farming* (1982). Although originally published in England, these books are available through distributors in the United States. Patterson's most recent works are *All about Bread* (1984) and *The Working Horse* (1985). *Home and office:* Beech Tree Farm, Wingfield, near Diss, Suffolk, England.

FOR MORE INFORMATION SEE: Contemporary Authors, Volume 103, Gale, 1982.

PETERSON, Lorraine 1940-

BRIEF ENTRY: Born July 10, 1940, in Red Wing, Minn. Teacher and author. Peterson received a B.A. from North Park College and Theological Seminary in 1962. That same year, she began teaching American history and English at a public junior high school in Glenview, Ill. She later taught English in Quito, Ecuador, and history at public schools in Minneapolis, Minn. Since 1981, she has taught both history and English as a second language at the American School of Guadalajara in Guadalajara, Mexico. As the author of four devotionals for teenagers, Peterson stated, "I love teenagers. . . . My goal as a writer is to try to help them through this difficult period of life by pointing out that Christian faith can be relevant to the teenager's world."

Among her books is *Real Characters in the Making* (Bethany House, 1985), which contains thirteen weeks of daily lessons based on the stories of thirteen well-known Old Testament characters. In the book, Peterson presents issues common to both contemporary teens and the Bible figures. She also wrote *Falling Off Cloud Nine and Other High Places* (Bethany House, 1981) in which, according to *Voice of Youth Advocates,* "each [devotional] offers a short paragraph describing the problem in a way teens will relate to." Peterson's other books are *If God Loves Me, Why Can't I Get My Locker Open?* (Bethany House, 1980, also published as a study guide, 1982, and a teacher's guide, 1983) and *Why Isn't God Giving Cash Prizes?* (Bethany House, 1982). *Home address:* c/o Gutierrez, Sorrento 825, Colonia Italia, Guadalajara C.P. 44-640, Mexico.

FOR MORE INFORMATION SEE: Contemporary Authors, Volume 113, Gale, 1985.

POGÁNY, William Andrew 1882-1955 (Willy Pogány)

PERSONAL: Born August 24, 1882, in Szeged, Hungary; came to United States in 1914; became naturalized citizen in 1921; died July 30, 1955, in New York, N.Y.; son of Joseph Stephen and Helena Paula (Kolis) Pogány; married Lillian Rose Doris,

December 9, 1908 (divorced, 1933); married Elaine Cox (a writer), 1934; children: (first marriage) John, Peter. *Education:* Attended Budapest Technical School for one year, and Budapest Academy of Art; also studied at art schools in Munich and Paris. *Politics:* Independent. *Residence:* New York, N.Y.

CAREER: Artist, illustrator, muralist, architect, sculptor, and stage and costume designer. Began illustrating books for children, London, England, circa 1906; moved to New York City, 1914, where he designed scenes, costumes and sets for the Metropolitan Opera House, on Broadway, and for several ballets; during the 1930s and 40s, worked in Hollywood as an art director for the film companies, United Artists, Warner Bros., Twentieth Century-Fox, Universal, and the Charles Chaplin Studios; illustrated magazine covers for *Metropolitan Magazine, Town and Country,* and *American Weekly,* 1940-51; painted portraits, beginning 1950. Instructor of art, New York City; lecturer in art, art schools throughout the United States.

EXHIBITIONS: Paintings represented in the permanent collection of the Hungarian National Gallery; executed murals at various locations, including the old Ziegfeld Theatre, New York City; the Heckscher Children's Theatre, New York City; Niagara Falls Power Co., Niagara Falls, Ontario; Glen Cove Children's Hospital, Glen Cove, N.Y.; William Randolph Hearst's estate, Wyntoon, Calif.; and John Ringling's residence, Sarasota, Fla.

MEMBER: Institute of Design Society of Mural Painters, Architectural League of New York, Beaux Art Institute of New York City, Salmagundi Club. *Awards, honors:* Gold medals from expositions in Budapest, Hungary and Leipzig, Germany; Gold Medal from the Panama-Pacific International Exposition in San Francisco, Calif., 1915, for "The Ride of the Valkyries"; Silver Medal of Honor from the New York Society of Architects, 1922; illustrator of Newbery Honor Book, Padraic Colum's *The Golden Fleece and the Heroes Who Lived before Achilles,* 1922; fellow, Royal Society of Arts (London).

WRITINGS—Under name Willy Pogány; all published by McKay, except as indicated: *Willy Pogány Children,* Harrap, 1914; (with wife, Elaine Pogány) *Peterkin* (juvenile; self-illustrated), 1940; *Willy Pogány's Drawing Lessons,* 1946, revised and enlarged edition, 1946, also published as *The Art of Drawing,* A. S. Barnes, 1969; *Water-Color Lessons, Including Gouache,* 1950; *Oil-Painting Lessons,* 1954.

Illustrator; under name Willy Pogány; all for young people: Ignacz Kunos, *Turkish Fairy Tales and Folk Tales,* Burt, 1901; George E. Farrow, *The Adventures of a Dodo,* T. Fisher Unwin, 1907; William J. Thomas, *The Welsh Fairy-Book,* F. A. Stokes, 1907, Dufour, 1963, reissued, Jones, 1979; Mary Augusta Ward, *Milly and Olly; or, a Holiday among the Mountains,* second edition, T. Fisher Unwin, 1907 (Pogány was not associated with earlier edition); Madalen G. Edgar, compiler, *A Treasury of Verse for Little Children,* Crowell, 1908, new edition, 1956; George W. Dasent, compiler, *Norse Wonder Tales,* Collins' Clear-Type Press, 1909; *Rubáiyát of Omar Khayyam,* Harrap, 1909, new edition, McKay, 1959; Nathaniel Hawthorne, *Tanglewood Tales,* T. Fisher Unwin, 1909.

Lillian Gask, *Folk Tales from Many Lands,* Crowell, 1910; H. de Vere Stacpoole, *The Blue Lagoon,* T. Fisher Unwin, 1910; Samuel T. Coleridge, *The Rime of the Ancient Mariner,* Crowell, 1910; Wilhelm R. Wagner, *Tannhäuser,* translated in poetic narrative form by T. W. Rolleston, Harrap, 1911; L. Gask, *The Fairies and the Christmas Child,* Harrap, 1912,

WILLY POGÁNY

also published as *Fairy Tales of Other Lands,* 1931; T. W. Rolleston, reteller, *Parsifal; or, The Legend of the Holy Grail,* Harrap, 1912; compiled by brother, Nándor Pogány, *The Hungarian Fairy Book,* F. A. Stokes, 1913; I. Kunos, compiler and translator, *Forty-Four Turkish Fairy Tales,* Harrap, 1913; W. R. Wagner, *The Tale of Lohengrin: Knight of the Swan,* adapted by T. W. Rolleston, Harrap, 1913; Frances J. Olcott, compiler, *More Tales from the Arabian Nights,* Holt, 1915; Leonard Fable, *The Gingerbread Man,* McBride Nast & Co., 1915; Charles Perrault, *Cinderella,* retold by Edith L. Elias, McBride Nast & Co., 1915; Burton E. Stevenson, compiler, *The Home Book of Verse for Young Folks,* Holt, 1915, revised and enlarged edition, 1929.

Padraic Colum, *The King of Ireland's Son,* Holt, 1916, reissued, Macmillan, 1967; Jonathan Swift, *Gulliver's Travels* (an abridged edition for children), edited by P. Colum, Macmillan, 1917, reissued, 1962; Gertrude Crownfield, *Little Tailor of the Winding Way,* Macmillan, 1917; P. Colum, *The Adventures of Odysseus and the Tale of Troy,* Macmillan, 1918, also published as *The Children's Homer: The Adventures of Odysseus and the Tale of Troy,* 1925, reissued, 1962; Helen Ward Banks, *Polly Garden,* Macmillan, 1918; Sara Cone Bryant, *Stories to Tell the Little Ones,* Harrap, 1918; F. J. Olcott, reteller, *Tales of the Persian Genii,* Harrap, 1919, new and enlarged edition, Houghton, 1931; Eleanor Louise Skinner and Ada Maria Skinner, *Children's Plays,* D. Appleton, 1919.

P. Colum, *The Children of Odin,* Macmillan, 1920, published as *The Children of Odin: The Book of Northern Myths,* 1962; Agnes McClelland Daulton, *Uncle Davie's Children,* Macmillan, 1920; P. Colum, *The Golden Fleece and the Heroes Who Lived before Achilles,* Macmillan, 1921, reissued, 1962; F. J. Olcott, editor and compiler, *The Adventures of Haroun Er Raschid, and Other Tales from the Arabian Nights,* Holt, 1923.

Out in the street the wind was bold;
Now who would house Him from the cold?

■ (From "A Christmas Folk Song" by Lizette Woodworth Reese in *My Poetry Book: An Anthology of Modern Verse for Boys and Girls,* selected by Grace Thompson Huffard and Laura Mae Carlisle. Illustrated by Willy Pogány.)

(From "The Story of the Fairy Rowan Tree" in *The King of Ireland's Son* by Padraic Colum. Illustrated by Willy Pogány.)

Richard F. Burton, *Kasidah of Haji Abdu el-Yezdi*, Coward-McCann, 1926; Pierre Louyes, *Songs of Bilitis*, translated by Alvah C. Bessie, Macy-Masius, 1926; Isidora Newman, *Fairy Flowers: Nature Legends of Facts and Fantasy*, Holt, 1926; Helen Hartness Flanders, *Looking Out of Jimmie*, Dutton, 1927; Margaret Loring Thomas, *George Washington Lincoln Goes around the World*, T. Nelson (London), 1927; *Willy Pogány's Mother Goose*, T. Nelson, 1928; Rosika Schwimmer, *Tisza Tales*, Doubleday, Doran, 1928; Lewis Carroll (pseudonym of Charles L. Dodgson) *Alice's Adventures in Wonderland*, Dutton, 1929; Heinrich Gebhard, *Fifteen Songs from Looking Out of Jimmie*, Dutton, 1929.

N. Pogány, compiler, *Magyar Fairy Tales from Old Hungarian Legends*, Dutton, 1930; F. J. Olcott, compiler, *Bible Stories to Read and Tell*, Harper, 1932; Elizabeth Barrett Browning, *Sonnets from the Portuguese*, Basil Blackwell, 1933, Crowell, 1936; Grace Thompson Huffard and Laura Mae Carlisle, compilers, *My Poetry Book: An Anthology of Modern Verse for Boys and Girls*, Winston, 1934, revised edition (with an introduction by Marguerite de Angeli), Holt, 1956; Helen von Kolnitz Hyer, *Wimp and the Woodle*, Sutton House, 1935; Blanche Ashley Ambrose, *Coppa Hamba*, Sutton House, 1935; Harriet Smith Hawley, *Goose Girl of Nuremberg*, Sutton House, 1936; Alexander Pushkin, *The Golden Cockerel*, retold by E. Pogány, T. Nelson, 1938; P. Colum, *The Frenzied Prince* (Irish legends), McKay, 1943; Phillis Garrard, *Running Away with Nebby*, McKay, 1944.

Other illustrated works: Johann W. Von Goethe, *Faust*, translated by Abraham Hayward, Hutchinson & Co., 1908; Gerald Young, *The Witch's Kitchen; or, The India Rubber Doctor*, Harrap, 1910; Heinrich Heine, *Atta Troll*, translated from the German by Herman Scheffauer, Sidgwick & Jackson, 1913; Joseph Anthony, *Casanova Jones*, Century, 1930; Edwin Arnold, *Light of Asia*, McKay, 1932; *Book Plates: Original Etchings by Willy Pogány*, Castle, 1940.

Also illustrator of the juvenile books *Hiawatha*, *Irish Legends*, *Bhagavad Gita*, *Robinson Crusoe*, and *La belle dame sans merci*. Contributor to *Le Rire* (Paris) and *Illustrated London News*, 1913.

SIDELIGHTS: Pogány was born in Szeged, Hungary in 1882, in the very center of the paprika industry. Although he studied to be a mechanical engineer at the Budapest Technical Institute, he quickly discovered that engineering was not for him. Enjoying drawing, Pogány entered the Budapest Academy of Art, but could not see any sense in finishing art school, either. "Art isn't an exact science like engineering, where standards are set. I realized that every artist has to set his own standards, so why should I go to an art school and accept the standards of other people secondhand. I quit art school and began to paint by myself." [Arthur Strawn, "Willy Pogány," *Outlook*, December 24, 1930.[1]]

Using money he received from art commissions, Pogány bought a railroad ticket to Paris. After a few months of hardship there, he began to make caricatures and humorous drawings for several French journals.

From Paris, Pogány went to London, married an English girl, and stayed for ten years, drawing book illustrations and murals. In 1914, Pogány came to the United States, where he made his home and became a naturalized citizen in 1921. Settling first in New York City, Pogány busied himself illustrating books, painting murals and portraits, doing etchings and sculpture, and designing stage settings and costumes for different shows and the Metropolitan Opera House.

During the 30s and 40s, Pogány worked in Hollywood as an art director for United Artists, Warner Bros., Twentieth Century-Fox, Universal, and the Charles Chaplin Studios. He was first invited to Hollywood to work for Samuel Goldwyn, de-

signing sets and costumes for a 1928 movie starring Gilda Gray. "At first I hesitated to accept the invitation. I did not know much about the technical side of motion picture production, and, no matter how curiously it may sound, I didn't know anything about photography, either. I had never taken a snapshot in all my life before going to Hollywood. Also I had heard rumors that speed was considered most important way down in Hollywood. And I like to work at a leisurely pace, I like the quiet of my studio.

"Then I learned that Gilda Gray was the star. I have known Gilda for more than ten years and she has always been one of the most charming of my friends. I admire her both as an artist and as a very human person. For her sake, as much as anything else, I undertook the journey to the Coast.

"There was, however, one other thing that faintly lured me. Or, rather, something that I had vaguely suspected (vaguely,

(From "The Death of Dermott O'Duivna" in *The Frenzied Prince: Being Heroic Stories of Ancient Ireland* by Padraic Colum. Illustrated by Willy Pogány.)

(From "In the Nursery" in *The Home Book of Verse for Young Folk,* selected and arranged by Burton Egbert Stevenson. Illustrated by Willy Pogány.)

because of my slender connections with the movies) but which I had never realized fully. Not until I arrived in Hollywood, anyway. And, to be quite frank, the realization of this suspicion filled me with pleasant surprise.

"The movies are still in their infancy—and I am not saying this disparagingly. Motion pictures have wide and infinite possibilities; the 'lot' is a territory where one can work free of traditions, with one's eyes on the future only. You don't know what this means to a painter who has had artistic ancestors for millenniums.

"In Hollywood I am not an epigon. There were no Rafaels, Rembrandts, Gainsboroughs, Michelangelos before me on the 'lots.' Their shadows do not fill me with awe and the glory of an immortal past. In Hollywood only the future exists.

"Aside from this, another delightful surprise was awaiting me. The speed of the picture studios was not irritating. It was not of the slave-driving variety—an impression created in me by disillusioned persons; or, shall we say, failures? Speed on the 'lot' is an expression of vitality, and consequently not annoying.

"As soon as I started work I discovered that my training in the technique of the theatre was of very little help to me. For there is a tremendous difference between the work of a scenic artist who designs for the stage and the work of the man creating sets for pictures.

"First of all, the stage designer creates his effects chiefly with colors. He does not consider the third dimension so carefully as the movie designer has to—because the third dimension is right there on the stage. But there are no colors in the movies. Only black and white, lights and shadows. You have to create your effects, the third dimensional effects, on a flat screen with chiaroscuro only. But then, again, Rembrandt and Michelangelo did great things with chiaroscuro. I may even add there is a similarity between the pictures and sculpture. For the sculptor has no colors at his disposal, either. He, too, creates his effects with lights and shadows only. Fortunately, I am [a] sculptor, too—although few people know it.

"Now, on the stage as well as in the movies, the effects are created by optical illusions. But on the stage we create these optical illusions with colors. A deep blue placed beside a lighter shade suggests depth and distance. You can't do this in the pictures. There you create the optical illusions by cheating in dimensions, if I may be permitted to use this expression.

"I was amazed when I first saw how primitive, and yet how expensive, the props for the production of the necessary optical illusions were. I, for one, consider the 'glass' shot as totally useless from the point of view of the artist. The miniatures are all right—but infinite possibilities are at one's disposal to develop and improve them. I'd retain them—applying to them

Bitterly Hypsipyle wept, but softly, for she would not have the others hear her weeping. ■ (From "The Voyage to Colchis" in *The Golden Fleece and the Heroes Who Lived before Achilles* by Padraic Colum. Illustrated by Willy Pogány.)

(From "The Happy Warrior" in *The Home Book of Verse for Young Folks,* selected and arranged by Burton Egbert Stevenson. Illustrated by Willy Pogány.)

a few other elementary principles, and principles not so elementary." ["Willy Pogány and Film Art," *New York Times,* January 1, 1928.[2]]

In 1933 Pogány divorced his first wife, Lillian Rose Doris, and married writer Elaine Cox the following year. The couple made their home in Hollywood for several years while Pogány worked there. ". . . I like Hollywood—partly, because of the nights down there which are the most beautiful anywhere on earth, and, partly, because I see the possibilities that are within the reach of the scenic artist. . . . I should like to do my modest bit toward putting these possibilities into reality. . . .

"The movies are no longer in an experimental stage. They offer much, they have grown to vast proportions, they are destined to fulfill a cultural mission in the life of humankind—but they are very far from the complete realization of their promises. People are beginning to demand more of the movies than what they are offering. And the demand must be met. The demand is for artistic development. Why not give it to them? The development of the movies should not be permitted to stop at the present stage. Witness the sad state of affairs

the radio and the phonograph are in as the result of their purely technical development.

"In order to achieve this aim, the artist must be given a more important position. First-class artists, real great ones, must be invited to participate in the production of films. I do not say there are no great artists down there now; there are—but only a few. And a few are not enough.

"And the artist should not be considered an inferior person. He ought to be at least as important as the actor—although he is as important as the director himself. Don't forget, movies are seen—and only the artist can create visible things. The future in the movies lies in giving the public food for their imagination—in giving them esthetic satisfaction. Consequently, imagination should be called into action—I don't mean fairy tales, though—but fantasy, vision, dreams. Bring out all in art. I have faith in the movies; one day they will realize that I am right."[2]

Highly diversified in his craft, Pogány also executed murals in various locations, including the Heckscher Children's Theatre in New York City. He illustrated numerous children's books, including the Newbery Honor Book *The Golden Fleece and the Heroes Who Lived before Achilles* by Padraic Colum, and *Magyar Fairy Tales from Old Hungarian Legends* by Nándor Pogány.

(From *The Blue Lagoon* by H. de Vere Stacpoole. Illustrated by Willy Pogány.)

(From *Running Away with Nebby* by Phillis Garrard. Illustrated by Willy Pogány.)

Pogány was also the author of a series of instructional art books, taught art in New York City, and lectured in art throughout the United States. He offered the following advice to would-be artists: "For your first attempt at painting choose a few simple objects like a bowl, a glass, and some apples. Arrange them on a table against a plain background such as a sheet of cardboard, a piece of material simply draped, or even the bare wall itself.

"See that your subject is lighted in such a way that there is plenty of contrast in light and shade.

"Sketch in your subject with charcoal. If you wish to make any corrections, use only a *chamois* for wiping off charcoal. Do not use cloth or erasers. When charcoal drawing is completed, it is ready to be fixed so that the charcoal adheres to the canvas and does not rub off.

"While painting studies, don't think to yourself, 'I am painting a glass bowl, an apple, a flower.' Concentrate only on *shapes, colors,* and *values.* Watch your complementary colors, and also notice how the *warm* and *cool shades* invariably follow each other.

And look at the house, the tragic house, the house with nobody in it. ■ (From "The House with Nobody in It" by Joyce Kilmer in *My Poetry Book: An Anthology of Modern Verse for Boys and Girls,* selected by Grace Thompson Huffard and Laura Mae Carlisle. Illustrated by Willy Pogány.)

"If you study these points as you paint, your subject will take form on the canvas before you realize it.

"A good picture needs *harmony* and *contrast.*

"Complementary colors will give *harmony.*

"Light and shade will make for *contrast.*

"The strongest contrast would be a *strong color* of *deep value* against a *light color* of *high value.*

"Darken *light shades* when approaching a *dark plane.*

"Lighten *dark shades* when approaching *lighter planes.*

"Shadow will always contain the *local color.*" [Willy Pogány, *Oil-Painting Lessons,* McKay, 1954.[3]]

Pogány was the recipient of numerous gold medal awards from international competitions at expositions in Leipzig, Budapest, and San Francisco. He was also awarded the Silver Medal of Honor from the New York Society of Architects. In his later years, Pogány worked primarily on portraits. "There is scarcely anything in this world that rivals the pleasure and satisfaction of painting a picture. There are no qualifying limits to this fascinating form of self-expression. You do not have to be an expert, nor do you have to feel that the fires of genius are burning within your soul. Many amateurs, and oftentimes children, have painted pictures that are decorative and appealing. The wonder world of the artist is open to all who feel the urge to paint.

"There are, however, certain fundamental mechanics in oil painting, and the question, 'How do I go about it?' would naturally arise in the mind of a beginner. Courage and confidence are two important factors in your approach to painting. Don't be discouraged by criticism. Oftentimes criticism can be helpful and constructive. Use it to advantage. *Paint bravely.*—Don't be afraid of spoiling a canvas now and then— (even the best of artists do that occasionally). Remember the old cliché 'We learn by our mistakes.'

"As to personal style, the only advice I would offer on this subject is 'Be yourself.' However, I might suggest occasional visits to Museums and Galleries. This will help to develop your taste and broaden your vision—besides giving you no mean enjoyment."[3]

Pogány died suddenly at his home at the Hotel Des Artistes in New York City on July 30, 1955, at the age of seventy-two. Just hours before he died he was working on plans for several stage sets for Broadway productions.

HOBBIES AND OTHER INTERESTS: Chess, soccer, swimming, and rowing.

FOR MORE INFORMATION SEE: Arts and Decoration, December, 1922, February, 1926, November, 1927; *International Studio,* October, 1925; "Willy Pogány and Film Art," *New York Times,* January 1, 1928; *American Magazine of Art,* August, 1928; *Wilson Library Bulletin,* January, 1929; Arthur Strawn, "Willy Pogány," *Outlook,* December 24, 1930; Bertha E. Mahony and others, compilers, *Illustrators of Children's Books: 1744-1945,* Horn Book, 1947; Stanley J. Kunitz and Howard Haycraft, editors, *Junior Book of Authors,* second edition, revised, H. W. Wilson, 1951; Richard W. Ellis, *Book Illustration,* Kingsport Press, 1952; Willy Pogány, *Oil-Painting Lessons,* McKay, 1954; *The National Cyclopedia of Amer-*

ican Biography, Volume 44, University Microfilms, 1967; Martha E. Ward and Dorothy A. Marquardt, *Illustrators of Books for Young People,* 2nd edition, Scarecrow, 1975; B. E. Mahony and Elinor Whitney, compilers, *Contemporary Illustrators of Children's Books,* Gale, 1978; *Rhode Island School of Design Bulletin Museum Notes,* April, 1979.

Obituaries: *New York Times,* July 31, 1955; *Publishers Weekly,* August 6, 1955; *Time,* August 8, 1955; *Wilson Library Bulletin,* September, 1955; *Britannica Book of the Year, 1956.*

POLLAND, Barbara K(ay)   1939-

PERSONAL: Born October 14, 1939, in Milwaukee, Wis.; daughter of Eugene Michael (a surgeon) and Margaret (a writer and nurse) Kay; married Peter David Polland, June 24, 1962 (divorced, 1978); children: Mark, Tamy. *Education:* National College of Education, B.Ed., 1961; San Fernando Valley State College, M.A., 1970; Claremont Graduate School of Education, Ph.D., 1983. *Office:* Department of Child Development, California State University, 18111 Nordhoff, Northridge, Calif. 91330.

CAREER: Assistant nursery school teacher in Shorewood, Wis., 1958; kindergarten teacher in Wilmette, Ill., 1961-62; organizer and teacher of kindergarten in Jackson, Wis., 1962-63; substitute teacher in elementary schools in Milwaukee, Wis., 1963-64, and Los Angeles, Calif., 1964-70; California State University, Northridge, associate professor of child development and educational psychology, 1970—. Volunteer tutor of handicapped children, 1964-66, counselor and tutor in Santa Monica, Calif., 1968, substitute teacher, 1970—. Licensed marriage, family and child counselor in California, with a private practice. Lecturer on children and effective, creative parenting and teaching, 1973—. Educational consultant for three Los Angeles schools, 1975—. Member of representative assembly of California Curriculum Forum, 1982-85. The Free Arts Clinic for Abused Children, board of directors, 1980—, member of executive board, 1983—.

MEMBER: Association for Childhood Education International, National Association for the Education of Young Children, United Professors of California, California Women in Higher Education, Southern California Association for the Education of Young Children (member of board of directors), California Association of Marriage Family Therapists, National College of Education Alumni Association, California State University, Northridge, Alumni Club, Kappa Delta Pi (Theta Eta chapter); Pi Lamda Theta; Phi Kappa Phi. *Awards, honors: The Sensible Book: A Celebration of Your Five Senses* was selected as a supplementary textbook for California public schools, 1975; Alumni Achievement Award, National College of Education, 1977; Distinguished Teaching Award from California State University, 1983.

WRITINGS: The Sensible Book: A Celebration of Your Five Senses, Celestial Arts, 1974; *Feelings: Inside You and Outloud Too,* Celestial Arts, 1975; *Decisions, Decisions, Decisions,* Celestial Arts, 1976; *Grandma and Grandpa Are Special People* (illustrated by Barbara Reinertson), Celestial Arts, 1983; *Guideposts for Growing Up,* Standard Education Corp., in press.

SIDELIGHTS: "Writing has always been an important outlet for me. During the storm and stress of growing up, I often shared my emotions with the pages of a personal journal. As an adult, I often find myself creating a clever thank you note

to a host and hostess while I'm in the midst of their party. When I see a beautiful flower or hear magnificent music, I try to find words to describe what I'm hearing, seeing, and feeling.

"Working extensively with children has helped me to hear the profound simplicity in their self-expression. Consequently, I try to use simple words to share complex emotions in my books. I hope that each book will stimulate communication between adults and children. We all have boundless capacity for growth when we share ourselves with each other.

"I use questions, statements, and photographs in my books to expand understanding of self and others. Letters expressing enthusiasm have arrived from children and adults and consequently I have felt encouraged to continue.

"Rather than lecture in the college classroom I have developed innovative approaches for learning course material. Adults as well as children like to be *actively* involved in the learning process. I have been invited to present these materials to parents, teachers, and on radio and television shows in many cities. The show hosts generally use one or more of my books as a springboard into discussion.

BARBARA K. POLLAND

I like to take walks with my grandpa. ■ (From *Grandma and Grandpa Are Special People* by Barbara Kay Polland. Illustrated by Barbara Reinertson.)

"A small private therapy practice gives me the opportunity to know a few people very well. Because this special kind of sharing so enriches me, I often wonder who gains the most—clients or therapist?"

HOBBIES AND OTHER INTERESTS: Arts and crafts, aerobic walking, gardening, psychic phenomena.

POLLOCK, Penny 1935-

PERSONAL: Born May 24, 1935, in Cleveland, Ohio; daughter of William Caswell (a candy maker) and Eleanor (a teacher; maiden name, Cadman) Morrow; married Stewart Glasson Pollock (a state supreme court justice), June 9, 1956; children: Wendy, Stewart, Jeffrey, Jennifer. *Education:* Mount Holyoke College, B.A., 1957; Kean College, M.A., 1973. *Religion:* Society of Friends (Quakers). *Home address:* Burnett Rd., Mendham, N.J. 07945.

CAREER: Dogwood School, Chester, N.J., assistant teacher, 1972-73; Village Nursery School, Brookside, N.J., head teacher, 1973-84. Lecturer at libraries and schools. Member of board of trustees of Mendham Township Public Library, 1979-83. *Member:* Society of Children's Book Writers, Patricia Lee Gauch Writers' Workshop, New Jersey Press Women, National Association for the Preservation and Perpetuation of Storytelling, New York Storytelling Center. *Awards, honors:* New Jersey Authors Award, 1983, for *Keeping It Secret*.

WRITINGS—Juvenile: Ants Don't Get Sunday Off (illustrated by Lorinda B. Cauley), Putnam, 1978; *The Slug Who Thought He Was a Snail* (Junior Literary Guild selection; illustrated by L. B. Cauley), Putnam, 1980; *Garlanda: The Ups and Downs of an Uppity Teapot* (illustrated by Margot Tomes), Putnam, 1980; *The Spit Bug Who Couldn't Spit* (illustrated by L. B. Cauley), Putnam, 1981; *Keeping It Secret* (illustrated by Donna Diamond), Putnam, 1982; *Stall Buddies* (illustrated by Gail Owens), Putnam, 1984; *Emily's Tiger* (illustrated by Judy Morgan), Paulist Press, 1985; *Water Is Wet* (illustrated with photographs by Barbara Beirne), Putnam, 1985. Contributor to *Cricket*.

WORK IN PROGRESS: An adventure story called *Mama Llama;* a book about a cow who has a need to "belong" and a three-legged cat who shows her the realities of life.

PENNY POLLOCK

SIDELIGHTS: Pollock says of her childhood: ''We were constantly on the move, trailing behind my adventure-loving father. Swarthmore, Pennsylvania, was our central home. From there, in the summer, we raced to Hiram, Ohio, or to the Jersey shore. One summer we camped out West, and there were jaunts to Mexico, Jamaica, and Tubac, Arizona. Some summers were spent in an apartment behind my father's nut and candy store on the boardwalk in Ocean City, New Jersey.

During the winter we lived on Star Island in Miami Beach. My father helped a snake farmer collect snakes on the Tamiami Trail. I sometimes went along.

''I have inherited my father's taste for adventure and my mother's sense of oneness with all living things. These feelings are important in my writing.

The name on her birth certificate said Mary Lou Spangler, but she was called Wisconsin. ■
(Detail of jacket illustration by Donna Diamond from *Keeping It Secret* by Penny Pollock.)

"Stories connect us to ourselves and to one another. Contrary to what we see on television, society is not unraveling. Fiction has the power to bind humanity together. The more I write, the more I feel the power of fiction. This power grows from such universal feelings as exultation, fear, and love. Children are comforted by shared emotions, and they hunger for stories of human triumph.

"Or perhaps I am comforting myself. In *Keeping It Secret* I deal openly with my hearing handicap as a way of saying to children that no one is perfect and that is okay. Once we accept our own limitations, we are free to accept those in others.

"I spend a lot of time talking with fifth and sixth graders about this point. The response is enormous. An inaudible sigh of 'I guess I'm all right after all' seems to rise up in the classroom. Children need to be reassured that although life is not perfect, it is wonderful—that although they are not perfect, they are wonderful. Because I believe this, I say it again and again.

"My books for younger children are mainly animal fantasies. They grow from a sense of oneness with all living things. My parents instilled this feeling in me. How I loved the search for the first skunk cabbage of the year!

"The characters in these books feel human to me. Ezra, the spittle bug, is a 'klutz.' That is, Ezra is not perfect. Writing about him, and his triumph, helped me find the courage to write about Wisconsin in *Keeping It Secret*. I did not notice this progression until recently.

"The importance of friendship runs through several of my books. Ezra, Garlanda, and Scarlett (*Stall Buddies*) learn that the essence of friendship is helping one another. That makes all the difference in life.

"Fantasy gives one more freedom than realistic fiction, but fantasy requires just as much research. It was not enough for me to care about my animal characters; I had to know about them, too. To learn more about insects, I turned to professors at Rutgers University for help. To learn more about trotters, I spent days in the barns at a track.

"Writing for children involves the wonderful challenge of telling children what it means to be human. The only way to meet this challenge is to share our feelings. This takes courage."

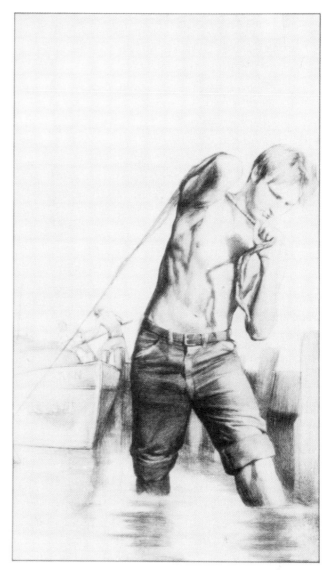

At low tide, Kuper had to wade ahead of the *Joan*, pulling at the anchor chain while his little crew pushed with poles. ■ (From *World War II Resistance Stories* by Arthur Prager and Emily Prager. Illustrated by Steven Assel.)

PRAGER, Arthur

PERSONAL—Agent: Alfonso Tafoya, 655 Avenue of the Americas, New York, N.Y. 10011. *Office:* 7 Washington Square N., New York, N.Y. 10003.

CAREER: Attaché at U.S. Embassy, Taipei, Taiwan and U.S. Consulate, Hong Kong, 1955-59; New York University, New York City, assistant professor of air science, 1959-62; Office of the Mayor, New York City, member of staff, 1962-82, assistant deputy mayor for policy, 1980—. Executive director, Royal Oak Foundation; consultant to Twentieth Century-Fox Film Corp. and Book-of-the-Month Club. *Military service:* U.S. Army Air Forces, 1943-46; became captain; received Distinguished Flying Cross. *Member:* The Coffee House, The Century Association. *Awards, honors:* Fellow of the Royal Society of the Arts.

WRITINGS: Rascals at Large; or, the Clue in the Old Nostalgia, Doubleday, 1971; *Underhanded Backgammon*, Haw-

ARTHUR PRAGER

thorn, 1977; *The Mahogany Tree: An Informal History of "Punch,"* Hawthorn, 1978; (with Emily Prager) *World War II Resistance Stories* (illustrated by Steven Assel), F. Watts, 1979.

Scripts: "Mousterpiece Theatre," Walt Disney Cable Television, 1983.

Contributor of articles and reviews to *Saturday Review, New York Times, Cosmopolitan, Ladies' Home Journal,* and *American Heritage.*

FOR MORE INFORMATION SEE: New Yorker, May 7, 1979; *New York Times Book Review,* July 1, 1979; *Economist,* August 11, 1979; *National Review,* December 21, 1979.

PUCCI, Albert John   1920-

PERSONAL: Born March 11, 1920, in Cleveland, Ohio; son of John Cloos and Sophie (Fumagalli) Pucci; married Gora Martino, September 12, 1955; children: Lisa, Marisa, Albert John. *Education:* Attended Brooklyn Academy of Fine Arts, 1936-41, and Pratt Institute, 1939-42. *Home:* 282 Hicks St., Brooklyn, N.Y. 11201.

CAREER: Artist and illustrator. Instructor in art, Pratt Institute Evening Art School. *Exhibitions:* Work has been exhibited at Audubon Artists Annual, 1951, Corcoran Gallery, 1951, National Academy of Design annual exhibitions, 1951, 1954, 1955, Biennial Brooklyn Artists, Brooklyn Museum, 1952, Associated American Artists Galleries, one-man show, 1954. Work is represented in the permanent collection of University of Kansas, Thayer Museum of Art. *Awards, honors:* First prize, National Academy of Design, 1955; *Across Five Aprils* was a Newbery Honor Book, 1965, and received the Lewis Carroll Shelf Award, 1966.

ALBERT JOHN PUCCI

ILLUSTRATOR—All for children: Irene Hunt, *Across Five Aprils,* Follett, 1964; Bernice Kohn, *Echoes,* Coward, 1965; Eleanor Vance, *Jonathan,* Follett, 1966; Ruth E. Partridge, *I Will Rejoice,* John Knox, 1968; Florence Laughlin, *Four to Get Ready,* Western Publishing, 1968; William I. Martin, *A Spooky Story,* Holt, 1970; Lilian Moore, *Riddle Walk,* Gar-

(From *Tail Twisters* by Aileen Fisher. Designed and illustrated by Albert John Pucci.)

rard, 1971; Janet Winn, *Home in Flames,* Follett, 1972; Aileen Fisher, *Tail Twisters,* Bowmar/Noble, 1973; Virginia Sutch, editor, *A Son Is Given,* John Knox, 1974; Merle Levy Bencheton, *A Magic Carousel,* Harcourt, 1976; A. Fisher, *Petals Yellow and Petals Red,* Bowmar/Noble, 1977; Rev. Francis J. Buckley, S.J. and Sister Maria de la Cruz, S.H., *Sharing God's Promises,* Sadlier, 1979; Rev. F. J. Buckley, S.J. and Sister M. de la Cruz, S.H., *Living God's Word,* Sadlier, 1979; Rev. F. J. Buckley, S.J. and Sister M. de la Cruz, S.H., *We Share Forgiveness,* Sadlier, 1981; Rev. F. J. Buckley, S.J. and Sister M. de la Cruz, S.H., *We Share Bread of Life,* Sadlier, 1981. Also illustrator of *The World So Big,* for Scott Foresman.

FOR MORE INFORMATION SEE: Sara Hammond, "Parttimer: Artist Arranges Time to paint Maine Coast," *Portland Press Herald* (Maine), August 29, 1985.

REYNOLDS, Malvina   1900-1978

PERSONAL: Born August 23, 1900, in San Francisco, Calif.; died of kidney failure, March 17, 1978, in Oakland, Calif.; daughter of David and Abigail (Shenson) Milder; married second husband, William (Bud) Reynolds (a carpenter and union organizer), April 15, 1934 (died, 1972); children: Nancy Schimmel. *Education:* University of California, Berkeley, A.B., 1925, M.A., 1927, Ph.D., 1939, postdoctoral study, 1951. *Politics:* Socialist. *Religion:* Jewish.

CAREER: Songwriter, performer, and political activist. Worked as a social worker, newspaper editor, tailor, and steelworker, before becoming a writer and performer of protest songs in the 1950s; owner, Schroder Music Co. (publisher), Abigail Music, and Cassandra Records. Appeared in concert tours, and on radio and television in the United States, Europe, and Japan. *Member:* American Society of Composers, Authors, and Publishers (ASCAP), American Federation of Musicians, American Federation of Television and Radio Artists, Sierra Club, Wilderness Society, Phi Beta Kappa.

WRITINGS—All songbooks: *Tweedles and Foodles for Young Noodles* (juvenile; illustrated by Jodi Robbin), Schroder Music, 1961; *Little Boxes and Other Handmade Songs* (illustrated by J. Robbin), Oak Publications, 1964; *The Muse of Parker Street: More Songs by Malvina Reynolds* (illustrated by J. Robbin), Oak Publications, 1967; *Cheerful Tunes for Lutes and Spoons* (juvenile; illustrated by J. Robbin), Schroder Music, 1970; *The Malvina Reynolds Songbook* (illustrated by Emmy Lou Packard), Schroder Music, 1974; *There's Music in the Air* (juvenile; illustrated by Elly Simmons), Schroder Music, 1976; *Morningtown Ride,* Turn the Page Press, 1984.

Recordings: "Malvina Reynolds," Folkways Records, 1960; "Another County Heard From," Folkways Records, 1960; "Malvina Reynolds Sings the Truth," Columbia, 1967; "Artichokes, Griddle Cakes, and Other Good Things" (juvenile), Pacific Cascade Records, 1970; "Malvina Reynolds," Century City Records, 1971; "Funny Bugs, Giggleworms, and Other Good Friends" (juvenile), Pacific Cascade Records, 1972; "Malvina," Cassandra, 1972; "Malvina—Held Over," Cassandra, 1975; "Magical Songs," Cassandra, 1978; "Mama Lion," Cassandra, 1980.

Also composer and lyricist of over forty songs, including "Morningtown Ride," 1957, "Little Boxes," 1962, "What Have They Done to the Rain?," 1962, and "Daddy's in the Jail," 1969. Author of newsletter, *Sporadic Times;* contributor

MALVINA REYNOLDS

to folk music journals; author of poetry; author of *Not in Ourselves, Nor in Our Stars Either,* a social commentary pamphlet, published by Schroder Music, 1975.

SIDELIGHTS: Reynolds was born in San Francisco, California on August 23, 1900, into a politically active family. Since both her father and mother were Socialists, it was not a surprise that one of her most cherished possessions was a photograph of her father with Socialist leader Eugene Debs. "Grandparents on my mother's side were pioneers who left Lithuania in the 70's and, rejecting the East Coast, came directly to San Francisco. My father came alone from Budapest when he was fourteen. I was born south of Market Street in San Francisco—now an area of small industries and wholesale houses, but then a respectable lower-class section of wooden railroad flats, a few of them still standing among the warehouses and plants. I have lived in this city or near it most of my life. As the saying goes in this town, 'Why should I go anywhere? I'm here already.'

"The bay and the hills around it are part of my natural environment, as they are of most of the three million who now inhabit the bay counties...." [Malvina Reynolds, "A Song of San Francisco Bay," *Natural History,* Volume 77, number 1, January, 1968.[1]]

Although Reynolds was an honor student at San Francisco's Lowell High School, she never graduated. Because her parents actively opposed World War I, the high school had planned to withhold her diploma at graduation. When Reynolds was warned of their intentions, she decided to skip the ceremony and persuaded the University of California to admit her without a diploma.

During her years at the University of California, Reynolds was elected to Phi Beta Kappa, earned an M.A. in 1927 and a doctorate in romance philology in 1939. "I was politically active in college and a known Socialist; as a result of that,

(From *The Muse of Parker Street: More Songs by Malvina Reynolds.* Illustrated by Jodi Robbin.)

Sarah's at the engine. . . . ■ (From *Morningtown Ride,* words and music by Malvina Reynolds. Illustrated by Michael Leeman.)

and all the other nasty things they suspected besides, I found myself on a sort of subliminal black list. I couldn't get a teaching job anywhere, being both a woman and a 'potential troublemaker.' Unfortunately, when I should have been out there fighting those battles for myself, I was determined to act out love stories instead. I was also really very timid, because after all I was a girl, I was supposed to be 'nice,' to be a lady, to meet a boy and get married. Not to do that back then was to be very much alone." [Amie Hill, "Malvina Reynolds: Time to Sing Her Praises," *Ms.*, June, 1975.[2]]

In 1934 Reynolds married a carpenter and social organizer named William (Bud) Reynolds. The marriage produced a daughter, Nancy. "Bud was one of the leaders of 'Hunger Marches' for the institution of Social Security in the 1930s, and also behind early antidraft movements. He was a real American Red, a quiet and devoted political person who still had more fun and played more tricks than anybody. He always bolstered my individuality, taught me not to be timid about singing, not to get hung up over whether my voice was pretty or not."[2]

Reynolds turned to song writing after having worked as a social worker, newspaper editor, tailor, and steelworker. For years she wrote and published poems until, in the 1950s, the poems turned into songs. Inspiration to write folk songs came from an old 78-rpm record, "Cherry Tree Carol." "Always I wrote poetry, and then I got hooked on the guitar bit and started singing folk songs. Pretty soon my poems began com-

ing out with tunes attached to them." ["Songster Malvina Reynolds Dies," *San Francisco Chronicle,* March 18, 1978.[3]]

Success in songwriting first came when her song "Turn Around" was recorded by Harry Belafonte in 1956. In 1957 Reynolds wrote the words for Woody Guthrie's song "Sally, Don't You Grieve," and with Allan Greene wrote "Turn Around," a song which was used in Kodak commercials for years. Although her song-writing career blossomed later in life—after she had been a mother, wife and student—her success continued for over twenty years. "I'd much rather be a songwriter than a college professor. I think like a songwriter. I guess that means I think in songs. I like to say in my songwriting what other people are thinking and feeling—say what's in their minds and hearts." ["Malvina Reynolds," *Encyclopedia of Folk, Country, and Western Music,* 2nd edition, St. Martin's Press, 1983.[4]]

In 1964 a folk song about conformity, "Little Boxes," made its mark on the music charts. Reynolds claimed that the song was written in two hours. In simple yet effective lyrics, the song earned her a reputation as a social critic, and made "ticky-tacky" part of everyday language. Its theme was developmental housing:

> "Little boxes on the hillside
> Little boxes made of ticky tacky
> All the same"

Later compositions by Reynolds protested nuclear power, war, and segregation. She wrote ''What Have They Done to the Rain,'' an antinuclear song popularized by folk singers Bob Dylan and Joan Baez.

> ''Just a little boy
> Standing in the rain
> The gentle rain that falls for years
> And the grass is gone
> The boy disappears
> And rain keeps falling like helpless tears
> And what have they done to the rain.''

Reynold's participation in anti-war and civil rights concerts and demonstrations of the sixties gave her the nickname ''The Singing Grandmother.'' ''I came along looking like their mothers and grandmothers and I understand. I know what's bugging them. I have sympathy. My friends ask me how I can be so tolerant of the kids. Maybe it's because they're other people's kids.''[4]

Reynold's songs have been performed by artists Pete Seeger, Judy Collins, Joan Baez, Harry Belafonte, Diana Ross, and others, and were used on the children's television programs ''Sesame Street'' and ''Mr. Dressup.'' ''I feel that everything that's wrong today stems from the basic contradiction that the institutions of production, which are actually social institutions run by many people, are in the hands of a few people who're only after profit.

''Violence and hostility are self-defeating. Maybe the time will come when it will make sense, like the American revolution. But we aren't near that time and the kids who think we are being romantic, imagining things that aren't so. They're making a big tactical mistake.''[3]

Reynolds continued writing songs, touring, lecturing, teaching, producing records and books, giving sermons in churches, and traveling throughout the world in the decade of the seventies. Her songs were translated for use in political demonstrations in countries as far away from the United States as Japan and Chile. At the age of seventy-five, she continued to maintain a full and active professional and personal schedule. ''Perhaps my only regret at this time of life is that I didn't start all this earlier. I should have been at it when I was twenty, but all I could think about was boys. . . . Men are wonderful, but in proportion. Now I'm usually so occupied with things that I never really think of my age; sometimes I'm even mildly surprised when I look in the mirror. The only real problem I have, besides the fact that things aren't as easy physically as they used to be, is that I can't get, say, a record company to invest in me because I have, quote, 'only a few years left.' They don't want to put any money into someone who 'doesn't have a future.' . . . Maybe I'd better write a song about it.''[2]

Reynolds died of kidney failure at the age of seventy-eight in Oakland, California. Before her death, she wrote her own obituary:

(Detail of photograph by Julie Thompson from the album cover of *Malvina and Friends Sing Magical Songs*. Words and music by Malvina Reynolds.)

**There was a little captain at the rudder,
Cum peedle um pum pump a day. . . .**

■ (From *Tweedles and Foodles for Young Noodles,* words and music by Malvina Reynolds. Illustrated by Jodi Robbin.)

"Celebrate my death for the
good times I've had,
"For the work that I've done
and the friends that I've made.
"Celebrate my death of whom it
could be said,
"'She was a working class woman
and a Red.'
"My man was the best, a comrade
and a friend,
"Fighting on the good side to
the very end.
"My child was a darling, merry,
strong and fine,
"And all the world's children
were mine."[3]

After her death, the Malvina Reynolds Radio Project was formed. The project consisted of a series of radio programs about Reynolds which was distributed to radio stations and libraries in the United States and abroad.

FOR MORE INFORMATION SEE: Time, February 28, 1964; Malvina Reynolds, "Song of San Francisco Bay," *Natural History,* Volume 77, number 1, January, 1968; Milton Okun, *Something to Sing About,* Macmillan, 1968; *Biographical Dictionary of American Music,* Parker Publishing, 1973; Amie Hill, "Malvina Reynolds: Time to Sing Her Praises," *Ms.,* June, 1975; Kathleen Bowman, *New Women in Entertainment,*

Creative Education, 1976; "Love It Like a Fool: A Film about Malvina Reynolds" (motion picture; also available as videocassette), New Day Films, 1977; *Sing Out,* September-October, 1979; *Encyclopedia of Folk, Country, and Western Music,* 2nd edition, St. Martin's, 1983. Obituaries: *San Francisco Chronicle,* March 18, 1978; *Time,* April 3, 1978; *Rolling Stone,* May 18, 1978.

RICHLER, Mordecai 1931-

PERSONAL: Born January 27, 1931, in Montreal, Quebec, Canada; son of Moses Isaac and Lily (Rosenberg) Richler; divorced from first wife, Catherine Boudreau; married Florence Wood, 1960; children: Daniel, Noah, Emma, Martha, Jacob. *Education:* Attended Sir George Williams University, 1949-51. *Religion:* Jewish. *Agent:* Lynn Nesbit, International Creative Management, 40 West 57th St., New York, N.Y. 10019; (for films) William Morris Agency, 1350 Avenue of the Americas, New York, N.Y. 10019.

CAREER: Author and screenwriter. Left Canada in 1951; freelance writer in Paris, France, 1952-53, and in London, England, 1954-72; returned to Canada, 1972—. Writer in residence, Sir George Williams University, 1968-69; visiting professor, Carleton University, 1972-74. Member of editorial board, Book of the Month Club, 1972—. *Awards, honors:* President's medal for nonfiction, University of Western Ontario,

MORDECAI RICHLER

1959; Canadian Council junior art fellowships, 1959 and 1960, senior arts fellowship, 1967; Guggenheim Foundation creative writing fellowship, 1961; *Paris Review* humor prize, 1967, for section from *Cocksure;* Canadian Governor-General's award for literature, 1969, for *Cocksure;* Canadian Governor-General's award and London Jewish Chronicle literature award, both 1972, both for *St. Urbain's Horseman;* Berlin Film Festival Golden Bear, Academy Award nomination, and Screenwriters Guild of America award for best comedy, all 1974, all for the screenplay, "The Apprenticeship of Duddy Kravitz"; Ruth Schwartz Children's Book Award from the Canadian Bookseller's Association and English Medal Award from the Canadian Library Association, both 1976, both for *Jacob Two-Two Meets the Hooded Fang;* Jewish Chronicle/H. H. Wingate Award, 1982, for "Joshua Then and Now."

WRITINGS—Novels: *The Acrobats,* Putnam, 1954; *Son of a Smaller Hero,* Collins (Toronto), 1955, Paperback Library, 1965; *A Choice of Enemies,* Collins, 1957; *The Apprenticeship of Duddy Kravitz,* Little, Brown, 1959; *The Incomparable Atuk,* McClelland & Stewart, 1963, published as *Stick Your Neck Out,* Simon & Schuster, 1963; *Cocksure,* Simon & Schuster, 1968.

Other: *Hunting Tigers under Glass: Essays and Reports,* McClelland & Stewart, 1969; *The Street: Stories,* McClelland & Stewart, 1969, New Republic, 1975; (editor) *Canadian Writing Today* (anthology), Peter Smith, 1970; *St. Urbain's Horseman,* Knopf, 1971; *Shoveling Trouble* (essays), McClelland & Stewart, 1973; *Notes on an Endangered Species and Others* (essays), Knopf, 1974; *Jacob Two-Two Meets the Hooded Fang* (juvenile; illustrated by Fritz Wegner), Knopf, 1975; (with Peter Christopher) *Images of Spain,* McClelland and Stewart, 1977; *Joshua Then and Now,* Knopf, 1980; *The Best of Modern Humor,* Knopf, 1983; *Home Sweet Home: My Canadian Album,* Knopf, 1984.

Screenplays: (With Nicholas Phipps) "No Love for Johnnie," Embassy, 1962; "Life at the Top," Royal International, 1965; (with N. Phipps) "Young and Willing," Universal, 1965 (released in England as "The Wild and the Willing"); "The Apprenticeship of Duddy Kravitz" (adapted from own novel), Paramount, 1974.

Contributor to Canadian, U.S., and British periodicals, including *New Statesman, Spectator, Observer, Punch, Holiday, New York Review of Books, Commentary, Encounter,* and *London Magazine.*

ADAPTATIONS—Motion pictures: "The Apprenticeship of Duddy Kravitz," starring Richard Dreyfuss, Paramount, 1974; "Jacob Two-Two Meets the Hooded Fang," starring Alex Karras, Cinema Shares International (Canada), 1977; "Joshua Then and Now," Twentieth Century-Fox, 1985.

Television: "The Trouble with Benny" (based on short story), Britain ITV, 1959; "Q for Quest" (excerpts from Richler's fiction), Canadian Broadcasting Corporation, 1963; "The Wordsmith" (based on short story), Canadian Broadcasting Corporation, 1979.

(From the movie "Joshua Then and Now," starring Alan Arkin and Eric Kimmel. Copyright © 1985 by RSL Entertainment Corp.)

Radio: "It's Harder to Be Anybody" (based on short story), produced on BBC and CBC radio, 1964.

Recordings: "Jacob Two-Two Meets the Hooded Fang" (one disc), read by Christopher Plummer, Caedmon Records, 1977.

Filmstrips: "The Street" (color animation), National Film Board of Canada, 1976.

Plays: "Duddy" (based on *The Apprenticeship of Duddy Kravitz*), Citadel Theatre, Edmonton, Canada, March, 1984.

WORK IN PROGRESS: A novel, *Gursky Was Here.*

SIDELIGHTS: **January 27, 1931.** Born in Montreal, Quebec, where he grew up in a working-class district on St. Urbain Street. ". . . In my day, St. Urbain Street was the lowest rung on a ladder we were all hot to climb. No, St. Urbain wasn't the lowest rung, for one street below came Clark, where they had no lane and had to plunk their garbage out on the street. Parked right before the front door. Immediately below Clark there came the fabled Main or, more properly, Boulevard St. Laurent. Levitt's delicatessen. Moishe's steak house. Richstone's bakery. The editorial office of the *Canadian Jewish Eagle.* The Canada, where you could take in three movies for a quarter, but sometimes felt gray squishy things nibbling at your ankles. The Roxy and the Crystal Palace, where they showed only two movies, but offered a live show as well. A forlorn parade of pulpy strippers. . . .

"Our world was largely composed of the five streets that ran between Park Avenue and the Main: Jeanne Mance, Esplanade, Waverly, St. Urbain, and Clark. . . . But on St. Urbain, our fathers worked as cutters or pressers or scrap dealers and drifted into cold-water flats, sitting down to supper in their freckled Penman's long winter underwear, clipping their nails at the table. Mothers organized bazaars, proceeds for the Jewish National Fund, and jockeyed for position on the ladies' auxiliary of the Talmud Torah or the Folkschule, both parochial schools. Visiting aunts charged into the parlor, armed with raffle books, ten cents a ticket. . . .

"I attended parochial school (studying English, modern Hebrew, and French), and after classes, three afternoons a week, I knuckled down to the Talmud with Mr. Yalofsky's class in the back room of the Young Israel Synagogue. Our parents were counting on us—a scruffy lot, but, for all that, the first Canadian-born generation—to elbow our way into McGill [University]. . . ." [Mordecai Richler, *Home Sweet Home: My Canadian Album,* Knopf, 1984.[1]]

1936-1946. Attended United Talmud Torah and Baron Byng High School.

1946. Parents separated. "My father was afraid of his father. He was afraid of my unhappy mother, who divorced him when I was thirteen. He was also afraid of his second wife. Alas, he was even afraid of me when I was a boy. I rode streetcars

(From the movie "The Apprenticeship of Duddy Kravitz," starring Richard Dreyfuss. Released by Paramount Pictures, 1974.)

on the sabbath. I ate bacon. But nobody was afraid of Moses Isaac Richler. He was far too gentle.

"The Richler family was, and remains, joyously Orthodox, followers of the Lubavitcher rabbi. So when my mother threatened divorce, an all-but-unheard-of scandal in its time, grim rabbis in black gabardine coats hastened to our coldwater flat on St.-Urbain Street to plead with my mother. But my mother, dissatisfied for years with her arranged marriage, in love at last, was adamant. The rabbis sighed when my father, snapping his suspenders, rocking on his heels, *speaking out,* stated his most deeply felt grievance. When he wakened from his Saturday afternoon nap there was no tea. 'I like a cup of hot tea with lemon when I wake up.'" [Mordecai Richler, "My Father's Life," *Esquire,* August, 1982.[2]]

1948-1950. Attended college; worked part-time as a reporter for the *Montreal Herald.* "I went to Sir George Williams College for two years. I was in an arts course, and I was an English major student. I did very badly in high school, but I was expected to go to Sir George Williams. I was very quickly disappointed. You see, when I went in the veterans were still there, and the people who became my friends were the veterans. There were some very good, very entertaining people among them. But they were leaving the next year, and suddenly I found that all the people I knew and liked had graduated. So I quit." ["A Conversation with Mordecai Richler," *Tamarack Review,* winter, 1957.[3]]

1951. Left Canada for Europe at the age of nineteen. ". . . I cashed in an insurance policy that my mother had been paying for for years—fifty cents a week. I remember now that one of the things I was afraid of at this time was that I did know some writers. These were the people who wrote for and edited *Northern Review,* and I thought it was very important and very good. But a great many of these people, after they got their B.A.s, seemed to go on to get an M.A. because the B.A. was worth nothing, and then they got their Ph.D.s, and then they taught. Maybe later they would write their novels. And I became quite frightened that if I got a B.A., I'd get an M.A. and then I might try for a Ph.D., and that would be the end. So I decided the best thing was to cut myself off and find out if I could write.

". . . [In Europe] I didn't know anyone, and the first three weeks were really miserable, because, you know, Paris is terribly friendless. . . . Life takes place in the streets, people at the other tables talking and obviously having a good time, and I knew nobody and I was very depressed and lonely and scared. Like most kids I had read a lot about Paris, I had read Hemingway, and it was a terrible disappointment to me at the very beginning."[3]

Began writing first novel, *The Acrobats.*

1952. Returned to Canada; worked as a radio news editor for the Canadian Broadcasting Corporation in Montreal.

1954. *The Acrobats* published. ". . . The very first novel I wrote . . . was called *The Acrobats.* It was published when I was 23. *The Acrobats* was a very impassioned novel about Spain. It was brought out by Putnam's, who were trying a new experiment in publishing at the time. They guaranteed you satisfaction or your money back on every book in their catalogue—every book but mine. . . . I went to Spain and wrote my first novel—and I was broke. . . . It was just a very young man's novel. Hopelessly derivative. Like some unfortunate collision of Sartre and Hemingway and Celine, all unabsorbed and undigested. I wasn't writing in my own voice at all. I was

imitating people." [Thomas R. Edwards, "Mordecai Richler Then and Now," *New York Times Book Review,* June 22, 1980.[4]]

Left Canada to live in London. Married Catherine Boudreau, but the marriage ended after a few years in divorce. "Some time after my return to Europe, where I was to remain rooted for almost two decades, I married a shiksa in London. My father wrote me an indignant letter and we became estranged again. But no sooner did the marriage end in divorce than he pounced, 'You see, mixed marriages never work.'

"'But, Daddy, your first marriage didn't work, and Maw was a rabbi's daughter.'

"'What do you know?'

"'Nothing,' I replied, hugging him."[2]

1955. *Son of a Smaller Hero* published. ". . . One of the things I was most concerned with in *Son of a Smaller Hero* was that it seems to me that class loyalties in Montreal were much stronger than so-called Jewish loyalties or traditions; that the middle-class Jew has much more in common with the middle-class Gentile than he has with the Jew who works for him in his factory. And some people obviously read my novel and thought it was anti-semitic.

". . . There was a violent reaction and I expected that and I expected people to be hurt; but what I didn't expect was abuse. My book largely wasn't reviewed in Canada, it was abused. I had written a serious book. In England it was well received. I don't mind people not liking the book, and some Jewish journals here attacked it. The *Jewish Observer* didn't agree with my arguments and thought it was unfortunate; but they treated it seriously, said that it was very well written. The Montreal *Star* said it should have been published as a paperback and sold under the counter. Now in the Yiddish papers it was also abused, but I don't mind this nearly as much because I think it sprang from deep feeling. These people were genuinely hurt."[3] Two years later, *A Choice of Enemies* was published.

1959. *The Apprenticeship of Duddy Kravitz* published. It was called a coming of age classic, and was taught in many Canadian schools. ". . . I'm more critical of my work and it displeases me more often. Now I think most good writers, and I think of myself as a good writer, are fundamentally in competition with themselves, and your next book is your best book. And I'm harder and harder on my own work. It's no longer a pleasure just to be published, and there was no novel as pleasurable to publish as my first and it's not my best novel by far, but that was a great pleasure. . . .

". . . I don't think I really found my own style until *Duddy Kravitz* and then it all became easier in a way because it was all my own. I felt confident then, for better or for worse this was the way I wanted to write. Until then I was all hit and miss and groping around. Possibly I began to write too early and I often think about that, . . . and I regret that . . . I haven't had a lot of nasty jobs and that sort of background to fall back on. I've been circulating among other writers and painters almost all my adult life, which is not a very good thing really, because it's a very special sheltered world. There are a lot of big competing egos and other things like that, but fundamentally it's a decent, easy, generous, civilized community to move in, but it can distort your vision of what other people's lives are like. I mean most of us have jobs we hate and every morning is agony, and that's what life is about, I think, in many ways. And you tend to forget that amidst all that your friends are having good or back luck but are doing what they want to do." [Graeme Gibson, *Eleven Canadian Novelists,* Anansi, 1973.[6]]

1960. Married Florence Wood. The couple had five children.

1961. Awarded Guggenheim Foundation Fellowship in creative writing.

1967. Father died. "After his last operation for cancer I flew to Montreal, promising to take him on a trip as soon as he was out of bed. The Catskills. Grossinger's. With a stopover in New York to take in some shows. But each time I phoned from London his doctor advised me to wait a bit longer. I waited. He died. The next time I flew to Montreal it was to bury him."[2]

1968. *Cocksure* was published. ". . . *Cocksure* is a satire dealing with caricatures and extremes and not with people."[6]

Became writer-in-residence at Sir George Williams University in Montreal. Awarded *Paris Review* annual prize for humor.

1972. Returned with his family to live in Montreal. Was visiting professor at Carleton University in Ottawa until 1974. "In Ottawa I have had my own experience of Canadian students, at Carleton University, where I was a visiting professor for two years.

"One morning, early in September . . . newly if uneasily ensconced in my professorial office, I set to interviewing applicants for the dubious course I was offering: English 298, a writing seminar. Outside my window there stretched the Rideau Canal.

"The students who drifted into my office that morning were engaging, and touchingly vulnerable, but I was shocked, even appalled, by how little most of them had managed to read. One young man in particular permanently endeared himself to me. I asked him, as I had all the others, 'What's the last novel you read?' But this groovy Aquarian wasn't going to be conned by a loaded question from an aging writer. He pondered. He searched the ceiling; he contemplated the floor. Finally, his eyes lit with triumph, he asked: 'Fiction or nonfiction?'" [Mordecai Richler, "Letter from Ottawa," *Harper's,* June, 1975.[7]]

Won the Governor-General's Literary Award and the London Jewish Chronicle literature award for *St. Urbain's Horseman.*

1974. Wrote the script for "The Apprenticeship of Duddy Kravitz," which was nominated for an Academy Award. "My wife and I were in Yellowknife, in the Northwest Territories, when Michael Spencer, beleagured head of the Canadian Film Development Corporation, telephoned from Montreal.

"'Cold out there?' he asked.

"'Forty-two below,' I lied, not wanting to disappoint.

"'Well, congratulations. You've just been nominated for an Academy Award.'

"The nomination was for having written the screenplay from my own novel, 'The Apprenticeship of Duddy Kravitz.' I didn't bother to call my editor, Bob Gottlieb, at Knopf, because I knew nothing would induce him to take out a full-page ad in

Variety, saying 'CONGRATS, MORT, FROM ALL THE GUYS AND GALS AT KNOPF,' but later in the afternoon I did have to telephone my old friend and former British editor, Tony Godwin, who now works in New York. He hadn't heard my news. And he wasn't impressed, 'Wouldn't it be embarrassing,' he ventured dryly, 'if you won?'" [Mordecai Richler, "O God! O Hollywood!", *New York Times,* May 18, 1975.[8]] That year Mario Puzo won the award for the best screenplay ("The Godfather, Part II").

About movies, Richler commented: "Films are modish and very overestimated. I don't think they have the depth of a novel. If I were going to be harsh about the film of 'Duddy Kravitz,' I would say it's a synopsis of the novel. Films are better than they were, and so they're overestimated—there's a new classic every two weeks. One thing that irritates me enormously is when people, talking about the film, say how pleased I must be to see it 'come to life.'" ["An Interview (?) with Duddy Kravitz's Creator," *Women's Wear Daily,* July 22, 1974.[9]]

1975. Wrote the award-winning juvenile book, *Jacob Two-Two Meets the Hooded Fang.* "I have five children who, when they were very young, were told again and again it was too early for them to read *Cocksure.* Or even *The Apprenticeship of Duddy Kravitz.* Well then, one of them asked, not unreasonably, isn't there anything of yours we are not too young to read? The short answer was no, but I also promised that one day I would write something that would be just for them; and that's how I came to write *Jacob Two-Two Meets The Hooded Fang.* The book was meant to be family fun, with certain built-in family jokes. It began, innocently enough, as a bedtime tale told to amuse our youngest child, Jacob, and as it made him (and even the others) giggle I started to write it down.

"As a child, I never read children's books myself, but cut my intellectual teeth on *Superman, Captain Marvel,* and *The Batman,* moving on from there to Ellery Queen and Perry Mason, and finally, at the age of twelve or thereabouts, to the first novel that I ever read, *All Quiet On The Western Front.* So my experience of children's books, such as it is, came to me from reading aloud to our children, an office that is usually

Mordecai Richler in 1974.

In the hidden children's prison he never, never saw the sun. ■ (From *Jacob Two-Two Meets the Hooded Fang* by Mordecai Richler. Illustrated by Fritz Wegner.)

filled by my wife. In reading aloud to them I was somewhat shocked to discover that a few classics old and modern, and the incomparable Dr. Seuss, aside, most children's books were awfully boring or insufferably didactic or sometimes both. These dreary, ill-written books were conceived for profit or to teach the kids racial tolerance, hygiene, or other knee-jerk liberal responses. In Canada, tiresome Eskimo or Indian legends seemed to be the rule. In contemporary children's stories parents were never hungover or short-tempered and the kids were generally adorable. I decided if I ever got round to writing a book for my kids its intention would be to amuse. Pure fun, not instruction, is what I had in mind.

"But I resisted sitting down to *Jacob Two-Two* for more than a year, because I also have a prejudice against children's books, too many of which are written by third-rate writers for children already old enough to enjoy at least some adult books. . . . I think bright children beyond the age of twelve are ready for the real stuff, properly selected.

"So *Jacob* was to be for the younger child, our Jacob actually, who was not yet ready for adult books. Writing it, really, was not very different than writing an adult novel, which is to say it was largely hard work, and, as is usually the case with me, went through many drafts. I did not worry overmuch about vocabulary, my feeling being that if a child didn't understand a word he could look it up in a dictionary. On the other hand, I did feel a rape scene might be inappropriate. I wrote it, first of all, for my own pleasure (and in fulfilment of a rash promise). Of course, I hoped, as I always do, that it would appeal

to a large audience, but that is never a consideration in the actual writing.

"The success of *Jacob Two-Two* has surprised, even embarrassed me. It was immediately accepted for publication in England and Canada and, after something like seven rejections in the U.S.A., was finally taken on there by my adult book publisher, Knopf." [Mordecai Richler, "Writing *Jacob Two-Two*," *Canadian Literature*, number 78, autumn, 1978.[10]] The award-winning book has been translated into several languages, and adapted into other media since its publication.

1980. Wrote *Joshua Then and Now*. Besides writing novels, Richler has also worked as a journalist, contributing articles to Canadian, American and British magazines and newspapers. ". . . I've been a writer since I was 20 or 21. I was published too early. Oh, at the time it was tremendous fun, you know. I was very pleased. But with hindsight, I wish I had not been published so easily or so soon, because novelist friends of mine who had to wait longer to publish can now draw on jobs they hated, the things they had to do to get by for years, and I haven't got that because I've been writing all this time. And so I find that between novels I like to do a certain amount of journalism, to get out into a world I only know by rumor. I find it necessary.

"Necessary in order to learn other idioms, to find out something about office life or sports life or whatever, because it has become more and more constricting to be a writer, with friends who are also writers or editors or journalists. It's a

(From the movie "Jacob Two-Two Meets the Hooded Fang," starring Alex Karras. Released by Cinema Shares International, 1977.)

diminishing world of experience. I find it necessary to get out and do all these things."[4]

FOR MORE INFORMATION SEE—Articles: *Tamarack Review,* winter, 1957; *Life,* March 15, 1968, July 9, 1971; *London Magazine,* May, 1968, August, 1968; *Saturday Night,* May, 1968, July, 1969, October, 1970; *New York Times Book Review,* May 5, 1968, June 22, 1980, September 11, 1983; *Times Literary Supplement,* January 23, 1969; *New Statesman,* January 31, 1969; *Best Sellers,* August 1, 1971; *Women's Wear Daily,* July 22, 1974; Donia Mills, "Richler: Movie Initiation of a Canadian Author Finding Honor in His Own Land," *Washington Star-News,* August 13, 1974; Jonathan Yardley, "Mordecai Richler: Humane Vision, Healthy Distrust," *Miami Herald,* September 22, 1974; *New York Times,* May 18, 1975; *Harper's,* June, 1975; *Canadian Literature,* number 78, autumn, 1978; *People,* August 25, 1980; *Esquire,* August, 1982; *Time,* April 30, 1984.

Books: George Woodcock, *Mordecai Richler,* McClelland & Stewart, 1970; G. David Sheps, *Mordecai Richler,* Ryerson, 1970; Robert Fulford, *Mordecai Richler,* Coles, 1971; Graeme Gibson, *Eleven Canadian Novelists,* Anasi, 1973; *Contemporary Literary Criticism,* Gale, Volume 3, 1975, Volume 5, 1976; *Authors in the News,* Gale, 1976; *Contemporary Novelists,* St. Martin's Press, 1976; *Contemporary Authors,* Volumes 65-68, Gale, 1977; Mordecai Richler, *Home Sweet Home: My Canadian Album,* Knopf, 1984.

RINARD, Judith E(llen) 1947-

PERSONAL: Surname is pronounced *Rine*-ard; born August 15, 1947, in Mason City, Iowa; daughter of Park (an administrative assistant in politics) and Phyllis (Palmer) Rinard. *Education:* Attended Drake University, 1965-66; University of Toronto, B.A., 1969. *Religion:* Unitarian-Universalist. *Home:* 8702 Manchester Rd., Silver Spring, Md. 20901. *Office:* National Geographic Society, 17th & M Sts. N.W., Washington, D.C. 20036.

CAREER: National Geographic Society, Washington, D.C., free-lance writer for *National Geographic,* 1970-72, staff writer, 1972—. *Awards, honors: Wonders of the Desert World* was named an Outstanding Science Book for Children by Childrens Book Council Joint Committee, 1976.

WRITINGS—All published by National Geographic Society: *Wonders of the Desert World* (juvenile), 1976; *Creatures of the Night* (juvenile), 1977; (contributor) Robert L. Breeden and Ron Fisher, editors, *Powers of Nature,* 1978; (contributor) R. L. Breeden and William R. Gray, editors, *Mysteries of the Ancient World,* 1979; (contributor) Ralph Gray, editor, *Wilderness Challenge* (juvenile), 1980; *Zoos without Cages,* 1981; (with Catherine O'Neill) *Amazing Animals of the Sea,* 1981; *Puppies,* edited by Donald J. Crump, 1982; *What Happens at the Zoo,* 1984.

SIDELIGHTS: "I have always enjoyed learning about nature, about plants and animals that live in many different parts of the world, about the sea, about mountains, forests, and wilderness areas where I have camped. I also enjoy learning about people and cultures different from my own, such as those of Spanish-speaking Latin Americans and North American Indians. I find that these subjects are my favorites when writing for children, and that children seem to enjoy reading and learning about these things as much as I do."

JUDITH E. RINARD

HOBBIES AND OTHER INTERESTS: Drawing and painting, travel, camping.

RYLANT, Cynthia 1954-

BRIEF ENTRY: Born June 6, 1954, in Hopewell, Va. Author of books for young people. Rylant received a B.A. from Morris Harvey College, a M.A. from Marshall University, and a M.L.S. from Kent State University. During her career, she has taught English part time at Marshall University, Ohio University at Ironton, and the University of Akron. She is the author of eight books for young people, two of which have won awards. In 1982 the American Library Association named *When I Was Young in the Mountains* (Dutton, 1982) a notable children's book for younger readers; in 1984 *Waiting to Waltz . . . A Childhood* (Bradbury Press, 1984) was named a notable children's book for older readers by the Notable Children's Books Committee of the Association for Library Service to Children.

Rylant's works of poetry and fiction stem from her upbringing in Appalachia. According to Rylant, "I grew up in West Virginia and what happened to me there deeply affects what I write. . . ." Referring to her grandparents, with whom she lived from ages four to eight, she stated, "The tone of my works reflects the way they spoke, the simplicity of their language, and, I hope, the depth of their own hearts." Rylant's first book, *When I Was Young in the Mountains,* is a series of reminisences of her childhood spent in the mountains. *Publishers Weekly* found that "... [Rylant] knows precisely how to tell a story that brings the reader into the special world of her recollecting." *Horn Book* mentioned the book's "gently rhythmic text" and "mood of rustic peacefulness." It was adapted into a filmstrip in 1983.

Among Rylant's other books is *A Blue-eyed Daisy* (Bradbury Press, 1985), a series of episodes about the experiences of eleven-year-old Ellie Farley who lives in a coal mining town in West Virginia. *School Library Journal* commented, "Through [Rylant's] understatedly elegant prose, readers come to know a beautiful person, easy to read about, but hard to forget." *Publishers Weekly* called it "an exquisite novel, written with love." Rylant also wrote *Miss Maggie* (Dutton, 1983), depicting the blossoming friendship between a young boy, Nat, and an elderly woman, Miss Maggie. Her other books (all published by Bradbury Press) are *This Year's Garden* (1984), *Every Living Thing* (1985), *The Relatives Came* (1985), and *Night in the Country* (1986). *Residence:* Akron, Ohio.

SARGENT, Sarah   1937-

PERSONAL: Born March 15, 1937, in Roanoke, Va.; daughter of Francis Atwell (a civil engineer) and Mary (a teacher; maiden name, DuPuy) Davis; married Seymour Sargent (a college teacher), August 25, 1962; children: Edgar, Alice. *Education:* Randolph-Macon Woman's College, B.A., 1959; Yale University, M.A., 1961. *Politics:* Democrat. *Religion:* None. *Home:* 627 Ceape Ave., Oshkosh, Wis. 54901. *Agent:* Dorothy Markinko, McIntosh & Otis, Inc., 475 Fifth Ave., New York, N.Y. 10017.

CAREER: Teacher of English at University of North Dakota, 1961-62, University of Vermont, 1963-67, University of Minnesota, 1967-68, University of Wisconsin-Oshkosh, 1968-72, 1975-78. *Awards, honors:* First place citation from Wisconsin Writers Council, 1979, for *Edward Troy and the Witch Cat;* *Weird Henry Berg* was listed among the best books of 1980 by *School Library Journal;* Juvenile Merit Award from Friends of American Writers and citation from Library of Congress, both 1980, for *Weird Henry Berg.*

WRITINGS—Juvenile: *Edward Troy and the Witch Cat* (illustrated by Emily McCully), Follett, 1978; *Weird Henry Berg* (Junior Literary Guild selection), Crown, 1980; *Secret Lies* (ALA Notable Book), Crown, 1981; *Lure of the Dark,* Four Winds, 1984; *Watermusic,* Clarion, 1986.

WORK IN PROGRESS: *The Solstice Son* (tentative title) and *The Seeds of Change* (tentative title), dealing with animal-human transformation in a swamp in the southern United States, both to be published by Bradbury.

SIDELIGHTS: "I am very interested in myth and in the various ways people add dimension to their lives by their participation in myths of one kind or another. *Secret Lies* is about a girl who shapes her reality by her commitment to soap operas

(Jacket illustration by Michael Garland from *Secret Lies* by Sarah Sargent.)

SARAH SARGENT

and romance novels. More recent books examine the relevance of older myths to our times—*Lure of the Dark* is about Norse myth and *Solstice Son* is about Celtic myth.

"*Weird Henry Berg* comes from my work [at Yale University] . . . in that I liked Old English literature quite a lot and took several courses in it. Real, as opposed to cute or invented, dragons figure into Old English poetry, which has always interested me. When I started to work on this book, I hauled out my old copy of *Beowulf* and attempted, feebly, to read swatches of the poem again. The point to that was not that I expected the book to show any direct influence from *Beowulf* or to allude to it. I wanted to remember that world, at once quite solid and still mysterious, full of caves and underwater dens and holes in the rocks where monsters of various sorts sit and watch the world of men.

"Fantasy, as far as I am concerned, is not a retreat from the world, but an extension of the possibilities we experience. There is a sense of a world not easily arranged into categories, of mystery around the edges of things, that I hope comes from the book as a whole. I think that the world is full of variety and ways of seeing besides our own and that we diminish ourselves if we don't remember that.

"Respect for animals and their individuality is an important value to me. I have known a lot of animals—beginning with a dog who got to be best friends with a duck. Now we have three guinea pigs in the basement, a very tough cat and a very timid dog on the first floor, and a rather delicate and aloof cat on the second. Our dog, who is enormous, twitches her nose delicately out the door, peering anxiously to see if the worst has arrived. Before her we had a Labrador retriever who loved to baby-sit for kittens.

"I've read fiction incessantly all my life. I read it mostly because it celebrates the dignity of individual lives—it refuses

to mass people into groups and generalize about them. My son spent . . . [a] summer reading Hofstadter's *Gödel, Escher, Bach: An Eternal Golden Braid* while listening to the Sex Pistols on his stereo. People, animals, all of us, not just Henry Berg, are weird, and it's that weirdness that makes us worth something.

"For me, writing fiction is not something that is under complete conscious control. It involves a dialogue between the conscious, order-producing side of my mind and the unconscious, image-producing side. Working this way, trying to open myself up to the possibilities of meaning that lie just below the surface in my material and in my mind, leads me automatically to work with myth because that is what myths are—attempts to dramatize and personify hidden forces in the world. I think the most important thing about my writing is the way it leads me to explore possibilities. Once words are typed onto a page, they start to be alive, to make suggestions, and to nudge me in directions I hadn't necessarily expected to move in. I am very interested in the way styles create worlds—in the power of language to shape realities."

SCHLEE, Ann   1934-

PERSONAL: Born May 26, 1934, in Greenwich, Conn.; daughter of Duncan and Nancy (Houghton) Cumming; married D.N.R. Schlee, July 27, 1957; children: Emily, Catherine, Duncan, Hannah. *Education:* Somerville College, Oxford, B.A., 1955. *Residence:* London, England. *Agent:* Deborah Rogers Ltd., 5-11 Mortimer St., London W1N 7RH, England.

CAREER: Tutor and writer. *Awards, honors:* Guardian Award commendation, 1977, for *Ask Me No Questions;* Guardian Award, and Carnegie Medal commendation, both 1980, for *The Vandal; The Vandal* was selected as a Notable Children's

ANN SCHLEE

Lum's mind was haunted by a dream. ■ (From *The Strangers* by Ann Schlee. Illustrated by Pat Marriott.)

Trade Book in the field of Social Studies by the National Council for Social Studies and the Children's Book Council, 1982; *Ask Me No Questions* was selected as a "Best Book" by *School Library Journal,* 1982.

WRITINGS—All juvenile, except as noted: *The Strangers* (illustrated by Pat Marriott), Macmillan, 1971, Atheneum, 1972; *The Consul's Daughter,* Atheneum, 1972; *The Guns of Darkness,* Macmillan, 1973, Atheneum, 1974; *Ask Me No Questions* (*Horn Book* honor list), Macmillan, 1976, Holt, 1982; *Desert Drum* (illustrated by J. Sewell), Heinemann, 1977; *The Vandal,* Macmillan, 1979, Crown, 1981; *Rhine Journey* (adult novel), Holt, 1981; *The Proprietor* (adult novel), Holt, 1983.

WORK IN PROGRESS: A third historical novel for adults.

SIDELIGHTS: Ann Schlee's historical novels for children are noted for their clear writing and deft characterization. Typically her stories deal with events in English history as seen through the eyes of a child or adolescent.

FOR MORE INFORMATION SEE: Times Literary Supplement, October 22, 1971, April 28, 1972, June 15, 1973, October 1, 1976; *Observer,* July 22, 1973, September 28, 1975, November 28, 1976; *Books and Bookmen,* October 1973; *Center for Children's Books: Bulletin,* October, 1974; *New Statesman,* November 5, 1976.

SCHNEIDER, Rex   1937-

PERSONAL: Born February 22, 1937, in Butler, Pa.; son of Cyril Leo and Alice (Jewell) Schneider. *Education:* Ball State University, B.S., 1959. *Home:* 70038 Treasure Island, Union, Mich. 49130. *Office:* P.O. Box 312, Union, Mich. 49130.

CAREER: Writer and illustrator. Sparrows Point High School, Baltimore, Md., art teacher, 1960-61; Logan School for Re-

tarded, South Bend, Ind., program director, 1961-63; Baltimore Association for Retarded Citizens, Baltimore, counselor, 1963-70; *Performance* (newspaper), Baltimore, graphic arts editor, 1970-72; free-lance artist, 1972—; Blue Mouse Studio, Union, Mich., owner, 1980—. Set and graphics director for "Voyage to Better Health" and "Classics 34" television programs for WNIT-TV in Elkhart, Ind. *Member:* Graphic Artist's Guild, Society of Children's Book Writers. *Awards, honors:* Silver medal from Atlanta International Film Festival, 1969, for "Peace Talks"; *The Wide-Mouthed Frog* was named a Children's Choice for 1982 by the International Reading Association.

WRITINGS—Self-illustrated: *The Wide-Mouthed Frog,* Stemmer House, 1980; *Ain't We Got Fun?,* Blue Mouse Studio, 1982; *That's Not All,* School Zone, 1985.

Illustrator: Emily Dickinson, *I'm Nobody, Who are You? Poems of Emily Dickinson for Children,* Stemmer House, 1978; Rosa Kohler Eichellberger, *Big Fire in Baltimore,* Stemmer House, 1979; Chris Buchman, *Movie Posters of the Silent Era,* Stemmer House, 1981; Jane Dickinson, *Wonders of Water,* Troll, 1983; Barbara Gregorich, *Jog, Frog, Jog,* edited by Joan Hoffman, School Zone, 1984; Keith Brandt, *Caves,* Troll, 1985; K. Brandt, *Transportation,* Troll, 1985.

Filmstrips: (With Chris Buchman) "Peace Talks," Buchanan Films, 1969; "Mexican Christmas," Encyclopaedia Britannica, 1984.

REX SCHNEIDER

January 13, 1934: **Reba Schlammkopf plays the organ at the Avalon Roller Rink with adroit artistry.** ■ (From *Ain't We Got Fun?* by Rex Schneider. Illustrated by the author.)

ADAPTATIONS: "The Wide-Mouthed Frog" (filmstrip), Society for Visual Education, 1982.

WORK IN PROGRESS: I Declare, a children's picture book; sequel to *Ain't We Got Fun?,* documenting history of Frogville, U.S.A.; *Mother Goose; Bazoody, the Alphabet Book; Wondrous Adventures of Tobri; Babbette Bubble; The Bb of Willie B. Bach;* a Somerset Maugham children's story.

SIDELIGHTS: The sight of Schneider sitting in the shade of a hemlock tree and surrounded by a curious assortment of animals while he draws them is not uncommon. As a youth in Pennsylvania, he maintained a harmonious community that included a goat, a cat, two dogs, two turkeys, several rabbits, and some chickens.

"This good fellowship with animals has influenced and accentuated my artistic endeavors. It has always been my view that, if given the chance, other living creatures would be as creative and foolish as their human kin—a view that is apparent in *Ain't We Got Fun?, I Want a Pet* and *That's Not All.*"

Schneider created, illustrated and published, through his own Blue Mouse Studio, *Ain't We Got Fun?,* a chronicle of life in Frogville, U.S.A. during the era of the great depression. He imbued its lovable cast of characters with his own persona: "Sometimes cynical, sometimes optimistic, sometimes a dose of devilish chicanery, and invariably—eccentric!"

And he created more frogs: a "Leapin' Lizards, It's a Frog Calendar" and "Reading Frog" bookplate for Antioch Bookplate Company; *Jog Frog Jog,* another full-color book for School Zone, and a frog puzzle, "A Family Swim," also for School Zone.

Schneider is concerned with authenticity in period architecture, clothing design, and all the "accessories of life." "Above all else, I would like to see a return to the tradition of quality illustrations for children's literature. Having been nurtured on a rich tradition of story-book illustrations of generations past, a heritage that served to inspire my own creativity, I am appalled by the attitude of the many publishers who place no value on aesthetics, one of the reasons for the steady rise of trash flooding the marketplace. The other reason being the 'marketing research' mentality of publishing houses and the dictatorship of chain bookstores. They seem to survey everyone but children and are only interested in what adults buy and not in what children enjoy or need."

He is quick to point out that "a perusal of the children's shelves in the bookstores is a depressing experience for any struggling but talented illustrator or writer because of the array of mediocrity put out by big publishers like Random House. One has to wonder how these great movers and shakers of publishing make their decisions. The only conclusion is that they don't look very hard or far for their artists.

"My only hope is that the serious children's book writer and illustrator doesn't give up and leave the field wide open for the opportunistic fakes!"

SCOTT, Sally (Elisabeth) 1948-

PERSONAL: Born May 30, 1948, in London, England; daughter of Paul Mark (a novelist) and N. E. Avery (a novelist) Scott. *Education:* University of York, Aegrotat degree, 1970. *Agent:* Bruce Hunter, David Higham Associates Ltd., 5-8 Lower John St., London, W.1., England.

CAREER: Writer and illustrator. *Member:* Society of Authors.

SALLY SCOTT

WRITINGS—Self-illustrated: The Elf King's Bride; or, How Prince Armandel Prevailed against the Twilight, MacRae, 1981; *The Magic Horse,* MacRae, 1985.

Illustrator: Paul Scott, *After the Funeral,* Whittington/Heinemann, 1980; Ruskin Bond, *Tales and Legends from India,* F. Watts, 1982.

WORK IN PROGRESS: Children's fantasy/adventure novel.

SIDELIGHTS: "As a child, I always seem to have been writing and drawing. I had written my first 'collection' of fairy tales—owing much to the *Arabian Nights*—by the time I was nine, and typed them out on my father's battered pre-war Remington portable. Books enriched my childhood, and the memory of some of them is still magical today, so that I have always regarded children's books as a very important issue, their influence not to be underestimated. As a writer, fantasy, fairy tale, myth and legend seem to be my roots; as an illustrator, I have always been deeply stirred by the artists of the 'Golden Age' of illustration—Rackham, Dulac, Kay Nielsen—although I prefer to work in black and white, Aubrey Beardsley and Harry Clarke being the artists in that medium that I most admire."

SIEBEL, Fritz (Frederick) 1913-

BRIEF ENTRY: Born December 19, 1913, in Vienna, Austria. Industrial designer, commercial artist, animator, and illustrator of children's books. Siebel grew up in Austria and Czechoslovakia and later attended the Academy of Art in Vienna. He served for two years in the Czech army before immigrating to the United States, where he worked in New York as a commercial artist and magazine illustrator. He was also involved in television animation, including the creation of the "Mr. Clean" advertising character. Seibel has used both full-color and pen-and-ink with color separation in over a dozen books for children. Among his illustrated works are *A Fly Went By* by Mike McClintock; *Tell Me Some More* by Crosby Newell Bonsall; *A House So Big* by Joan Lexau; *Amelia Bedelia, Thank You, Amelia Bedelia,* and *Amelia Bedelia and the Surprise Shower,* all by Peggy Parish.

FOR MORE INFORMATION SEE: Illustrators of Children's Books: 1957-1966, Horn Book, 1968; *Illustrators of Books for Young People,* Scarecrow, 1975.

SKOFIELD, James

BRIEF ENTRY: Born in Karachi, Pakistan. A poet and author of children's books, Skofield received a B.A. from Wesleyan University where he was awarded the Academy of American Poets Prize in 1978. To date, he has produced three works of fiction for children, all written in a poetic style. In his first book, *Nightdances* (Harper, 1981), a little boy hears the "windmusic" and slips outside in the autumn night to dance under the moon. Soon he is joined by his parents, and they all dance until they grow tired. Skofield later wrote *Snow Country* (Charlotte Zolotow Books, 1983), in which Sister, Small Brother, and their grandparents (Old Woman and Old Man) encounter the first snow of winter on the grandparents' farm. *Publishers Weekly* observed, "Skofield . . . [etches] in the reader's mind the wonders wrought by winter. . . ." *School Library Journal* noted the "warmth and security of the text."

In Skofield's most recent work, *All Wet! All Wet!* (Charlotte Zolotow Books, 1984), a Junior Literary Guild selection, a young boy sets out for a walk in the woods on a rainy day. Wearing a yellow slicker and carrying an umbrella, the boy is depicted only in the illustrations as the text is written from the woodland animals' viewpoint. According to *Horn Book*, ''The text describes in hushed tones the actions of the animals as they seek shelter from the storm.'' *Booklist* found that ''Skofield paints some lovely word pictures . . . ,'' while *School Library Journal* described the book as ''gentle . . . [and] evocative.'' Skofield is also the translator of Irina Korschunow's *The Foundling Fox: How the Little Fox Got a Mother* (Harper, 1984). *Residence:* New York, N.Y.

SLOGGETT, Nellie   1851-1923
(Nellie Cornwall, Sarah L. Enys, Enys Tregarthen)

PERSONAL: Born December 29, 1851; died in 1923; buried in Padstow, Cornwall, England.

CAREER: Author of children's books.

WRITINGS—Under pseudonym Nellie Cornwall: *Daddy Longlegs, and His White Heath Flower*, T. Woolmer (London), 1885; *Grannie Tresawna's Story*, T. Woolmer, 1886; *Hallvard Halvorsen; or, The Avalanche: A Story of the Fjeld Fjord and Fos*, S. W. Partridge (London), 1887; *Twice Rescued; or, The Story of Little Tino*, John F. Shaw (London), 1888; *Mad Margrete and Little Gunnvald: A Norwegian Tale*, T. Woolmer, 1889; *Sprattie and the Dwarf; or, The Shining Stairway*, C. H. Kelly (London), 1891; *Tamsin Rosewarne and Her Burdens*, S. W. Partridge, 1892; *Little Bunch's Charge; or, True to Trust*, S. W. Partridge, 1894; *Joyce's Little Maid*, Religious Tract Society (London), 1896; *Little Annie*, Charles H. Kelly, 1897; *The Maid of the Storm*, S. W. Partridge, 1897; *The Hill of Fire*, Religious Tract Society, 1901; *The Little Don of Oxford*, John F. Shaw, 1902; *Little Gladwise: The Story of a Waif*, S. W. Partridge, 1909.

Under pseudonym Enys Tregarthen: *The Piskey-Purse: Legends and Tales of North Cornwall* (illustrated by J. L. Pethybridge), Wells Gardner (London), 1905; *North Cornwall Fairies and Legends*, Wells Gardner, 1906; *The House of the Sleeping Winds, and Other Stories, Some Based on Cornish Folklore (*illustrated by Nannie Preston), Rebman (London), 1911; *Piskey Folk: A Book of Cornish Legends* (illustrated with photographs by William McGreal), compiled by Elizabeth Yates, John Day, 1940; *The Doll Who Came Alive* (illustrated by Nora S. Unwin), edited by Yates, John Day, 1942, reprinted, John Day Junior Books, 1972; *The White Ring* (illustrated by N. S. Unwin), edited by Yates, Harcourt, 1949.

Under pseudonym Sarah L. Enys: *Perpetual Calendar of Cornish Saints, with Selections of Poetry and Prose Relating to*

Never a day passed but it found Nan sitting on the verge of the cliff with her tiny face resting in the hollow of her hands, gazing seaward. ■ (From *The White Ring* by Enys Tregarthen. Illustrated by Nora S. Unwin.)

Jyd showed the doll all the fascinating games of which she had told her. ■ (From *The Doll Who Came Alive* by Enys Tregarthen. Illustrated by Nora S. Unwin.)

Cornwall, A. W. Jordan (Truro, England), 1923; (compiler) Francis de Sales, *St. Francis de Sales Every Day in the Year: A Perpetual Calendar,* Girls' Friendly Society (London), 1925; (compiler) William Bottrell, *Cornish Drolls,* W. Brendon & Son (Plymouth, England), 1931.

SIDELIGHTS: Born on December 29, 1851 in Padstow, Cornwall, Sloggett was raised in this coastal area in the westernmost corner of England. After her father died, she and her mother lived with her aunt and uncle and two cousins in their house. The Rawles family had been a shipbuilding seafaring family, and their home reflected their travels.

Tragedy struck young Sloggett at the age of seventeen when she developed a form of spinal paralysis. Doctors were unable to give her relief from almost continual suffering and absolutely no hope for recovery. For the remainder of her life, she was incarcerated in her bedroom in her cousin's home, Yatala.

Although Sloggett was limited as to where she could go physically, she read widely, traveling to other places in her imagination. She kept a sequence of diaries, in which she described in detail the view from her window—the birds she saw, the flowers, and the changing of seasons.

In 1885, her first book was published under one of her pseudonyms, Nellie Cornwall. From then on Sloggett began to write in earnest—novels, stories, poems, and plays, publishing them under the pseudonyms Nellie Cornwall, Sarah L. Enys, and Enys Tregarthen. At first she wrote of distant places, but gradually she began to focus on her surroundings. Her interest centered around her village in Cornwall, and she began to collect and record the folk tales of the region, especially tales of the piskeys, Cornwall's own particular fairy folks.

Sloggett's pen kept the fairy folk of Cornwall from being forgotten. Leaning on an elbow in her bed, she wrote her stories, although she was in almost constant pain. By the time of her death in 1923 at the age of seventy-two, she had written numerous books, collections of poetry, and calendars.

Fifteen years after her death, in 1938, Elizabeth Yates visited Sloggett's home in Padstow upon the request of Bertha Mahony Miller, the editor and compiler of *Illustrators of Chil-*

dren's Books. During her visit there, Yates was given an account of the author's daily life by Sloggett's cousin.

In an article for *Horn Book,* Yates described her visit to Sloggett's room. ''. . . This was the little room to which, through the years, so many people had come—children with their expectant faces and their fistful of wild flowers, old people with their tales of the past, the Vicar making his weekly call. And when they could not come, they wrote letters.

''They laid their contributions of the world before her; and she replied, telling of her ideas for books, her thoughts on religion and the world, her news of mutual acquaintances, and always she asked her friends to relay to her any stories, weirds or legends they might come across in their travels, especially those that were tucked away in the memories of old people and in danger of being lost forever. Her friends were aware of her suffering, but they did not hesitate to bring their own sorrows and cares to her, thinking that these would pale before hers.

''There are letters from publishers saying, 'Have you any other manuscripts for us to look at this year'—and one from a lawyer who was doing his best to protect her in the matter of copyright. She needed his interest, for that was the time when the copyright of a book was sold outright for fifteen or twenty guineas and a writer had little protection.

''Presents often came to her—books in the post, a birthday cake so December 29 would still have its aura, tiny pressed flowers mounted on paper, and a notebook in which the donor thought Nell might care to record the conversations with her distinguished circle of visitors. Increasingly through the years the feeling grew that 'the little lady of Padstow,' as she came to be called, was peculiarly blest.

'''I hope you will accept my good wishes for your birthday,' one wrote. 'You are in many ways a favored being and I hope you will be spared to brighten the lives of many people for years to come and to add to the literature of the West Country.'

''So Miss Rawle [Sloggett's cousin] told us of the life the upper room had once seen and showed us the letters, faded now and worn by much handling. . . .

''The light was growing dusky in the room so Miss Rawle brought in a lamp. Then she reached under the bed and drew out a small old-fashioned trunk.

'''These are writings of my cousin's that have never been published,' she said; then she looked at us more closely, 'I think she would want you to have them now and so I give them to you.'

''We had no thanks that were adequate, but before our fumbling words Miss Rawle continued to smile.

'''You're welcome,' she said. 'I don't need them.'

''In the trunk we found what we had so long been seeking— legends and tales as Cornish as the wind blowing over the moors or the sea pounding against the cliffs. They were bound in brown paper, neatly tied together and written by hand. The paper had yellowed, in places the ink had faded. There was a thick old smell of dust, but the stories themselves were fresh and glowing, alive with their peculiar magic—the magic made by one who could remember what it was to be a child.'' [Elizabeth Yates, ''Enys Tregarthen,'' *Horn Book,* May, 1949.']

Two stories and a collection of Cornish legends were compiled and edited by Elizabeth Yates from the unpublished writings of Nellie Sloggett. Using Sloggett's pseudonym, Enys Tregarthen, the books were published in the 1940s as *Piskey Folk: A Book of Cornish Legends, The Doll Who Came Alive,* and *The White Ring. Piskey Folk* was illustrated with photographs by Yates' husband, William McGreal.

FOR MORE INFORMATION SEE: Horn Book, May, 1950; Elizabeth Yates, ''How Enys Tregarthen's Cornish Legends Came to Light,'' in *The Horn Book Magazine: A Horn Book Sampler on Children's Books and Reading,* edited by Norma R. Fryatt, introduction by Bertha Mahony Miller, Horn Book, 1959.

SPARKS, Beatrice Mathews 1918-

PERSONAL: Born January 15, 1918, in Goldberg, Idaho; daughter of Leonard Clarence (a painter) and Vivian (Johns) Mathews; married La Vorn G. Sparks (an investor); children: La Vorn G., Jr., Suzette Sparks Pembleton, Cynthia. *Education:* Attended University of California, Los Angeles, and Brigham Young University. *Religion:* Church of Jesus Christ of Latter-day Saints (Mormons). *Home and office:* 174 West 4750 N. University Ave., Provo, Utah 84601.

BEATRICE MATHEWS SPARKS

CAREER: Youth counselor, 1955—; writer. Teacher in division of continuing education at Brigham Young University; music therapist in youth division at Utah State Mental Hospital. Guest on television and radio programs; public speaker.

WRITINGS: Key to Happiness, Deseret, 1967; *Go Ask Alice,* Prentice-Hall, 1971; *Voices,* Times Book Co., 1978; *Jay's Journal,* Times Book Co., 1979. Author of columns, ''Today,'' in *California Intermountain News,* ''What's New on the Malibu,'' in *Malibu Monitor,* and ''News and Views,'' in *Santa Monica Outlook.*

ADAPTATIONS—Motion pictures: ''Go Ask Alice'' (television), Metro Media, 1972; ''Jay's Journal,'' Casa Blanca Films.

WORK IN PROGRESS: One Little Indian, the story of Spark's American Indian foster child; *My Friend,* on the childhood of Jesus; *The Great Adult Abdication,* for Times Book Co.

SIDELIGHTS: ''Since 1955 I have been working with kids who have problems. I have found them at Utah State Mental Hospital where I was a therapist, at Brigham Young University where I taught special classes, and at seminars and youth conferences. I have talked to mixed groups at runaway houses and school assemblies. My husband and I drove from San Francisco to New York, taking a northern route, and returned via Los Angeles on a southern route. In all, I talked with well over one thousand young people, privileged kids, underprivileged kids, and 'in-betweens.' I talked to scholars and non-readers; those who were conformers and those who were rebellious. Hurting kids are everywhere!

''Alice is fifteen, white, middle class. She diets. She dates. She gets decent grades. She fights with her younger brother and sister. She has her own room. She thinks someday she'd like to get married and raise a family. Alice turns on to acid. She digs it. Alice's parents don't know what's going on. They cannot help her. The difference between Alice and a lot of other kids on drugs is that Alice keeps a diary. After Alice's death I put her diary into book form, *Go Ask Alice.*

''Jay is an exceptionally intelligent and articulate boy, with all the advantages of a prosperous and loving home; but he is also unhappy, confused, self-pitying, guilty, bored, and lonely. He gets in over his head in the eerie and dangerous world of the occult. At the age of sixteen Jay shoots himself, leaving behind his raw and haunting message—what scared and troubled him, what he couldn't tell his parents, what he couldn't tell anyone, except his journal, published as *Jay's Journal.*

''*Voices* documents with horrifying honesty the lives of four teenagers: Mary, Mark, Milly, and Jane, who, in their poignant, futile struggle to be loved and cared about, settled for something far less. They tell their own stories in their own words, about what it is like to deal with homosexuality at school, to be high on drugs at the dinner table with two unsuspecting parents, to be fourteen years old and introducing a

(From the television movie ''Go Ask Alice,'' starring Jamie Smith-Jackson and Mimi Saffian. Presented on ABC Movie of the Week, January 24, 1973.)

younger sister to amphetamines, to join a cult and live through the agony of deprogramming.

''My books are all 'message' books in the sense that I sincerely believe we cannot isolate today's kids from today's problems. We can hope to educate them so they will accept as a privilege their right to free agency, will take responsibility for their own actions, and will make intelligent decisions concerning their own lives.

''I started *The Great Adult Abdication* after a young student body president said: 'Kids don't publish the porno mags, make the skin flicks, bankroll the midnight auto supply, run the massage parlors, . . . own the breweries, allow one out of five kids to graduate from high school functionally illiterate.' Through my books I try to present young people, many of whom feel they walk frighteningly alone, unsupported, unprotected, and unrepresented.''

Go Ask Alice has been translated into sixteen languages, *Jay's Journal* into five languages, and *Voices* has also been translated into other languages.

FOR MORE INFORMATION SEE: Jackson Sun, September 5, 1971; *Christian Science Monitor*, November 1, 1971; *School Library Journal*, March 15, 1972, October, 1979; *Television Weekly*, October 22, 1973; *New York Times*, September 19, 1975; *Kalamazoo Gazette*, September 28, 1975; *Kirkus Reviews*, June 1, 1978; *Hollywood Press*, October 13, 1978; *Teen*, January, 1979; *Chronicle of Higher Education*, February 20, 1979; *Booklist*, October, 1979; *Los Angeles Times*, October 29, 1979.

STOCKTON, Francis Richard   1834-1902 (Frank R. Stockton; Paul Fort, John Lewees, pseudonyms)

PERSONAL: Born April 5, 1834, in Blockley, Penn.; died of a cerebral hemorrhage, April 20, 1902, in Washington, D.C.; buried in Woodlands Cemetery, in Pennsylvania; son of William Smith (a writer) and Emily Hepzibeth (a school administrator; maiden name, Drean) Stockton; married Marian (some sources cite Mary Ann) Edwards Tuttle (a teacher), in 1960. *Education:* Attended public schools in Philadelphia, Pa. *Residence:* ''The Holt,'' at Convent Station near Morristown, N.J., later ''Claymont,'' near Charles Town, W.Va.; and New York (winters).

CAREER: Novelist, short-story writer, editor. After graduating from high school, Stockton became a wood engraver and draftsman; in the late 1860s, became free-lance writer for several newspapers and periodicals; joined the staff of *Hearth and Home* in 1869; about 1872, joined editorial staff of *Scribner's Monthly* (later *Century*); from 1873-1881, was assistant editor for *St. Nicholas;* beginning in 1881, full-time author of short stories and novels and contributor to numerous periodicals. *Member:* Century Club, Authors Club. *Awards, honors:* Lewis Carroll Shelf Award, 1963, for *The Griffin and the Minor Canon*, and 1969, for *The Storyteller's Pack: A Frank R. Stockton Reader.*

WRITINGS—All under name Frank R. Stockton; for children: *Ting-a-Ling* (fairytale collection; title story first appeared in *Riverside Magazine for Young People*, 1867; illustrated by E. B. Bensell), Hurd & Houghton, 1870, published as *Ting-a-Ling Tales* (illustrated by Richard Floethe), Scribner, 1955;

FRANCIS RICHARD STOCKTON

Round-About Rambles in Lands of Fact and Fancy, Scribner, Armstrong, 1872; *What Might Have Been Expected* (illustrated by Sol Eytinge and others), Dodd, 1874, reprinted, Books for Library Press, 1972; *Tales Out of School*, Scribner, Armstrong, 1875, new edition, 1903; *A Jolly Friendship*, Scribner, 1880; *The Floating Prince, and Other Fairy Tales*, Scribner, 1881; *The Story of Viteau*, Scribner, 1884; *The Bee-Man of Orn, and Other Fanciful Tales*, Scribner, 1887, published as *The Bee-Man of Orn* (illustrated by Maurice Sendak), Holt, 1964; *Personally Conducted* (travel book; illustrated by Joseph Pennell and others), Scribner, 1889.

The Clocks of Rondaine and Other Stories (illustrated by E. H. Blashfield and others), Scribner, 1892; *Fanciful Tales*, edited by Julia Elizabeth Langworthy, Scribner, 1894; *New Jersey: From the Discovery of the Scheyichbi to Recent Times* (history), D. Appleton, 1896, reissued as *Stories of New Jersey*, American Book Co., 1896, reprinted, Rutgers University Press, 1961; *Captain Chap; or, The Rolling Stones* (illustrated by Charles H. Stephens), Lippincott, 1897, published as *The Young Master of Hyson Hall* (illustrated by Virginia Davisson and Charles H. Stephens), Lippincott, 1900; *A Storyteller's Pack* (collection; illustrated by Peter Newell, E. W. Kemble, and others), Scribner, 1897, published as *The Storyteller's Pack: A Frank R. Stockton Reader* (illustrated by Bernarda Bryson), 1968.

Buccaneers and Pirates of Our Coasts (history; illustrated by George Varian and B. West Clinedinst), Macmillan, 1898 [later edition illustrated by Bernard Krigstein, Looking Glass Library, 1960, new edition, Macmillan, 1967; adaptation published as *Stories of the Spanish Main* (illustrated by G. Varian and B. W. Clinedinst), Macmillan, 1913; *Kate Bonnet: The Romance of a Pirate's Daughter* (illustrated by A. J. Keller and H. S. Potter), D. Appleton, 1902; *The Queen's Museum, and Other Fanciful Tales* (illustrated by Frederick Richardson), Scribner, 1906; *The Poor Count's Christmas* (with illustrations from drawings by E. B. Bensell), Stokes, 1927 [later edition illustrated by Mary Weedon, privately printed, 1964]; *The Reformed Pirate: Stories from "The Floating Prince," "Ting-a-Ling," and "The Queen's Museum"* (illustrated by Reginald Birch), Scribner, 1936; *The Griffin and the Minor Canon* (fairytale; illustrated by M. Sendak), Holt, 1963; *Old Pipes and the Dryad* (fairytale; illustrated by Catherine Hanley), F. Watts, 1968.

For adults; all fiction, exception as indicated: (With wife, Marian Stockton) *The Home: Where It Should Be and What to Put in It* (nonfiction), Putnam, 1873; *Rudder Grange,* Scribner, 1879, reprinted, 193?; *The Lady, or the Tiger? and Other Stories* (illustrated by Wladyslaw T. Benda; title story first appeared in *Century,* November, 1882), Scribner, 1884, reprinted, Scholarly Press, 1977; *The Transferred Ghost,* Scribner, 1884; *The Casting Away of Mrs. Lecks and Mrs. Aleshine* (illustrated by George Richards), Century, 1886; *Stockton's Stories: A Christmas Wreck and Other Stories,* Scribner, 1886, reprinted, Books for Libraries Press, 1969; *The Late Mrs. Null,* Scribner, 1886, reprinted, 1907; *The Hundredth Man,* Century, 1887; *The Dussantes* (sequel to *The Casting Away of Mrs. Lecks and Mrs. Aleshine),* Century, 1888 [later edition published as *The Casting Away of Mrs. Lecks and Mrs. Aleshine [and] The Dussantes,* Appleton-Century, 1933, reprinted, Dover, 1961]; *Amos Kilbright: His Adscititious Experiences, with Other Stories,* Scribner, 1888, reprinted, Books for Libraries Press, 1972 (contains "The Reversible Landscape," "Dusky Philosophy," and "Plain Fishing"); *The Stories of*

On his first attempt his vigorous efforts nearly upset the boat, but he succeeded at last. . . . ■ (From *The Young Master of Hyson Hall* by Frank R. Stockton. Illustrated by Virginia H. Davisson.)

the Three Burglars, Dodd, 1889; *The Great War Syndicate,* Dodd, 1889, reprinted, Literature House, 1970.

Ardis Claverden, Dodd, 1890; *The Merry Chanter,* Century, 1890; *The House of Martha,* Houghton, 1891; *The Squirrel Inn,* Century, 1891; *The Rudder Grangers Abroad and Other Stories,* Scribner, 1891, reprinted, Books for Libraries Press, 1969; *My Terminal Moraine,* Collier, 1892; *The Watchmaker's Wife, and Other Stories,* Scribner, 1893; *Pomona's Travels* (sequel to *Rudder Grange),* Scribner, 1894; *The Adventures of Captain Horn,* Scribner, 1895; *A Chosen Few: Short Stories,* Scribner, 1895, reprinted, Books for Libraries Press, 1969; *Mrs. Cliff's Yacht,* Scribner, 1896; *The Girl at Cobhurst,* Scribner, 1898; *The Great Stone of Sardis,* Harper, 1898, reprinted, Blemont Tower Books, 1976; *The Associate Hermits,* Harper, 1899; *The Vizier of the Two-Horned Alexander* (illustrated by Reginald B. Birch), Century, 1899; *The Novels and Stories of Frank Stockton,* 23 volumes, Scribner, 1899-1904.

Afield and Afloat, Scribner, 1900; *A Bicycle of Cathay,* Harper, 1900; *John Gayther's Garden and the Stories Told Therein,* Scribner, 1902, reprinted, Books for Libraries Press, 1970; *The Captain's Toll-Gate,* D. Appleton, 1903; *The Magic Egg and Other Stories,* Scribner, 1907, reprinted, Books for Libraries Press, 1970; (contributor) *My Favorite Novelist* (essays), privately printed, 1908; *Fable and Fiction: Frank Stockton,* selected by J. I. Rodale, Story Classics, 1949; *Best Short*

Captain Cephas had brought over a bundle of things from his house. ■ (From *A Storyteller's Pack* by Frank R. Stockton. Illustrated by E. W. Kemble.)

Stories, Scribner, 1957; *The Science Fiction of Frank Stockton: An Anthology,* Gregg Press, 1976.

Also illustrator of *Poems,* written by brother, Thomas Hewlings Stockton, 1862. Under pseudonyms Paul Fort and John Lewees, contributor of articles and short stories to *St. Nicholas;* also contributor to additional periodicals, including *Southern Literary Messenger, Lippincott's, The Youth's Companion, Round Table, Saturday Press, Vanity Fair,* and others.

ADAPTATIONS—Movies and filmstrips: "Fantasy" (motion picture), adaptation of "Old Applejoy's Ghost," Paramount, 1927; "The Lady, or the Tiger?" (motion picture), Metro-Goldwyn-Mayer, 1942, Marshall Grant-Realm Television Productions, 1949, Encyclopaedia Britannnica Educational Corp., 1969; "The Lady, or the Tiger?" (filmstrip with casette), Listening Library, 1977.

Plays: "The Lady, or the Tiger?" (operetta; libretto by Sydney Rosenfeld), first produced in New York at Wallack's Theatre, May 7, 1888; Lewy Olfson, "The Lady, or the Tiger?" published in *Plays,* May, 1962; Adele Thane, "Old Pipes and the Dryad," published in *Plays,* January, 1964; "The Apple Tree" (three one-act plays, which included the one-act play "The Lady, or the Tiger?"), first produced at the Shubert Theatre, New York, N.Y., October 18, 1966; Eleanor Harder and Ray Harder, "Good Grief, a Griffin" (operetta), adaptation of *The Griffin and the Minor Canon,* Anchorage Press, 1968; Lewy Olfson, "The Transferred Ghost," published in *Classics Adapted for Acting and Reading,* Plays, 1970; "Marathon 81" (four one-act plays, which included a one-act play that Shel Silverstein loosely based on Stockton's "The Lady, or the Tiger?"), first produced at Ensemble Studio Theater, May, 1981 (later produced as "Wild Life," at the Vandam Theatre, May 2, 1983).

Francis Richard Stockton. From a portrait by Mrs. Dora Wheeler.

"I'll go first," said Mrs. Lecks, "and show you how." ■ (From the *Casting Away of Mrs. Lecks and Mrs. Aleshine* by Frank R. Stockton. Illustrated by George Richards.)

Recordings: "The Lady, or the Tiger? [and] The Discourager of Hesitancy," read by Judith Anderson, Caedmon, 1970; "The Lady, or the Tiger?" in "Tales for a Winter's Night," read by John Carradine, Pelican Records, 1976; "The Casting Away of Mrs. Lecks and Mrs. Aleshine," American Forces Radio and Television Service, 1978.

SIDELIGHTS: **April 5, 1834.** Frank Stockton was born in Blockley, a suburb of Philadelphia, Pennsylvania. The third child of his father's second marriage, he was lame from birth, one leg shorter than the other. He came from a literary family. His father, William S. Stockton, was a prominent Methodist writer. "Serving an apprenticeship to literature, if the first stages of a literature life may be so called, began in my case at an earlier age than at which any boy or girl should be apprenticed to an ordinary trade. My first literary composition was not strictly original, for it came through a desire to get from my favorite authors more than they could give me.

"When I began a book that I liked, I didn't want the story ever to stop. I remember some volumes by Miss Jane Porter, extraordinarily thick and fat, which delighted me merely to look at, because even the most rapid reader would require a long, long time to get to the end of such books.

"Now, *Charles O'Malley* was one of my favorite books, but it ended before I was satisfied with the story, and I think my first literary composition of any importance was an addition to this novel. I undertook the extension of the book in company with two young friends, one of whom suggested incidents for the new chapters, and the other drew some startling illustrations.

"As I grew older, Dumas and Hans Christian Andersen became my favorite authors, and my first literary work which was successful enough to get into print was a short story of French life written in the closest and the most conscientious imitations of Dumas; In fact, had anyone mistaken it for a translation of that author or even from any French writer, I should have considered it the highest praise.

"But this piece of work did not please me long. Reading it in print, it occurred to me that there was really nothing in it which I could truly claim as my own, and I was also very much afraid that there was nothing in it which any French authors who had ever had his work printed would be willing to father; besides, my companions praised it very mildly; It was plainly their opinion that Dumas could have written the story better." [Frank Stockton, "How I Served My Apprenticeship as a Man of Letters," *The Youth's Companion*, Volume 70, March 5, 1896.[1]]

1840. Attended grammar school in Philadelphia. As a child Stockton showed talent for writing and drawing. "I was very young when I determined to write some fairy tales because my mind was full of them. . . . These were constructed according to my own ideas. I caused the fanciful creatures who inhabited the world of fairy-land to act, as far as possible for them to do so, as if they were inhabitants of the real world. I did not dispense with monsters and enchanters or talking birds and beasts, but I obliged these creatures to infuse into their extraordinary actions a certain leaven of common sense." [Frank Stockton, *The Storyteller's Pack: A Frank R. Stockton Reader*, Scribner, 1968.[2]]

1848. Entered Central High School in Philadelphia. At school, Stockton won a prize for a story submitted to a contest held by *The Boys' and Girls' Journal*. During his high school years, Stockton's interest in writing included poetry as well as short stories. One of his first attempts at poetry began, "My love she hath a black eye; / Her lips are cherry red."

1852. Graduated from Central High School; became apprenticed to a wood engraver. Stockton did not abandon his literary interest completely, however. Following graduation, he joined a literary society of young men, many of whom were Central graduates.

As he gazed upon his bees hovering about him, . . . he said to himself, "They know just what they have to do, and they do it, but alas for me! I know not what I may have to do." ■ (From *The Bee-Man of Orn* by Frank R. Stockton. Illustrated by Maurice Sendak.)

For about five years, Stockton and his brother John met weekly with members of "The Forensic and Literary Circle," to read and discuss their original compositions. "I had always a great liking for fairy-tales, especially those of Hans Christian Andersen, and when I came to compose, I constructed a good many stories before I wrote any—I was naturally inclined to follow at a very, very great distance the path of that great master. But it was not long before a book came into my hand, a collection of fairy-tales, written by a literary man who was evidently a close student of Andersen, and his stories, although very good indeed, so closely resembled the work of the author of 'The Ugly Duckling' that I saw plainly the danger which lie[s] before the earnest student whose essays work in his master's line.

The Griffin now thought that he ought to visit the sick and the poor; and he began to go about the town for this purpose.... ■ (From _The Griffin and the Minor Canon_ by Frank R. Stockton. Illustrated by Maurice Sendak.)

"I think the first encouragement my literary work ever received was given to these early fairy-tales. I belonged at the time to a literary society composed of youths, many of whom possessed high intellectual tastes and ambitions. They read a great deal, generally the English classics, and those who wrote inclined toward poetry. The first use I intended to make of my fairy-tales was to read them before this society and I did so with some doubts as to their reception. . . . But there was no reason for my fears; the tales were well received, and some of the members of the most advantaged stage of thought took occasion to say pleasant things about them.

"This was great encouragement; if such young men—in my thoughts, I omitted the adjective—were satisfied with my work, there was no reason why editors should condemn it; I therefore tried an editor, and with success. The stories were printed but at the same time a demurrer was entered against being considered legitimate fairy-tales. Another piece of work which I did about this time was of an entirely different character. It was not intended for young readers, nor for those older readers who take pleasure in work designed for the young. It was addressed to those who were in love, or who were liable at any time to fall in love, and who would therefore take an interest in lovers in a story.

"But I wanted to make it different fom the ordinary love story; therefore I treated it after a fashion which pleased me and

(From *The Vizier of the Two-Horned Alexander* by Frank R. Stockton. Illustrated by Reginald B. Birch.)

Without the slightest hesitation he went to the door on the right, and opened it. ■ (From *The Lady, or the Tiger? and Other Stories* by Frank R. Stockton. Illustrated by Wladyslaw T. Benda.)

which was diametrically opposed to the method I had employed in the fairy-tales. Into the incidents and among the characters of real I introduced an element of fancy, and this so utterly ruined the story for the ordinary editor that it was not until I had sent it to nearly all the magazines in the United States that I succeeded in getting it printed, in the *Southern Literary Messenger* of Richmond."[1]

September 1, 1855. First published story, "The Slight Mistake," appeared in the *Philadelphia American Courier*. That same month his short story "Kate" appeared in the *Southern Literary Messenger* magazine. "This acceptance, though without pecuniary results, was a practical advantage to me, for I was asked to write a short serial for that magazine, which, although the scene was laid in France, was not treated after the manner of Dumas."[1]

April 30, 1860. Married Marian Edwards Tuttle.

1869. Became assistant editor to Mary Mapes Dodge, editor of *Hearth and Home* magazine. "In the course of time I entered the life of journalism and this, instead of assisting me in my strictly literary work, greatly interfered with it. When I was engaged in affairs which had no connections whatever with literature, composition and writing in my leisure hours were a recreation and a rest; but after a day of work upon a daily newspaper I had little inclination, even if I had had the strength and the time, for writing stories and tales.

"But journalism was an excellent training for my subsequent literary work; I learned much of the mechanism of composition, and much of the habits, customs and influences of that sphere of intellectual activity which may be termed the lobby of literature.

"But time passed on, and I passed on from the office of a daily paper to that of a weekly. This was a great change, and my new position might almost be called the first step in a business-like literary career."[1]

1870. *Ting-a-Ling,* a series of fairy tales, was published. Became a steady contributor to *Riverside,* a magazine for children. "My first book was a long time in growing. It came up like a plant by the wayside of ordinary avocation, putting forth a few leaves at a time; and when at last it budded, there was good reason to doubt whether or not it really would blossom. At length, though, it did blossom, in red, brown, green and blue.

"It was a book for young people, and was called *Ting-a-Ling.* It was made up of fairy stories, and when these first went out, each by itself, to seek a place in the field of current literature, it was not at all certain that they would ever find such a place. The fairies who figured in these tales were not like ordinary fairies. They went, as it were, like strangers or foreigners, seeking admission in a realm where they were unknown and where their rights as residents were some time in being recognized.

"I was far away in the backwoods of Virginia when I received the first copy of my first book, and what author has forgotten the first copy of his first book? Mine was of handsome proportions, bound in crimson cloth, and embellished with glittering plumes. It was delicately illustrated, beautifully printed, and I could imagine no home which would not be made brighter by the possession of the book, even if it were never read." [Martin I. J. Griffin, *Frank R. Stockton: A Critical Biography,* University of Pennsylvania Press, 1939.[3]]

1873. Named assistant editor to the newly formed *St. Nicholas* magazine. ". . . I left the office of the weekly periodical in order to enter that of a monthly magazine. Here the field of literary opportunity opened widely ahead. The magazine offered me a chance of printing work of greater pretention, and possibly of greater value, than that which could be admitted into the crowded columns of a weekly paper.

"Long-continued reading of manuscripts submitted for publication, which were almost good enough to use, but not quite up to the standard of a magazine, cannot but be of great service to anyone who proposes a literary career.

"Just before I entered the office of the magazine I was greatly interested in writing for a comic paper, and for this I composed a Christmas story in which the elements of the fantastic so permeated the real life of the characters that the tale was a decided extravaganza. The comic journal died just before the intended appearance of the story, and I was greatly pleased to have the manuscript accepted by the editor of the magazine to which I soon after became attached."[1]

1874. "Rudder Grange," a collection of stories, was first published in *Scribner's* magazine. "The discovery that humorous compositions could be used in journals other than those termed

comic marked a new era in my work. Periodicals especially devoted to wit and humor were very scarce in those days, and as this sort of writing came naturally to me, it was difficult, until the advent of *Puck,* to find a medium of publication for writings of this nature. I contributed a good deal to this paper, but it was only partly satisfactory, for articles which make up a comic paper must be terse and short, and I wanted to write humorous tales which should be as long as ordinary magazine stories. I had good reason for my opinion of the gravity of the situation, for the editor of a prominent magazine declined a humorous story (afterward very popular) which I had sent him, on the ground that the traditions of magazines forbade the publication of stories strictly humorous. Therefore, when I found an editor at last who actually *wished* me to write humorous stories, I was truly rejoiced. My first venture in this line was 'Rudder Grange.' And, after all, I had difficulty in getting the series published in book form. Two publishers would have nothing to do with them, assuring me that although the papers were well enough for a magazine, a thing of ephemeral nature, the book-reading public would not care for them. The third publisher to whom I applied issued the work, and found the venture satisfactory." [Frank R. Stockton, "A Memorial Sketch," in *The Captain's Toll-Gate,* D. Appleton, 1903.[4]] The serial was published in book form in 1879.

1878. Eyesight began to fail. Stockton found that he could not read continuously for any length of time without great pain.

(From the operetta "The Lady, or the Tiger?" starring De Wolf Hopper. Opened in New York at Wallack's Theatre, May 7, 1888.)

This recurring eye infection caused him to relinquish his position on *St. Nicholas* magazine. He turned to free-lance writing, dictating his stories to his wife and later to a secretary.

1882. "The Lady, or the Tiger?" appeared in *Century* magazine. This story became an overnight sensation causing Stockton's name to become a household word, as fans debated the outcome of the hero of the tale. "When I first planned the sketch of 'The Lady, or the Tiger?' I did not propose making a fictional problem of it. In fact I did not intend to write it or publish it. Its origin was due to the request of a friend in Nutley, New Jersey, who . . . gave an evening entertainment, some of the features of which were literary. As one of the guests asked to assist in the performances of the evening, I was requested to tell a story. I therefore set about composing one, and 'The Lady, or the Tiger?' was the ultimate result. I did not, however, tell the story at that party. When the appointed evening arrived it was not finished, and so far as I am concerned it is in that condition now.

"During the first construction of the story I had no thought but that I should finish it, state which door was opened by the young man in the arena, and give the reason why his lady-love, the princess, directed him to the one portal rather than to the other.

". . . At last I concluded to write it for publication without attempting to give any conclusion, and to leave the solution of the problem to those who might read it and care to think it out for themselves. I did not fear that I should indicate in any way that I had a personal bias in favor of the one or the other solution, for no such bias existed in my mind. I found, however, that it was not an easy sketch to write, for before I felt satisfied that I had put the question properly I had constructed it . . . several times.

"I remember very well the circumstances under which it was put on paper beneath some trees on a broad lawn of an old mansion in Amelia County, Virginia. Near by was a small house, called in that part of the country an office, which I used as a study. This building, intended for summer use, was raised a few feet from the ground, and was supported by wooden piers, and in the intervals of dictation I watched the efforts of a small moccasin snake, which was under the house, endeavoring to catch a toad. The toad, if fascinated at all, was only partly under the influence of its charmer, and seemed to have sense enough to hop about outside the line of the building, while the snake appeared afraid to venture beyond its protecting shadows. When I had finished my work a boy was sent to drive the snake from under the house and kill it, but I never heard whether, before its death, the snake got the toad or the toad got away.

"When the story was offered for publication its availability was a matter for consideration, for the reason that it did not belong to any of the classes of literary matter usually published in magazines. It was not a story, nor an essay, nor a practical article. . . .'' [Frank Stockton, "How I Wrote 'The Lady, or the Tiger?'," *Ladies' Home Journal*, November, 1893.⁵]

As readers pondered the feasible answer to the question, "Who came out of the door,—the lady, or the tiger?," Stockton's popularity in the field of American literature grew. Solutions to the story flooded into *Century* magazine offices and to Stockton's home. Indeed, fan letters to Stockton continued sporadically throughout the remainder of his lifetime. "Of course I replied to these letters, saying that I could not tell the writers what I did not know. In return I was made the subject of not a few severe attacks; according to some of them a writer

is famous who excites the interest of his reader without subsequently satisfying the resulting desire for full information. No notice being taken of my request for cooperation and assistance from those who might be better able than I to determine the action of my heroine, it was as if a searcher for the north pole, having failed to reach his objective point, had requested of other explorers some information based upon their explorations, and had received in return nothing but abuse for not being able to tell them the way to reach the pole.''⁵

1884. Three collections of short stories were published and all became successful. Stockton was considered the leading American humorist of the 1880s. ". . . If I am about to write a fairy tale, I must get my mind in an entirely different condition·from what it would be were I planning a story of country life of the present day. With me the proper condition often requires hard work. The fairy tale will come when the other kind is wanted. But the ideas of one class must be kept back and those of the other encouraged until at last the proper condition exists and the story begins.

"I have been thinking why it is that very often the work of an author of fiction is not as true as the work of an artist, and I have concluded that the artist has one great advantage over the author of fiction, and over the poet even. The artist has his models for his characters—models which he selects to come as near as possible to what his creations are going to be. The unfortunate author has no such models. He must rely entirely upon the characters he has casually seen, upon reading, upon imagination. . . .

"The best artists have live models to work from. But your writer of fiction—how, for instance, can he see a love scene enacted? He must describe it as best he can, and, although he may remember some of his own, he will never describe those.

"I think the beautiful young heroine of fiction generally gives the author of love stories a great deal of trouble. Such ladies exist, and their appearances may be described; but it is very difficult to find out what they would do under certain conditions necessary to the story, and therefore the author is obliged to rely upon his imagination, or upon the few examples he has met with in his reading, where men or women have delivered love-clinics at their own bedsides, or have had the rare opportunities of describing them at the bedside of others. For this reason people who are not in love, and whose actions are open to the observations of others, are often better treated by the novelist than are his lovers. I have sometimes thought that a new profession might be created—that of 'literary model.' Of course we would have none but the very highest order of dramatic performers, but such assistance as they might be able to give would be invaluable. Suppose the writer wanted to portray the behavior of a woman who has just received the tidings of the sudden death of her rejected lover. How does a writer, who has never heard such intelligence delivered, know what expressions of face, or what gestures, to give to his heroine in this situation? How would the intense, high-strung, nervous woman conduct herself? How would the fair-haired, phlegmatic type of women receive the news? The professional literary model might be enormously useful in delineating the various phases assumed by one's hero or heroine." [Edith M. Thomas, "Real Conversations—III: A Dialogue between Frank R. Stockton and Edith M. Thomas," *McClure's* magazine, November, 1893.⁶]

1890. Bought "The Holt," Stockton's home in Convent Station, New Jersey.

"What is this little girl in for?" he asked. . . .

"Piracy," he answered. ■ (From "Prince Hassak's March" in *The Storyteller's Pack: A Frank R. Stockton Reader.* Illustrated by Bernarda Bryson.)

(From the one-act play "The Lady, or the Tiger?" in the stage production of "The Apple Tree," starring Barbara Harris who won a Tony Award for her performance. Opened on Broadway at the Shubert Theatre, October 18, 1966.)

1899. Sold "The Holt" and bought "Claymont," near Charles Town, West Virginia, on land that had been owned by George Washington.

April 16, 1902. Stricken with a cerebral hemorrhage during a banquet held in his honor by the National Academy of Sciences, he died four days later. "Whatever merit my methods of expression may possess, is due, I believe, to my constant, earnest, and ever-anxious desire to make my readers understand what I mean." [George Bainton, editor, *The Art of Authorship: Literary Reminiscences, Methods of Work, and Advice to Young Beginners,* James Clark, 1890.[7]]

FOR MORE INFORMATION SEE—Juvenile: Frank Stockton, "How I Served My Apprenticeship as a Man of Letters," *The Youth's Companion,* Volume 70, March 5, 1896; Stanley J. Kunitz and Howard Haycraft, editors, *The Junior Book of Authors,* H. W. Wilson, 1934; S. J. Kunitz and H. Haycraft, editors, *American Authors, 1600-1900: A Biographical Dictionary of American Literature,* H. W. Wilson, 1938; Elizabeth Rider Montgomery, *Story behind Great Stories,* McBride, 1947; Laura Benet, *Famous Storytellers for Young People,* Dodd, 1968; "A Discussion of Frank Stockton's 'The

Lady, or the Tiger?'" (filmstrip), Encyclopaedia Britannica Educational Corp., 1970; D. L. Kirkpatrick, editor, *Twentieth-Century Children's Writers,* St. Martin's, 1978.

Adult: George Bainton, editor, *The Art of Authorship: Literary Reminiscences, Methods of Work and Advice to Young Beginners,* James Clark, 1890; Edith M. Thomas, "Real Conversations—III: A Dialogue between Frank R. Stockton and Edith M. Thomas," *McClure's* magazine, November, 1893; Frank Stockton, "How I Wrote 'The Lady, or the Tiger?'," *Ladies' Home Journal,* November, 1893; Martin I. J. Griffin, *Frank R. Stockton: A Critical Biography,* University of Pennsylvania Press, 1939; Frank Stockton, *The Storyteller's Pack: A Frank R. Stockton Reader,* Scribner, 1968; Henry L. Golemba, *Frank R. Stockton,* Twayne, 1981.

How long a time lies in one little word!
Four lagging winters and four wanton springs
End in a word. . . .

—William Shakespeare
(From *King Richard the Second*)

STRETE, Craig Kee 1950-

PERSONAL: Born in 1950 in Fort Wayne, Ind.; married Countess Irmgard Von Dam, 1984. *Education:* Wright State University, B.A., 1974; University of California, Irvine, M.F.A., 1978. *Home:* Hollywood, Calif. *Agent:* Virginia Kidd Literary Agent, 538 East Harford St., Milford, Pa. 18337; Curtis Brown Ltd., 575 Madison Ave., New York, N.Y. 10022; Kirby McCauley Ltd., 425 Park Ave. S., New York, N.Y. 10016; International Creative Management, 40 West 57th St., New York, N.Y. 10019.

CAREER: Fiction writer and playwright. Screenwriter under pseudonyms for major episodic television series during the 1970s. In de Knipscheer, Munich, foreign rights and international acquistions editor, 1980—; *East West Players Newsletters,* managing editor, 1984-85. *Member:* Author's League of America, Society of Children's Book Authors, Dramatists Guild, Directors Guild of America, Writers Guild of America, Society of Ethnic Literature in Translation (co-founder and director).

AWARDS, HONORS: Nebula Award nomination, 1975, for science fiction story "Time Deer"; *When Grandfather Journeys into Winter* was chosen notable trade book in the field of social studies by the Children's Book Council, 1979, was nominated for a Golden Sower Award by the University of Nebraska, and won the Fourteenth Annual Georgia Book Award from the University of Georgia; Dutch Children's Book Award nomination for *Grootvaders Reisdoel;* first place in the Dramatist Guild/CBS New Plays Programs for "Paint Your Face on a Drowning in the River"; Hugo Award nomination; Native American Students Association, minority grant in aid, 1976-78.

WRITINGS—For young people: *The Bleeding Man and Other Science Fiction Stories,* introduction by Virginia Hamilton, Greenwillow, 1977; *Paint Your Face on a Drowning in the River* (novel), Greenwillow, 1978; *Uncle Coyote and the Buffalo Pizza,* In de Knipscheer (Holland), 1978; *When Grandfather Journeys into Winter* (illustrated by Hal Frenk), Greenwillow, 1979; *Grootvaders Reisdoel,* In de Knipscheer, 1980; *Met de Pijn die het Liefheeft en Haat,* In de Knipscheer, 1983.

Other: *If All Else Fails, We Can Whip the Horse's Eye and Make Him Cry and Sleep* (short stories), introduction by Jorge Luis Borges, In de Knipscheer, 1976, Doubleday, 1980; *In Geronimo's Coffin,* In de Knipscheer, 1978; *Spiegel Je Gezicht,* In de Knipscheer, 1979; (with Jim Morrison) *Dark Journey* (poetry), In de Knipscheer, 1979; *Two Spies in the House of Love* (novel), In de Knipscheer, 1981; *Dreams That Burn in the Night* (short stories), Doubleday, 1982; *Burn Down the Night* (novel), Warner Books, 1982; *To Make Death Love Us,* Doubleday, 1985; *Death on Spirit House,* Doubleday, 1986; *Death Chants,* Doubleday, 1986; *Night Walker,* Harper, 1986.

Plays: "Paint Your Face on a Drowning in the River," produced by East West Players in Los Angeles, Calif., May,

CRAIG KEE STRETE

1984; "A Sunday Visit with Great Grandfather," produced by American Indian Community House, 1984; "The Arrow That Kills with Love," produced by American Indian Community House, 1984. Also author of "Dark Walkers," "Love Affair," "Knowing Who's Dead," "In the Belly of the Death Mother," and "Horse of a Different Technicolor."

Screenplays: "Somebody Shot My Horse," A. W. G. Productions, 1972; "Killing Moves," Cine Milano, 1975; "Honor Code," Ebrixton Films, 1976; "Blodets Rost" (title means "Voice of Blood"), Masterman Productions, 1978; "Sous les toits de nuit" (title means "Under the Roofs of Night"), Lyceum Cinema Internationale, 1978.

Author of radio plays "Saturday Night at the White Woman Watching Hole," and "The Bleeding Man."

Contributor of stories to magazines, including *If, Galaxy,* and *Playboy.*

WORK IN PROGRESS—Juvenile: *Boy with Indian Eyes, Secret of the White Head Hawk, Buffalo Brother, When Old, Many Coyote Sang the World into Being, How Tree Frog Got His Magic.* For adults: *Nightlands* (story collection); *Horse of a Different Technicolor* (six one-act plays); *Light That Brings the Dark,* for Doubleday; *The Man Who Danced with Wild Horses;* "The Night Brother," a full-length play about Siamese twins; "As If Bloodied on a Hunt before Sleep," a play with an Amerindian theme.

HOBBIES AND OTHER INTERESTS: Creative writing, native American fiction, South American writers, Carribean literature, short fiction, surrealism, contemporary novel, native American art, mythology of Eastern Woodlands Indians.

FOR MORE INFORMATION SEE: Peter Nicholls, *The Encyclopedia of Science Fiction: An Illustrated A to Z,* Grenada, 1979.

SUTCLIFF, Rosemary 1920-

PERSONAL: Born December 14, 1920, in West Clanden, Surrey, England; daughter of George Ernest (an officer in the Royal Navy) and Nessie Elizabeth (Lawton) Sutcliff. *Education:* Bideford School of Art, 1935-39. *Politics:* "Vaguely Conservative." *Religion:* Unorthodox Church of England. *Home:* Swallowshaw, Walberton, Arundel, Sussex, England.

CAREER: Author, 1945—. *Member:* P.E.N., National Book League, Society of Authors, Royal Society of Miniature Painters. *Awards, honors:* Carnegie Medal commendation, 1955, for *The Eagle of the Ninth,* 1957, for *The Shield Ring,* 1958, for *The Silver Branch,* and 1959, for *Warrior Scarlet; New York Herald Tribune*'s Children's Spring Book Festival honor book, 1957, for *The Shield Ring,* and 1958, for *The Silver Branch;* Hans Christian Andersen Award honor book, 1959, for *Warrior Scarlet,* and Highly Commended Author, 1974; Carnegie Medal, 1960, for *The Lantern-Bearers:* International Board on Books for Young People Honor List, 1960, for *Warrior Scarlet: New York Herald Tribune*'s Children's Spring Book Festival Award, 1962, for *Dawn Wind;* Lewis Carroll Shelf Award, 1971, for *The Witch's Brat;* Boston Globe-Horn Book Award for outstanding text, and Carnegie Medal runner-up, both 1972, both for *Tristan and Iseult; Heather, Oak, and Olive: Three Stories* was selected one of Child Study Association's "Children's Books of the Year," 1972, and *The Ca-*

ROSEMARY SUTCLIFF

pricorn Bracelet was chosen, 1973; Order of the British Empire, 1975; *Boston Globe-Horn Book* Honor Book for Fiction, 1977, for *Blood Feud;* Other Award, 1978, for *Song for a Dark Queen,*

WRITINGS—All children's books, except as noted: *The Chronicles of Robin Hood* (illustrated by C. Walter Hodges), Walck, 1950; *The Queen Elizabeth Story,* Walck, 1950; *The Armourer's House* (illustrated by C. Walter Hodges), Walck, 1951; *Brother Dusty-Feet* (illustrated by C. W. Hodges), Walck, 1952; *Simon* (illustrated by Richard Kennedy), Walck, 1953; *The Eagle of the Ninth* (ALA Notable Book; illustrated by C. W. Hodges), Walck, 1954; *Outcast* (illustrated by R. Kennedy), Walck, 1955; *The Shield Ring* (ALA Notable Book; illustrated by C. W. Hodges), Walck, 1956, new edition, 1972; *Lady in Waiting* (adult novel), Hodder & Stoughton, 1956, Coward, 1957; *The Silver Branch* (illustrated by Charles Keeping), Oxford University Press, 1957, Walck, 1958; *Warrior Scarlet* (ALA Notable Book; illustrated by C. Keeping), Walck, 1958, new edition, 1966; *The Lantern-Bearers* (ALA Notable Book; illustrated by C. Keeping), Walck, 1959; *The Rider of the White Horse* (adult novel), Hodder & Stoughton, 1959, published as *Rider on a White Horse,* Coward, 1960; *The Bridge-Builders,* Blackwell, 1959.

Knight's Fee (ALA Notable Book; illustrated by C. Keeping), Walck, 1960; *Houses and History* (illustrated by William Stobbs), Batsford, 1960; *Dawn Wind* (ALA Notable Book; *Horn Book* honor list; illustrated by C. Keeping), Oxford University Press, 1961, Walck, 1962; *Rudyard Kipling* (adult), Bodley Head, 1960, Walck, 1961, revised edition, Bodley Head, 1965; (reteller) *Beowulf* (ALA Notable Book; *Horn Book* honor list; illustrated by C. Keeping), Bodley Head, 1961, Dutton, 1962, new edition published as *Dragon Slayer: The*

Story of Beowulf, Penguin, 1976; *Sword at Sunset* (adult novel; Literary Guild selection), Hodder & Stoughton, 1963, Coward, 1964; (reteller) *The Hound of Ulster* (ALA Notable Book; *Horn Book* honor list; illustrated by Victor Ambrus), Dutton, 1963; *A Saxon Settler* (illustrated by John Lawrence), Oxford University Press, 1965; *Heroes and History* (illustrated by C. Keeping), Putnam, 1965; *The Mark of the Horse Lord* (ALA Notable Book; *Horn Book* honor list; illustrated by C. Keeping), Walck, 1965; (reteller) *The High Deeds of Finn MacCool* (*Horn Book* honor list; illustrated by Michael Charlton), Dutton, 1967; *The Chief's Daughter* (illustrated by V. Ambrus), Hamish Hamilton, 1967; *A Circlet of Oak Leaves* (illustrated by V. Ambrus), Hamish Hamilton, 1968; *The Flowers of Adonis* (adult novel), Hodder & Stoughton, 1969, Coward, 1970.

The Witch's Brat (ALA Notable Book; *Horn Book* honor list; illustrated by Richard Lebenson), Walck, 1970; *Tristan and Iseult* (ALA Notable Book; *Horn Book* honor list; illustrated by V. Ambrus), Dutton, 1971; *The Truce of the Games* (illustrated by V. Ambrus), Hamish Hamilton, 1971; *Heather, Oak, and Olive: Three Stories* (includes *The Chief's Daughter* and *A Circlet of Oak Leaves;* illustrated by V. Ambrus), Dutton, 1972; *The Capricorn Bracelet* (illustrated by Richard Cuffari), Walck, 1973; *The Changeling* (illustrated by V. Ambrus), Hamish Hamilton, 1974; (with Margaret Lyford-Pike) *We Lived in Drumfyvie,* Blackie, 1975; *Blood Feud* (*Horn Book* honor list; illustrated by C. Keeping), Oxford University Press, 1976, Dutton, 1977; *Shifting Sands* (illustrated by Laszlo Acs), Hamish Hamilton, 1977; *Sun Horse, Moon Horse,* (*Horn*

Book honor list; illustrated by Shirley Felts), Bodley Head, 1977, Dutton, 1978; *Song for a Dark Queen,* Pelham Books, 1978, Crowell, 1979; *The Light Beyond the Forest: Quest for the Holy Grail* (illustrated by S. Felts), Bodley Head, 1979, Dutton, 1980.

Frontier Wolf, Oxford University Press, 1980, Dutton, 1981; *Three Legions: A Trilogy* (contains *The Eagle of the Ninth, The Silver Branch,* and *The Lantern-Bearers*), Oxford University Press, 1980; *The Sword and the Circle: King Arthur and the Knights of the Round Table* (illustrated by S. Felts), Dutton, 1981; *Eagle's Egg* (illustrated by V. Ambrus), Hamish Hamilton, 1981; *The Road to Camlann: The Death of King Arthur* (ALA Notable Book; illustrated by S. Felts), Bodley Head, 1981, Dutton, 1982; *Blue Remembered Hills: A Recollection,* Bodley Head, 1983, Morrow, 1984; *Bonnie Dundee,* Bodley Head, 1983, Dutton, 1984. Also author of radio scripts for BBC Scotland.

WORK IN PROGRESS: Flame Coloured Taffeta.

SIDELIGHTS: **December 14, 1920.** Born in West Clanden, Surrey, England. "When anybody asks me where I was born, or when I am called on to provide that information in filling in a form, I admit with a distinct sense of apology that I was born in Surrey. Why the sense of apology I do not know. Surrey is quite as rich in history and, at least in parts, quite as beautiful in its own way as any other country in England. I can only think that it is because my father, like all the best

We ran the *Red Witch* down into the water and set off on our river-faring once again. ■ (Jacket illustration by Michael Eagle from *Blood Feud* by Rosemary Sutcliff.)

Aboard the *Paralos* was all the ordered bustle of departure, ropes being cast off, rowers in their places at the oars. ■ (From *A Crown of Wild Olive* by Rosemary Sutcliff. Illustrated by Victor Ambrus.)

sailors except Nelson, was Devon born and bred, and my mother was born in Dorset; and because of that, I grew up with the feeling that the West Country is the only right and proper place in which to have one's beginnings.'' [Rosemary Sutcliff, *Blue Remembered Hills*, Morrow, 1983.[1]]

1923. Father, a naval officer, transferred to Malta. ''When I was not much past three years old, my father was ordered to join the *Benbow* of the Mediterranean Fleet. . . .

''To this day the name 'Malta' means bells to me. Bells ringing, not as the church bells ring in this country, but clashing all together, tossing and falling and fountaining above the rooftops and through the narrow streets. And I see the blue of a night sky through a mosquito net; and somehow superimposed on that, the top of an orange-tree triumphant with flaming golden fruit peering at me over the broken coping of a sunlit wall.

''At the centre of it all was our house in Sliema, rented furnished from two very great and gracious ladies, who refused, at the end of our time there, to have the inventory checked, saying that they should not dream of so insulting my mother. The outside of the house is gone from me, but the inside was grey; a greenish underwater grey filled with shadows and coolness; with quiet, tall, immensely dignified rooms whose stone floors were washed daily with paraffin in the water to discourage the ants and other creepy-crawlies. They were washed by our maid Lucille Azzipadi, who I remembered for one dramatic pronouncement, made with flashing eyes and hands on hips, in some time of strife at home: 'My fader, he *debbil* man!' ''[1]

Sutcliff contacted Still's disease, a form of infantile paralysis which often kept her confined and in the close care of her mother. ''All my friends had nannies, which shows how much the world has changed in half a century; for we were the children of very ordinary naval and army officers with nothing but their pay. But I never had a nannie of my own. That was because I was still being ill—ill in patches and better in patches, and sometimes very ill indeed, as the arthritis burned its way along, and attack and remission followed each other during all the time that we were in Malta. My mother would not trust me to another woman's care.

''How I wished sometimes in later years that she had!

''My mother was one of those people, generally, I think, women, capable of great love and great self-sacrifice, but not capable of giving these things without demanding a return. During those years, she devoted herself to me to an extent which I sometimes think must have come hard on my father. She was not really beautiful, certainly not pretty, but she had one of those enchanting, changeable faces that can put on beauty, and lose it, and find it again as quickly as the changing lights of a March day; and a mass of golden hair. . . .''

''She was wonderful, no mother could have been more wonderful. But ever after, she demanded that I should not forget it, nor cease to be grateful, nor hold an opinion different from her own, nor even, as I grew older, feel the need for any companionship but hers. If this seems a terrible thing to write, I can argue only that it is the truth, and if I left it comfortably unwritten, I could not give a true picture of our relationship, which was a very close one, almost as close at times as she thought it was, and as she would have liked it to be. But it was never, after the very early years, an easy one. Very few of the worthwhile things in this world are all that easy.''[1]

1925. Returned to England with her family. ''At 66, Norfolk House Road I had my first experience of wireless, my initiation into the joys of 'Children's Hour.' In the dining-room there was a large black box covered with white dials like staring eyes, the property of my cousins, who were already on the edge of being grown up. And one afternoon, the lights on and the curtains drawn for tea, I was sat down in front of it, and a pair of earphones fitted over my head. It was telling a story. After the first moment of surprise, I sat enthralled. The story is for the most part lost to me, but I do remember that it concerned the adventures of some elves, and that at one point one of the elves had the misfortune to slide down the handle of a silver ladle into a soup tureen. He said, 'Where am I?' and they said, 'You're in the soup!' This, the first joke that ever I remember, struck me as being so exquisitely funny

that I rolled about and came perilously near to wetting my knickers.''[1]

Sutcliff was educated at home and read to extensively by her mother: "When I was about six mother decided that the time had come for me to learn to read. And that was when she made her mistake. Instead of merely sitting me down in front of *Peter Rabbit, The Secret Garden* or the Jungle Books and telling me to get on with it, she provided a dreadful book about a Rosy-Faced Family who Lived Next Door and Had

He was built crooked, with a hunched shoulder and a twisted leg that made him walk lopsided like a bird with a broken wing. ■ (From *The Witch's Brat* by Rosemary Sutcliff. Illustrated by Richard Lebenson.)

Cats that Sat on Mats, and expected me to get on with *that*. I was outraged—I, who had walked the boards with the Crummles, and fought beside Beowulf in the darkened Hill of Heriot. I took one look, and decided that the best way of making sure that I should never meet the Rosy-Faced Family or any of their unspeakable kind in the future was not to learn to read at all. So I didn't, and my mother never quite had the hardness of heart to stop reading to me. We had lessons and lessons and lessons; and we got practically nowhere."[1]

1926. Father transferred to South Africa; Sutcliff went with mother to visit her uncle on Headley Down.

"We arrived a few days before the 5th of November, and Uncle Acton decided that we should have our own fireworks party, since I had never experienced one before, and went into Hazlemere to buy the fireworks. The night came, clear and with a touch of frost to mingle with the scent of pine trees and wood smoke in the air; exactly what a Guy Fawkes' night ought to be. And my mother and Miss Edes and I wrapped in rugs were installed in the open-sided garden shed, while Uncle Acton took his stand with his box of fireworks on the patch of rough lawn in front of us."[1]

1930. Father retired; family settled in Devonshire. "My schooldays proper had begun. And, oddly enough, I was all

for it. I had no real desire to learn to read, but the dignity of schoolgirlhood appealed to me strongly. So there, on a day, was I, my chest swollen with the importance of myself and the occasion, passing for the first time through the doorway of Miss Beck's Academy.

". . . Miss Amelia Beck had no teaching qualifications whatsoever, save the qualifications of long experience and love. She was the daughter of a colonel of Marines, in her eighty-sixth year when I became one of her pupils; and for more than sixty years, in her narrow house overlooking the Lines at Chatham, she had taught the children of the dockyard and the barracks. She accepted only the children of service families.

"From a tattered old volume of Grimm's *Fairy Tales* passed round among us, we learned to read, even I, at long last, discovering suddenly what the mystery was all about. I have no recollection of the actual process; I do not know how or why or when or wherefore the light dawned. I only know that when I went to Miss Beck's Academy I could not read, and that by the end of my first term, without any apparent transition period, I was reading, without too much trouble, anything that came my way.

"After we left Chatham, Miss Beck and I wrote to each other until I was quite grown up and she had long since retired, for

Out of the heart of the blue radiance there began to grow a little tree. ■ (From *The Capricorn Bracelet* by Rosemary Sutcliff. Illustrated by Richard Cuffari.)

The whole village seemed gathered in the central space.... ■ (From *The Outcast* by Rosemary Sutcliff. Illustrated by Richard Kennedy.)

she lived into her late nineties. And then the time came when I wrote as usual, and there was no answer to my letter, and no answer to the next letter either. And I knew, even before I wrote to the old housemaid to ask for news, that all of us, scattered over the face of the earth like Kipling's *Slaves of the Lamp*, had lost our Miss Amelia Beck, and a tiny part of our own lives with her.

"For the next few years hospital alternated with school as my point of contact with other children. I departed at intervals, eight or ten times it must have been, to the Princess Elizabeth Orthopaedic Hospital in Exeter for operations that attempted with varying success to repair the damage left by Still's Disease."[1]

1934. Enrolled in art school. "I left school at fourteen, which you could do in those days. It was painfully obvious that it was not going to be the least use my staying on any longer. The only subject I was any good at was art—I had been good at that since I was five and began decorating my plasters with rather magnificent robins in brown and red chalk. So I left St George's and went to Bideford Art School, which really was an art school, and an extremely good one at that time.

"Everybody was eighteen or more, except me. At fourteen, I was very much the baby of the art school; the others were all

nice to me, . . . but of course they didn't include me in anything. So art school for me really was all work and no play. Not that I am complaining; I loved the work, and I stuck to it harder than I had ever stuck to anything before. I did a full three-year stint, taking the General Art Course. The white plaster casts of classical statuary I made studies of, from the North, South, East and West, in pencil, charcoal, oils and water colours. I did Still Life, Portraiture, Composition and Design. I did Life—occasionally we had a paid girl model for that, but more often it was a young fisherman from the Quay, posing bashfully in a G-string for 7/6d. an hour. Once it was a hard-up divinity student who, for some unknown reason, having taken off everything else, refused to take off his shoes, socks or sock-suspenders."[1]

1938. "When I was seventeen, I fell in love with my cousin Edward. At least, I thought I did.

"It was the last summer before the war, and he came to spend part of his leave with us. I had seen him very occasionally since the Sheerness days, but those few occasions have left no particular mark on my memory. And now suddenly, there he was, a lieutenant in the navy, and with war beginning to loom, which made him seem a prospective hero. I was young for my age, and had not yet grown out of hero-worship. He was almost the first young man I had ever spoken to; and certainly

The wagon heaved and jolted through the ruts, swaying like a ship in a gale, so that Simon felt more sick and dizzy.... ■ (From *Simon* by Rosemary Sutcliff. Illustrated by Richard Kennedy.)

They sat on for a while, quietly drinking their wine, and talking of the prospect of fair weather for the harvest.... ■ (From *The Silver Branch* by Rosemary Sutcliff. Illustrated by Charles Keeping.)

he was the first who ever appeared to notice that I was a girl. He opened doors for me and got up when I came into the room, and looked at me intently and as though my opinions mattered when we talked to each other. And I was his slave, just as surely as I was at five years old when he noticed that I was human and brought me unlawful coconut from Sheerness Fair.

"We went for picnics and for days out in the car, as we always did in time of summer visitors. . . . The end of Edward's leave came and he went back to his ship. I wore a tiny photo of him cut out of a snapshot in a silver locket round my neck and never took it off day or night, and another year went by. I was eighteen, and on that beautiful September Sunday in 1939 the war came.

"We settled down into the wartime routine that was to last for six years. Living in the depth of the country, so far from any target area, in some ways we never saw the war at all. We had only three jettisoned bombs within a mile of us from first to last; and my mother and I both had a regretful feeling that we were missing out on something that the rest of the country was sharing, though there must have been many in the same case as ourselves. That is not to say that they were easy years for either of us. We had our full share of the anxieties of women with their menfolk away at the wars.

". . . There being, apparently, no other war work that I could do, I had managed to get myself on to the team of a dictatorial old lady who collected handicraft materials and sent them out to prisoner of war camps and camp hospitals in Germany, and I was generally working out tapestry designs and painting them on to canvas for her. It was funny sort of war work, but better than nothing.

"Sometimes I would have a painting job on hand, and my mother would drop me off at the Art School, while she did the shopping on her own. I was no longer a student, having finished my General Art Course the year before the war, but by courtesy of Mr Sharpe, my old headmaster, I was allowed the use of an empty room whenever I had a sitter. For by now I was a professional miniature painter.

"I was quite a good one. Technically I was a very good one; but technique is not everything. I began to get sitters; and since the petrol situation made it impossible for people to get out to us, and Bideford was a good central point, I had this arrangement with Mr Sharpe. I painted children for the most part. Oh, the awfulness of trying to paint children, who can never sit still for a second, even when being told stories; and even more, the awfulness of their mothers, who are never satisfied, and who equate blue eyes and duckling yellow hair with beauty! But as the war went on, I began to get more and more work to do at home from photographs; husbands and sons in the uniform of one or other of the services. And then, sadly, more and more often, photographs of husbands and sons who would not be coming home again.

"I suppose it must have been around the middle of the war that I began to get the itch to write. Almost from the beginning I felt cramped as a miniature painter and I think my first urge to break out into writing was the result of this. One can write as big as one needs; no canvas is too large to be unmanageable.

"So I began to scribble, at first purely for the pleasure of scribbling, and without any idea of getting published. It was a delight, a way of escape, and in early years it had the added attraction of being a forbidden delight, a way of escape that must be kept secret. My family knew that I could paint, but—

who shall blame them, remembering my school record—they had no faith whatever in my ability to write.''[1]

1946. Began writing for publication. ''Not long after the war, I started on a book which I did intend for children, a re-telling of the Celtic and Saxon legends on which my mother had brought me up. Beowulf, Cuchulain, Geraint and Enid, Gawain and the Loathely Lady, about a dozen in all. And writing them, I began for the first time to think about the possibility of getting published, the strange alchemy which would turn a private scribble on foolscap, made for one's own joy in the making, into a book to be opened to the world and read by other people. It seemed that in a sort of way that would be to bring what one had written to birth, and the pregnancy would be just as private and just as much a delight as ever.

''When they were finished, I sent the whole collection, copied out in my best long-hand, to my old friend Colonel Crookenden, to see what he thought of them. Why Crooky, I am not sure; I could scarcely have chosen anybody less bookish.

''. . . A day or two after receiving my parcel of legends, Crooky chanced to find himself at some social gathering next to the daughter of an old friend, who, born, as it were, into the Cheshire Regiment, had lately married into the Oxford University Press. He told her about the legends and issued his orders, 'I shall send them to you tomorrow, and you will show them to your husband.' . . . The stories arrived, the girl did as she was bid. And by and by I received a very kind letter from the Oxford University Press, saying that they didn't want them—which somewhat surprised me since I had known nothing at all that went before.

''So, the Oxford University Press did not want my British legends. But the very kind letter went on to suggest that I should try my hand at writing a *Robin Hood* for them.

''And that was how it all began.''[1]

1950. First two children's books were published. ''I had finished *The Chronicles of Robin Hood* by that time, and sent it to a typing agency, where I think it must have been lost, because it was eighteen months and a great many letters later that it returned to me. In the interval I set to work again, and the result was *The Queen Elizabeth Story. The Q.E.S.* was a book for little girls, too cosy and too sweet, as were the next two or three books to follow it, before I found, as it were, my own voice. But it was a real book whereas *Robin Hood* was a foster-child, it was my own, bone of my bone, flesh of my flesh. . . .''[1]

Sutcliff is best known for her historical novels. ''Writing historical fiction is one of those things that happened, I suppose,

Sutcliff, about 1980.

because I had so much read to me when I was small. I don't always enjoy writing. It's too much like hard work. But I have no wish to write modern books. I don't think I could write modern books. To me half the fun of writing a book is the research entailed. I love trying to piece together historical background and to catch the right smell of the period. Every period has very much its own subtle difference in smell, and the whole atmosphere changes a little bit every few years through history. It's a fascinating exercise to try and catch this difference.

"Usually I prepare myself by getting a great many books together from the county library. This acts like a snowball. Every book has a bibliography and I get a great many more books from each bibliography. I just go on until I am completely embedded in the period and place that I'm writing about. Generally the plot comes from the historical background, not the other way around. The two things gradually move together in my mind as I get the research further, so that the plot grows with it, if plot it can be called—I'm not very good at plots. They just grow fairly naturally, side by side.

"I keep a little red exercise book with notes and get a new one each time I'm writing a book. In this I write down all that I'm going to write about the characters, real and imaginary. I gradually think these people out, what their personal appearance is going to be, any kind of odd tricks and habits and likes and dislikes that they've got, their backgrounds, anything I can think of that makes them into real people, so that if one walked around behind them they would have a back view as well as a front view. By the time I've got all this locked together, they've become kind of acquaintances. As I write about them, I get to know them better. By the time I've finished a book, our acquaintance has ripened and I know them as one knows a person whom you've known through the years and got to know very well." [Cornelia Jones and Olivia R. Way, editors, *British Children's Authors: Interviews at Home,* American Library Association, 1976.[2]]

1963. Published *Sword at Sunset.* "After I'd written *Sword at Sunset,* I did an edited version for children, and they made me cut certain things—details of the battles, because they were too violent; and the fact that two of the soldiers were homosexuals, which was in fact a most natural thing to happen, and part of being a warrior. I discovered later that lots of children had been reading the adult version and loving it!

"And if the child is caught by your book, his imagination is caught, even if the relationship is complicated; they don't mind being stretched, they sort of hop along in your wake, and understand what they can. They can understand kind of through the pores of their skin; things that are beyond them mentally they can very often take in intuitively. But one can't count on that." [Justin Wintle and Emma Fisher, editors, *The Pied Pipers,* Paddington Press, 1975.[3]]

Sutcliff remarked about her writing career: "Well, I get a lot of fan letters, generally saying: How did you come to be a writer, how long does it take you, how can I become one; sometimes they inquire anxiously about particular characters—did so-and-so find a nice wife, and this kind of thing, which I find really rather touching, because one feels they have become really involved, and the people are real to them. One fan letter I had once, years and years ago, said, broadly speaking: Dear Miss Sutcliff, I enjoy your books very much, and I hope that when you are dead you will go on writing books and I can go on reading them."[2]

Sutcliff lives in a sprawling house in Sussex, England, where she doesn't write regular hours, but keeps a general writing schedule, working on and off from morning until suppertime.

HOBBIES AND OTHER INTERESTS: Archaeology, anthropology, primitive religion, making collages and costume jewelry.

FOR MORE INFORMATION SEE: Margaret Meek, *Rosemary Sutcliff,* Walck, 1962; Muriel Fuller, editor, *More Junior Authors,* H. W. Wilson, 1963; Roger Lancelyn Green, *Tellers of Tales,* F. Watts, 1965; Brian Doyle, *The Who's Who of Children's Literature,* Schocken Books, 1968; *Horn Book,* December, 1970, December, 1971, October, 1972; Martha E. Ward and Dorothy A. Marquardt, *Authors of Books for Young People,* 2nd edition, Scarecrow, 1971; John Rowe Townsend, *A Sense of Story: Essays on Contemporary Writers for Children,* Lippincott, 1971; Virginia Haviland, *Children and Literature: Views and Reviews,* Lothrop, 1974.

Edward Blishen, editor, *The Thorny Paradise,* Kestrel, 1975; Justin Wintle and Emma Fisher, editors, *The Pied Pipers,* Paddington Press, 1975; *School Bookshop News,* March 4, 1976; Cornelia Jones and Olivia R. Way, *British Children's Authors: Interviews at Home,* American Library Association,

His listeners nodded, and huddled closer to the long fires, and here and there a man glanced behind him into the shadows. ■ (From *Beowulf,* retold by Rosemary Sutcliff. Illustrated by Charles Keeping.)

The City seemed a city in a fairytale, every ledge and cranny deep in sparkling frosted snow. . . . ■ (From *The Armourer's House* by Rosemary Sutcliff. Illustrated by C. Walter Hodges.)

1976; Ann Block and Carolyn Riley, editors, *Children's Literature Review,* Volume 1, Gale, 1976; Dennis Butts, editor, *Good Writers for Young Readers,* Hart-Davis, 1977; D. L. Kirkpatrick, *Twentieth-Century Authors,* Macmillan (London), 1978; "Meet Your Author: Rosemary Sutcliff," *Cricket,* March, 1980; *Children's Literature in Education,* summer, 1981, winter, 1982; *Times Literary Supplement,* April 22, 1983; Rosemary Sutcliff, *Blue Remembered Hills: A Recollection,* Morrow, 1984.

THEROUX, Paul   1941-

PERSONAL: Born April 10, 1941, in Medford, Mass.; son of Albert Eugene and Anne (Dittami) Theroux; married Ann Castle (a radio producer), December 4, 1967; children: Marcel Raymond, Louis Sebastian. *Education:* Attended University of Maine, 1959-60; University of Massachusetts, B.A., 1963; Syracuse University, further study, 1963.

CAREER: Soche Hill College, Limbe, Malawi, lecturer in English, 1963-65; Makerere University, Kampala, Uganda, lec-

turer in English, 1965-68; University of Singapore, Singapore, lecturer in English, 1968-71; professional writer, 1971—. Visiting lecturer, University of Virginia, 1972-73. *Awards, honors:* Robert Hamlet one-act play award, 1960; *Playboy* Editorial Award, 1971, 1976; Literature Award, American Academy of Arts and Letters, 1977.

WRITINGS—Novels; published by Houghton, except as indicated: *Waldo,* 1967; *Fong and the Indians,* 1968; *Girls at Play,* 1969; *Murder in Mount Holly,* Alan Ross, 1969; *Jungle Lovers,* 1971; *Saint Jack,* 1973; *The Black House,* 1974; *The Family Arsenal* (Book-of-the-Month Club selection), 1976; *Picture Palace,* 1978; *The Mosquito Coast,* 1982.

Other books; published by Houghton, except as indicated: *V. S. Naipaul: An Introduction to His Work,* Africana Publishing Corp., 1972; *Sinning with Annie and Other Stories* (collection of stories), 1972; *The Great Railway Bazaar: By Train through Asia* (travel), 1975; *The Consul's File* (collection of stories), 1977; *A Christmas Card* (juvenile; illustrated by John Lawrence), 1978; *London Snow* (juvenile; illustrated with wood engravings by J. Lawrence), 1979; *The Old Patagonian Express: By Train through the Americas,* 1979; *World's End and Other Stories,* 1981; *The London Embassy,* 1983; *The Kingdom by the Sea: A Journey around Great Britain,* 1983, large print edition, G.K. Hall, 1983; *Sailing through China,* 1984; *Half-Moon Street,* 1984; *The Imperial Way,* 1985.

Contributor of fiction to *Encounter, Atlantic Monthly, Playboy,* and other periodicals; contributor of reviews to *New York Times, Times* (London), and other periodicals in the United States and England.

ADAPTATIONS: "Saint Jack" (movie), New World/Shoals Creek/Playboy/Copa de Oro, 1979; "Mosquito Coast" (movie), starring Harrison Ford, produced by Saul Zaentz, 1985.

SIDELIGHTS: Born in the Boston suburb of Medford, Massachusetts, Theroux was raised as the third child of seven born to a shoe-leather salesman and a former school teacher. From

PAUL THEROUX

the age of fourteen he held aspirations of becoming a writer. "You can't hide very easily in a large family, but there was always privacy in reading. The earliest books I read as a child were about travel. Books about fur trapping in Hudson Bay, about catching animals in Africa, being a doctor up the Amazon—that kind of book.

"Reading ought to be a pleasure. It ought to take you away. I could never, for example, write a book like *Ordinary People* or *Kramer vs. Kramer*. I find books about unhappy families and divorce tedious and depressing. If you're going to spend a year or two writing a book, you have to be interested in and amused by your material." [Joseph Barbato, "Books Should Take You Away," *Express,* June, 1982.[1]]

After graduating from college, Theroux taught in Italy before joining the Peace Corps, which sent him to Africa. Since then, he has lived a good portion of his adult life outside the United States. ". . . I grew up in Massachusetts, and I was educated in Massachusetts—and couldn't afford to do a lot of traveling. Then I went to Africa in 1963, and I've never effectively been back since then, although I own a house in [Massachusetts] and I go back every summer.

(Jacket illustration by Jerry Pinkney from *Fong and the Indians* by Paul Theroux.)

"In late 1971, I decided that I was going to make a living as a writer—or fail. I had published five books by then, and I came to England.

"My wife is English, so when it came time to settle it didn't frighten me to live in the West Country of England. I didn't come here thinking that this would be a good place to write, but it just struck me that it would be a nice place to stop for a bit. Actually, it amazes me that so much time has passed. . . ." [Paul Theroux, "'I Sell More Books in the United States, but I'm Understood' in England," *U.S. News & World Report,* December 17, 1979.[2]]

About England, he remarked: "Money isn't really a very important thing in this country, so you can't buy services, and people who serve you aren't interested in money. Privacy is greatly valued. It's a place I would recommend to a person who wanted to write, because a writer here is regarded in a different way from a writer in the States.

"Here writing is seen as a profession—unmagical—and no one here associates a writer with someone who is going to break the bank. In the States, it's very difficult to describe yourself as a writer without explaining how you make ends meet.

"One of the reasons I stayed on here is because no one has said, 'Isn't it time you left?' British society is very easy to live in but impossible to gain entrance to: You're regarded as 'that West Indian' or 'that American' or something exotic; you are 'the gentleman in the parlor.'

Saint Mary's on the river was a dark steeple against the yellow light from the Chelsea Flour Mill on the far bank. ■ (From *London Snow: A Christmas Story* by Paul Theroux. Wood engraving by John Lawrence.)

"One could live here a long time and be very happy and yet not take an active part in the society, whereas a foreigner who goes to the United States quickly and assertively becomes an American. Living in England has enabled me to retain my American identity.

"I think I'm taken seriously as a writer here and am treated in a kindly way. I was asked to give a lecture at the Royal Geographical Society, but I've never been asked by the equivalent society in America. I've won prizes here for books, but I've never won anything in the States.

"I sell more books in the States, but perhaps I'm understood here. At least I'm getting a lot of friendly attention. . . .

"I like living here, but I'm not British. So I'd be kidding myself if I said, 'Yes, I'll put roots down and stay'—because I can't. Fortunately, it's not necessary to be British in order to live here, whereas in every other country you would have to adopt the style or the posture of the people you are living among. The British don't require that of you; in fact, they forbid it.

"In years to come, I'll slowly gravitate back to the States. As the children grow older, I'll be spending more and more time there, and I think probably I've already begun to phase myself out of England. It would be self-delusion to do otherwise. But, in an important sense, England made me."[2]

In 1975, Theroux boarded a train at London's Victoria Station and began a four-month trip that took him through Asia. The trip was described in his book, *The Great Railway Bazaar,* which became a best seller. It was one of the few travel books to gain such popularity. "Ever since childhood, when I lived within earshot of the Boston and Maine, I have seldom heard a train go by and not wished I was on it. Those whistles sing bewitchment: railways are irresistible bazaars, snaking along perfectly level no matter what the landscape, improving your mood with speed, and never upsetting your drink. The train can reassure you in awful places—a far cry from the anxious sweats of doom airplanes inspire, or the nauseating gas-sickness of the long-distance bus, or the paralysis that afflicts the car passenger. If a train is large and comfortable you don't even need a destination; a corner seat is enough, and you can be one of those travelers who stay in motion, straddling the tracks, and never arrive or feel they ought to—like that lucky man who lives on Italian Railways because he is retired and has a free pass. Better to go first class than to arrive, or, as the English novelist Michael Frayn once rephrased McLuhan:

Theroux at Brighton during his travels around the British coastline researching *The Kingdom by the Sea.*

'the journey is the goal.' But I had chosen Asia, and when I remembered it was half a world away I was only glad.

"Then Asia was out the window, and I was carried through it on these eastbound expresses marveling as much at the bazaar within the train as the ones we whistled past. Anything is possible on a train: a great meal, a binge, a visit from card players, an intrigue, a good night's sleep, and strangers' monologues framed like Russian short stories. It was my intention to board every train that chugged into view from Victoria Station in London to Tokyo Central. . . ." [Paul Theroux, *The Great Railway Bazaar: By Train through Asia,* Houghton, 1975.[3]]

Theroux's second book about train travel, *The Old Patagonian Express,* described his trip from Boston to the tip of South America. Although Theroux has written several books of fiction, his name is synonymous with the literature of train travel. ". . . A person should travel not only to find out about the present but to find out about the future. A grand tour today should be the opposite of what it was in the past. It should avoid museums, cathedrals, castles and ruins. It should go where human life is, to places that throw you images of the future. It should be an intense experience of time, but not historical time, not high culture. Not an experience of seeing the underside of life, because we're closer to it now than we've ever been. I think that by looking closely at New York, or conversely at India, Laos or parts of Chicago, you see the

The cabin had a shadowy haunted look. ■ (From *A Christmas Card* by Paul Theroux. Illustrated by John Lawrence.)

pattern of what the future holds for us: a society that is unsafe, difficult, lacking in distribution of things like water, fuels, food; a society in which transportation is bad and security a little shaky. The future has already arrived in Burundi; it has also arrived in Japan. It's a hundred years ago in Burundi, and perhaps it'll always be that; it's tomorrow morning in Japan. There's a date that you can assign to all places. Maybe in Malaysia it's 1956. In Afghanistan it might be 1910. In Tokyo it might be 1982—or 1984. Travel should be an experience of time. Not an evasion of reality but a confrontation with it. The trouble with most travel today is that it's done by the very old, people who are retired, on whom it makes an impression but who won't make much of a difference." [Anthony Weller, "Paul Theroux," *GEO* magazine, November, 1983.[4]]

One of Theroux's latest travel books centered around a walking trip, not a trip by train. *The Kingdom by the Sea: A Journey around Great Britain* recorded his impressions of the British coast. ". . . Walking is the ideal way to travel in any country, and if I had the time, if I didn't have to make a living, that's definitely what I'd do; I'd just walk. Twenty miles a day on foot is the ideal rate. You leave a place in the morning, have lunch in another place and sleep in another place. And you keep moving. This is what I've just done, actually, for my new travel book. I've walked around the coast of Britain—not just England but Wales, Scotland, Northern Ireland. If it was raining I took a bus or a train, but it's such an easy country to travel in that you constantly have to slow yourself down. I went on the assumption that there was a coastal path that went entirely around Britain. And what I want to do now is write about Britain as it's never been written about before. More books have been written about Britain than about perhaps any other country on earth, but it's still very much an unknown place because of people's received impressions. People come looking for Dicken's England, Thackeray's England, cookie-box England. In order to write well you have to rid yourself of accepted notions of a place."[4]

Theroux's literary output includes novels, books for children, short stories, poetry and, of course, travel books. When asked what reaction he wants from the readers of his books, he answered: ". . . I want people to burst into tears, I suppose, or be thrilled. Or to give the book to someone else and say, 'Read this book, I hope you like it as much as I do.' Because offering a person a book is like offering him a destination. You say, 'Take this and you'll be happy.' We're all trying to find something that will give the world a sense of order. And that's what fiction does. In the case of my travel books, if a person says to me, 'Your book made me want to go there,' that always makes me feel I've failed. He should say, 'I'm glad I read your book, now I don't have to go there.' That's an important distinction. In a sense the travel writer is traveling for the reader. The book should be an intense experience of the place, and the reader should receive the experience as freshly and directly as I have."[4]

About his choice of professions, Theroux remarked: "Writing made me a free man. No other profession could have done that. When you think that writing is something you do by yourself, that you're making something out of nothing, it's like a conjuring trick in one sense—there *is* nothing like it. Except, I suppose, painting, composing music, the other creative professions. All of those make you free. They free you from dogma, they free you from every sort of earthly constraint, they give you a tremendously vivid dream life, and they add to your sense of joy and liberation. And that's the only point of going on living, being able to feel that as your time on earth progresses you're becoming steadily more free. You can't feel as if you're subject to someone else's will. I suppose that's why rich people buy an island or a jet plane. In a material sense they want to be free, and they're trying to do it with money. But it is possible with the imagination.''[4]

FOR MORE INFORMATION SEE: Harper's, May, 1967; *Kenyon Review,* September, 1967; *New Yorker,* November 11, 1967, November 8, 1969; *Time,* August 23, 1968; *Christian Science Monitor,* September 5, 1968; *Saturday Review,* September 28, 1968; *New York Times Book Review,* November 3, 1968, September 28, 1969, November 5, 1972, September 8, 1974, August 24, 1975, July 11, 1976; *Times Literary Supplement,* June 12, 1969, November 17, 1972, April 27, 1973, March 26, 1976; *Books Abroad,* summer, 1969, winter, 1971; *National Observer,* October 6, 1969; *Virginia Quarterly Review,* winter, 1969, winter, 1970; *New Republic,* November 29, 1969; *Punch,* December 10, 1969.

London Magazine, January, 1970; *Life,* May 21, 1971; *New York Times,* May 29, 1971, August 23, 1977, May 31, 1978; *National Review,* June 29, 1971, November 10, 1972; *Book World,* August 8, 1971, September 15, 1974; *Choice,* July, 1973; *Encounter,* July, 1973; *New Statesman,* October 4, 1974, October 17, 1975; *Spectator,* October 12, 1974; *Hudson Review,* winter, 1974; Paul Theroux, *The Great Railway Bazaar: By Train through Asia,* Houghton, 1975; *Contemporary Literary Criticism,* Gale, Volume 5, 1976, Volume 8, 1978; *Detroit News,* June 4, 1978; P. Theroux, "'I Sell More Books in the United States, But I'm Understood' in England," *U.S. News & World Report,* December 17, 1979; Joseph Barbato, "Books Should Take You Away," *Express,* June, 1982; Anthony Weller, "Paul Theroux," *GEO* magazine, November, 1983.

WEGEN, Ron(ald)

BRIEF ENTRY: Born in New Jersey. Artist, author and illustrator of books for children. Wegen graduated from New York City's Pratt Institute and has lived in several different cities around the world, including London, Rio, and Rome. A versatile artist, he produces paintings, jewelry, sculpture, and pottery. Among Wegen's seven self-illustrated children's books are *Sand Castle* (1977), *Where Can the Animals Go?* (1978), and *Sky Dragon* (1982), all published by Greenwillow. In 1983 he was the recipient of the New Jersey Authors Award for his story *The Halloween Costume Party* (Clarion Books, 1983). For younger preschoolers, Wegen's wordless picture book *Balloon Trip* (Clarion Books, 1981) was described by *School Library Journal* as "magnetic . . . , fresh, and memorable." *Publishers Weekly* agreed, calling it "an adventure exciting to share in boldly colored pictures." Wegen is also the illustrator of *There's No Such Place as Far Away* by Richard Bach. *Residence:* New York and Bogatá, Columbia.

WEISS, Ellen   1953-

PERSONAL: Born December 7, 1953, in New York, N.Y.; daughter of Jack (an accountant) and Leatie (a writer and kindergarten teacher; maiden name, Taber) Weiss; married Ken Goldstrom (a ceramist), September 21, 1980. *Education:* Pratt Institute, B.F.A., 1975. *Residence:* Cambridge, Mass.

CAREER: Author and illustrator, 1975—. Designed sheet music covers and artwork for lyric books in New York City, 1976; designed and illustrated a series of rubber stamps for Boston-

ELLEN WEISS

based company, 1981-82. Teacher of a course on illustrating children's books. Also worked in advertising. Illustrations exhibited in the "Original Art Show" of original children's book illustrations, Master Eagle Gallery, New York City, 1983. *Awards, honors:* Garden State Children's Book Award for "Easy-to-Read Books" from the New Jersey Library Association, 1979, for *Heather's Feathers;* Parents' Choice Award for Illustration from Parents' Choice Foundation, 1984, for *The Vingananee and the Tree Toad.*

WRITINGS—For children; self-illustrated: *Clara, the Fortune-Telling Chicken,* Windmill Books, 1978; *Millicent Maybe,* F. Watts, 1979; *Things to Make and Do for Christmas,* F. Watts, 1980.

Illustrator: Leatie Weiss, *Heather's Feathers,* F. Watts, 1976; LouAnn Gaeddert, *Your Night to Make Dinner,* F. Watts, 1977; L. Weiss, *Funny Feet!,* F. Watts, 1978; Verna Aardema, reteller, *The Vingananee and the Tree Toad,* Warne, 1983; L. Weiss, *My Teacher Sleeps in School,* Warne, 1984; Beatrice Schenk deRegniers, *So Many Cats!,* Clarion, 1985; Maria Polushkin, *Baby Brother Blues,* Bradbury, 1986. Contributor of illustrations to magazines, including *Day Care.*

SIDELIGHTS: "Ever since I was little I knew that what I wanted to do *most* was to write and illustrate children's books. Soon after I learned to hold a crayon, I began to staple sheets of paper together and draw on them so I could create books. Drawing and creating characters was the most fun then, and it still is.

"Often I will create a character and write a story around that character. This happened with *Clara, the Fortune-Telling Chicken.* I was visiting Chinatown in New York City one day and wandered into a penny arcade. This is where I met Clara. She was a real live chicken, locked in a cage. I put a quarter in the slot on the side of the cage; a light went on inside the cage; Clara pressed a button, and out popped my fortune card.

Soon Millicent had eaten too much of this and too much of that. She could not fit into her clothes.

She had bought too much of this and too much of that. There was hardly enough room left for Millicent!

(From *Millicent Maybe* by Ellen Weiss. Illustrated by the author.)

I thought it was rather sad to see poor Clara locked up in the cage, pressing buttons all day long for people who wanted their fortunes told. But still the idea of the fortune-telling chicken stayed with me, and I decided to write a story about her.

"When I wrote *Millicent Maybe,* I created Millicent the alligator-lady *after* I had written the story. Many of the people I am close to (and myself, too, I'm afraid) were dealing with the same problem that Millicent has in the story—that is, making up one's mind. The subject of decision making and the inability to make up one's mind seemed a good one for me to write about. That story is straight from my heart. It is my favorite of the books I've written.

"I like to write about feelings and experiences I remember having when I was as young as the kids who read my books. I feel close to my childhood, so things that happened many years ago are still very vivid in my mind. I'd like to think that my stories touch the people who read them in some way. If they make children giggle and put smiles on their faces, I feel I've accomplished something. If my stories generate discussion afterward, I'm equally thrilled. If I've gotten my point across in a way that is not moralistic, I feel I've been successful. I want children to have a *great* time when they read. I want them to go back to my stories time and time again and enjoy them as much as they did the first time. If they have as much fun with my characters as I have creating them in words and pictures, I've accomplished a lot."

HOBBIES AND OTHER INTERESTS: "In my free time I try to go folkdancing whenever I can. I learned how to folkdance when I was about thirteen years old and have been folkdancing

ever since. I do Israeli, Russian, and Slavic folkdances and I love it. I love doing the steps and listening to the music from the different countries."

WHITE, E(lwyn) B(rooks)   1899-1985

OBITUARY NOTICE—See sketch in *SATA* Volume 29: Born July 11, 1899, in Mount Vernon, N.Y.; died of Alzheimer's disease, October 1 (another source cites September 30), 1985, in North Brooklin, Me. Essayist, poet, editor, and author of books for adults and children. White was regarded by many as the best essayist of modern time. Early in his career, he was a reporter with the *Seattle Times* and served as production assistant and copywriter for an advertising agency. He joined the *New Yorker* in 1926, where he wrote the editorial essays in the "Notes and Comment" section for twelve years and edited parts of the "Talk of the Town" section. He was a staff writer with the magazine until about 1975 and a contributing editor until his death. White is often credited with giving the *New Yorker* the writing tone that made it one of the best-written magazines in the nation.

White's contribution to children's literature was also noteworthy. His first book for children, *Stuart Little,* was published in 1945, followed by *Charlotte's Web* in 1952. *Trumpet of the Swan* appeared in 1970. White received numerous awards for his juvenile works, including the Lewis Carroll Shelf Award and Laura Ingalls Wilder Medal. In 1953 *Charlotte's Web* was selected a Newbery Honor Book. Like *Stuart Little* and *Trumpet of the Swan, Charlotte's Web* is considered a classic among children's books. White's adult works include *The Lady is Cold; Is Sex Necessary? or, Why You Feel the Way You Do*, written with James Thurber; *World Government and Peace: Selected Notes and Comment, 1943-1945;* and *The Second Tree from the Corner.* White also revised William Strunk Jr.'s *The Elements of Style*, a text on grammatical usage and composition that is required reading for many students. In 1978 White was awarded a Pulitzer Prize Committee special citation for the full body of his work.

FOR MORE INFORMATION SEE: American Writers, Scribner, 1974; *Dictionary of Literary Biography*, Volume 22: *American Writers for Children, 1900-1960*, Gale, 1983; *Twentieth-Century Children's Writers*, 2nd edition, St. Martin's, 1983; Scott Elledge, *E. B. White: A Biography*, Norton, 1984. Obituaries: *Detroit News*, October 1, 1985, October 2, 1985; *Detroit Free Press*, October 2, 1985; *Publishers Weekly*, October 11, 1985.

WIGHT, James Alfred 1916-
(James Herriot)

BRIEF ENTRY: Born October 3, 1916. Veterinarian and author. Readers of all ages have enjoyed the best-selling books written by Wight, under the pseudonym James Herriot, that chronicle over forty years of his life as a country vet in the uplands of Yorkshire, England. Published in America by St. Martin's, the tetralogy begins with *All Creatures Great and Small* (1972), a title taken from the famous Anglican hymn. Appropriately, the sequels are *All Things Bright and Beautiful* (1974), *All Things Wise and Wonderful* (1977), and *The Lord God Made Them All* (1981). Herriot's memoirs commence with his first harrowing year as a newly qualified vet surgeon during the late 1930s and continue through the early days of his marriage, the turbulent years of World War II when he served in the RAF, and the post-war years.

Critics agree that Herriot's anecdotes, written simply yet eloquently, carry universal appeal. As *Library Journal* noted: "[His] literary skill is uncanny in its mixture of humor, sympathy, joy, and sorrow—he has a rare gift of insight into the lives of animals and people." "Some of the stories are funny," added *Publishers Weekly*, "some sad and others—like life—mixtures of both." Nelson Bryant, writing for the *New York Times Book Review*, summed up the eternal charm of Herriot's work: "Reading him, one is reminded that there are . . . country places where the wind blows clean, places where men and women find pleasure in hard work and simple living." The four Herriot books have been translated into every European language and others, including Japanese. *All Creatures Great and Small* was adapted for television, and *All Things Bright and Beautiful* appeared as a motion picture in 1979.

In 1984 Herriot produced his first picture book, *Moses the Kitten* (St. Martin's). Illustrated by Peter Barrett, it is the true story of a little black kitten who was found nearly frozen among the rushes of a pond. Adopted by a nearby farm family, the kitten astounded all by becoming the thirteenth member of a litter of suckling piglets. Herriot recently completed his second picture book, entitled *Only One Woof* (St. Martin's, 1985). Also illustrated by Barrett, it tells the tale of an unusually quiet sheep dog. *Home:* Mire Beck, Thirlby, Thirsk, Yorkshire Y07 2DJ, England.

FOR MORE INFORMATION SEE: American Veterinary Medical Association Journal, August 1, 1979; *Contemporary Authors*, Volumes 77-80, Gale, 1979; *Contemporary Literary Criticism*, Volume 12, Gale, 1980; *Time*, June 29, 1981; *The Writers Directory: 1984-86*, St. James Press, 1983.

WILKS, Michael Thomas 1947-
(Mike Wilks)

PERSONAL: Born March 20, 1947, in London, England; son of Thomas and Lucy Wilks. *Education:* Attended Junior Art School, Sutton, Surrey, England, 1960-63, and Croydon College of Art, 1963-67. *Politics:* None. *Religion:* None. *Home and studio:* 4 North Rise, St. Georges Fields, London W2 2YB, England. *Agent:* Carol Smith, The Carol Smith Literary Agency, 25 Hornton Court E., Kensington High St., London W8 7RT, England.

CAREER: Worked as designer and art director, London, England, 1967-70; Turner, Wilks, Dandridge Ltd. (design consultants), London, founding partner and creative director, 1970-75; Harrow School of Art, London, lecturer in design studies, 1975-79; free-lance design consultant, 1975-79; writer, 1979—.

WRITINGS: (Under name Mike Wilks, with Sarah Harrison) *In Granny's Garden* (juvenile fantasy; self-illustrated), Holt, 1980; (under name Mike Wilks) *The Weather Works* (juvenile fantasy; self-illustrated), Holt, 1983.

Illustrator; all under name Mike Wilks: Alan Sillitoe, *The Incredible Fencing Fleas* (juvenile fiction), Robson Books, 1978; Brian W. Aldiss, *Pile: Petals from St. Klaed's Computer* (poetry), Holt, 1979; Lionel Davidson, *Under Plum Lake* (juvenile fantasy), J. Cape, 1980.

WORK IN PROGRESS: The Ultimate Alphabet Book, under name Mike Wilks, publication by Holt.

SIDELIGHTS: "I live and work alone. I work between twelve and fourteen hours a day, seven days a week. A typical book will take me three or four years to complete."

(From *Pile: Petals from St. Klaed's Computer* by Brian W. Aldiss. Illustrated by Mike Wilks.)

WILLIAMS, Kit   1946(?)-

PERSONAL: Born about 1946, in Romney Marshes, Kent, England. *Education:* Educated in England.

CAREER: Worked in factories, circa 1965-72; artist, 1972—; writer. *Military service:* Royal Navy, circa 1961-65; in electronics.

WRITINGS—Self-illustrated: *Masquerade,* J. Cape, 1979, Shocken, 1980, new edition published as *Masquerade: The Complete Book with Answers and Clues Explained,* Workman, 1983; *Book without a Name,* Knopf, 1984.

WORK IN PROGRESS: Paintings; another children's book.

SIDELIGHTS: Born in Romney Marshes, Kent, England. "It was not till I was 11 years old that people realized little Kit Williams could neither read nor write and was headed for diggin' and double diggin' and trench diggin' and double trench diggin'. I was what they now call dyslectic. At 15, I managed to decipher a written appraisal by an English teacher: 'I know he's alive because I've seen him breathing.'" [Israel Shenker, "A Treasure Awaits Anyone Who Solves *Masquerade* Riddle," *Smithsonian,* December, 1980.[1]]

As a schoolboy, Williams had a talent for working with his hands, making radio and television sets as well as rockets. "I was almost put off art at school but I always knew I could do it. Thinking visually was useful in physics, and I spent my time building television sets and sending up rockets. When I left school—without any 0 levels—my mother was so fed up she sent me off to join the Navy." [Susan Raven, "The Man of *Masquerade,*" *London Sunday Times,* June 20, 1982.[2]]

1961-1965. Joined the Royal Navy. Stationed in the Far East as an electronics repairman. "When I went down to the sea in ships I thought it was a very romantic thing to do. I was at sea for four years and I thought I can't go any further with these electronics. I decided to become a philosopher and I went to the ship's library and took out all the books on philosophy I could find and started reading them." [Taken from the book jacket of *Masquerade* by Kit Williams, Schocken, 1980.[3]]

"I read Nietsche and Marx and Russell for two days. No good. Then I decided to be the first visual philosopher. I started painting and never looked back. That was onboard the aircraft carrier *Victorious.* She's in razor blades now! Everyone round me was playing cards—I couldn't do that. To keep steady when the ship was moving, I used to tie down the canvas and the seat I was sitting on; I even tied my arm to an armrest.

KIT WILLIAMS

They thought I was very strange, but my divisional officer somehow understood. He gave me a tiny compartment to paint in. He thought it was better than letting me fiddle around with the ship's computer, which had to look after 24 aircraft.''[2]

Williams eventually bought himself out of the Navy, for 200 pounds—''my life's savings, enough to have bought a car!''[2] For the next ten years, he toured the coast of England in a caravan, moving when the police moved him on, taking less and less demanding jobs so that he could conserve his energy. Working for a time on navigational computer development for the Concorde took too much of what he called ''thinking time,'' so he turned to menial work, sweeping floors and erecting TV antennas. Williams then married an art student, whom he supported while she studied. Soon Williams took to painting again, and through a self-motivated study of art history discovered English painters Blake, Samuel Palmer and Stanley Spencer. ''I felt related to them, I identified with them, though today, Botticelli is my man.''[2]

Williams first exhibited his work in Bristol. ''Nobody came to the preview. I vowed I would never show my work again.''[2]

The following year, Williams lived in Whitstable, where he often collected driftwood on the shore. Sometimes he would construct little boats, put his address inside, and push them out to sea, hoping to get replies from far off lands. ''That must have been 1971. In the end, somebody in England picked one up and wrote to me, thinking I was a child. When I wrote back saying, 'Actually, I'm on the dole,' this chap—a young man about to go to Cambridge University—came to see me. And it was he who brought me an entrance form for the John Moores exhibition in Liverpool.''[2]

Williams submitted an intimate picture of two people and a picture of a Morris Minor parked on a river bank. The latter painting was one of eighty selected from 800 entries and was bought by one of the Moores family before the exhibition even opened. The Portal Gallery in London saw his work in the Liverpool show and approached Williams, asking to exhibit his work. After his second exhibition at the Portal in 1976, Tom Maschler, chairman of the publishing house of Jonathan Cape, invited him to do a children's book. Maschler commented, ''Kit was living 100 miles from London, but I went to see him on an instinctive feeling that he could produce something exceptional. I don't know how I got that feeling, but I did from the painting I saw [at the Portal Gallery].'' [David Sharp, ''The Reward at the End of the Read,'' *Publishers Weekly*, July 6, 1984.[4]]

According to Williams: ''It all began in **1976** when Tom Maschler came to see me. He had seen my paintings at the Portal Gallery in London and wanted to know if I would illustrate a children's book. *Illustrate* a children's book! I explained I was a painter and not an illustrator, and anyway I wouldn't want to draw pictures for someone else's story. So he suggested I write a story of my own. I'd never written anything in my life, and so I said 'no' to that too. He left saying, 'I bet you can do something with books that no one has every done before.' And those words stuck in my mind.

''One day some weeks later, an idea came to me while I was eating breakfast, but I told it to go away. I was much too busy to be bothered with ideas for books. Then I started thinking about what books are and how they work. By dinner time that first idea was back with a friend, and soon the whole room was full of ideas. I couldn't resist the thought of a book that a lot of people would want to examine closely. I rang up Tom Maschler and said I would need £3,000 to do it. He didn't

seem to understand completely how it would work but he very bravely sent me a contract straight away.

''What I wanted to do was to retain the format of a book but then do something different. If I was going to spend two or three years doing sixteen paintings, I didn't want them to be just flicked through and put down. That's why the perspective is odd in some of the *Masquerade* pictures, and why others overlap their borders. Sometimes things come straight out at you. All to make you look really closely. The riddles and the treasure are also partly to make people look. Little did I know how hard they were going to look!

''When I was a child there were competitions on cereal packets that pretended to be treasure hunts. They always seemed such disappointing gimmicks because the puzzles weren't exciting and the treasure wasn't worth the hunt. I thought I would do something for my lost childhood and make a real treasure from gold, bury it in the ground, and use riddles to lead people to it.

''I did various experiments with map co-ordinates and bits of string in fields but I couldn't find a simple and accurate way to pinpoint the treasure. It would have to be marked by something already there. A monument, for example. I've always been fascinated by astronomy and I worked out a way of using a monument like the upright pointer on a sundial. The treasure could be buried where the end of the shadow was on a certain day in the year. I liked the idea of the equinox because it gives you two days each year, spring and autumn, when the shadow is exactly the same length. I remembered visiting a place called Ampthill Park when I lived near Bedford, where there's a cross about 18 feet high commemorating the first of Henry VIII's six wives, Catherine of Aragon. When I went to Ampthill to check [how] everything would work, I found a small stone a few yards away from the cross with these words from Psalm 104 on it:

> 'O Lord how manifold are thy works!
> in wisdom hast thou made them all:
> the earth is full of thy riches.'

''That settled it. Ampthill was the perfect place. It wasn't famous for anything—then! Catherine of Aragon introduced lace-making to Bedfordshire, and the rhyme 'Jack be nimble, Jack be quick,' which I used for Jack Hare in the Isaac Newton picture, is an old lace-makers' song. And Jonathan Cape's address is *Bedford* Square, so the name of the nearest big town would be printed in every copy of the book.

''Solving the master riddle that pointed to where the treasure could be found should depend on a relationship of words *and* pictures. I wrote out a sentence of about twenty words defining exactly, to within a few inches, where the gold would be buried. Once I had that sentence, I worked out how to put it into the construction of the pictures. All I had in mind for a story when I began to paint was the idea of a messenger going through the elements of earth, air, fire and water. The hare fitted because it isn't a cuddly animal, like a rabbit, and it can run very fast.

''For me the crucial picture was the one which appears first in the book. I had been painting all day every day, even at weekends, becoming more and more obsessed and inward-looking. It was December, and the combination of the fumes from my paraffin heater in the workshop and the water dripping on the polythene tent I'd built to keep condensation off while I worked was driving me slightly crazy. At night I spent hours staring at the moon through my telescope and observing

(From *Masquerade* by Kit Williams. Illustrated by the author.)

the moonlit landscape so that during the day I could convey the quality of moonlight in the painting. It was then that the story came to me: the hare should be the messenger of the moon. Only later did I discover that the hare is a messenger in legends and folklore in many countries.

"Each of the pictures in *Masquerade* is like a big fat novel: there are plots and sub-plots and things going on that aren't even hinted at in the text. And I enjoyed putting in some personal jokes too: the names Lionel Levy and Eric Lister, which appear in 'Jack in the Green,' are the names of the owners of the Portal Gallery where I exhibit my paintings, and Tom Maschler's name is on the removal van in the aerial view of Tewkesbury. I was painting the man drinking tea on Silver Jubilee Day, and so I put the Queen's head on the tea caddy. The little girl with the Penny-Pockets Lady is the daughter of the chemist in my village, and I painted her as the girl swimming, as I imagine she'll look when she's sixteen.

"Some things came out of the pictures to fit the story in an almost magical way. I'd just finished the paintings of Isaac Newton and the puppet on the beach at the end of the book when a friend showed me the quotation on Isaac Newton's statue in Cambridge: 'All my life I seem to have been only like a boy playing on the sea-shore. . . .' It fitted perfectly, so I put it in the story. The girl who worked at the gold merchant's in Birmingham where I bought the gold was called Dawn, so I thought I'd write her into the story where the moon

Photograph of *Masquerade*'s buried treasure unearthed. ■ (From *Masquerade: The Complete Book with Answers and Clues Explained* by Kit Williams.)

makes the jewel 'with a little gold taken from the dawn sky.' I wonder if she's ever read the book!

"Writing the text only took about three weeks as I already had it clear in my head. Now I had to make the jewel and bury it. I had never made jewellery [sic], although I'd worked in brass, steel and copper. My methods were unsophisticated and sometimes unconventional, using old-fashioned tools, like an Archimedes drill. From one piece of gold I cut the outline of the hare, five and a half inches from nose to tail, then sawed out and drilled the filigree work within the body. The other piece of gold was enough to make the hare's legs, ears, and tail, which I riveted to the body. Everything else—the bells and their tongues, the chains, the tiny animals—had to be made by melting down the remaining scraps of gold, beating them into coin shapes, then cutting them out.

"The stones I chose were a ruby for the hare's eye, turquoise in the flowers on the body and a large moonstone for the back of the moon. The faces of the sun and moon are made of faience, a substance the ancient Egyptians used a lot. I had to experiment for ages because the facial expressions changed so much as the faience cooled and hardened.

"The first time I gave the whole thing a good polish it looked a bit plain in some places, so I engraved the gold with tools my grandfather, a gunsmith, had left me. Though the gold and precious stones cost less than £1,500, the pendant was valued at £5,000 when I'd finished it. I suppose it must be worth a small fortune now.

"I also had to make a special container out of clay in the shape of a hare. I engraved the words 'I am the keeper of the jewel of Masquerade which lies waiting safe inside me for you or eternity' on the side of the pot and fired it in a kiln. Then, under the lights of television, I wrapped the gold in paper, put it in the pot, poured in hot wax and put on the lid. As the wax cooled it hardened and sealed the jewel in. It was very moving.

"On the night of **August 7th, 1979,** I set off with Bamber Gascoigne, who was chosen to witness the burial. Once at the right spot, I cut a turf about ten inches square with my knife, then dug down until I'd made a hole to the depth of my elbow. There was a moment of panic when my trowel hit rock, but it turned out to be just a small stone. In went the pot with the gold, then the earth and the turf. I watered the spot to encourage the grass to grow again. As Bamber and I shook hands over the burial ground, the moon came out from behind a cloud and, I like to think, shone down a blessing on us.

"Six weeks later the book was published and the world went crazy! People seized on everything I had put in the book and lots of things I hadn't. One poor woman had her garden invaded as people spotted the topiary hare in the aerial view of Tewkesbury. A man hid in the grounds at Sudbury Hall in Derbyshire (which is the swimming girl picture) so that he could dive in the lake in front of the house after dark.

"Sudbury Hall is an example of the strange coincidences which seem to surround *Masquerade*. I painted the house from an old photograph—I've never been there—taken before the white dome was gilded. Treasure hunters were intrigued to find it was actually gold. And there is a stone frog in the grounds, just like the one I put in the shop window picture. To make people even more certain they were on the right track, there happened to be an exhibition of marionettes and toys there when *Masquerade* was published. The organizers of the exhibition had fun arranging alphabet blocks in the display to

**Sir Isaac grabbed the strings of gravitational force that bound Jack to his destiny and
PULLED—. ▪** (From *Masquerade* by Kit Williams. Illustrated by the author.)

spell out other places near by so that treasure hunters wouldn't dig up the grounds.

"All these stories I heard secondhand—or read about in newspaper articles. Very soon I had my own evidence of what I'd started. Letters began to pour in. I had phone calls in the middle of the night and muddy people carrying spades turned up at my door. One man wrote to me from Switzerland to say that his family had urged him to spend their savings on a journey to England, where he ended up on a remote and dangerous clifftop in Cornwall. Taking his life in his hands, he had shinned down the cliff face, and then got cut off by the incoming tide. A woman who wrote asking me to pay her fare to somewhere else in the British Isles actually lived only a mile from where the treasure was buried. Someone was even convinced he could reach the treasure if he found out my real name. Kit Williams, he declared, was just an anagram of 'I will mask it.'

"Then suddenly, on Friday, **February 19th, 1982,** a map turned up in the post which changed everything. We were woken up, as usual, by the dog barking at the postman and my wife Eleyne went down to get the letters and make the tea. Besides two fat parcels of letters from America, there were six letters Eleyne recognised as coming from known *Masquerade* treasure-hunters, and another one which she brought upstairs. I opened it as casually as I'd opened thousand upon thousand in the past. There it was, a letter with a map like a child's drawing, but enough for me to know someone had cracked it.

"I felt elated and relieved. That simple drawing would prove to everyone that it was not impossible to find the jewel. The letter was just signed 'Ken.' I'd always promised to contact anyone who discovered the burial place. I leapt out of bed, rang the number in the letter and asked for Ken. When I told him his solution was correct, he said he couldn't dig it up that day because he had a cold. Not the reaction I'd expected!

"Ken became really excited later in the day when he phoned back and explained how he'd found the spot which had eluded everyone else. He had been on the search for nearly eighteen months. Early on, he had arrived at Catherine of Aragon from ONE OF SIX TO EIGHT under the first picture in the book. He decided this was an important clue and did some research into her life. He made hundreds of expeditions to Kimbolton Castle in Cambridgeshire, where she died. He also believed from the Dance in Time picture that the equinox was important for measuring distance.

"The clever bit—though it short-circuited my method—was to spend a lot of time investigating my own life and discovering I had lived near Bedford and in Kent. Even so, the search got nowhere. Twice he gave the book away, and each time went out to buy another copy to begin all over again.

"One day when he was driving home, he decided to stop to give the dog a run and turned off the road at Ampthill Park. He didn't know then that a monument to Catherine stood there. It was the dog who discovered the stone with the 'All the riches of the earth' verse on it. Could this be it? That night, he read in the *Shell Guide* that one of the pair of stone crosses he'd been looking at in the afternoon had been put up in honour of Catherine of Aragon in 1773. That settled it. He was sure that providence and his dog had led him to the buried treasure.

"For three nights Ken tried to get underneath the stone, convinced the treasure lay there. But it wouldn't budge. He then concentrated on Catherine's Cross instead. He was a bit worried by what he thought were signs of digging near the cross,

but it only made him more certain he was in the right place. Remembering the equinox, he got a friend to help him work out how the sun would cast a shadow of the cross on any particular day. He dug a small hole and found nothing. It was at this point he sent me the map for confirmation.

"When he next went back to the site he got a real shock. A fresh hole had appeared close by. He dug like crazy until he was standing in a trench 8 feet long and 2 feet wide. Still there was no sign of the treasure. Next day Ken checked his measurements and found they led to the middle of his trench. By now he was convinced someone had already dug up the treasure. There seemed to be no alternative to announcing that an unknown person had found the treasure and kept quiet about it.

"On Tuesday morning, four days after I'd received his letter, Ken rang again. 'Look, don't tell the press yet. What if someone went along with a metal detector where I dug and found it? I'd feel a real Charlie. I might have missed it in the dark.' Ken's plan was to go back in the *daytime*, pretending to be a workman. He went prepared with some poles and tape, put up a makeshift fence and dug again, in full daylight. He told passers-by he was investigating subsidence.

"I was at a friend's house on Wednesday, February 24th when Eleyne rang to say there had been a new development. 'I think you should come home.' New development? I thought Ken must have been arrested! I rang him up. He'd found it—at a quarter to three that afternoon. What a relief! Apparently the casket had been just under the surface where he'd dug at night. He had missed it in the dark and reburied it. The sun was shining for the first time for days, and the shadow of the cross was very clear. I love the idea of the moon shining on the burial and the sun shining as it was unearthed. As Ken filled in the hole, the Bedfordshire Army Cadet Corps came along for training. Ken soon had them marching up and down his trench to firm the soil back in!

"Ken wanted me to be there when he took the golden hare out of its casket and was happy to wait until arrangements were made to record the momentous event. But the following day no one could get through to him. Had he disappeared with the jewel in fright? So far, I hadn't either seen the casket or checked the site for myself. How could I be sure Ken had actually found it?

"For once the explanation turned out to be simple. He had been taken suddenly into hospital. An illness that bothered him from time to time had been aggravated by all those nights of digging. He'd be out again in about a week. We agreed to meet as soon as he got back home. Days of suspense followed. Then at last, on Sunday, March 7th, Tom Maschler and I drove out to see him.

"As the world now knows, Ken had the jewel all right, and we planned the day of announcement over a glass of whiskey in Ken's cottage. For personal reasons, he wanted to retain his anonymity and agreed to speak to one newspaper and one television programme, but afterwards to vanish from the limelight. It was only right to respect his wishes. He said he wouldn't think of selling the golden hare—not for some years anyway. He'd spent eighteen months looking for it and wouldn't be parted from it now.

"The thing Ken hadn't unravelled was the master riddle I'd hidden in the book. He had discovered some important clues, so it wasn't just a fluke that he'd found the jewel. He'd got some of the confirmers as well. The word CULMINATION

Ambrose's little kitchen was as warm and cosy as fresh baked bread. ▪ (From *Book without a Name* by Kit Williams. Illustrated by the author.)

The wood seemed to be drawing her towards it. . . . ■ (From *Book without a Name* by Kit Williams. Illustrated by the author.)

on the border to the last picture in the book, for instance, meant originally 'to be on the meridian'—the point where the sun is at its highest in the sky. The shadow cast by the cross at the time of the equinox would be accurate to the inch. Ken saw through some of my red herrings too. Many people have spent hours on the numbers in the football pitch in the aerial picture of Tewkesbury, but Ken, who is an engineer, recognised them as atomic numbers for chemical elements. Translated into letters, they spell: FALSE NOUU THINK AGAIN. Of all the people who wrote to me, a girl of twelve was one of only four to see this.

"I didn't tell Ken how to get the rest of it. It seemed a shame to spoil the fun for everyone else by announcing how to crack the code before anyone had managed to work it out. But a letter from a teacher in Manchester, which arrived at my home just as th[e] paperback edition of the book was going to press, changed all that. He was the one who had sent Ken into a frenzy by digging a hole near by at Ampthill. Failing to find the treasure on that dig, Mike and his friend John had decided to wait—too long as it turned out—for the equinox on March 20th to pinpoint the spot. Still, the quest had been fulfilled, for theirs was the first completely correct solution to reach me.

"It had taken them less than a year to solve it and they first reconnoitered the site in January 1982. Mike returned with his wife to dig their hole on the night of February 18th, when Ken's letter to me was safe in the post. They were in no doubt they had the right answer and wrote to me after hearing the news about Ken's discovery." [Taken from the introduction by Kit Williams to *Masquerade: The Complete Book with Answers and Clues Explained*, Workman, 1983.[5]]

"It is a great shame they did not get in touch with me sooner. But I was thrilled when I heard from them. I'd been so depressed that the treasure had been found *without* the code having been worked out. They are still the only people who have cracked it.

"I've always held—and the teachers agree—that the mystery was not esoteric, that a child of 10 could do it, with a lot of perseverance. Perhaps that need to stick to it is why the puzzle is more of a cult with the middle-aged."[2]

Williams lives in a tiny cottage in Gloucestershire with his second wife, Eleyne, a handloom weaver, whom he met on a train in September, 1980 and married three months later. They share their cottage with Bramble, a border collie and two cats, Willie and Kali. Though *Masquerade* sold over a million copies, Williams says he would never want to change his lifestyle. The Williams now have a car, a studio for Eleyne and a workshop for Kit, but the cottage still has no central heating. "I spent 10 years almost on the breadline, making do with scraps and leftovers—and I could still do it. Money means that I can't use that skill, which means I've also had a pleasure removed."[2]

Masquerade has been translated into French, German, Italian, Japanese and Dutch. The sixteen original paintings from the book sold out within four days of their exhibition and Williams' new works sell for upward of $10,000. "When I first knew about the money from the book I got grand. My accountant told me, 'You've got to buy a Porsche. You've got to live abroad to avoid taxes.' Then I saw a beautiful house, with an orchard, a stream running through the orchard, an old mill behind it, with a lake and woods. I thought, 'This is me. I'll sit on the veranda and I'll watch the gardener tending my garden.' But after a while my cottage said to me—this in plaintive tones—'Oh, you're not leaving me.' and I realized I

Williams holding the mahogany box that contains the only titled copy of *Book without a Name.*

don't need the beautiful house, I don't want to live abroad, I don't need the Porsche. I've got my little van, and it carries the firewood."[1]

About the worldwide reaction from his readers, Williams commented, "The Americans are great guessers. Their method was to quickly flip through the book: *Stonehenge*. One woman in Atlanta must have written me 5000 letters, each with a different place. She was trying the elimination game.

"The Japanese wanted to know about the philosophy of the book and how it related to English history.

"The Germans were very gothic—joining lines and analyzing pictures in the way that art historians would do.

"The English were very private. People would sidle up to me, give me a nudge and say something like a tiny quote from Shakespeare, or 'Underneath the second stone by the green tree.' They would whisper absolutely obscure things in my ear and wander off with a smile on their faces as if they thought they had conquered me."[4]

Williams, whose monofocal vision gave him problems as a schoolboy, describes how his particular way of seeing influences his paintings. "Each eye sees separately and with no coordination, not a single image but two images, two channels that remain separate. I can look at a thing with one eye while using the other to paint what I see with that other eye. I've learned to use my disability very well, and I'd never have it straightened out."[1]

June, 1984. Williams' second book, *Book without a Name*, published simultaneously in England and America. In the new work Williams challenged his readers to discover the book's title and to express it without using the written word. The prize was to be the only titled copy of the book in the world, sealed within a curious and exquisite mahogany bee box of finely wrought honeycomb marquery, guarded by a queen bee of pure gold. The cover of the book is a facsimile of the cover of the box. Williams explained, "You must translate the title into another form . . . such as a painting, a song on a tape, a statue or whatever else you can think of. The title is not esoteric but describes real objects, so that you've got something to sink your teeth into."

Williams' plan was to exhibit all the entries and on May 25, 1985 choose a winner on the basis of creativity. He commented, "It'll be whichever one impresses me the most."

The idea for *Book without a Name* was inspired by readers' responses to *Masquerade*. "All of the answers were incredibly good. Some of the solutions were much better than mine. I even got poems and pictures, although I asked for none of that. It started me thinking, 'Gosh, if I asked people to do something incredible, what will happen then?' This time I wanted to see what the creative mind of the world is like."

Williams prohibited written responses so that the contest would be open to everyone. "Once a Japanese person has gotten the Japanese title, he then translates it into some other form, into music or painting, or something understandable by me. Things other than the written word are international. They also transcend age groups. A tiny child can be as inventive, or even more inventive, than an art-school lecturer. We have a special warehouse waiting for the submissions."[4]

1985. The title for *Book without a Name* was revealed to be *The Bee on the Comb*. The winning entry was submitted by Stephen Pierce, a native of Leicester, England and a designer of amusement parks. Williams awarded Pierce the hand-crafted box, which went on display along with the prize-winning entry as well as all of Williams' original paintings from the book at the Portal Gallery in London, for the month of July, 1985.

Williams also chose fifty of the most interesting submissions for a special exhibition at the Usher Gallery in Lincoln, England, July, 1985.

FOR MORE INFORMATION SEE: Chicago Tribune, February 13, 1980; *People,* February 18, 1980; *Time,* March 3, 1980, March 29, 1982; *Los Angeles Times,* October 22, 1980; Israel Shenker, "A Treasure Awaits Anyone Who Solves *Masquerade* Riddle," *Smithsonian,* December, 1980; *New York Times Book Review,* February 1, 1981; *Newsweek,* March 30, 1981, March 29, 1982; *New York Times Magazine,* November 15, 1981; *New York Times,* March 15, 1982; *Washington Post,* March 15, 1982; *Detroit News,* March 16, 1982; Susan Raven, "The Man of *Masquerade*," *London Sunday Times,* June 20, 1982; David Sharp, "The Reward at the End of the Read," *Publishers Weekly,* July 6, 1984.

WOOD, Audrey

BRIEF ENTRY: Born in Little Rock, Ark. Author and illustrator of children's books. Wood comes from a family of artists, including her father, grandfather, and great-grandfather. In addition to writing and illustrating children's books, Wood has owned and operated a book and import shop. Among her numerous books is *The Napping House* (Harcourt, 1984), illustrated by her husband, Don Wood. It was named a notable children's book for young readers by the Notable Children's Books Committee of the Association for Library Service to Children. The book is a cumulative rhyme, on the order of "The House That Jack Built." In the story, grandma goes to take a nap on a rainy day. Then, one after the other, a child, dog, cat, and mouse join her in bed, piling one on top of the other. Nap time soon comes to an end when a "wakeful flea" appears and bites the mouse, which sets off a chain reaction that sends everyone tumbling out of bed. *Wilson Library Bulletin* commented that Wood "exhibits the same knack as old-time folk narrators," while *Bulletin of the Center for Children's Books* deemed the book "an engaging cumulative tale."

Wood wrote and illustrated *Tugford Wanted to Be Bad* (Harcourt, 1983). In the story, Tugford, a boy mouse, tries to become an outlaw like the ones he sees in the movies and steals a bank shaped like a kitty out of his mother's closet. In the end, Tugford decides that being a real outlaw isn't much fun. *Publishers Weekly* remarked, "[Wood's] pictures . . . are a joy for the Let Me Read Book crowd to follow. . . ." Her other books include *Magic Shoelaces* (1980), *Balloonia* (1981), and *The Princess and the Dragon* (1982), all self-illustrated and all published by Child's Play. Wood's latest work is *King Bidgood's in the Bathtub* (Harcourt, 1985). *Residence:* Santa Barbara, Calif.

WOOD, Don 1945-

BRIEF ENTRY: Born in 1945. Artist and illustrator. Wood received a B.A. from the University of California at Santa Barbara and an M.F.A. from California College of Arts and Crafts. During his career, he has worked as a lumberjack, a sailmaker, and has executed paintings for the pay television show "Faerie Tale Theatre." He is now a full-time illustrator for magazines and picture books. In 1984 he received the Golden Kite Award for his illustrations in *The Napping House* (Harcourt, 1984), written by his wife, Audrey Wood. The book was also named a *New York Times* Best Illustrated Children's Book in 1985. Critics have praised Wood's work in the book, noting his unique use of color and light in helping to develop the story. *Wilson Library Bulletin* observed, "Don Wood creates the counterpart of narrative crescendo by slowly developing color intensities." According to *New York Times Book Review,* ". . . Wood's moonlight blue and pink pictures develop their own sly visual drama. . . ." Wood also illustrated *The Moon Flute* and *Quick as a Cricket,* both by Audrey Wood. *Residence:* Santa Barbara, Calif.

CUMULATIVE INDEX TO
ILLUSTRATIONS AND AUTHORS

Illustrations Index

(In the following index, the number of the volume in which an illustrator's work appears is given *before* the colon, and the page on which it appears is given *after* the colon. For example, a drawing by Adams, Adrienne appears in Volume 2 on page 6, another drawing by her appears in Volume 3 on page 80, another drawing in Volume 8 on page 1, and another drawing in Volume 15 on page 107.)

YABC

Index citations including this abbreviation refer to listings appearing in *Yesterday's Authors of Books for Children,* also published by the Gale Research Company, which covers authors who died prior to 1960.

Author Index

The following index gives the number of the volume in which an author's biographical sketch, Brief Entry, or Obituary appears.

This index includes references to all entries in the following series, which are also published by Gale Research Company.

YABC—*Yesterday's Authors of Books for Children: Facts and Pictures about Authors and Illustrators of Books for Young People from Early Times to 1960*, Volumes 1-2

CLR—*Children's Literature Review: Excerpts from Reviews, Criticism, and Commentary on Books for Children*, Volumes 1-9

SAAS—*Something about the Author Autobiography Series*, Volumes 1-2

Author Index

Author Index

Author Index